THE POLARIZERS

Postwar Architects of Our Partisan Era

SAM ROSENFELD

University of Chicago Press
Chicago and London

The University of Chicago Press, Chicago 60637
The University of Chicago Press, Ltd., London
© 2018 by The University of Chicago

Published 2018
Printed in the United States of America

26 25 24 23 22 21 20 19 18 17   1 2 3 4 5

ISBN-13: 978-0-226-40725-8 (cloth)
ISBN-13: 978-0-226-40739-5 (e-book)
DOI: 10.7208/chicago/9780226407395.001.0001

Library of Congress Cataloging-in-Publication Data

Names: Rosenfeld, Sam (Political scientist), author.
Title: The polarizers : postwar architects of our partisan
    era / Sam Rosenfeld.
Description: Chicago ; London : University of Chicago
    Press, 2017. | Includes bibliographical references and
    index.
Identifiers: LCCN 2017009027 | ISBN 9780226407258
    (cloth : alk. paper) | ISBN 9780226407395 (e-book)
Subjects: LCSH: Political parties—United States. |
    Polarization (Social sciences)—United States. | United
    States—Politics and government—1945-1989. | United
    States—Politics and government—1989-.
Classification: LCC JK2265 .R67 2017 |
    DDC 324.273/13—dc23
LC record available at https://lccn.loc.gov/2017009027

♾ This paper meets the requirements of ANSI/NISO
Z39.48-1992 (Permanence of Paper).

For Erica

CONTENTS

INTRODUCTION

In America, nationally successful politicians tend to be a practical sort. By necessity, they tackle the political constraints of the moment pragmatically. But on occasion, such politicians have been prompted to take the long view about how the political system functions, and how they think the two major parties should behave. During the middle of the twentieth century, a particular set of questions about the parties came up again and again—questions that, from our own age of hyperpartisanship, might seem difficult to take seriously. Should the two major parties reflect distinctive philosophies and agendas? If the parties held many of the same beliefs, was that good or bad for democracy? Public officials disagreed over the answers.

In 1944 President Franklin Roosevelt turned to an aide and declared, "We ought to have two real parties—one liberal, and the other conservative." This was a provocative claim at the time given the ample number of Democrats who were more conservative than many Republicans. Roosevelt made that remark while pursuing secret inquiries into orchestrating a top-down party realignment, by forging an alliance with his moderate, internationalist Republican opponent of 1940, Wendell Willkie, on behalf of a new party that would combine the liberal wings of the existing Democratic and Republican parties. Such a configuration would have pushed conservative Republicans and the large minority of conservative Democrats to ally in a single new party as well. Willkie responded favorably to the idea, lamenting the current state of affairs in which "both parties are hybrids."[1]

Fifteen years later, in 1959, Vice President Richard Nixon took the opposite tack. "It would be a great tragedy," he told a California audience, "if we had our two major political parties divide on what we would call a conservative-liberal line." This would be a tragedy because "one of the attributes of our political system has been that we have avoided generally violent swings in Administrations from one extreme to the other. And the reason we have avoided that is that in both parties there has been room for a broad spectrum of opinion."[2]

Four years after that, Attorney General Robert F. Kennedy—then embroiled in a conflict pitting his brother's administration against fellow Democratic leaders in the South over segregation—expressed a sentiment similar to Nixon's in a discussion with the journalist Godfrey Hodgson. "With some vehemence," Hodgson later recalled, Kennedy insisted that, since "the country was already split vertically, between sections, races, and ethnic groups," it would be "dangerous to split it horizontally, too, between liberals and conservatives." Down that path "lay the rift between haves and have-nots, and the ideological politics of Europe."[3] The jumble of crosscutting partisan and ideological alliances helped to ensure national stability and political inclusion, he argued.

Just a few years later, South Dakota senator George McGovern disagreed with Nixon and Kennedy, and agreed with Roosevelt and Willkie. In 1969 a journalist asked him what he thought about "a realignment of American parties to something a little closer to the British system, with conservatives in one party and liberals in another." He responded that, "on balance, it would serve the national interest and serve the interests of our party."[4] Demonstrating that this view itself crossed ideological lines, a fellow senator with radically different politics, Jesse Helms of North Carolina, later concurred with McGovern by calling for "a general realignment into Conservative and Liberal parties, by whatever names."[5]

Politicians were not the only ones with views on this subject. "It is now time," an Arkansas man wrote to California senator William F. Knowland in 1956, "to get all the right-wingers on one side, and all the left-wingers on the other."[6] Many ordinary midcentury Americans agreed—but many more did not. Between the 1930s and the

1970s, George Gallup's polling firm periodically surveyed Americans, posing questions like this: "It has been suggested that we give up the present Republican and Democratic Parties and have two new parties, one for the Liberals and one for the Conservatives. Would you favor this idea?"[7] Across four decades, those who said yes never reached even one-third of the total.

Gallup has long since stopped asking Americans that question, just as contemporary politicians rarely opine in public about its subject. That is because what had been a matter of speculation is now reality. By the end of the twentieth century, Franklin Roosevelt and George McGovern and Jesse Helms had gotten their wish, while Richard Nixon and Robert F. Kennedy and, it seems, consistent majorities of Americans did not. The two major American political parties are now sorted quite clearly along ideological lines. The most liberal Republican member of Congress has amassed a voting record that is consistently to the right of the most conservative Democrat.[8] And when politicians and the public alike now speak out about parties and their role in politics, they are much more likely to lament incivility, gridlock, and dysfunction. They attribute those qualities to "polarization."[9] But polarization runs deeper than rude behavior and hostile politicking. It's rooted in ideology.

A slew of institutional changes have accompanied the ideological sorting of the parties. Contemporary parties are not only more cohesive and distinct than at midcentury. They are also more disciplined when in power, and more centralized in their internal authority at the national level. These developments have helped to give contemporary politics the distinctive character of high-stakes warfare. Indeed, much of what Americans bemoan about their polarized politics, from increasing "extremism" to seemingly pointless partisan bickering to the breakdown of norms of cooperation and civility across the aisle, are largely secondary consequences of one key development: the parties are now chiefly distinguished from each other by their contrasting agendas and worldviews. The parties' increasing internal cohesion makes them more disciplined and oppositional, and the forces of ideological zeal and partisan team spirit now reinforce each other. The days when politicians and voters belonged to "hybrid" parties and were pulled in varying directions at once are long gone.

This book shows how an ideologically defined two-party system took hold in the United States. National politics in the middle of the twentieth century involved historically high levels of bipartisanship in government, weak and balkanized party structures, and partisan attachments that were defined more by ties of tradition and communal affiliation than by policy issues and ideology. But the dawn of the twenty-first century saw levels of partisan discipline in Congress unseen since the Gilded Age, the emergence of robust national party organizations, and an electorate that was sorted into two parties defined by ideology. In this shift, American party politics gained a programmatic cast and logic long considered alien to the country's political traditions. That change in the relationship between partisan and ideological politics lies at the root of modern party polarization.

But this is not something that just happened. Individuals brought this change about deliberately. The party system we have today is not simply the byproduct of structural developments like mass demographic shifts or technological change; it was a political project carried out by specific people—men and women who had reasons to think that forging disciplined, programmatically distinct parties would solve endemic problems they saw in American politics. A wide variety of people, from small-town citizens to presidents, played roles in this change. But at the heart of the emergence of our polarized party system were ideologically driven thinkers, activists, and politicians in the middle ranks of American politics. They were the men and women, sometimes pursuing short-range goals, sometimes explicitly seeking long-range systemic change, who worked over the course of decades to remake the parties in their image. Ultimately, they succeeded.

Today's pundits wring their hands about polarization and yearn for the halcyon days of bipartisan comity. Yet pundits of the mid-twentieth century saw that very bipartisanship as the key problem in American politics. They argued that the lack of clarity between the parties stifled progress while blurring accountability to the voters. Polarization was their *solution* to this problem. They thought making parties "real" in the sense that Roosevelt had meant—unified behind distinct policy agendas that were clear to voters—would invigorate democracy and improve policymaking. Their ideas influenced the views of key political actors on both the left and right in the ensuing decades.

An ascendant postwar generation of educated, issue-driven liberal activists, thrilling to Adlai Stevenson's presidential campaigns and powering the stormy tenure of national Democratic chairman Paul Butler, battled to wrest control of Democratic Party organizations from traditional political machines. They also fought with national party leaders they deemed overly beholden to conservative southerners. At the same time, conservatives ranging from North Dakota senator Karl Mundt to South Carolina politico Greg Shorey advocated a partisan realignment that would formalize an ideological coalition of southern whites and northern Republicans. Later, congressional and party reformers worked to make the political system more permeable and responsive to ideological activism. Capitalizing on those institutional reforms, left-liberal movement activists like Michael Harrington and Heather Booth struggled in the 1970s to create a coalition between the cultural Left and a reconstituted labor movement. At the same time, New Right architects within the GOP such as Paul Weyrich and Phyllis Schlafly brokered a lasting alliance of social and economic conservatives. By effectively drawing new party lines across a wide array of issues, those activists helped in turn to catalyze a partisan resurgence over the last two decades of the century and beyond— a resurgence that took many political observers utterly by surprise.

Today, the party system offers voters genuinely meaningful programmatic choices, but the constitutional reality of separated powers all but guarantees frequent gridlock and occasional crisis. Voters lament the ill effects of polarized parties operating in a fragmented political system, even as their own political behavior grows ever more predictably defined by partisan and ideological loyalties. New issues, as they become salient, swiftly turn into grist for the mill of partisan conflict. Think of how technical legislative provisions like, say, an individual mandate to buy private health insurance, or obscure government institutions like the Import-Export

Bank, turned from sleepy bipartisan policies to ideological light-ning rods seemingly overnight. The system's relentless logic of line-drawing proves hard to escape. To paraphrase Leon Trotsky, you may not be interested in polarization, but polarization is inter-ested in you.[10]

What follows is the story of a momentous change in American politics. In telling that story, I alternate focus between liberal and conservative activists and party builders. The first four chapters chronicle intellectual and political developments in the exception-ally depolarized mid-twentieth century. Chapters 5 through 7 ana-lyze the 1970s as a decade of underappreciated dynamism, flux, and experimentation in American party politics that tightened the alignment between the policy positions and the partisan af-filiations of political activists and elites. Chapter 8 and the con-clusion chronicle the unpredicted resurgence of partisanship and the transformation of national policymaking resulting from this alignment, from the Reagan years to today. A bibliographic essay positions these developments within contemporary scholarship on parties and political history.

We can't understand our contemporary polarized era without understanding its origins. Because the rancor of current Ameri-can politics inspires so much popular discontent, a note of nostal-gia suffuses much discussion of reforming the system or revers-ing the tide of partisanship. The story of polarization's architects and their motivations for action—which were often compelling and soundly democratic—cautions against wistful longing for a bygone era of statesmanlike civility and bipartisan compromise. The de-polarized midcentury system did as much to suppress as facilitate democratic decision-making on important issues, and the systems' myriad challengers had their reasons. The polarizers' story also helps us to recast common understandings of the last half-century of American politics, illustrating how activists on both the left and the right engaged in a shared project of party reconstruction that had transformative consequences for policymaking and politi-cal culture. Americans still wage their democratic struggles in the world that the polarizers made.

1

THE IDEA OF RESPONSIBLE
PARTISANSHIP, 1945-1952

On November 4, 1952, Adlai Stevenson lost handily to Dwight Eisenhower in the presidential election, ending twenty years of Democratic control of the office. Over 80,000 people wrote Stevenson in the immediate aftermath of the election.[1] One of them was the political scientist E. E. Schattschneider.

The Wesleyan professor had read newspaper reports that Stevenson was assuming the mantle of leader of the Democratic opposition, and he wrote to express his hope that this leadership would embody "a more active effective sense than that implied in the expression 'titular head' of the party." He credited Stevenson with having "done very much to interpret for the nation the idea of party government and party responsibility" and implored him to build upon the popular following and policy agenda he had established in the campaign and sustain them in opposition.[2]

What end would this leadership serve? "The function of the Democratic party as an opposition party," Schattschneider wrote, "is to remain, first, a liberal party, and second . . . to help the public understand the meaning of the liberal alternatives" to the coming Republican rule, which he was sure would be brief. Moreover, structural developments, particularly "the breakup of the Solid South, which seems now to be near at hand," might allow for a newly *effective* party governance when the Democrats returned to power. Thus the party should prepare now for that power and responsibility by mounting a cohesive opposition.

Adlai Stevenson responded to this letter, as he responded to the many others articulating similar arguments in the winter of 1952,

FIGURE 1. Joe Parrish, *Chicago Tribune*, February 18, 1957. © Chicago Tribune. Used by permission.

with a courteous and noncommittal note of thanks, after which, it appears, the politician and the professor never communicated again.[3] In itself, the exchange meant little. But it hinted at a postwar intellectual and political story with lasting consequences.

Schattschneider, a lifelong student of American parties, was associated more closely than any other scholar with a specific outlook on how they should function, summed up by two terms he used in the letter: "party government" and "party responsibility." Proponents of responsible party government sought to nationalize the structures of American parties that had long been patchworks of state and local organizations. They promoted programmatic parties, organized around policy positions rather than ties of tradition, patronage, or personality. And to secure democratic accountability in a system that provided voters with only two real options, they sought ways to ensure that the two parties' respective programs were at once coherent and mutually distinct. The goal, as a Schattschneider-led committee of the American Political Science Association (APSA) wrote in 1950, was a system in which the parties "bring forth programs to which they commit themselves and . . . possess sufficient internal cohesion to carry out these programs."[4]

This was a theory with intellectual roots in the turn of the century, later taken up by a set of advocates influenced by their political experiences of the 1930s and 1940s. The modern national state created by the New Deal and World War II brought with it a new politics centered on issues of federal policy. Franklin Roosevelt's presidency reshaped American liberalism as a public philosophy of government activism. But, crucially, that liberalism only partially defined the program and personnel of the *party* that Roosevelt led—a party that contained factions opposed to various aspects of the New Deal agenda. Liberal Democrats, frustrated with the obstacles to effective policymaking posed by dissident elements of their own party, would thus prove the most eager proponents of responsible party notions in the ensuing decades.

Seeking to ensure that the Democratic Party would "remain, first, a liberal party," such liberals targeted those Democrats whose partisan identity was not tied to the New Deal. These included the declining ranks of nonideological patronage-based organizations as well as the conservative party leaders of the Solid South. The southern bloc compromised the coherence and effectiveness of the Democratic Party in Congress and made mischief in conventions and national committee deliberations. Thus, liberals pushed for party discipline in Congress and majority rule within national party affairs. Schattschneider's heralding of two-party competition in the South, meanwhile, hinted at a logical end product of these intraparty struggles: a realigned party system structured by coherent policy agendas, consisting of one broadly liberal and one broadly conservative party.

The doctrine of responsible party government was most clearly articulated in the 1950 APSA report, *Toward a More Responsible Two-Party System*, whose critics responded in turn with a vigorous defense of traditional American parties as valuable forces for stabilization and inclusion. This scholarly dispute helped to set the terms of debate for conflicts that would soon erupt in the rough-and-tumble world of party politics. Indeed, the questions it touched on—about the proper function of parties, their connection to policy and ideology, and their role in the political system—were to recur in American politics for another half century.

THE NEW DEAL'S INCOMPLETE REVOLUTION

When Franklin Roosevelt enticed Wendell Willkie in 1944 with his vision of "two real parties—one liberal and the other conservative," a top-down party realignment seemed a tantalizing possibility.[5] Some mistimed press leaks, a spate of cold feet, and, most important, Willkie's sudden death that October all compelled the president to abandon this pursuit. But the mere fact of his overture signified how the New Deal era had provided a new impetus for the ideological realignment of the parties.

The New Deal transformed American politics but only *partially* transformed American parties. This sparked a revival of responsible party doctrine as both an idea and a plan of action. Government activism during the Roosevelt years centered political conflict on federal policy and inspired a new belief in the power of state intervention in markets and society. But though Roosevelt's massive electoral victories occurred under the Democratic label, the New Deal was less a party program than the agenda of a congeries of interest groups, social movements, experts, and public officials, some entirely disconnected from Democratic organizations.[6] The New Deal's effect on the Democratic Party was dramatic, shifting its electoral center of gravity to the North, associating its national agenda with the president's liberalism, and compelling a limited but real degree of centralization in its internal affairs.[7] Countervailing developments, however, compromised Roosevelt's leadership over his party—most important, the emergence by 1938 of an effective obstructionist coalition of Republicans and conservative Democrats. Those Democrats were mainly southern, disproportionately senior, and empowered by the congressional committee system. In his famous "purge" campaign that year, Roosevelt intervened in the primary contests of leading conservative Democrats in a largely failed effort to replace them with pro–New Deal alternatives. Roosevelt explained this effort to radio audiences in explicitly ideological terms, saying that, as "head of the Democratic Party," charged with carrying out "the definitely liberal declaration of principles" in the 1936 platform, he was obligated to support liberal Democrats over conservative ones whenever possible.[8]

Four years later, Schattschneider hailed the purge campaign as "one of the greatest experimental tests of the nature of the American party system ever made."[9] Its failure did not put an end to liberals' interest in party realignment.[10] The dramatic year of 1948, for example, saw upheaval within the Democratic coalition followed by a polarized general election. In a stunning demonstration of the growing party clout of northern liberals, insurgent activists at the 1948 Democratic convention succeeded in adding a forceful civil rights plank to the platform, prompting four delegations from the South to bolt and mount a third-party presidential bid. For the general election, Harry Truman's political strategists devised an aggressively liberal campaign strategy, mobilizing core New Deal constituencies like organized labor in the name of securing and expanding Franklin Roosevelt's legacy. Truman's upset victory, accomplished without the Deep South's support, accompanied the election of a slew of energetic liberal newcomers to Congress. It seemed to herald an era in which Democrats could compete nationally without their southern conservatives.[11]

Related developments helped to channel left-liberal energies into the Democratic Party and grow a constituency for stronger discipline and ideological cohesion within it. The New Deal oriented politics around national issues while the pressures of domestic anticommunism took their toll on radical agrarian and labor politics; both developments hastened the decline of regional third-party movements, such as Minnesota's Farmer-Labor Party, after World War II.[12] The national Progressive Party disintegrated, while the anticommunist Americans for Democratic Action (ADA) consolidated its position as an elite liberal satellite of the Democratic Party.[13] A similar dynamic affected the political strategy of the labor movement. After flirting with third-partyism, industrial labor leaders like Walter Reuther abandoned the effort by 1947 in favor of integration into the Democratic coalition.[14] Their long-range strategy was to partner with liberal and civil rights activists within Democratic ranks, compel the exit of illiberal blocs (chiefly southern conservatives), and achieve an ideological realignment.[15]

Meanwhile, the failures of Truman's second term—the grinding frustrations of congressional obstruction and partisan disarray that crippled the Fair Deal domestic agenda—prompted liberal Democrats to scrutinize the institutional and political roadblocks to effective party governance.[16] Into this setting stepped a group of political scientists, eager to help.

THE PRESCRIPTION OF PARTY RESPONSIBILITY

The doctrine of responsible party government originated in the scholarly writings of Progressives like Woodrow Wilson and Henry Jones Ford. In part, the New Deal and World War II–era intellectual revival of the doctrine reflected classic Progressive concerns, such as modernizing public administration and rationalizing the politics of national policy.[17] Making the parties more cohesive and programmatic was bound up in a broader reform project aimed at adapting America's cumbersome and antiquated constitutional structure to the needs of a modern industrial and military state. Thomas Finletter, a New York lawyer and diplomat who served as Truman's Air Force secretary, typified this reformist impulse in his 1945 book *Can Representative Government Do the Job?*, which warned that the political drift and division fostered by American federalism and the separation of powers imperiled the national interest in an era of global crisis. He advocated closer legislative–executive branch coordination and the abolition of such legislative "anachronisms" as the Senate filibuster, the autonomy of committees, and the seniority system, all of which impeded action and fragmented authority. Giving presidents the power to dissolve Congress and coordinating the terms and election schedules of the House, Senate, and presidency, meanwhile, would help to produce that "party discipline which alone in representative government can constitute an effective bridge between the Executive and Congress and alone can bring them to work together harmoniously."[18]

As Finletter's prescriptions hinted, the British parliamentary system loomed large as a model in postwar reformist thinking, particularly among liberal admirers of the postwar Labor Party under Clement Attlee. The Attlee government's implementation of a sweeping program of social provision and nationalization stood in stark contrast to the deadlock and disappointments of Truman's Fair Deal.[19] British intellectuals like Harold Laski contributed to comparative analysis of the two party systems, while young American scholars like Samuel Beer studied the dynamics of British politics for applicable lessons.[20] "I was much influenced by the British example of strong party government getting things through the legislature," Beer recalled. "I thought, well, that's what we need: A political party which has a program that's been explained to voters who then choose this program rather than another."[21]

To these strands of responsible party thinking, Elmer Eric Schattschneider would add both an overarching framework and a potent voice of hardnosed realism—a highly un-Progressive celebration of the raw and messy aspects of real-life democratic politics. Writing in a distinctively terse, aphoristic style, Schattschneider celebrated the restless power-seeking energies of the political parties even as he sought to transform them. He believed in the centrality of parties as organizers of conflict and generators of governing agendas, in part because he was skeptical about ordinary voters' capacity to comprehend complex policy issues.[22] As Schattschneider wrote, "the people are a sovereign whose vocabulary is limited to two words, 'Yes' and 'No.' Moreover, they are a sovereign that can only speak when spoken to."[23] In contrast to the Progressives, he felt that this made the parties all the more important. Progressive antipartyism had been "formulated in language which seems to condemn all partisanship for all time," he pointed

out, but was in fact directed at a distinctly corrupt and reactionary political era.[24] Its legacy was a "folklore of politics" that venerated independence to a fault. "Independence per se is a virtue, and
party loyalty per se is an evil. We cling to this notion" even in the
face of evidence that "independence is a synonym of ineffectiveness in a game in which teamwork produces results."[25] The worthy
Progressive goal of issue-based politics would best be achieved,
Schattschneider argued, through stronger and more programmatic parties.

Schattschneider similarly eschewed the Progressive tendency
toward formalism and institutional reform. Though the fragmented constitutional structure fostered similar fragmentation in
the parties, he believed that a new commitment among partisans
to unity could trigger far-reaching changes in the entire political
system. His priority was thus political: to will discipline and organization into existence on behalf of programmatic national parties.
In turn, the ceaseless electoral competition between those parties
would have the happy byproduct of smashing the boss rule of urban
machines and the southern gentry.[26]

The intellectual force of Schattschneider's arguments and his
infectious enthusiasm as a teacher and scholar brought him a devoted following in the 1940s.[27] "You're the prophet," his protégé
Austin Ranney wrote in 1948. "I never expect to cease being a disciple."[28] Other influential devotees included Steven K. Bailey, who
alternated between stints in government and academia throughout the 1950s; James MacGregor Burns of Williams College; and
Hubert Humphrey's circle of publicly active political scientists at
the University of Minnesota. Neither Schattschneider nor his allies
could claim to speak for the discipline. (Harvard's V. O. Key, for
one, was both somewhat skeptical of responsible party doctrine
and also more broadly influential.) But Schattschneider's effectiveness at intellectual networking played a role in his appointment
as chair of the APSA's new Committee on Political Parties in 1947.
Indeed, he had indirectly inspired the creation of the committee
by publishing an article in 1946 concerning partisan dynamics in
Congress.[29] His analysis intrigued three scholars working in federal agencies at the time, Fritz Morstein Marx, Bertram Gross, and

Paul T. David, who thought a comprehensive case might be made for responsible party reforms under the imprimatur of a national commission.

Establishing that committee was one way that political scientists sought to provide prescriptive expertise in the service of planning and reform in the early postwar years—a commitment that was not to last. As the APSA put it in a 1945 manifesto, part of political scientists' task was to "spread as widely as possible a knowledge of what good government is and what its benefits are to all citizens."[30] An immediate model for the parties committee was the Committee on Congress, which had exerted modest influence on the Legislative Reorganization Act of 1946. The Committee on Political Parties' stated mission was to "study the organization and operation of national political parties and elections, with a view to suggesting changes that might enable the parties and voters to fulfill their responsibilities more effectively."[31] The group circulated a series of position memos in 1947, then held meetings over the course of 1948 and 1949.[32]

Though Schattschneider did not personally dominate the activities of the committee, responsible party doctrine certainly drove its assumptions and approach. All of the most active participants, among them Schattschneider, Gross, Marx, Louise Overacker, and Clarence Berdahl, were committed to encouraging better disciplined, more programmatic, and more nationally oriented parties. There were few dissident members, though most of the group did strongly differ from Schattschneider's view that efforts to spread mechanisms of democratic participation *inside* the parties were irrelevant at best and pernicious at worst. The others believed instead that intraparty democracy bolstered programmatic cohesion—a position that survived in the committee's eventual report, *Toward a More Responsible Two-Party System*. Though Fritz Marx was the report's primary author, the APSA committee leader's spirit was well reflected by the confident declaration in the foreword that "the weakness of the American two-party system can be overcome as soon as a substantial part of the electorate wants it overcome."[33]

Toward a More Responsible Two-Party System, an accessible 100-

page document released to considerable fanfare in the fall of 1950, framed the problem of irresponsibility this way: "Historical and other factors have caused the American two-party system to operate as two loose associations of state and local organizations, with very little national machinery and very little national cohesion." This meant that either party, when in power, "is ill-equipped to organize its members in the legislative and executive branches into a government held together and guided by the party program." Lest Americans resign themselves to muddling through, the report warned that modern conditions rendered the situation truly "grave," for "it is no longer safe for the nation to deal piecemeal with issues." The authors were emphatic that parties should be organized around issues—"the choices provided by the two-party system are valuable to the American people in proportion to their definition in terms of public policy"—and attributed the new policy-oriented basis of partisanship to the New Deal: "The reasons for the growing emphasis on public policy in party politics are to be found, above all, in the very operations of modern government."[34]

The committee suggested reforms along three dimensions of party operations: developing policy positions, ensuring discipline and cohesion, and centralizing national power. It advocated a fifty-member party council that would manage continuing affairs and steer the formulation of the platform while devising positions on new policy issues between conventions. Notably, the council would also act as a disciplinary board authorized to "make recommendations to the National Convention, the National Committee or other appropriate party organs with respect to conspicuous departures from general party decisions by state or local party organizations." As a further means to foster integration, cohesion, and deliberation over policy programs, the committee recommended that national party conventions take place biennially. Concerning Congress, the committee recited what by that time had become a standard litany of reform proposals to rationalize, if not quite parliamentarize, both chambers: curbing the autonomy of committees and the sanctity of seniority; centralizing authority in the party leadership; and abolishing that iconic countermajoritarian institution, the Senate filibuster.[35]

IN DEFENSE OF INDISCIPLINE

The APSA report was intensely controversial, setting the terms of debate about American political parties for much of the next decade.[36] One testament to its impact was its success in motivating the committee's opponents to mount a vigorous defense of American parties as they had traditionally functioned.

These critics largely rearticulated the main lines of argument laid out a decade earlier by Pendleton Herring in *The Politics of Democracy*. Herring agreed that American parties were not suited to generating coherent and distinct programs, but he did not see that as a problem. "Our present system does not mean the negation of policies because the parties seem so similar in viewpoint," he wrote. "There is ample room for positive programs, but our parties are not the channels best suited to their initiation." Instead, interest groups and activists in society better served that role. The parties functioned less as policy channels than as arenas in which "differences of viewpoint . . . may in large measure be either disregarded or compromised"; thus, the parties served as forces for stability, integration, and incremental, pragmatic change.[37]

Herring argued that loose, nonprogrammatic parties suited not only America's fragmented constitutional order but also a diverse population composed of a jumble of crosscutting group interests. As the younger pluralist David Truman put it in his massively influential 1951 work *The Governmental Process*, in systems like America's featuring undisciplined parties, the channels of access to power "will be numerous, and patterns of influence within the legislature will be diverse" and "constantly shifting."[38] The value of a system dominated by incremental and fragmented bargaining among interests was implicit in Truman's account and explicit in many others. Strongly majoritarian visions of comprehensive mandates and responsible parties, to such analysts, were unwelcome in part because they were so unrealistic. Indeed, the acute *danger* posed by party alignments based on deep ideological or group cleavages was a central theme in another influential contemporary defense of American parties, Herbert Agar's *The Price of Union*.[39]

Critics of the APSA report sounded anew these cautionary notes. "How much party centralization do we want?," T. William Goodman asked. Expressing doubt that most voters ever consciously associated their vote with support for a given party's platform, and invoking Madisonian reservations about the potential for majority tyranny, his answer was clear: not nearly as much as the Committee on Political Parties wanted.[40] The most notable voice in this chorus was Schattschneider's erstwhile "disciple" Austin Ranney, who had become "more and more skeptical about the applicability, the reality, of the Schattschneider prescription." Herring's and Agar's work helped attune him to the political necessity of concepts like "consensus and majority forbearance and minority acquiescence" that responsible party proponents often sidelined.[41] Ranney published a critique of the committee's report challenging its presumption that Americans' fundamental democratic commitment was to effective majority rule. In fact, he countered, a sensitivity to minority rights and to the prevention of unchecked control of the full government by any given majority was deeply ingrained in American political culture. Indeed, "the same popular beliefs about government which sustain our present anti-majoritarian constitutional system will continue to sustain . . . our anti-majoritarian party system."[42]

What little direct evidence existed of Americans' views of the party system, moreover, showed general hostility to the prospect of a programmatic party realignment—though the committee report claimed that the scrambled ideological lines of the parties was "a serious source of public discontent."[43] Gallup polled Americans in 1947: "It has been suggested that we give up the present Republican and Democratic Parties and have two new parties, one for the Liberals and one for the Conservatives. Would you favor this idea?" Thirteen percent said yes. In 1950 Gallup asked, "Would you like to have the Republican party officially join with the Southern conservative Democrats in a new political party?" Majorities of Republicans, northern Democrats, and Southern Democrats all answered in the negative.[44]

In the face of such polling data, committee members likely would have responded that their aim was to *educate* citizens about the virtues of strong, responsible parties. Yet their report was notably coy on the subjects of ideology and realignment. Though the implication may have been obvious in, say, their claim that "the sort of opposition presented by a coalition that cuts across party lines, as a regular thing, tends to deprive the public of a meaningful alternative," the report's drafters deliberately avoided an explicit discussion of realignment. Strategic calculation drove this decision. Paul David recalled that it was "obvious when the report was being written that most of the proposed reforms would be impossible or unlikely unless some realignment occurred, especially in the South." When he therefore suggested addressing the subject head-on, however, Marx and his colleagues resisted, suggesting instead that realignment would happen naturally: "if the Democratic party went ahead firmly with the development of the programmatic views that were held by a majority of the party, then the southern dissidents would eventually find themselves so out of place that they would leave the party."[45]

If such deliberations indicated an awareness that responsible party government would entail a more ideologically defined system, they sought to downplay this theme publicly. The final report even claimed that "needed clarification of party policy *in itself* will not cause the parties to differ more fundamentally or more sharply than they have in the past." Since such clarification would produce a more realistic, policy-focused public discussion, "the contrary is much more likely to be the case."[46] In his critique T. William Goodman expressed incredulity at this obvious fudge. "If parties are not 'to differ more fundamentally or more sharply' in the future than in the past," he asked, "what is all the hullaballoo about? How will the voters have any clearer choices than they have had?"[47] The report deepened its own ambiguity with an artful formulation on ideology. "Increasing concern with their programs" will not "cause the parties to erect between themselves an ideological wall," the committee wrote. "There is no real ideological division in the American electorate, and hence programs of action presented by responsible parties for the voter's support could hardly be expected to reflect or strive toward such division."[48] This statement was pregnant with the assumptions and vocabulary of midcentury liberal thinking about a national consensus, but it raised the question of what *would* motivate and shape the construction of two alternative party programs, if not some differing set of principles or "ideology."

Far from being clear on this point, Schattschneider betrayed just such a thin conception of political disagreement. What mattered to him was simply the existence of a choice between programs and the ability of a party to carry its program out. The formulation of the programs and their mutual distinctiveness would be byproducts of the parties' competition for votes. He could even write approvingly of the often-muddled results of this process.[49] Ideology and principle played little role in his self-consciously pragmatic conception of politics. Partisan competition was for him the all-powerful mechanism.[50] But his unexamined assumptions about the sources of political belief had implications for party competition. As one critic noted prophetically, disciplined national parties might produce *more* rather than less one-party dominance in localities, given the uneven distribution of political beliefs across the country.[51] Moreover, the most zealous advocates of programmatic politics in the 1950s—the amateur foot soldiers of party responsibility—would be precisely those most drawn to a political language of principle and ideological conviction.

The controversy over *Toward a More Responsible Two-Party System* was largely confined to academics in the early 1950s, though the report did circulate elsewhere. Its publication garnered front-page coverage in the *New York Times* and a supportive editorial in the *Washington Post*.[52] Schattschneider traveled to Washington at Hubert Humphrey's invitation to discuss the report with labor activists and party leaders.[53] Truman administration officials showed the report to the president, who agreed with certain specific recommendations (like enhancing the party's research capacities) but thought the party council idea impractical.[54] Some of the report's language also influenced activist organizations. A 1951 ADA pamphlet suggested possible topics for discussion at chapter meetings, including: "Should we have responsible political parties?"[55] Still, the report's early political impact was modest.

During those same years, however, a groundswell of grassroots political activism with a distinctly programmatic ethos attended Adlai Stevenson's rise to Democratic leadership. His presidential campaign in 1952 drew an influx of reformist liberals into state and national Democratic organizations. One such Stevenson booster, an energetic national committeeman from Indiana named Paul Butler, came across *Toward a More Responsible Two-Party System* in 1952, on the eve of his rise to power within the Democratic National Committee. Butler took the report to heart, and as DNC chairman would soon pursue something of an experiment in responsible party leadership.

2

DEMOCRATS AND THE POLITICS OF PRINCIPLE, 1952-1960

The apostles of responsible party doctrine in the postwar years tended to be liberal Democrats frustrated with the party's internal divisions and contradictions. Nominal party leader Adlai Stevenson would play a partial, even unwitting role in advancing the vision of a more disciplined and coherent party. An introspective patrician rather than a party warrior—and an ideological moderate to boot—Stevenson nonetheless served as a vessel for programmatic liberal energies in the 1950s. His two campaigns for president facilitated, on the one hand, the coalescence of a powerful cadre of policy intellectuals and, on the other hand, a major grassroots influx of activists committed to Democratic party reform as well as substantive, issue-based politics. Both constituencies wanted to make American party politics more national in scope, programmatic in orientation, and disciplined and cohesive in structure.

The Democratic struggle for party responsibility was less visible in Stevenson's campaigns than in nascent efforts to reform Congress, skirmishes in the national conventions, and, most vividly, the long and controversial tenure of Democratic National Committee (DNC) chairman Paul Butler. Between late 1954 and 1960, Butler institutionalized a key reform proposal—an official party council—and articulated an increasingly explicit vision of vigorous opposition. His actions drew him into ceaseless public conflicts with southern Democrats, urban bosses, and congressional leaders Sam Rayburn and Lyndon Johnson, men who shared a starkly different outlook on the value and function of parties.

These intra-Democratic struggles proved inconclusive in the

FIGURE 2. Bill Sanders, *Greensboro Daily News*, July 8, 1959. Used by permission, Sanders Cartoon Commentary.

Eisenhower era, but they raised crucial questions about the nature of political conflict and the relationship between parties and principles. Pitting liberals against conservative southern Democrats, such conflicts were bound up in the politics of race. The fight for civil rights would prove to be the great dynamic force for nationalizing power within the Democratic Party, bolstering its capacity for internal discipline and eventually, ushering in the ideological realignment of both parties. But that process would involve more conflict and take more time than reformers anticipated. In the 1960s, issue-driven and ideological activism would rock the party with explosive force. But the origins of that activism, and that approach to party politics, could be found in the allegedly staid 1950s.

PAUL BUTLER, ADLAI STEVENSON, AND THE AMATEUR SPIRIT

That national party chairmen rarely have been historically significant players in American politics is testament to the structural weakness of the national committees. The title of a leading assessment of the party committees summarized their peculiar position: *Politics without Power*.[1] Paul Butler did not transcend the limits of his post or transform it in an enduring manner. But his unusually energetic effort to do just that, driven by both substantive commitments and responsible party theory, served to highlight dynamic tensions within the Democratic coalition and the party system.

Butler was a lawyer from South Bend, Indiana, who had risen through the Democratic ranks in a state marked by strong two-party competition. In his native setting he was not a good-government reformer. He was, however, a devoted New Deal liberal, and despite his modest reform bona fides, he owed his ascension within the DNC to a new breed of Democrats who saw in him a kindred spirit. "Paul had observed the discontent brewing in the Party in many states over the ineffectiveness of the old politics," recalled Michigan party chairman Neil Staebler, "and was determined to bring the new approach into the National Committee."[2]

What was "the old politics"? What was "the new approach"? Staebler evoked a dynamic current that ran through Democratic politics in a slew of states and cities in the 1950s. At the vanguard of this change was a generation of predominantly middle-class liberal party activists—the "club Democrats." In state after state beginning in the late 1940s, the club Democrats came into conflict with existing party machinery and leadership, unless they took over with little resistance at all.

These power struggles took place amid the postwar acceleration of a trend that had begun during the Progressive Era: the long-term decay of transactional, nonprogrammatic local and state party organizations—that is, machines. New Deal financial and political largesse had prompted a short-term revival of urban party organizations (specifically Democratic ones) in the 1930s and 1940s. But the machines' Indian summer did not long outlast World War II.[3] Postwar observers recognized the decline as it happened. Journalist John Fischer, who had worked on the Stevenson campaign in 1952, described the "almost total collapse of the party organization" across the country that had hindered that campaign's efforts: "The city machines turned out to be a toothless and rheumatic team of dragons," he wrote, "far gone in senility and fatty degeneration. The old-time bosses . . . found they could no longer deliver the votes."[4]

Myriad forces drove the slow unraveling of the parties' classic patronage model. Economic growth and the creation and expansion of a national welfare state reduced the demand among voters for the services offered by the old machines. Civil service reforms in states and cities, meanwhile, removed public sector jobs from political control, drastically depleting the machines' main supply of material incentives for party work. ("Grandma no longer needed to see her precinct captain about that pension," Fischer wrote in explaining the machines' decline. "Instead she talked to a brisk civil servant with a Vassar degree in the neighborhood Social Security office.")[5] Finally, party organizations were no longer the only way people got political information: increased access to education along with the advent of new media—most important, television—hampered parties' ability to prescribe voting choices. To be sure, well into the 1950s voting behavior continued largely to be structured by stable partisan affiliations formed early in life, with issues and ideology playing marginal roles.[6] But the long-range trends were destabilizing those patterns, while setting the context for more visible, immediate changes among the parties' activist ranks.

The pattern recurred in several states in the late 1940s and early 1950s. Young, educated New Deal liberals, motivated largely by national issues, forged alliances with organized labor and racial minorities to square off against sclerotic, generally nonideological Democratic organizations. There was the California Democratic

Council, launching pad for future liberal congressional stalwarts like George Miller, Phil Burton, and Henry Waxman, which produced in the 1950s a zealous and energetic DNC committeeman in Beverly Hills attorney Paul Ziffren.[7] The liberal Democratic Organizing Committee of Wisconsin swamped and supplanted the existing state party leadership through primary fights in the late 1940s.[8] The Michigan Democratic Club formed in the wake of liberals' failed efforts to oust the state party leadership in 1946. Through painstaking statewide organizational work by Neil Staebler in alliance with labor leaders Gus Scholle and Walter Reuther, the club launched G. Mennen "Soapy" Williams to a record six terms as governor starting in 1948.[9] In states like New York and Illinois that had more robust existing machines capable of defending themselves, new reformers and clubs still managed to establish beachheads from which they became meaningful players in party activities. Even in one-party Texas a vigorous liberal cadre, inspired initially by the Stevenson campaigns, established the Democrats of Texas in 1957 as a base for Senator Ralph Yarborough, providing the left flank of a three-way factional division within the state party.[10]

Contemporaries described such activists as "New Look" Democrats.[11] What distinguished them from other partisans? A leading observer, James Q. Wilson, contrasted these "amateur Democrats" with nonideological professionals, writing, "The amateur takes the outcome of politics—the determination of policies and the choice of officials—seriously, in the sense that he feels a direct concern for what he thinks are the ends these policies serve and the qualities these officials possess." By contrast, public policy to the professionals was merely "the by-product of efforts that are aimed, not at producing the good society, but at gaining power and place for one's self and one's party." Parties under professional control served as "neutral agents which mobilize majorities for whatever candidates and programs seem best suited to capturing public fancy."[12] A key implication of this distinction was that the amateur's attention to issues of public policy made him at least a potential advocate for a party system organized around coherent agendas—that is, responsible party government. The authors of *Toward a More Responsible Two-Party System* had heralded the emergence of just such a type of activist helping to "break down the patronage-nomination-election concept of party" and to build programmatic parties in its wake.[13] As the 1950s progressed, advocates like Schattschneider and Burns similarly welcomed signs of ascendant issue-based voting and party activism.[14]

No development proved more galvanizing to the emergence of that activism in the 1950s than Adlai Stevenson's first campaign for president. Stevenson was in many ways an unlikely vessel for such liberal energies. His positions on issues ranging from civil rights to economics were more conservative than those of the activists manning the Draft Stevenson movement and populating Stevenson clubs in 1952, as well as those of policy advisors and speechwriters like Arthur Schlesinger Jr. and John Kenneth Galbraith. What endeared him to the new breed of activists was his political style and posture toward the party machinery. His intelligence and evident aversion to the grubby business of old-fashioned politicking struck a chord with amateurs whose interest in politics was, to use Wilson's term, "purposive" and ends-focused rather than transactional.[15] In this sense the Stevenson followers' proud adoption of the pejorative "egghead" label reflected not merely their dominant social characteristics, but a particular and increasingly pervasive disposition toward politics.[16]

Butler, an early Stevenson supporter who was first elected national committeeman in 1952, built a reputation among DNC members as an energetic and innovative proponent of issue-based, program-oriented party politics, traveling endlessly to foster intraparty communication while proposing organizational reforms that stemmed directly from the work of the APSA Committee on Political Parties.[17] Butler had learned of the committee while working on a proposal for a 1954 midterm national party convention.[18] He argued that a midterm convention would generate publicity for the party while helping to keep it engaged on national issues and a coherent program.[19] The response to the proposal at the DNC Executive Committee illustrated the fault lines that would later define Butler's chairmanship. Chairman Stephen Mitchell and several reformist committeemen expressed interest. But Pittsburgh mayor

David Lawrence, a powerful machine boss, articulated a skepticism shared by many professionals when he pointed out that to "have a convention and have the linen washed out over television" might exacerbate rather than resolve intraparty tensions.[20] Unity-minded professionals, conservative southerners, and congressional leaders jealously guarding their dominance over policy all voiced opposition.[21] One congressman called the idea "asinine."[22] A committee appointed to consider the idea dismissed it on logistical grounds.[23]

Similar factional lines were evident in Butler's 1954 bid to succeed Mitchell as DNC chairman. Unlike his two main rivals for the job—Harry Truman's favored candidate, Mike DiSalle of Ohio, and the urban bosses' pick, James Finnegan of Pennsylvania—Butler lacked a powerful patron. He was the only candidate to actively campaign for the job, personally calling 93 of the 105 DNC members to solicit their vote.[24] In the December election, Butler secured the support of reformist committee members from states like California, Wisconsin, Michigan, and Minnesota, while Finnegan and DiSalle split the machine-dominated East Coast.[25]

Surprisingly, however, Butler also swept the votes of southern committee members, the region least committed to responsible party reforms, nationalized parties, or issues-based politics. In an uncharacteristically cynical gambit, Butler had made a secret pledge in a closed-door meeting with Georgia Democratic chairman John Sammons Bell: "I do not consider the question of segregation a political issue," read the note that bore Butler's signature. "I see no reason for any chairman of our party at any level to project segregation into our political discussions."[26] Expediency appears to explain Butler's signature, since he was progressive on civil rights and critical of the South's role in the party. As we will see, a mid-fifties intraparty détente on racial issues soon broke down, and Butler would become the civil rights camp's outspoken advocate.

Butler's early years as chairman saw little movement on civil rights, but a number of initiatives reflected the issues-based, programmatic orientation of his core allies. He appointed Neil Staebler as chairman of a new Advisory Committee on Political Organization (ACPO), which offered suggestions on party structure, worker training, and communication. Several of ACPO's recommendations reflected a belief in issue-based partisanship. District and regional issues conferences would foster the circulation of "a common body of information and argument for party members," while televised town hall meetings could publicize those positions.[27] ACPO also recommended measures promoting disciplined commitment to party programs, such as a Platform Review Committee operating between conventions that would report to the DNC concerning "the manner in which the Democratic Party Platform is being implemented."[28]

Butler's own conception of the relationship between program and party reflected responsible party theory. In a 1959 speech, he explained why a modern party must be "first and foremost an 'issue-oriented' organization—one held together primarily by belief in and devotion to some commonly held, clearly enunciated principles that provide motivation for political action."

> The extent and nature of the modern means of mass communication, the increased educational level of the population, the increasing importance of nationalizing trends as regards both section and nationality, the expanding participation of citizens in the processes of political parties and the growing importance of governmental programs in the Nation's economy and the everyday life of the citizen are all increasing the emphasis on the power of issues, principles, and ideas as the forces which are most responsible for the attraction and lasting attachment of new people to the banners of political parties. Party leaders are fast discovering, some the hard way, that political organizations based solely on patronage, personal favors, and the power and prestige of public office no longer enjoy the tremendous effectiveness they once possessed.

Using a term that would gain currency a decade later, Butler explained that "the 'new politics' places a premium on principles and demands greater attention be given to issues." Wherever the party takes "a hard-hitting approach based on issues designed to clarify the differences between our party and the opposition, we are making steady and often phenomenal progress."[29]

Neither the midterm convention nor the platform review committee came to pass during Butler's tenure, but a related reform—also with origins in the APSA report—did. The Democratic Advisory Council (DAC), which had a broad policy purview, was Butler's crowning innovation, an experiment that achieved an outsized impact precisely by sharpening rather than papering over the party's internal tensions.

FROM BRAIN TRUST TO PARTY COUNCIL

The core driver behind the DAC was not Butler but an unofficial network of intellectuals, politicians, and ex–New Dealers associated with Stevenson and known as "the Finletter group," after its social center and patron, ex–Air Force secretary Thomas Finletter.[30] The group owed its existence to the liberal drive to publicize a positive, distinct Democratic program in the Eisenhower years. A chorus of such voices urged Stevenson to maintain a national presence after his loss in 1952, starting with his adviser, Arthur Schlesinger Jr.[31] Resolutions passed after the election by Stevenson clubs and state and local parties pledged continued activity on behalf of his national agenda.[32] *Saturday Review* editor Norman Cousins suggested that Stevenson help establish a High Council for the Democratic Party to develop issue positions, while Hubert Humphrey urged him to sustain a vigorous, public advocacy of liberal principles and to combat the party's right wing.[33] Stevenson heeded the call in 1953 and 1954 by authorizing an informal stable of experts, writers, and politicians to produce detailed memos and speech material for party officials.

It was fitting that Tom Finletter would lead such an effort. A hardliner on military matters but a staunch liberal domestically, he generally encouraged boldness in the party's policy pronouncements. More significant was his abiding intellectual interest in strengthening the lines of accountability and partisan cohesion in the political system. Finletter had advocated a partial parliamentarization of government in his book *Can Representative Government Do the Job?* and the Democrats' ouster in 1952 sharpened his focus on the problem of opposition.[34] "The idea of a 'cabinet,' an organization in opposition, a shadow organization, was in my mind for a long time," he recalled.[35]

The research and communication capacities of this brain trust provided not only Stevenson but other leading Democrats with a steady supply of ammunition for attacking the policies of the Eisenhower administration and articulating alternatives. Arthur Schlesinger and John Kenneth Galbraith were leaders and informal coordinators of the ad hoc, ever-changing roster of participants.[36] The group's output between 1953 and 1956 was often reactive, responding to issues and agendas set by congressional Republicans or the Eisenhower administration. But collectively the papers circulated by the group amounted to a coherent articulation of Cold War liberal orthodoxy—hawkish and internationalist, aggressively Keynesian, and committed to enhancing New Deal–vintage activism in labor relations, health care, social insurance, and agriculture. This was primarily *northern* Democratic doctrine, advocated without the threat of veto from southern or other conservative party professionals.[37] By 1955 the "Finletter group" was a phrase and a phenomenon readily discussed in the press. The *Christian Science Monitor* described the group as the "secretariat of a shadow-government . . . one of the most interesting innovations in the evolution of the United States political system.[38] Soon enough, the DNC under Paul Butler's stewardship would absorb the group's approach, and much of its key personnel, into a formal party apparatus.

The Democrats' recapture of Congress in the 1954 midterms intensified calls to publicize a party program. Stevenson sought to formalize the Finletter group's activities with a salaried director.[39] From elsewhere in the DNC came renewed attention to policy promulgation and to the sticky subject of coordinating with the congressional leadership. After the midterms, Truman aide and DNC special counsel Charles Murphy suggested that the committee work with congressional leaders to develop a policy agenda for the party, arguing that "it is not enough to wait for Eisenhower's recommendations and vote them up or down."[40] He sent Butler a dossier of material for a Democratic legislative program and strategized about how they might share it with the congressional leadership "without undue ruffling of feelings" or provoking suspicions of "mischievous interference."[41]

Murphy's fears on this latter score were prescient. The conflict that flared up in the later 1950s between Paul Butler and Sam Rayburn and Lyndon Johnson encompassed clashes over strategy, ideology, and personality. Underlying all of them, however, were the institutional barriers to cohesive party agendas inherent in the American system. Policymaking authority for the "out party" (the party lacking control of the presidency) belonged to congressional officials, each of whom was directly responsible to local constituents rather than to a collective party organ. The drafters of the 1950 APSA report had been well aware of this predicament when they cast their proposal for a Party Council not as an incursion on congressional prerogative but rather as an instrument of integration that incorporated a large congressional contingent.[42] But the very divisions the council was meant to heal made establishing such a body difficult. Frustration would compel liberals to begin addressing this dilemma, and electoral defeat would embolden them to act.

The frustration stemmed from the performance of congressional Democrats during the Eisenhower years, first in the minority and especially in the majority during the 83rd Congress (1955–56). The political strategy adopted by Rayburn and Johnson was well publicized, and its watchword was cooperation with Eisenhower. They surmised that the president's immense personal popularity, combined with policy divisions between his administration and the Old Guard majority of congressional Republicans, necessitated a constructive Democratic posture. Democrats should seek opportunities to find common ground with the president, which would exacerbate fractures within the GOP. This implied that congressional leaders should work to blur programmatic differences between the parties while avoiding issues that divided Democrats.[43] Rayburn and Johnson took their recapture of Congress in 1954 as vindica-

tion. "We are going to look upon the president's recommendation with kindliness," Rayburn said upon reclaiming the Speaker's
gavel, "because he is the leader of our country. We are not going
to be against [his program] just because a Republican President
has recommended it."[44] Throughout 1955 and 1956, newspapers
depicted the "bipartisan love match" and "Capitol Hill armistice"
governing executive–legislative relations."[45] Assessing congressional politics prior to the 1956 party conventions—typically a time
ripe with partisanship—William S. White marveled that "little that
is stark and unarguably clear stands to differentiate the parties as
they enter the final weeks of this session."[46]

For liberals, that was just the problem: it was both politically
and substantively perverse for Democratic leaders to insulate
Eisenhower from the taint of congressional Republicans' conservatism while melding the Democratic agenda with his own. What
the party needed was a program that contrasted with Eisenhower's
while revealing his moderate image to be window-dressing. In a
widely circulated 1955 memo, Schlesinger described how Eisenhower's "bear hug" of congressional Democrats—a strategy "designed to obscure and minimize the issues between the parties"—
might "result in squeezing a good deal of the vitality out of the
Democratic appeal." Democrats needed instead to "clarify the differences between the parties," in part by passing an array of bills
intended to draw presidential vetoes.[47] This strategy spoke directly
to the tricky question of how to apply responsible party principles
to a system where power was often divided between the parties. By
passing bills doomed to veto, liberals would help amass a record
to run on in the next election, while the very process of commit-
ting to a bold agenda could resolve intraparty ideological divisions.
Both goals were anathema to Rayburn and Johnson, the latter explaining to Harry Truman in late 1956 that he would construct his
legislative agenda in reaction to the president's declared priorities
rather than independently, and would pursue only what was pass-
able.[48]

When Stevenson lost the presidential election that year by even
bigger margins than in 1952, a wave of Democratic recrimination ensued. "The election of 1956 was over before the campaign

began," ex-senator Herbert Lehman argued. "The Democrats in Congress failed to make the issues during the 18 months we were in control. On the contrary, almost everything the leadership did during that time was designed to prevent any controversial issue from being seriously joined or vigorously debated."[49] The fact that Eisenhower made gains among key Democratic constituencies, particularly African Americans and union members, illustrated to liberals the costs of letting two congressional southerners dictate party strategy.[50] The domination of committees by southerners far more reactionary than Johnson or Rayburn, moreover, posed even more of an electoral burden. One party boss summarized the predicament faced by northerners when trying to get out the labor and black votes for Stevenson that year: to counter the Democrats' appeal, the Republicans "just say 'Eastland'; they say 'Barden'; and that answered all kinds of arguments."[51] (Mississippi senator James Eastland was the white-supremacist chairman of the Judiciary Committee; North Carolina congressman Graham Barden the anti-union chairman of the House Education and Labor Committee.) These were not new complaints, but Stevenson's second loss at last prompted action to institutionalize a party voice outside of Congress.

Surprisingly, the Democratic Advisory Council was born of mixed amateur and professional parentage. The central mover on its behalf was California's Paul Ziffren, who epitomized those "new look" liberal committeemen devoted to issues-based politics and loyal to Paul Butler. But two powerful big-city professionals, former Illinois Cook County boss Jacob Arvey and Pittsburgh mayor David Lawrence, joined Ziffren in proposing the council in late November.[52] They suggested a two-part resolution: first, a reaffirmation of the contents of the 1956 Democratic platform and a call for the Democratic congressional majorities to enact it; and second, authorization for the chairman to establish an advisory committee made up of the full DNC Executive Committee as well as party leaders from Congress, state and local government, and elsewhere. The group would meet from time to time to "coordinate and advance efforts in behalf of Democratic programs and principles."[53]

Predictably, the Executive Committee members most skeptical
of this proposal were southern. Camille F. Gravel Jr. of Louisiana,
who was racially moderate and loyal to the national party, worried
that "we might be playing with political dynamite if we try to take
the position in this committee that we should advise the members
of Congress and the Senators as to what sort of legislative program
they should adopt." Assuring the committee that "we are going
to have trouble with our states in the South," Gravel questioned
whether "the Executive Committee . . . should adopt a resolution
in the face of major conflicts we apparently have within the Democratic Party." Even the symbolic reaffirmation of the platform gave
him pause. He reminded his colleagues of how much unhappy
compromise had been required to secure agreement to that platform in the first place. This prompted Arvey to interject that he saw
nothing wrong "in asserting our belief in the principles which we
adopted in our last Democratic Convention. We either meant those
things at that time, or we did not." Gravel was dubious:

> GRAVEL: 110 members of the Democratic House are from the
> South.
> ARVEY: Just a minute, they were elected on the Democratic plat-
> form, were they not?
> GRAVEL: Parts of it.
> ARVEY: Well, parts of it.
> (*Laughter*)
> GRAVEL: I mean seriously, now that—
> ARVEY: My friend, let me finish. We either have a National Party or
> we do not have.

Gravel's fellow southerner on the Executive Committee, Sallie
Baker Everett of North Carolina, echoed his skepticism, but both
agreed to join the others in passing the resolution, which authorized Butler to extend invitations to twenty Democrats. Butler hoped that he could secure cooperation from congressional
leaders, though he allowed that he had a better shot with Rayburn
than with Johnson. When Ziffren acknowledged the likelihood that
"Mr. Johnson will view this with less than enthusiasm," DNC trea-

surer Matthew McCloskey chimed in: "That's an understatement." "That's the understatement of the year," Gravel added, to laughter.

The congressional leaders' response to the Democratic Advisory Council was, indeed, immediate and negative. Johnson told Rayburn that the council idea "opened up a real hornet's nest" and "is capable of deepening divisions within the Democratic Party."[54] He suggested that all members of the congressional leadership refuse to join the council on the grounds that membership would conflict with their obligations to colleagues.[55] Rayburn expressed this to Butler, whose follow-up pleading fell on deaf ears.[56] The leaders' refusal to join the council dissuaded most other congressmen from joining, along with two southern governors. The council seemed to be stillborn.

But Butler, characteristically persistent, pressed on without the congressional leaders, asking Charles Murphy to draw up an organizational plan and bylaws.[57] The Executive Committee made Butler chairman of the DAC, authorizing him to appoint an organizing committee and hire an executive director.[58] Significantly, on two early occasions the full DNC endorsed the initiative. In February it ratified the establishment of the council over the objections of several southern members.[59] In May southerners pushed a resolution requiring full committee approval for any DAC policy declaration; it was defeated 67 to 26.[60] The DAC rested on a strong foundation of DNC support.

Those committeemen and -women who backed the DAC largely shared its view that the national committee should contribute to party policy. The congressional party, they argued, could not exercise a monopoly on policy during nonconvention years, not only because institutional constraints compromised its effectiveness, but also because doing so shut out millions of Democrats who were not represented by their party in Congress. "The Democratic Party is not just a Congressional party, it is a National party," Stevenson declared in justifying the DAC. "To be an effective opposition, the Democratic Party must have a broader base than the Democrats in Congress."[61] Maryland committeeman Phil Perlman argued that, given the regional biases of the congressional party, "on many policy matters, if not all of them, the Democratic National

Committee is more truly representative of the entire Party."[62] The council's executive director, Charles Tyroler, put it more bluntly decades later: the DAC's founders were "goddamned tired of the presidential wing of the party—the liberal, national-oriented wing of the party, stalwarts of it, who controlled 60 percent of the electoral votes—not being listened to in the off-years. Everybody was listening to Sam and Lyndon. Who were they but a couple of Texas politicians?"[63]

Rayburn and Johnson may have just been a couple of Texans, but their opposition to the DAC—and its ripple effects—rendered the council's membership much more monolithically liberal than originally intended. Indeed, the two senators who bucked their leaders to accept Butler's invitation at the outset, Estes Kefauver and Hubert Humphrey, epitomized the council's ideological cast. Humphrey had long served as a leader of the Senate Democrats' liberal bloc, and just as the DAC took shape in 1957 he sponsored a comprehensive legislative program in conjunction with Eugene McCarthy's introduction of a similar manifesto in the House.[64] In addition to Kefauver, Humphrey, and the fourteen ex-officio members from the DNC's Executive Council, the DAC's membership included figures such as Truman, Stevenson, and Soapy Williams, joined in later years by the likes of Herbert Lehman, governors Pat Brown and Orville Freeman, labor chief George Harrison, and, eventually, 1960 presidential hopefuls Stuart Symington and John F. Kennedy. This was a body with real stature. But it was also the mouthpiece of a specific party faction.

What did the DAC actually do? Its core function, like that of the Finletter group, was issuing policy statements. It interpreted its mandate in the same broad manner as had the APSA report in suggesting that it "make more specific or reformulate the party principles in their application to current situations."[65] Between January 1956 and June 1960, the DAC produced a total of sixty-one statements.[66] Ranging from lengthy essays to short reactions to current events, they emerged from the work of advisory committees comprising academics and activists, including groups on foreign affairs, economic policy, labor, natural resources, and civil rights. Conflicts emerged within some advisory committees, but they were differences of degree. The DAC's published output reflected members' shared support for military buildup, criticism of Eisenhower's approach to foreign and domestic policy, and advocacy of Keynesian management and more equitable social provision. The most significant subset of DAC statements, by dint of its sheer distance in tone and content from the congressional party's output, was undoubtedly civil rights.

As a vehicle for transmitting a distinct and relatively coherent policy agenda to a national audience, the DAC was a success. It commanded widespread and prominent press attention.[67] National and local newspapers alike routinely covered its pronouncements, often reprinting their full text and frequently portraying them as official party positions. On occasion journalists even assessed the council's institutional significance. "The U.S. political system has been often criticized for its failure to produce a coherent and challenging opposition between national elections," the *Dayton Daily News* editorialized in 1957. "For that reason, the Democratic hierarchy rates an 'A' for effort for taking up the chore."[68] Two years later the *Christian Science Monitor* declared the DAC "a significant development in the political evolutionary process."[69]

Such press reports spoke directly to Butler's vision. Over his tenure, Butler had increasingly articulated a commitment to party responsibility. Years of pitched conflict within his party and frustration with the fragmented machinery of national lawmaking had sharpened his diagnosis of the party system's ailments. In an extraordinary address in the summer of 1958, Butler offered an analysis that would have sounded familiar in a political science seminar but hardly constituted the typical rhetoric of party chairmen.[70] He ticked off some of the main components of party irresponsibility, including "loose party organization in the relationship of the state group to the national level . . . loosely organized national conventions and national committees, and the lack of mechanics to provide statements of official policy." The system's crowning failure, however, was the "total lack of disciplinary authority in implementing the provisions of the party platform." He knew that the DAC could not eradicate the structures fostering indiscipline, but it could help compensate for it.

The impediments to party responsibility did not end with the institutional elements Butler identified. Major ideological conflicts rent the party as well—substantive divisions that aligned with and thus compounded the institutional divisions and ensured that the DAC could never truly be more than a factional mouthpiece.[71] That Butler invariably viewed such complications as goads to further action made his tenure a source of inspiration for some and exasperation for others.

What accounted for this heedless persistence of Butler's, a trait that struck many as downright eccentric? Those who knew him emphasized both his earnestness and guilelessness, a tendency to commit fully to abstractly reasoned plans without sensing the controversy they would likely engender. Katie Louchheim, the savvy head of the DNC Women's Division and a powerful player in the party, recalled him as a moody micromanager who never seemed to anticipate making enemies but was, she wrote, "afraid of no one."[72] Sidney Hyman portrayed Butler as the personal embodiment of the amateur spirit in modern American politics—the egghead as party boss: "Tall, thin, an abstainer from both smoking and drinking, he impresses most of those who meet him as an intense and innocent man, scholarly and stubborn.... He seems lacking in all the back-slapping, yarn-swapping minor arts of politics. All this makes the 'old pros' uncomfortable in his presence.[73]

Those pros, Truman among them, never ceased trying to oust Butler, while the base of his support lay among reformist committeemen who shared his outlook and commitment to issue-based politics. That commitment won him the support of liberals nationally. The symbolic stakes in Butler's clashes with Rayburn and Johnson explain why Johnson's aide George Reedy once advised his boss to take a public attitude toward Butler's pronouncements akin to that of "a tolerant father toward a wayward son who drinks too much, necks too much, and gets himself hauled off into police court too many times for speeding. Any comments should be amused and tolerant and delivered with a smile—and should be held to a minimum."[74] That advice would be sorely tested in the late 1950s.

PARTIES, PRINCIPLES, AND THE DILEMMAS OF OPPOSITION

A Broadway hit came to Washington in June 1959. *Sunrise at Campobello* depicted a young Franklin Roosevelt's heroic struggle with polio, offering a showcase for actor Ralph Bellamy. The capital's Democratic Central Committee sponsored a gala opening at the National Theater and invited Democratic luminaries and party activists to it.[75] At one point in the play, Bellamy read aloud a letter Roosevelt wrote in 1922, warning that "this country will be enduring Republican presidents for a long time unless we rip the barnacles off the Democratic organization and make it a progressive and modern political party." The audience exploded into unexpected applause.[76]

The familiar pattern of congressional electoral gains followed by liberal frustration at the Democrats' legislative performance recurred after the 1958 midterms, with one difference. The party's gains that election were *massive*.[77] Capitalizing on a recession and mobilizing organized labor against a slew of state-level right-to-work proposals, Democrats picked up forty-eight House and thirteen Senate seats—and virtually all of the new members were liberals from outside the South. Liberals now constituted not only a majority of the Democrats in Congress but nearly a majority of the full House and Senate. The pressure was thus higher than ever for Democrats to pursue liberal policies. The DAC's postelection statement, "The Democratic Task in the Next Two Years," called on Democrats to pass a gamut of bills covering, among others, foreign aid, defense spending, public housing, federal aid to education, rural electrification, the enforcement of desegregation and voting rights statutes in the South, Social Security expansion, the repeal of Taft-Hartley's right-to-work provisions, and a minimum-wage hike.[78]

Rayburn and Johnson, as usual, responded dismissively, a reflection not merely of pique but also of the stark fact that the filibuster, the seniority system, and Congress's committee structure ensured the conservative coalition's continued power even in the face of swollen liberal ranks.[79] By the end of the first session of Congress, Democrats had passed fewer than a third of the council's suggestions, and indeed the most important bill produced by the 86th Congress turned out to be the labor-regulating Landrum-Griffin Act.[80] Liberals reached new peaks of outrage toward congressional leaders, expressed not merely in spontaneous applause from theater audiences but in jeremiads from the likes of ADA and the National Committee for an Effective Congress.[81] The DAC issued a harsh analysis of "The Current Legislative Situation," which urged Congress to stop attempting "to water-down proposals to the limits of what the president might accept. . . . The Congress should not be intimidated by threats of Presidential veto. The American people are entitled to have the lines definitely drawn."[82]

Rayburn and Johnson defended their approach—*not* to draw definite lines—with both pragmatic and normative arguments. The practical case was simple. Institutional obstacles notwithstanding, the scrambled ideological contours of *both* parties at the time virtually guaranteed that legislative strategies had to be bipartisan to succeed. Ad hoc alliances of liberal Democrats and Eisenhower Republicans on certain issues alternated with conservative coalition action on others. In this fluid legislative terrain, party labels did little to structure conflicts. Johnson's press secretary recalled, "there were practically no circumstances under which Johnson would countenance a 'Democratic' bill" during his years as majority leader.[83] Such an aversion guaranteed Johnson's rejection of the DAC as a concept. "Republicans who will vote for certain types of Democratic legislation," he wrote to Rayburn, "are highly unlikely to vote for that legislation . . . advanced by a committee whose sole objective is to sponsor a Democratic ticket that will elect a Democratic Congress in 1958 and Democratic President in 1960."[84] He retained this outlook even after 1958.

Johnson and Rayburn's objections also stemmed from institutional culture: the set of norms and mores that defined virtuous behavior in Congress. Those mores tended to emphasize attitudes antithetical to vigorous discipline and programmatic commitment. The social world and professional values of midcentury congressmen and senators were focused around collegiality, compromise, deference, and bipartisanship. "Integrity crosses party lines," a Republican told one scholar studying the issue. "You rely on some of your Democratic colleagues equally."[85] The intensely self-conscious internal culture of the Senate in particular venerated civility, reciprocity, and a peculiar combination of individualism and conformity.[86] It instilled a primary commitment to the Senate as a body. As William S. White put it, the Senate type is "a man for whom the Institution is a career in itself, a life in itself, and an end in itself."[87] That meant, in turn, that lawmaking should always take priority over partisan efforts. As a young Senator Robert Byrd told Butler in 1959, "We are here to legislate—not to make a political record," which helped ensure that "our party is big enough for the liberals, the conservatives, and the middle-of-the-roaders."[88]

Such a congressional culture not only challenged responsible partisanship but also buttressed an alternative vision of American parties as big tents that mitigated rather than clarified conflict. As one analyst put it, Butler's commitment to implementing responsible party principles betrayed a disastrous misunderstanding of the American system, where federalism and the separation of powers demanded that parties serve as "arenas of compromise"—decentralized "multi-group associations with liberal and conservative wings."[89] To those skeptical of the responsible party vision, like the critics of the APSA committee report, the very "irresponsibility" of American parties was a feature rather than a bug. During the Eisenhower era, scholars further elaborated a Madisonian argument for loose, inclusive parties: Each party incorporated a portion of all the various groupings in the population, thus tempering conflicts between them while protecting minority rights.[90] "The parties have been the peacemakers of the American community," Clinton Rossiter wrote in his bestselling *Parties and Politics in America*, "the unwitting but forceful suppressors of the 'civil-war potential' we carry always in the bowels of our diverse nation. Blessed are the peacemakers, I am tempted to conclude."[91]

This defense of traditional parties was of a piece with postwar pluralist models in political science that portrayed politics as the ad hoc, incremental, and nonideological negotiation of group interests. In his study of reform Democrats, James Q. Wilson cast a critical eye on such activists' commitment to a politics of principle, issues, and outcomes—their belief that "the ends of government and the incentives for political action ought to be identical." Wilson, greatly influenced by his collaborations with Edward C. Banfield studying the rough and tumble of American urban politics, preferred a system of unprincipled professionals and nonideological voters, in which "public policies are the by-product of political self-seeking."[92]

Ideology—the politics of principle—occupied an ambiguous place in this discourse, too. Celebrators of the American party system at times sidelined ideology in their own arguments, while at other times they celebrated *the system's* sidelining of ideology. They alternated between, on the one hand, arguing that the parties' nonideological orientation reflected a real consensus and, on the other hand, celebrating the parties for their role in mitigating Americans' potential for ideological strife. When Lyndon Johnson argued that "what the man on the street wants is not a big debate on fundamental issues; he wants a little medical care, a rug on the floor, a picture on the wall," he implied that Americans shared core premises and sought from politics only incremental improvements. But when, in nearly the same breath, he intoned that "the biggest threat to American stability is the politics of principle," he conveyed a fear that ideological conflict was in fact all too possible.[93] In this he echoed currents of midcentury thought among consensus-oriented intellectuals and chastened ex-radicals like Daniel Bell, who wrote with some regret about the "end of ideology" in the postwar era but concluded that "the tendency to convert concrete issues into ideological problems, to invest them with moral color and high emotional charge, is to invite conflicts that can only damage society."[94]

Similarly, Johnson's Senate ally Thomas Dodd of Connecticut combined optimism with alarm in a 1960 speech that condemned Democratic reformers' recklessness "when they try to whittle away at the deliberative process, when they attack the committee system of the Congress ... when they propose binding party platforms and binding party caucuses."[95] Dodd warned against paving the road to the British system, which he cast as a heinous party dictatorship that crushed independent judgment and divided the country. Such ominous warnings, though, jibed awkwardly with his complacent belief in an American consensus. "The extreme liberals in the

Democratic Party and their conservative counterparts in the Republican Party," Dodd mused, "are fond of issuing manifestos calling for a repudiation of the moderate elements in each party and thus presenting the voters with a clear choice." The reason they always fell on deaf ears was simple:

> We live in a country which has an essentially sound system of government, a basically just social system, a growing and prosperous economy, a happy relationship between church and state, a satisfactory arrangement between workers and employers, and the absence of bitter conflict between the so-called classes. Why then should there be a doctrinaire division, a fundamental conflict between the two parties? Why should people resent the fact that our parties offer similar solutions to most problems? Why should there be a call for disagreement, merely for the sake of disagreement?

Dodd's questions conjured an image of social peace and consensus. Hindsight affords us the knowledge of just how soon afterward the explosion of the long civil rights struggle into a mass movement of direct action and moral reckoning would shatter that picture.

Such knowledge is not only relevant for critically engaging postwar assumptions about consensus and ideology; it is also central to understanding how the American party system eventually did transform. Responsible party innovations like the DAC were doomed to a life of factional controversy so long as deep ideological fissures remained in the parties, while the existence of those divisions helped in turn to entrench an array of cultural and intellectual bulwarks against party responsibility. The gradual emergence of issue-based party activism and voting behavior created the possibility of ideological realignment in American parties and produced a set of constituencies potentially committed to it. But a key catalyst for that eventual realignment—and a major fulcrum of party transformation as it actually took place—turned out to be civil rights.

CIVIL RIGHTS, INSTITUTIONAL REFORM,
AND THE SPECTER OF REALIGNMENT

Within the DNC Butler's initial posture toward civil rights was compromised. His election in 1954 had depended on a coalition of northern reformers and highly unreformist southerners. Once in office, Butler was conciliatory toward the South, partly reflecting Stevenson's position at the time.[96] But Butler's personal views on civil rights were liberal, and he and other Democrats were increasingly compelled to marry their substantive commitment to civil rights with their commitments to party nationalization and discipline. Nationalization in this sense did not mean the geographic expansion of the party but rather the centralization of institutional power in national organs dominated by the party's growing liberal majority.

Leading Democrats' substantive position on civil rights evolved as a result of pressure from activists and national events. Black officials like Michigan congressman Charles Diggs and National Association for the Advancement of Colored People (NAACP) executive secretary Roy Wilkins lobbied Butler relentlessly regarding DNC policies and voting conditions in the South.[97] Other reformist Democrats did so as well. As a state chairman wrote to Stevenson in 1956, increasing numbers of northern Democrats were "persuaded that the southern Democratic base no longer is a reality and that efforts to restore it are fatal to success in the north and the west," an assessment with clear implications for the party's position on civil rights.[98]

For many Democrats the substantive commitment was not merely strategic. Mid-level activists who did so much to shape party policy in the north—issue-based amateurs, unionists, urban reformers—held disproportionately liberal views on civil rights. As a pro-civil rights pressure force in the Democratic Party, they had little counterpart within the GOP, notwithstanding the number of Republican officeholders espousing moderate to liberal positions on racial issues.[99] More and more Democrats concluded that a commitment to liberalism demanded a commitment to civil rights. The rout of Stevenson in 1956 and later southern resistance to the

Supreme Court's *Brown v. Board of Education* decision helped convince Butler of the same. During the Little Rock desegregation controversy in 1957, he declared that "the Democratic Party will not be deterred in its stand for civil rights by any threat of a third party in the South."[100] The DAC condemned Arkansas's governor and later established an Advisory Committee on Civil Rights, headed by Eleanor Roosevelt, which called for the 1960 platform to explicitly endorse picketing and sit-down demonstrations.[101]

Substantive conflict over civil rights had important institutional consequences. The so-called loyalty oath controversy enhanced the power of the national party to set conditions on state party behavior.[102] In the Dixiecrat revolt of 1948, the ballots of four southern states listed, under the Democratic label, electors pledged to the States' Rights Democratic Party nominee. To prevent this from recurring, Michigan senator Blair Moody authored a resolution requiring states to list the national party's presidential ticket on their ballots under the Democratic label or otherwise lose delegate credentials at the national convention. Three southern states refused to comply in 1952 and others expressed opposition on federalist grounds.[103] In 1953 a DNC panel revisited the rule. Its proposal, adopted and aggressively enforced by Butler, made state party chairmen responsible for ensuring that the national ticket appear properly on all ballots and required a stringent loyalty pledge from national committee members. The new rule set a precedent for the nationalization of party authority, for it demonstrated that, in the words of the DNC's counsel, "the state party is not acting by and for itself, but as a part of a national party and, linked with all other states parties, in a national effort."[104] This proved to be a wedge for subsequent transformative national reforms.[105]

Civil rights politics also contributed to party nationalization and reform by motivating a more intensive effort to restructure Congress. The litany of suggested congressional reforms—curbing seniority, subordinating the authority of committee chairmen, and abolishing the Senate filibuster—was largely the same as that in the 1950 APSA report. But civil rights threw into relief the connection between southern conservative power and the structure of Congress, since southern Democrats controlled key legislative chokepoints. The conservative coalition's obstructive capacity was never better demonstrated than during these fights, and this bipartisan alliance diminished the luster of bipartisanship itself to increasing numbers of liberals. As a result, they were more inclined toward reforms that fostered greater party coherence.[106] The NAACP began lobbying for filibuster reform in 1949 and joined with labor and other activists in such efforts during every Congress in the 1950s. Liberals inserted a call for "improved Congressional procedures so that majority rule prevails" into the party platform.[107] The DAC's first policy statement endorsed filibuster reform, meanwhile, and conflict over the committee system provided subtext to its clashes with congressional leaders. The council advocated not only policies that conservative chairmen opposed but also the kind of overarching party *program* that a fragmented committee system could not sustain.

A related development, similarly catalyzed by civil rights, was the organization of a liberal Democratic bloc in Congress built around "McCarthy's Mavericks," the informal caucus in the House that supported Eugene McCarthy's proposed party manifesto in 1957.[108] Efforts to formalize this faction and bolster its capacity in areas such as whip operations, coordinated floor speeches, and committee testimony culminated in the 1959 formation of the 120-member Democratic Study Group (DSG).[109] At the outset, the DSG gave voice to liberal representatives' criticism of their congressional leaders for being "more content . . . to keep peace between the North and South than to push the Democratic Party's aims." An early DSG report analyzed the conservative coalition's makeup and operations, while the staff distributed talking points and speech material to combat it.[110]

Unsurprisingly, both Butler's staff and the DAC engaged directly with the DSG.[111] The combined efforts of the DAC, the DSG, key senators, and allied advocates amounted to a phalanx of liberal policy activism that directly influenced the party's unprecedentedly aggressive 1960 platform.[112] This feat of policy generation seemed to approach Schattschneider's vision of responsible partisanship, despite the fact that it took place without the support of congressional leaders and amid deep divisions in the party.

Civil rights exacerbated those divisions like nothing else, and thus fueled interest not only in institutional reform but in realignment of the parties. In October 1958, after reiterating his repudiation of Arkansas governor Orval Faubus's stance on school desegregation, Paul Butler received a typical outpouring of angry correspondence from conservative Democrats.[113] "What are you trying to do, make Arkansas go Republican?" one elderly Iowan asked, while a Texan wrote to declare he was "beginning to think that maybe it would be a good idea if the South did quit the Democratic Party."[114] These warnings were meant rhetorically. But the threat was beginning to lose its sting among many liberals who, for the first time since FDR's purge campaign, were willing to contemplate leaving the South to the GOP.

Advocacy of ideological party realignment spread from responsible party scholars to major liberal interest groups in the later 1950s, thanks in part to civil rights' intensification of sectional discord among Democrats. As late as 1955, speculation about realignment had an airily abstract quality. James MacGregor Burns, writing that year in the *New York Times*, argued that long-range economic development in the South could diminish the region's exceptional qualities, thus facilitating two-party competition along liberal-conservative lines.[115] He did not depict this process as either a "bolt" or a "purge" spurred by civil rights conflicts. But by 1958, Democratic politicians could earn praise from liberal activists and journalists by taking positions that might alienate the white South. The *New Republic* deemed the DAC's postelection policy manifesto that year "electrifying. They told the South if it wanted to bolt, to go bolt. Just like that." The magazine hoped that the DAC's efforts would eventually lead the country to "have coherent political parties like other nations, instead of foggy coalitions."[116]

Key elements of the labor movement echoed this vision. At its constitutional convention in 1959, the United Auto Workers (UAW) passed a resolution calling for "a real realignment" of the party system and "a clear demarcation" between a liberal party and a conservative one. Americans could then "vote for a clear-cut program ... with the full assurance that when elected that party will carry out

its liberal program without qualification, compromise or delay."[117]
This amounted to a tempered version of the political strategy developed among labor activists associated with the socialist Max
Shachtman. Since the late 1940s, Shachtman had shared Walter
Reuther's commitment to working within the Democratic Party.
But, compelled by the civil rights conflicts of the later 1950s and
under the influence of Burns's writings, Shachtman now articulated a more elaborate political project for labor radicals: unite with
civil rights and liberal forces, aggravate tensions within the Democratic coalition, and compel an exodus of reactionary southerners
and urban bosses.[118] By 1959 Shachtman had convinced the Socialist Party to endorse the strategy, called simply "realignment."[119]

Closer to the political mainstream, meanwhile, Butler experienced firsthand the dynamic by which tensions over civil rights
could prompt discussions of realignment. In 1958 Butler voiced
concern about southern dominance of the congressional committee system, then described civil rights as an issue that would be addressed "without compromise" in the 1960 platform. As for southern Democrats who disagreed? "Those people in the South who are
not deeply dedicated to the policies and beliefs, in fact the philosophy, of the Democratic Party will have to go their own way," taking
"political asylum wherever they can find it, either in the Republican Party or a third party."[120] The outcry was swift. House campaign chairman George Smathers of Florida told Butler to "pipe
down," while Mississippi's Jamie Whitten warned that the South
truly would bolt if such talk kept up.[121]

Criticism came not merely from southern conservatives, but
also from northern machine elements and those officials, like
Harry Truman, sensitive to their views. Even among urban bosses
who supported civil rights legislation, Butler's moralistic rhetoric
and ideology zeal were anathema. At several points during Butler's tenure, an alliance of southerners and northern machine
leaders attempted to oust him, using controversies over Butler's
public statements as pretexts. Truman supported the first such
effort, in the summer of 1957, which included among the plotters
Jacob Arvey, David Lawrence, and New York's Tammany boss Car-

mine De Sapio.[122] Most of the same participants mounted another "dump Butler" effort two years later, after Butler had broadcast his intention "to try to influence the Democratic leadership of the Congress to come along with the national program, rather than the more conservative and moderate program which they are trying to follow."[123] Southern Democrats rushed en masse to denounce the chairman, while Sam Rayburn curtly retorted that "Mr. Butler can do the talking and we'll do the acting and make the record."[124] Rayburn's response in private correspondence was more aggressive. He advised one donor to the DNC to hold off on a contribution so as to avoid demonstrating "endorsement of [Butler's] criticism of Congress."[125]

Butler owed his survival to continued support among most DNC members as well as liberals across the country. The 1959 ouster attempt collapsed in the face of a clear pro-Butler majority. One committeeman explained, "we admire his integrity and courage. He is a symbol of the liberal feeling which is dominant in the party."[126] Many activists and officials specifically endorsed his antisouthern comments.[127] In a floor speech Michigan senator Pat McNamara defended Butler and castigated congressional timidity. "Leadership of the 86th appears to be more like leadership of the minority of the majority," he said. "Or perhaps it is leadership of the majority of the minority. In any event, it is looking less like leadership of the majority party in Congress."[128] Johnson and Rayburn's efforts to accommodate disparate Democratic factions prevented them from carrying out a legislative agenda supported by "the majority of the majority." Increasing numbers of Democrats, however, sought a new approach.

The midcentury responsible party theorists had outlined a prescriptive model of partisan change along three lines. They sought the nationalization of party operations and political contests. They wanted policy issues and mutually distinctive party programs to be the central elements of national politics. And they advocated the development of sufficient discipline within the parties to enable them to carry out coherent programs when in power. Along all

three of those dimensions, the 1950s saw the emergence of necessary though not sufficient conditions for the transformation of the
party system.

Such developments were only latent by decade's end, however. The Democratic Party's standard-bearer in 1960 occasionally connected a theory of party politics to his overarching critique
of Eisenhower-era drift. "Legislative leadership is not possible
without party leadership," John F. Kennedy declared, condemning
efforts to "blur the issues and differences between the parties."[129]
But he lacked interest in thoroughgoing party leadership. He made
it clear that the DAC would cease operation upon his election, and,
later, after considering the reformist Neil Staebler to replace Butler, opted instead for Washington senator Henry Jackson, followed
by Connecticut machine boss John Bailey.[130] Meanwhile, his selection of the Texan Johnson as a running mate followed the familiar
lines of Democratic coalitional logic. The campaign against Nixon,
then adopting the moderate positioning of Eisenhower's "Modern
Republican" brand, featured notably little in the way of clear-cut
divisions on ideology or issues. The resulting electoral map showed
little evidence of a fraying of the Democrats' coalition, excepting
Mississippi's vote for Strom Thurmond. The forces that would
bring transformative changes to the party system, in other words,
were not yet in evidence at the national level—and Paul Butler, who
died unexpectedly of a heart attack in 1961, would not live to see
such changes.

But signs abounded for those who knew where to look. They
could be seen in the civil rights movement, whose rhetoric of moral
transformation promised an equivalent transformation of political
institutions. They could be seen in the language of middle-class reform clubs, like the inaugural declaration of Tom Finletter, Eleanor
Roosevelt, and Herbert Lehman's New York Committee for Democratic Voters. "The day of boss rule and boss power . . . is nearing its
end," it proclaimed in 1959, advocating "the principles of democracy within all the reaches of the Democratic Party organization
of New York."[131] And they could be seen in the words of the party
chairman Kennedy replaced. Years before a more famous speech
insisted that moderation in pursuit of justice was no virtue, Paul

Butler sounded a similar note. "The Democratic Party is not a party of accommodation or attainability or compromise," he declared in 1959. "People who are willing to accommodate themselves and the objectives of the Democratic Party to existing obstacles . . . do not typify the real spirit, the true courage or the genuine zeal of our Party." Most dangerous of all: "The Democratic Party is a party of principle."[132]

3

A CHOICE, NOT AN ECHO, 1948-1964

In the early postwar decades, Democrats did not have a monopoly on internal arguments over principle in partisanship. Indeed, Republican National Committee (RNC) leaders did their counterparts one better during the inaugural gathering in 1959 of their own party council, the Republican Committee on Program and Progress. They put the very question of whether or not parties should stand for anything up for debate.

To stimulate discussion, the group's chairman brought in a young political scientist to offer a provocative challenge. "This Committee is charged with the task of formulating principles and objectives to guide the Republican Party," Robert Goldwin began, but he wanted to make a case that "it is neither possible nor desirable for a major political party to be guided by principles."[1] Goldwin proceeded to lay out the basic argument for the big-tent American party tradition—a case that, he assured the assembled Republicans, was "a commonplace feature of books on the American political system."

The reasons that so many analysts "say it is a good thing for the nation as a whole that neither of our two major parties stands for anything in particular" were myriad, Goldwin explained. A two-party system in a large, heterogeneous nation forced both parties to seek majorities through appeals to many of the same groups. Federalism and the separation of powers, moreover, crippled national party discipline and cohesion. "With both parties including liberals and conservatives within their ranks," Goldwin said, "those differences which would otherwise be the main campaign

"—Thus We May See Eye to Eye on This Knotty Problem"

FIGURE 3. Hugh Haynie, *Louisville Courier-Journal*, February 27, 1959.
© Gannett-Community Publishing. Used by permission.

issues are settled by compromise within each party." American elections "have the effect of unifying the nation rather than dividing it on ideological or class lines. . . . Our national unity would be weakened if the theoretical differences were sharpened." Given these arguments, Goldwin challenged the members: "Are there good reasons even so why this Committee ought to try to formulate principles and objectives for the guidance of the Republican Party?"

The ensuing discussion was tortured. Committee members blanched reflexively at the idea that parties should not have principles but struggled to explain why. Some interpreted "principle" simply to mean integrity, with one surmising that "it was not where you stood on a particular issue that was a matter of principle, but *that* you stood." Others acknowledged the inevitable diversity of a broad-based, majority-seeking party while still insisting that an underlying philosophy defined the GOP. But, pushed by Goldwin to identify the principles that distinguished the party from Democrats, members faltered. Most of them eventually settled on the idea that both Democrats and Republicans shared core premises and ultimate goals, while differing on the methods to achieve them.

The committee's near-consensus, in other words, insisted on the existence of a basic *American* consensus. One member rejected that assumption outright. The premise that "we all have the same objectives" was a false one, insisted Stephen Shadegg of Arizona. "We have men who have no desire to be self-sufficient, who have been conditioned by twenty years of our philosophy to depend on someone else." What Shadegg meant by "our philosophy" was the prevailing New Deal–era belief "that man is significant materially, to be fed, housed, cared for, doctored, buried, have his worries removed." This conflicted directly with Shadegg's concept of "the dignity of the individual, which is such that man has a spiritual need to do these things for himself. . . . This is a basic conflict, I believe, between the collectivists who are in control of the Democrat Party and the philosophy of the Republican Party which we have somehow neglected." Shadegg cast this conflict in stark terms. "What we are talking about," he said, "is the nature of man, really."

Political conflict in the United States did involve a clash of core premises, Shadegg was arguing. It went deeper than mere questions of governmental technique. This philosophical divide was also a partisan divide—or it could be, if Republicans would reaffirm their commitment to principles that too many had "neglected" out of misguided expediency. Shadegg's words were pointedly dissonant. The Committee on Program and Progress was a project instigated by Dwight Eisenhower and administered by RNC chair Meade Alcorn and the liberal GOP businessman Charles Percy, and its staff and membership largely reflected the moderate political outlook to which the president had attached the moniker "Modern Republicanism."[2] Shadegg was in the minority as a representative of the party's conservative wing. In his professional life Shadegg was Senator Barry Goldwater's campaign manager and something of an intellectual alter ego. In five years he would help Goldwater articulate a national political message that doubled as a commentary on the place of ideology in a two-party system. "This will not be an engagement of personalities," Goldwater would say in announcing his presidential bid in 1964, but "an engagement of principles." Shadegg's insistence that a philosophical divide in postwar America demanded partisan expression would reverberate in Goldwater's promise: "I will offer a choice, not an echo."[3]

As among Democrats, so too did political divisions among Republicans reflect competing visions for the party and clashing views about partisanship itself. But the situations were not identical. Ideological divisions within the comparatively homogenous GOP were shallower than those wracking Democrats. Responsible party doctrine proved less directly influential in shaping conservatives' thinking. And as a chronic minority, Republicans had different issues to debate than Democrats who grappled with the dilemmas of a baggy majority coalition. Liberal Democrats mainly sought clarity and cohesion through the removal of a dissident sectional faction—a politics of subtraction—whereas moderate and conservative Republicans alike had to focus on the task of majority-making—a politics of addition.[4]

Factional disputes over political strategy took on ideological coloring, as ubiquitous conservative charges of "me, too" posturing by GOP politicians prompted deeper questions about the very existence of an American consensus. Against the backdrop of declining political machines and a resurgent conservative intellectual movement, GOP politics in the later 1950s witnessed intensifying clashes between supporters of a moderate, Eisenhower-centered partisan vision and issue-driven amateur activists on the right.

The Solid South—solidly non-Republican, that is—was central to the party's debate. Conflicting ideological visions aligned with conflicting postures toward the South, especially regarding civil rights. The alignment was a mirror image of the one defining Democratic factionalism. Republican advocates of a coherent ideology for the party were disproportionately conservatives seeking formal alliance with southern whites, in part through opposition to civil rights. Conversely, those most committed to retaining their party's traditional advocacy of civil rights were mainly moderates opposed to both parties' ideological sorting. The sectional question was part of a national story, moreover: the eventual breakup of the Solid South depended on the growth of a conservative movement advocating ideological partisanship.

As the long history of that southern debate helps illustrate, the eventual conservative capture of the GOP, long cast as a story that begins with the movement for Goldwater's 1964 campaign, actually originated in intellectual conflicts, party developments, and strategic choices made during the previous two decades.[5] Years of intraparty conflict amid a changing postwar landscape helped to produce, by the early 1960s, a party constituency receptive to rejecting American consensus and affirming the centrality of ideology. That this constituency proved incapable of forging an electoral majority in 1964 only delayed rather than prevented the system's eventual transformation.

"ME, TOO": PARTY THEORIES IN THE DEWEY-TAFT WARS

The political revolution wrought by the New Deal affected the Grand Old Party along with the Democrats. Populist western progressives disappeared as a faction in the 1930s and 1940s as some abandoned their Republican label while others followed their foreign policy isolationism by adopting a more orthodox conservatism. Stalwart Midwestern Republicans, disproportionately rural, overwhelmingly Protestant, and hostile to the New Deal, soon dominated the party's reduced congressional ranks. Simultaneously, the eastern progressive Republican tendency—urban, paternalistic, internationalist—revived under a new "moderate" label thanks in part to the increase in government–business co-operation during the war and the need to compete with the Democrats' electoral juggernaut through similar promises of government activism.[6] Stalwarts' strongholds were Congress and the professional ranks of most state parties and RNC memberships. Moderate leaders tended to be found among big-state governors and senators building statewide coalitions that included urban and labor constituencies.

The three presidential contests of the 1940s—all considered at the time to be winnable by the Republicans—helped sharpen a division within the party that would take on increasing ideological coloring in the postwar decades. Wall Street attorney Wendell Willkie failed to unseat Franklin Roosevelt in 1940 but succeeded in consolidating moderate elements within the GOP. Willkie's campaign also fueled stalwarts' sense that Tweedledee/Tweedledum campaigns downplaying policy differences with the Democrats were electoral losers.[7] New York governor Thomas E. Dewey emerged as the moderate faction's leader in the early 1940s and, aided by a tenacious and media-savvy political operation based in Albany, secured the presidential nomination in 1944. Dewey's campaign deemphasized issues outright, while his control of the party platform guaranteed that on Social Security, health care, and labor law, differences between GOP and Democratic positions were minimal. That election's "outstanding characteristic," a *New York Times* editorial summarized, was "the promise by both parties of all the good things to come from a benign and endless generous Government."[8] Dewey's defeat left his party demoralized over its endemic minority status and divided about the course forward.

Those divisions intensified in the later 1940s, embodied by the pitched rivalry between Dewey and Ohio senator Robert Taft. When the GOP captured control of Congress in 1946, its congressional leadership, including Taft, exercised impressive discipline over the rank and file, sustaining a conservative if hardly counter-revolutionary policy stance.[9] The legislative centerpiece of the 80th Congress was the Taft-Hartley Act, which amended existing labor law to outlaw the closed shop, allow states to pass right-to-work laws, legalize federal injunctions against some strikes, and tilt speech regulations in management's favor. Congressional Republicans' near unanimity in voting for the bill belied deep misgivings among moderates about the actual policy.[10] Backed by the conservative coalition, Taft-Hartley was a crosscutting issue of the bipartisan era and a key flashpoint for intra-Republican struggles in the run-up to 1948.

Outside of Congress, Taft- and Dewey-aligned forces battled for control of state party operations and the RNC. Dewey, flush with cash from financial and industrial interests, eventually secured the 1948 nomination over Taft. With two moderate big-state governors—Dewey and California's Earl Warren—on the ticket and another big-state moderate, Hugh Scott, installed as RNC chair, 1948 was the apogee of the Dewey wing's power within the party. The platform that year was brief, general, and focused on the middle ground. It offered a Goldilocks-like maxim for the "just right" amount of public policy: "Maximum voluntary cooperation between citizens and minimum dependence on law; never, however, declining courageous recourse to the law if necessary." It briefly and namelessly touted the 80th Congress's "sensible reform of the labor law" while pledging "continuing study to improve labor-management legislation," advocated the expansion of Social Security benefits, and touted federal action on civil rights, voting rights, and the desegregation of the military.[11]

Dewey's shocking 1948 defeat, even as the incumbent Democrat faced an independent challenge from an important sector of the New Deal coalition, unleashed a new, more intense round of Republican recrimination and soul-searching. H. L. Mencken's cutting postelection characterization of Dewey's campaign strategy—"to chase what appeared to be the other fellow's ambulance"—found amplification among Taftites ready to publicize their frustration.[12] House Republicans, who lost 75 seats and thus the majority in 1948, established a policy committee soon after the election with the mandate to "guide the minority to a firmer national policy.[13] Taft wrote a confidant that Dewey could have won "if he had put on a real fight on the issues" rather than offer pallid bromides and paeans to character.[14] Hugh Scott solicited the views of GOP precinct workers in the run-up to the RNC's first postelection meeting. "Why don't you me-too guys who are running the party try dropping dead?" wrote one typical correspondent.[15] Senate Minority Leader Kenneth Wherry spoke out at that meeting against "those who say we should revitalize the party by turning to the radical left and by out-promising New Dealers. A 'me-too' policy is the road to ruin for our party and for our nation."[16]

Soon domestic anticommunism emerged as a new point of conflict among Republicans. Taftites were committed to a robust internal security program and the purging of Communist sympathizers from the public sector. As the Red Scare intensified, moreover, so did those Republicans' support for Wisconsin senator Joseph McCarthy and his brutal tactics.[17] On the moderate side, Margaret Chase Smith rallied six fellow senators behind a Declaration of Conscience, which she read on the Senate floor in June 1950.[18] If these moderate opponents of McCarthyism emphasized the importance of sober leadership and unity in national security, the McCarthyite conservatives—including an extraordinary new cadre of young conservative intellectuals and activists galvanized by this debate—saw in it a vehicle for infusing partisan politics with crusading moral conviction and meaningful line-drawing.[19]

Thus, like postwar Democrats, the GOP at the dawn of the 1950s faced a factional divide that was also an ideological one— increasingly so as the decade wore on.[20] As with the Democrats, these Republican factions developed contrasting views of the roles that partisanship, issues, and ideology should play in the political system. After repeated presidential defeats and ubiquitous charges of "me, too" temporizing, moderate Republicans had the tougher case to make. Political pragmatism remained central to their argument. In the first RNC meeting after the 1948 election, moderate committeeman Victor Anderson agreed with the Taft supporters that expediency should not require Republicans to cease being Republicans, but "on the other hand, we are not required by consistency to commit political harikari by an over-zealous and ceremonious insistence upon the doctrines of laissez faire." The consequence of such arguments, however, was an unavoidable vagueness in moderates' prescription for their party's ideological identity, as Anderson himself showed. "America," he declared,

"needs a soundly liberal, or if you prefer . . . a progressively conservative party." Where Anderson sought party unity by combining liberalism and conservatism, another Deweyite advocated jettisoning both in favor of a purely partisan affinity. "We must stop
identifying each other as 'liberals' or 'conservatives' or 'reactionaries,'" Indiana congressman Cecil Harden insisted, urging all to
claim "but one label . . . the label of the Republican Party."[21]

But some moderates offered a more affirmative argument,
grounding their big-tent advocacy in a theory of the proper role of
parties. As the minority faction among both rank-and-file activists
and national officials, these moderates most often echoed conservative Democrats in celebrating the flexible and nonprogrammatic
aspects of the American party tradition. Dewey himself, the moderates' postwar standard-bearer, offered the most forceful case in
February 1950, laying out his thoughts on the American two-party
tradition and his own vision for the Grand Old Party.[22] Dewey
traced his brand of Republican governance back to the Whig tradition that dominated the GOP program in its initial decades as well
as to the regulatory initiatives instituted during Theodore Roosevelt's presidency, emphasizing that Republican governance historically encompassed active state intervention.[23]

He devoted much more time, however, to a general defense of
parties' traditional failure to adhere to any particular programmatic approach, including the one he preferred. Dewey celebrated
rather than lamented the fact that, "in the sense of a unified organization with a national viewpoint on major issues," neither party
could be described as "real." "There are wide divergencies of opinion in each of the two great parties . . . because each party repre-
sents a composite spectrum of roughly similar interests." Dewey
countered the "me, too" charge by explaining that two-party competition in a heterogeneous nation ensured that "no single religion
or color or race or economic interest is confined to one or the other
of our parties. . . . The result is that since the Civil War the parties
have not been too far apart on most fundamentals of our system."

Dewey knew all too well that "this similarity is highly objectionable to a vociferous few. They rail at both parties, saying they represent nothing but a choice between Tweedledee and Tweedledum."

They sought to purge moderates and liberals from the GOP and "have the remainder join forces with the conservative groups of the South."

> Then they would have everything very neatly arranged, indeed. The Democratic party would be the liberal-to-radical party. The Republican party would be the conservative-to-reactionary party. The results would be neatly arranged, too. The Republicans would lose every election and the Democrats would win every election.

For reasons he hardly intended, those last words would prove among Dewey's most famous, one of those unprescient gems of midcentury political prognostication offered by occupants of a complacent center. But Dewey's electoral prediction was a side note to his main argument against ideological realignment in America: his conviction that "the resemblance between the parties and the similarities which their party platforms show are the very heart of the strength of the American political system."[24]

If moderate Republicans echoed conservative Democrats in their normative arguments about the workings of the party system, conservative Republicans could often sound like liberal Democrats. Similarly occupying a majority position within their party's activist ranks, conservative Republicans advocated party adherence to their views in order to draw stark distinctions between the GOP and the Democratic Party. The intellectual foundations for conservatives' argument differed somewhat from that of liberal Democrats. Such Democrats embraced the doctrine of responsible party government precisely because it connected party coherence to a streamlined system of majoritarian, activist governance. Yet conservative Republicans more typically couched their critiques of New Deal liberalism in language venerating the wisdom of the constitutional tradition and condemning the aggrandizement of centralized governmental power. Members of the party that had toiled in the congressional minority for most of the past several decades were also more reflexively disposed toward an emphasis on minority rights rather than majority rule in lawmaking.[25] A few notable conservatives of the period, including the economics writer Henry Hazlitt and former president Herbert Hoover, disputed the statist subtext of much responsible party theory and embraced its prescription for party government.[26] Such voices were exceptional, however.

But if the factional warfare between Taft and Dewey had not turned conservative Republicans into advocates of parliamentary-style governance under disciplined parties, it had prompted them to sharpen an argument for issue-based politics and distinct party programs. The corollary to this argument was a critique of non-substantive partisan affiliations. "A political party," Taft declared, "is not just an organization in which men of completely different points of view join because their parents or their friends belonged to that party, or because they became members through youthful and forgotten prejudices."[27] Policy substance mattered. A belief in programmatic politics also implied opposition to a political strategy based on individual candidates' personal electoral appeal. Sharpening the ideological contrast between Republicans and Democrats would help to enable Americans to "vot[e] for ideas rather than built-up personalities," as conservative writer Felix Morley put it.[28]

Republican debates over strategy and the politics of personality only intensified in the wake of Dewey's decision to take himself out of presidential contention in 1952, for his successor as the moderates' favored candidate turned out to be a figure of truly extraordinary personal appeal. After heavy courting from both parties, General Dwight D. Eisenhower entered the race against Taft for the Republican presidential nomination backed by much of Dewey's campaign machinery and his organizational support in the Republican Governors Association and among eastern party donors. Eisenhower's strategic vagueness on policy issues came in for the same criticism from Taft supporters that Dewey's had before him. "The Republican voters of this country," National Republican Senatorial Committee chairman Everett Dirksen wrote in 1952, "are entitled to know whether the candidate, who only a few months ago wouldn't say whether he was a Democrat or Republican, is now an advocate of Democratic or Republican national policies."[29] But the allure of a personally popular candidate proved hard to resist after such a prolonged political drought for the party.

Eisenhower's campaign operatives fanned out during the spring of 1952 to line up support among state party leaders through promises of patronage and assistance in local matters.[30] Nowhere did the battle between the Eisenhower and Taft campaigns for delegate pledges prove more intense and decisive than in the South, which sent one-sixth of the total delegates at the national convention. Eisenhower's campaign managers had deliberately sought to cultivate delegates who opposed the Taft-leaning "old guard" in states like Texas, Louisiana, and Georgia, in the process involving themselves in internecine local factional squabbles within thinly institutionalized state party organizations. Most of the ninety-eight delegate seats that were contested before the Credentials Committee at the convention that summer belonged to southern states, and the bruising battle for them ultimately tipped the nomination in Eisenhower's favor.[31]

That the southern delegate fights proved particularly rife with opaque dealmaking—and devoid of anything resembling arguments over policies or ideology—was fitting. The virtual eradication of a popularly backed Republican organizational presence in most parts of the South following Reconstruction had rendered state parties empty shells, a collective regional "holdover organization functioning only for the power it could wield in national conventions," as one scholar put it.[32] The legacy of that nineteenth-century expulsion for twentieth-century GOP politics was a quadrennial display of regional engagement at its most ruthlessly pragmatic and insular. Eisenhower's campaign manager recalled that the leaders of southern state Republican parties "represented almost no one at home," surviving off of federal patronage directed their way in exchange only for nominating support at conventions.[33]

While the 1952 nominating fight highlighted the GOP's organizational weakness in the region, the national political context was changing in ways that signaled the potential for momentous transformations in southern alignments. The great post–New Deal flourishing of the conservative coalition in Congress highlighted the Right's potential national power. Simultaneously, southern support for Democratic presidential candidates was slowly eroding, as illustrated by the States' Rights Democratic Party's capture of four Deep South states in 1948 and Eisenhower's eventual 49 percent showing in the southern popular vote in 1952. The prospect of a southern Republican Party that was not a shell but rather a viable organization was becoming increasingly apparent. And thus, just like postwar Democratic debates over ideology and partisanship, intra-Republican debates touched unavoidably on the subject of party realignment in Dixie—and the explosive issues of race and civil rights.

THE SOUTHERN CROSS

"I am a Southerner by birth and tradition," G. Wartham Ages of Memphis wrote to RNC chairman Guy Gabrielson in 1949, "but nearly all my life I have been an independent in politics, and especially so since Roosevelt destroyed the Democratic Party." Like conservatives throughout the country, Ages attributed Thomas Dewey's defeat the previous year to "his promise to do everything that the New Dealers were doing but to do it better." He also attributed "all that has been accomplished in the 80th and 81st Congresses to defeat Truman's program" to "a combination of the conservative members of Congress from the North and South." This observation compelled a question—one that increasing numbers of conservatives asked in the postwar decades. "Why not make that combination a real and permanent factor rather than a temporary one for expediency only?"[34]

Giving partisan shape to the conservative coalition had been a goal for some northerners and southerners alike since its inception during the late New Deal. As southern congressional resistance to Franklin Roosevelt's legislative agenda had spread and solidified, conservative Republicans made tentative inquiries into building electoral inroads into the region.[35] "I realize it is hard for those who have been active leaders in one party to change their allegiance,"

Taft told a Nashville audience in 1948, "but I suggest to the people of the Southern States that you lead your leaders into the Republican Party."[36] But the strength of existing partisan ties in the electorate and the absence of enduring, interlocking relationships among activists and partisan elites in the northern Republican and southern Democratic parties rendered such ideas purely theoretical through the 1940s.

Indeed, the southern revolt against the national Democratic Party that did eventually emerge during that decade—the Dixiecrat campaign of 1948—illustrated the region's continued aversion to the Republican label, even as it revealed the extent of political change underway there. Structural factors driving the revolt would make the region increasingly ripe for political realignment. The impact of the New Deal and World War II in sparking regional development, agricultural mechanization, and industrialization in the South challenged the region's one-party politics. The stirrings of political activism among both working-class whites and African Americans exiting agricultural labor and emboldened by wartime service helped to provoke, in reaction, a closer political alliance between agricultural elites and industrial and commercial businessmen in the South.[37] Those elites viewed with alarm the growing electoral strength of African American Democrats in the North and the rapid rise of racial liberalism to the forefront of the New Deal–Fair Deal ideological agenda. This looming specter was best epitomized by the wartime Fair Employment Practices Commission (FEPC) and President Truman's postwar support for its permanent operation.

The civil rights threat prompted a reevaluation of the party system and the South's place in it. Charles Wallace Collins, an Alabama lawyer, political activist, and propagandist for white supremacy, portrayed the fight over the FEPC and other Truman-endorsed civil rights measures as a harbinger of a broader partisan breakdown in his hugely influential 1947 treatise, *Whither Solid South?* "The South finds itself in the anomalous position of being the chief support of a political party which intends to put her through a second Reconstruction," he wrote.[38] Given the fact that there was now "a 'liberal' and a 'conservative' wing to each major party," Collins's preferred solution to the southern predicament was the forging of a "new two-party alignment" in which the respective wings would sort into a Liberal Party and a Conservative Party and the latter would protect the southern racial order.[39] But if political leaders proved incapable of bringing about such a realignment, Collins laid out a second-best alternative, one that became the blueprint for the States' Rights Democratic Party campaign of Strom Thurmond the following year: a regional third-party bid intended to deny any candidate a majority of electoral votes, thereby throwing the decision to the House of Representatives where southerners could influence the outcome.

The legacy of the 1948 Dixiecrat campaign, both for southern political strategy and for the shaping of postwar American conservatism, was mixed. The party's disappointing electoral performance provided further testimony to the continuing strength of traditional partisanship. (It won only in the four southern states whose ballots listed Thurmond as the Democratic nominee.) And the scope of the Dixiecrats' ambition had been modest to begin with. Rather than an attempt to ideologically realign the party system, the revolt was merely a venture to restore one faction's unique position within that system. But precisely because it failed to achieve that goal, increasing numbers of political actors in the coming years began to envision national rather sectional partisan strategies for combatting racial and economic liberalism.

While southern conservatives struggled over political strategy in the wake of the 1948 election, northern conservatives in the GOP pursued new efforts at forging an electoral alliance with the South as part of their factional struggle with moderates. At the center of the most significant of such efforts was South Dakota senator Karl Mundt, a close ally of Joe McCarthy in the early postwar years.[40] Mundt's crusading anticommunism lent a sense of urgency to his interest in reconstructing partisan alliances. Amid a global spread of collectivism, he thought, the fragmentation of conservative forces in America had enabled the creeping socialistic bent of the New Deal–Fair Deal agenda to drive policy unchecked. "Present political groupings," he declared, "appear to be based much more upon geographical, traditional, or historical factors than upon a grouping around basic economic, social, and political concepts."[41] Such foggy alignments muffled the voice of American conservatism at just the moment it was most needed. Southern realignment was essential, he wrote, not only "for our two-party system, but also for the most effective fight possible against Communism in America."[42]

Starting in 1949 Mundt began corresponding with a circle of fellow senators and GOP aides on the subject, including the fellow anticommunist militant Owen Brewster of Maine and the recently retired Albert Hawkes of New Jersey. Two New York–based Republican activists, J. Harvie Williams and John Underhill, spent the summer of 1949 soliciting support from northeastern businessmen and Republican donors to fund a "Citizens' Political Committee" to explore the idea of party realignment through a North-South conservative alliance.[43] Their prescribed strategy for such a union began with a reorganization of partisan control in Congress.[44] Mundt argued for a presidential focus instead.[45] Republicans, he said, should nominate a 1952 ticket composed of a Republican and a Southern Democrat—Mundt suggested Georgia's Richard Russell or Virginia's Harry Byrd—and directly woo alienated southerners in their platform and campaign appeals. A victory for the ticket would quickly compel a formal reorganization within both Congress and the national parties. Beginning with a swing through the Northwest in the winter of 1949 and 1950 and continuing with multiple speaking tours across every southern state, Mundt devoted much of the next two years to appealing to southerners to help "bring about a permanent realignment of party forces in this country . . . so that henceforth in each of our 48 states the people would have a clear cut choice in all elections."[46]

Mundt's speaking tours helped provide the impetus for the formal launch of a Committee to Explore Political Realignment in September 1951.[47] The committee commissioned Williams and Underhill to draft a full report on the rationale and prospects for an ideological sorting of the parties, which eventually resulted in an eighty-page treatise, "Liberty and the Republic: The Case for Party Realignment."[48] The committee included several northern ex-senators and ex-governors, while the leading southerner was Donald Richberg, a former New Deal official turned conservative legal scholar. Most conservative political elites in the South still proved reluctant to pursue openly the idea of a formal proto-partisan alliance with Republicans.[49]

Nevertheless, southern audiences welcomed the Yankee senator's message during his tours. Standing ovations were typical. The audience at one 1951 address gave Mundt "not mere applause . . . but ear-splitting level yells," according to Mississippi's *Jackson Daily News*.[50] Charles Wallace Collins wrote to Mundt to express his support.[51] National conservative voices like radio personality Fulton Lewis Jr., writer Felix Morley, and newspaper editor William Loeb all joined in the encouragement.[52] Speaking at the annual Mississippi Economic Council in 1951, Raymond Moley, another conservative ex-New Dealer, heralded the coming dissolution of the South's one-party system, cribbing from V. O. Key's mammoth recent study of southern politics to describe the southern state Democratic organizations as "merely a holding company of transient squabbling factions."[53] An ideological realignment of the two parties, Moley argued, would finally render southern politics meaningfully coherent and issues-based and connect southern goals to the national political system.

All of this discussion was mere abstraction if it did not face squarely the most potent source of the rift between southern Democrats and their national party: civil rights for African Americans. Mundt made the policy implications of realignment clear when he repeatedly declared that a conservative alliance could be possible only if the Republicans gave "some thought to southern concepts in the writing of the platform" and avoided including "any of the planks which are understandably repugnant to the people of the South."[54] The planks he meant, in the 1948 platform drafted by the Dewey forces, were the endorsements of federal legislation challenging Jim Crow practices in the workplace and polling place. As Moley bluntly put it, realignment depended on getting "Republicans to forego their past practice of baiting the South by support of a Federal civil rights program."[55]

Postwar Republican positions on federal civil rights measures aligned with the party's factional split. Opposition was disproportionately found among Taftites opposed to all manner of federal activism in social policy and answering to few African American constituents. Taft had long expressed private skepticism about courting black votes, writing in 1945 that it was hopeless to try since a measure like the FEPC bill "violates any possible party philosophy we could adopt."[56] Three years later he warned a Tennessee crowd that Truman "would center in Washington the entire field of control over questions involving civil rights, without even considering the proper functions of the Federal Government, the states, and local communities in dealing with different features of the problem."[57] Taftites opposed a permanent FEPC throughout the 1940s and stripped draft language endorsing aggressive civil rights measures out of a 1950 statement on party principles.[58] Mundt's advocacy of jettisoning altogether the civil rights tradition that had been the GOP's birthright was not mere opportunism in pursuit of party realignment, but a stance that was ideologically and politically congenial to many Republican conservatives.

That stance was expressed explicitly in terms of federalism rather than white supremacy. As the Birmingham newspaperman John Temple Graves put it in heralding an ideological party realignment, "an obstacle in the path of this national political line-up is the impression given a great many Americans that the States' Rights movement in the South is nothing but race hate in political action, and is a sort of political first cousin to the Klan."[59] Deracializing the language of southern conservatism—and of opposition to civil rights legislation in general—was a prerequisite for realignment. "The South must be led by men less identified with the Negro question and more identified with the national revolt against federalism in general," he wrote.[60] Taftite Republicans were partners in this rhetorical project. RNC chairman Guy Gabrielson startled many political observers in the early 1950s by making direct appeals to the Dixiecrats, but he did so on race-neutral ideological grounds. "Our friends call themselves States' Righters and we call ourselves Republicans," he declared in Alabama in 1952. "But they oppose corruption and so do we."[61] Mundt endorsed white southerners' framing of their own opposition to federal action on civil rights. "Southerners have no desire to hold the Negro down," he insisted. "They want to promote programs in an area where by evolution and education they must work out a harmonious adjustment."[62]

To pro–civil rights Republicans, such positions were as morally objectionable as they were strategically dubious. In 1951 Mundt debated liberal Republican congressman Clifford Case in the pages of *Collier's* magazine on the question, "Should the GOP Merge with the Dixiecrats?"[63] Case offered practical objections to the idea, but the heart of his argument was substantive. "I do not want victory at the price of party character," he wrote, echoing Margaret Chase Smith's recent dissent against her party's embrace of McCarthyism. Case agreed that two-party politics would soon come to the South, but believed history and morality alike required that it come about through "a progressive Republican party which will align itself with, and provide a rallying point for, the progressive forces in Southern labor, industry, and agriculture—not with the Dixiecrats." Antiracism was a central pillar of Case's vision for a southern Republicanism that "really believes that the Negro is not an inferior person to be dealt with kindly but kept in his place."

Case proceeded, however, to make a broader normative point about the American party system. Like Thomas Dewey the year before, he offered a note of caution to "those who, whether on doctrinaire grounds or because they are dazzled by the prospect of temporary political or economic advantage, would re-form our two great parties along separate interest groupings and ideological lines." Achieving such a reformation, he argued, would strike at the defining quality of the American two-party system, namely the fact "that our two great political parties do not divide the people into separate interest or ideological groups." Case's essay revealed the logic by which, under the midcentury alignment of political and ideological forces, a moderate Republican's forceful, principled argument for civil rights could also amount to a celebration of the *absence* of principle in the division of the two parties.

The same logic explained why Mundt's ideological enemies in

the opposing party frequently endorsed his proposal for realignment. Mundt engaged in a radio debate with leading liberal Democrat—and noted responsible party advocate—Hubert Humphrey in July 1951. On the question of ideological realignment, their "debate" turned out to be anything but. Humphrey stated up front that he agreed with Mundt's "propos[al] that we get the political parties cleaned up or cleared up on the basis of issues. . . . I welcome it, because I would like to have the American people truly know what the political parties stand for."[64] Mundt appeared on the *Eleanor Roosevelt Show* the same year, where the former First Lady told her guest, "I agree with you when you say that our present parties confuse people. . . . I made a suggestion somewhat similar to that [for party realignment] also some time ago."[65]

In the short term, however, conservatives would prove no more capable than liberals of reconstructing the party system along ideological lines. The shuttering of the Committee to Explore Political Realignment less than a year after its creation was illustrative.[66] "I am not willing to raise a substantial amount of money from people all over the country," Hawkes wrote to Mundt, "until I feel we have some kind of a plan that justifies their contributing the money and justifies us in expecting to spend it wisely and effectively."[67] Such a plan was missing. A surfeit of political caution disinclined large numbers of political leaders—North and South—from enlisting in the cause. At this early stage in southern conservatives' break with the national Democratic leadership, too many were still invested in existing arrangements, and too few northern and southern activists, political funders, and politicians had developed ties with each other, to make a short-term political breakthrough realistic.[68] Virginia's powerful Democratic senator Harry Byrd, for example, launched his own campaign in the South against Truman's civil rights policies in 1951 and called for the reinstatement of the old two-thirds requirement for Democratic presidential nominating conventions that had given Dixie veto power before 1936.[69] But despite repeated meetings with Hawkes and other leaders involved in the committee, Byrd resisted joining an explicit campaign for party realignment.[70]

Explaining the "standoffish" attitude of many southern conservatives to party realignment, one journalist cited not only the pull of tradition and lingering suspicions of Republicans, but also the continued uniqueness of the South's place in the political system. "Southerners exert a vital balance-of-power role in national affairs, particularly in the Congress," he wrote, "and do all right on patronage, public works, and other items of Federal aid, too."[71] That unique role depended on sectional solidarity, just as, from southern elites' perspective, the maintenance of Jim Crow depended on preventing party competition in the South that could lead to efforts to mobilize African Americans electorally. National party realignment threatened to disrupt that political solidarity. To most southerners in the 1950s, the risks of such a disruption outweighed the potential benefits.[72]

Nevertheless, stirrings from the South in 1952 indicated that increasing numbers in the region were beginning to change their calculations. Eisenhower's southern support was strongest in the urbanized and comparatively moderate peripheral states.[73] But disenchantment with the national Democratic Party had grown sufficiently to compel increasing numbers of strong conservatives to jump ship as well. From the Virginian Donald Richberg to the Texas oil baron Jack Porter to South Carolina governor James F. Byrnes, conservative southern activists, donors, and public officials mobilized on behalf of a Republican presidential candidate in numbers never seen before.[74]

Two developments would help to compel more southerners to join such apostates in the years to come. First, as the region grew economically and drew increasing numbers of northern transplants, traditional partisan attachments loosened and began more closely to resemble national patterns. Second, American conservatism itself attained a new coherence and self-conscious movement spirit, and as a result helped to empower the Right in its battles within the GOP. That national Republican right would advocate a political posture toward the South much more in keeping with Karl Mundt's Dixie courting than Clifford Case's progressivism.[75] Ironically enough, both of these developments would commence during the tenure of an exceptionally popular and avowedly moderate Republican president.

"PRINCIPLE IS BASIC": THE CONSERVATIVE
MOVEMENT IN THE AGE OF CONSENSUS

Conservative Republicans had reason to feel embattled during Dwight D. Eisenhower's presidency. Contrary to Eisenhower's reputation as a grandfatherly executive amiably carrying out his tenure in a nonideological manner, his "hidden-hand" leadership was actually driven by sharp political and partisan instincts and Midwestern small-government convictions.[76] But despite those convictions, Eisenhower's outlook on the GOP's future emphasized substantive accommodation to the New Deal state and a political image makeover. Increasingly over his two terms, Eisenhower pursued both high-profile and *sub rosa* political activities on behalf of a vision for the Republican Party that was sharply at odds with the interests of the party's conservatives.

Eisenhower's substantive views shaped his brand of Republicanism. Ideologically, he combined a fervent internationalism with a view of domestic policy that venerated what he termed "the Middle Way." "The critical problem of our time," he wrote to a friend in 1954, "is to find and stay on the path that marks the way of logic between conflicting arguments advanced by extremists on both sides on almost every economic, political, and international problem that arises." In the realm of social policy, this meant "establishing some kind of security for individuals in a highly specialized and industrialized age" without "push[ing] further and further into the socialistic experiment."[77] His substantive disagreements with Republican conservatives took early form in the well-publicized fight with congressional isolationists over a proposed constitutional amendment to restrict the scope and process of treaty ratification.[78] It continued with conservative grumbling over his appointment of Earl Warren as Chief Justice of the Supreme Court. In the electoral arena Eisenhower actively promoted several moderates to run for House and Senate races.[79] The protracted battle within the administration over whether or not to jettison Richard Nixon from the ticket in 1956 was similarly colored by ideological factionalism, as the California Cold Warrior's place on the 1952 ticket had been due to his closeness to the party's right wing. Though Nixon stayed on,

Eisenhower was by then newly committed, in his words, to "build-[ing] up a strong, progressive Republican Party in this country. . . . If the right wing wants a fight, they're going to get it."[80]

In an unhappy irony for his cause, Eisenhower's efforts ulti-mately did a great deal to shape, cohere, and motivate the post-war conservative movement that eventually captured the Repub-lican Party. William F. Buckley and other intellectual architects of the postwar conservative movement forged their analysis and movement partly through combat with those who expounded on Eisenhower-style moderation, chief among them the law professor-turned-administration official Arthur Larson. At the grassroots level, demographic and social developments similar to those driving the rise of a new kind of liberal activist inside the Democratic Party also enabled the flourishing of amateur activism on the Republican right. Those activists derived motivation and missionary zeal from the very fusionist conservative ideology that Buckley and others were disseminating. The first stirrings of this newly powerful confluence of intellectual leadership and grass-roots energy were felt in internal party initiatives that Eisenhower encouraged in the hopes of bolstering moderate Republicanism. Those stirrings would turn into a storm of conservative activity in the 1960s that powered Barry Goldwater's ascension to the presi-dential nomination.

"Boy oh boy oh boy, does that Arthur Larson bear keeping one's eye on!," editorialized *National Review* in September 1956.[81] That magazine's writers and editors kept close eyes indeed on the man whom the *New York Times* called Eisenhower's "chief theo-retician" and *Meet the Press*'s moderator called the White House's "ideologist-in-chief." Larson, like Eisenhower a Midwestern-raised Republican, was a legal scholar of the welfare state before serving as undersecretary of labor, director of the United States In-formation Agency, and eventually, chief presidential speechwriter.

Larson articulated his view on the alignment of forces in the contemporary political system in a bestselling treatise in 1956, warmly endorsed by the White House.[82] (Larson's book, William F. Buckley quipped, "had the singular distinction of being read by President Eisenhower.")[83] *A Republican Looks at His Party* promised to establish "two key political facts of mid-century America," the first being that "we have greater agreement than ever before in our history on fundamental issues," the second that the Eisenhower administration's philosophy and policies reflected that agreement.[84] Ike's approach charted a third way between what Larson termed the "1896 ideology" of laissez faire and the "1936 ideology" of proto-socialism. It acknowledged that an urbanized industrial society now required concerted federal action in many realms of life that had traditionally been left to states, localities, and the private sector. It also, however, limited federal action to those realms in which local or private initiatives could not meet the need. The formula prescribed "as much government as necessary, but not enough to stifle the normal motivations of private enterprise."[85]

How did such an approach work in a two-party system? Larson disavowed European-style party politics, "with its left-right arrangement of political status. . . . In this country, we have alignments formed according to a complex system of sectional, local, traditional and interest groupings." The cumulative product of such fragmented alignments was the "American Consensus" approach to policy that Larson endorsed. But though "there is no American Center Party as such, and there probably never will be," Larson predicted that Republicanism in the Eisenhower mold could forge an enduring majority for years to come. This was because the Democrats actually contained within their coalition the most extreme promoters of both the 1896 and the 1936 ideologies, positioning a reformed GOP to "capture the political center."[86]

Larson used the term "New Republicanism" to describe this project. By the time Eisenhower hit the campaign trail in 1956, after delivering a nomination acceptance speech at the GOP convention that Larson had written, "Modern Republicanism" had become the more popular phrase. On the night of his second victory over Adlai Stevenson, Eisenhower declared that "modern Republicanism has now proved itself. And America has approved of modern Republicanism."[87]

*Dis*approval of modern Republicanism helped to shape the politics and vision of the postwar conservative movement. William F. Buckley, Brent Bozell, James Burnham, Frank Meyer, William Rusher, and the rest of the mid-1950s intellectual circle around *National Review* saw the ideological scrambling of the two-party system as the means by which a collectivist liberal elite could sustain itself in power. "The most alarming single danger to the American system," declared the *National Review*'s inaugural issue, "lies in the fact that an identifiable team of Fabian operators is bent on controlling both our major political parties—under the sanction of such fatuous and unreasoned slogans as 'national unity,' 'middle-of-the-road,' 'progressivism,' and 'bipartisanship.'" In the face of that threat, the new journal would stand "without reservation" on the side of a "two-party system that fights its feuds in public and honestly."[88] In that vein, the magazine declined to endorse Eisenhower in 1956, and in the ensuing years made good on the promise to track the exploits of the president's court philosopher, Larson, as he rose in prominence. "Modern Republicans," wrote the magazine, "are—*as a matter of principle*—*against* principle."[89] For that reason, they were to blame for both the GOP's failure to recapture Congress in 1956 and, most grievously, the party's mammoth congressional losses in the 1958 midterms. "An organization needs people and money, but before that it needs a purpose," Brent Bozell explained in 1958, augmenting conservatives' substantive critique of Modern Republicanism with their longstanding argument against me-tooism. "With the Republican Party deprived of a distinctive policy, the party organization was deprived of a reason for existing and working."[90]

Buckley offered his most thorough formulation of the connection between building a conservative ideological movement and recasting the party system in his 1959 book *Up from Liberalism*. He attacked the era's atmosphere of ideological dissolution, issuing a call to reject consensus politics and revive ideology that in certain ways anticipated arguments of the New Left. Though "America, fashionable observers say, is a non-ideological nation," Buckley warned of the danger that looms "when a distrust of doctrinaire social systems eases over into a dissolute disregard for principle" and when Americans demonstrate a "failure to nourish any orthodoxy at all." Larson's Modern Republicanism claimed to identify a coherent line of thought driving the seeming mishmash of centrist policymaking, but "in permitting so many accretions, modifications, emendations, maculations, and qualifications" to its alleged tenets, it had proven "simply not useful as a philosophy of government distinctive to a single faction in American life."[91] A two-party system made a coherent and distinctive philosophy all the more necessary. Our "challenge," Buckley wrote, was "to restore principles to public affairs." Doing so required factional battle inside the GOP, which in turn called for a vigor derived from intellectual coherence: "The conservative movement in America has got to put its theoretical house in order."[92]

The way in which Buckley and other midcentury conservative intellectuals had set about doing just that constituted one of the more thoroughgoing and self-conscious projects of ideological construction in American history. The "fusionism" of the postwar conservative project, to use Frank Meyer's term, merged the economic libertarianism of Hayek with cultural traditionalism and a militant and morally charged anticommunism.[93] At a theoretical level, intellectuals worked to show how those outlooks fit together into a coherent conception of the relationship of individuals to the state and society. But Buckley the activist was always explicit in asserting the practical necessity of fusion as a matter of coalition politics. In *Up from Liberalism*, he endorsed the centrality of a "negative response to liberalism" as the organizing rationale of conservative unity, and used a nautical metaphor to describe an approach to disparate political issues that put them all "in range" of a single conservative outlook. "There is a point from which opposition to the social security laws and a devout belief in social stability are in range," he wrote, "as also a determined resistance to the spread of world Communism—and a belief in political non-interventionism. . . . That is the position, generally speaking, where conservatives now find themselves on the political chart."[94] The task was to mobilize such conservatives into an ideological movement capable of achieving real political impact.

The grassroots and organizational manpower for that movement had several sources. One was the conservative core of Republican activists and professionals referred to as the "Taft wing" prior to the Ohio senator's death in 1953. When, four years later, Eisenhower acknowledged in his private notes that his candidacy had been "forced down the throats of a lot of people in '52," these rank-and-file conservatives at the base of the party were who he was describing: "Some will never forget it. . . . There is so much resentment, and these people will never give up." In the years between Taft's death and Goldwater's national ascendency, such rank-and-file conservatives lacked an agreed-upon standard-bearer. But even while politically leaderless, Republican conservatives articulated increasingly hard-edged critiques of Eisenhower Republicanism and support for polarization. One 1957 RNC survey of Midwestern party officials found sentiments that were typified by one respondent's suggestion to "Register all 'Modern Republicans' as Democrats."[95]

Beyond the enduring core of Taftites among the party's rank and file was the emergence, over the first two postwar decades, of a right-wing corollary to the "amateur Democrats" of James Q. Wilson's analysis: a great flourishing of organization-building and political activism by largely middle-class issue-driven conservatives. These "suburban warriors" populated the sprawling new developments of the booming postwar Sunbelt, and their activism gave grassroots force to the fusionist ideology that Buckley and his fellow intellectuals helped construct.[96] Locally rooted anticommunist groups, linked through national networks of organizations and syndicated media and radio programs like the *Dan Smoot Report* and the *Manion Forum on Opinion*, compelled millions of Americans to connect the global Cold War struggle to domestic political issues and ideological conflicts.[97] Christian conservative groups like Spiritual Mobilization, the Freedom Clubs, and Fred Schwarz's Christian Anti-Communism Crusade gave powerful organizational form to the ideological melding of religious conservatism, Cold War hawkishness, and domestic free-market orthodoxy.[98] At the day-to-day heart of much of this activism was a cohort of conservative women—educated wives and mothers of the postwar boom—who organized the book clubs, arranged the speakers' series, and galvanized community activism on behalf of local and national issues alike.[99]

The manner in which this amateur spirit began to penetrate the party system likewise had some parallels to the club Democrats. Some existing para-party organizations at the state level, like the California Republican Assembly, found themselves taken over by conservative insurgencies starting in the late 1950s, while conservatives in other states built new independent Republican groups from scratch.[100] And movement funders such as Roger Milliken, Lemuel Boulware, and J. Howard Pew took tentative initial steps to form and bankroll national mass-membership organizations dedicated to conservative advocacy.

One locus for issue-driven and ideological party activism on the right, however, had no parallel among liberal Democrats. Intense ideological warfare—and eventual conservative triumph—in the Young Republican and College Republican organizations at both the state and national level revealed Republican youths to be the canaries in the coalmine of future party transformations. Key conservative movement activists and party operators had cut their teeth in Young Republican National Federation politics in the early postwar years, notably William Rusher and the campaign operative F. Clifton White.[101] By the time of the 1957 Young Republicans convention, committed conservatives representing a Midwestern-Sunbelt regional coalition had secured control of the national organization. Two years later, the federation passed a platform plank that explicitly denounced Eisenhower Republicanism.[102]

By the late 1950s, then, grassroots elements within the Republican Party, in auxiliary organizations, and in civil society increasingly espoused a consciously ideological movement spirit. The political mobilization of that spirit began, ironically, within Eisenhower's initiatives to remake the national GOP along Modern Republican lines. Eisenhower's ambition as a party leader far exceeded his capacity to change the ideological outlook of the party's most engaged activists, and thus his efforts to secure Modern Republicanism had the profoundly unintended consequence of empowering the Republican right.

"I still have a job of re-forming and re-vamping the Republican Party," Eisenhower wrote upon his reelection in 1956. Building organizational capacity from the precinct level up would serve to provide "a strong basis for the Modern Republicanism that will best represent the interests of all the people."[103] To pursue his party-building agenda, the president and his appointed RNC chairman Meade Alcorn called for six regional conferences of party workers and officials in 1957 to discuss party organization and program, culminating in a Republican National Conference in Washington that summer. All seven meetings proved to be riven by ideological division, with conservative Republicans mobilizing to voice their criticism of the Modern Republican agenda. At the National Conference, the president only managed to deepen rather than mollify the division when he denied that intra-Republican disagreements "concerned our basic principles" and chastised Republicans who "have a talent for magnifying and advertising our differences."[104]

Eisenhower and Alcorn's next party-building initiative, launched in the aftermath of the GOP's devastating losses in the 1958 midterms, provided further occasion for those "magnifiers of difference" to showcase their talent. In early 1959 Alcorn appointed a Republican Committee on Program and Progress—known as the Percy Committee after its moderate chairman, Charles Percy—and tasked it with "providing the Republican Party with a concise understandable statement of our Party's long-range objectives in all areas of political responsibility."[105] The new committee was similar to the Democratic Advisory Council (DAC) under Paul Butler. Both were responses to electoral losses that had seemed to reveal the need for a clearer and more identifiable national policy program. But if the DAC became a vehicle for the Democrats' dominant liberal faction to amplify its agenda, the Percy Committee served as an effort by elite Modern Republican proponents to secure a moderate brand for their party. The president believed that the GOP's electoral misfortunes derived not only from a moribund organization and poor candidate recruitment, but also, relatedly, from a conservative program that failed to project youth, vigor, or optimism. The Percy Committee, intentionally stacked with party outsiders and tasked with devising consensual policy positions on such themes as "The Impact of Science and Technology" and "Economic Opportunity and Progress," was intended to remedy this by institutionalizing Modern Republicanism.[106]

Though Percy and RNC staffers worked to strike a nonideological tone for the proceedings, participants from both the Modern Republican and conservative factions made the deepening fissures within the party unmistakably clear. Thomas Kuchel typified the moderates' arguments in his address at a March 1959 session. The California senator, whom then-Governor Earl Warren had originally appointed to fill Richard Nixon's seat, made a point of celebrating Warren's tenure as Chief Justice, including the *Brown v. Board of Education* decision, as part of a venerable party tradition of progressivism. Kuchel urged congressional Republicans to abandon their alliance with southern Democrats against pro-labor and pro-civil rights legislation. But he insisted even to "those of you who disagree with some of the philosophy that I espouse" that the Republican Party "is big enough to have and . . . strong enough to have men of a conservative point of view, and I think it is big enough and strong enough to have men and women in it of a moderate to liberal point of view."[107]

A forceful, if oblique, counterargument came later in the same session, during a presentation by the new chairman of the National Republican Senatorial Committee who also happened to be the rapidly rising star of American conservatism. By 1959 Arizona's Barry Goldwater had already achieved conservative renown for the consistency—so unusual in a professional politician—with which he framed his positions on disparate issues within an overarching ideological vision. An across-the-board antistatist conservative, Goldwater was particularly notable in the Senate for his hostility to organized labor and the populist, proworker rhetoric he employed in the service of denouncing union leadership. His smashing reelection victory in 1958 in the face of a concerted labor-backed effort to unseat him bucked the anti-Republican trend that year and won him newfound national attention.[108]

Goldwater insisted to the Percy Committee that a party comeback did not require a reversal of position on labor policy or any other core issue. In his description of the 1958 successes in Arizona, he emphasized the primacy of a clear party program over the individual attributes of any of the candidates. He cited analyst Samuel Lubell's postelection work surveying voters to find out why the state "went against the trend. Voter after voter interviewed said they voted for us because they knew what we stood for. . . . Our position in Arizona was unambiguous and uncompromising, and it was clearly conservative, afraid neither of the word, nor its connotations." Goldwater combined his analysis of that campaign with a historical argument about the strategic daftness of "me, too" party policies. The conclusion he reached directly contrasted with Kuchel and others' defense of party heterodoxy. "Principle is basic. That is the first consideration," Goldwater insisted. "It is axiomatic that a party must finally deteriorate into nothing if it becomes obsessed with technique and forgets its basic meaning and purpose. . . . The trouble is not that we are Republican. The trouble may be that we are not Republican enough."[109]

A day later, during the discussion on principles and partisanship with political scientist Robert Goldwin, Goldwater's aide Stephen Shadegg insisted that a fundamental ideological divide over the very "nature of man" defined contemporary America's politics, if not yet its parties. For a committee dominated by Modern Republicans, Goldwater and Shadegg were skunks at the garden party. But their argument for ideological battle galvanized more party activists than did the committee's bromides. The committee's final report, published in book form as *Decisions for a Better America* in 1960, covered a laundry list of policy issues but did little to dispel Modern Republicanism's reputation for vague philosophical straddling. Conservative Republicans saw in the report's lack of ideological coherence and distinctiveness only capitulation and crypto-liberalism—"the ultimate, it may be hoped," Goldwater speechwriter Karl Hess later wrote, "in the lemming-like Republican urge to accept Democratic programs, tacitly approve Democratic principles, but to propose implementing them in a more businesslike manner." *Decisions for a Better America* barely made a ripple among political readers and commentators. Another book released in 1960—a compendium of Goldwater's speeches and writings polished by William F. Buckley's brother-in-law and released as *The Conscience of a Conservative*—took aim at the statist New Deal philosophy that reflected "the view of a majority of leaders of one of our parties, and of a strong minority among the leaders of the other." Over half a million copies were in print by year's end.[110]

"EVERYTHING SHOULD BE AN ISSUE": THE GOLDWATER MOVEMENT, 1960–1964

The tributaries of conservative activism flowing through the later 1950s first converged behind the political leadership of Barry Goldwater in 1960. Conservative intellectuals alarmed at the chameleonism and opportunistic leftward drift of Richard Nixon, the party's likely presidential nominee, looked to Goldwater as the vessel for ideological energy. "The situation of conservatism in the United States," Frank Meyer wrote to his fellow *National Review* editors in May 1960, "presents a sharp contrast between the steady growth of conservative influence on the intellectual level and the cumulative debacle on the political level." Only the "emergence of Barry Goldwater as a principled conservative" on the national scene "gives us a public political symbol . . . in the political arena."[111] The emerging conservative stronghold of young Republican organizations mobilized early and dramatically on behalf of a "Draft Goldwater" movement for vice president, starting in the Midwestern Federation of College Young Republican Clubs. Within half a year, the student campaign took on a new organizational form, Young Americans for Freedom, at a meeting at William F. Buckley's Connecticut estate.[112] And finally, within formal GOP ranks, a delegate drive to nominate Goldwater for the presidency materialized in the heart of Dixie, at the South Carolina Republican convention.

That South Carolina would provide the triggering action—"the catalytic agent," in F. Clifton White's words—that launched Goldwater toward an active candidacy helps to underscore the centrality of civil rights politics to the conservative ascendency within the GOP.[113] The alignment of the party's left-right ideological division with competing positions on civil rights, already close in the early postwar years, had tightened further in the wake of *Brown v. Board*, massive resistance, and the beginnings of the civil rights movement's "classical" phase of direct action against Jim Crow.

Racial conservatism was as much a component of movement leaders' fusionist intellectual project as economic orthodoxy and moral traditionalism. In the later 1950s *National Review* and other conservative organs helped to refine and legitimize "color-blind" states-rights and constitutional arguments against federal intervention on civil rights.[114] The *Conscience of a Conservative* typified this emerging line in the two chapters it devoted to "States' Rights" and "Civil Rights," respectively.[115]

That ideological work dovetailed with a nascent effort at Republican party-building in South Carolina, on hard-edged conservative terms. The Palmetto State proved a first mover in this regard, and a rebuke to contemporaneous efforts by Eisenhower and the RNC. The president and Meade Alcorn pursued "Operation Dixie," a significant initiative to build southern GOP organizational capacity while eschewing segregationist appeals and deepening party inroads among young urban professionals in the peripheral South.[116] What happened in South Carolina was different, and a harbinger of how conservative Republican advances would be made in other southern states.[117] Northern transplants proved central to the emergence of conservative Republicanism in South Carolina. Gregory D. Shorey Jr., a Massachusetts native, owner of a sports equipment company, and rock-ribbed conservative, had risen through the South Carolina GOP ranks in the 1950s as one of several younger activists battling a patronage-oriented Old Guard. As party chairman in 1960, he worked with a fellow northern migrant, the textile magnate and Republican financier Roger Milliken, to assure a surprise vote at the state convention pledging all fourteen presidential delegates to Goldwater. As Milliken told a local journalist, the vote was "designed to call attention of GOP bigwigs and Nixon personally of conservative sentiment in these parts."[118] Unsurprisingly for Yankee businessmen like Shorey and Milliken, Goldwater's antilabor stances and economic conservatism were as significant components of his ideological appeal as his opposition to civil rights legislation.

Though conservative Republicans' pursuit of this kind of southern strategy met with loud opposition from GOP moderates, a basic imbalance in the factional politics of civil rights was already apparent by 1960. To be sure, key Republican officials crusaded aggressively on behalf of civil rights. New York governor Nelson Rockefeller withheld his endorsement of Richard Nixon in 1960 until he could secure a strong civil rights plank in the platform in the infamous (to conservatives) "Treaty of Fifth Avenue."[119] Moreover, as typified by President Eisenhower's dispatching of federal troops to Little Rock, Arkansas, in 1957 to enforce the *Brown* decision, Republican governance in the executive branch in the later 1950s, while insufficient in the eyes of civil rights activists, was hardly calculated to win the political allegiance of segregationist southerners.[120]

Nevertheless, support for civil rights was more prevalent at the elite level, where Republican officeholders worked to sustain multiracial electoral coalitions, than it was in the middle range of party activists and officials. At least as early as the immediate postwar years, northern Democratic activists showed at once more pervasive and more intense support for civil rights than their Republican counterparts. "Basically and sociologically," Theodore White wrote in 1956, "Republican state organizations are unlikely to go out for the predominantly working class Negro unless flogged into it by the White House." As one RNC official told his chairman two years later, "How many Republicans would sit down in their own home and break bread with a Negro? I've done it, but even I don't say much about it for fear other Republicans would look down their nose at me."[121] Eisenhower's sole African American White House aide, E. Frederic Morrow, grew sufficiently frustrated by the GOP's half-hearted outreach efforts to black voters and activists to voice his criticism publicly in 1959, lamenting that blacks lacked "a full-fledged part" in the party and "a voice in party councils."[122] The lack of a sizeable activist bloc for whom civil rights advocacy was a salient and central concern led the Nixon campaign in 1960 to err further on the side of caution against alienating southern whites. The campaign neglected black mobilization, and Nixon avoided public interaction with civil rights activists.[123] Already in 1960, as a consequence both of the balance of pressure within the party base and the developing political landscape for pursuing new voters, the GOP's racial strategy was beginning to tilt in the direction that

Barry Goldwater, one year later, would articulate to an audience in Atlanta. "We're not going to get the Negro vote as a bloc" in coming elections, the senator declared, "so we ought to go hunting where the ducks are."[124]

At the 1960 convention Goldwater electrified attendees with his speech while organizers of the draft effort sought to win open support from delegates outside of South Carolina and Arizona. The would-be candidacy of this scourge of "me-tooism" fizzled in Chicago, clearing the way for the determinedly nonideological general election race between Nixon and John F. Kennedy. As in 1956, *National Review*'s staff debated whether or not to publish an endorsement in the general race. William Rusher, always the most caustic in evaluating the GOP's potential as a movement vessel, argued strongly against offering one. "I think that both major parties, as presently constituted, are simply highly efficient vote-gathering machines," he wrote. "It is pointless to upbraid such a machine for failing to concern itself with principles." Rusher held out hope for the independent emergence in the coming years of a "new and more highly ideologized political party."[125]

As it would happen, just such an ideologized party seemed to appear, with deceptive speed, by 1964. And contrary to Rusher's prediction, the party was that very "machine" itself, the GOP. It would, however, prove significantly less efficient than usual at vote-gathering that year.

Prior to that election, the GOP's internal deliberations reflected the persistence of a factional division over ideology and strategy. Moderates pointed to electoral shortfalls in urban centers of the industrial North in accounting for Nixon's razor-thin loss to Kennedy. Officials allied with Nelson Rockefeller, then the party's moderate standard-bearer, called for staking out progressive party positions on issues like civil rights, government-supported medical care, and labor law as a means of cutting down Democrats' dominance among union members and African Americans.

Partly to avoid exacerbating intraparty divisions, party leaders tended toward more organizational approaches to party renewal. This was typified by the RNC's Committee on Big City Politics, established in 1961 under the leadership of a renowned guru of nuts-and-bolts party-building, Ohio party chairman Ray Bliss. Explicitly tasked by the RNC to "work on campaign techniques and not on Party philosophy," the committee prescribed a set of enhancements to precinct organization and party staffing in metropolitan areas as the key to boosting electoral competitiveness.[126] Party leaders' aversion to confronting divisive policy issues head-on meant that northern urban inroads could be pursued at the same time that the GOP expanded its investment in Operation Dixie. "The apparent contradiction between wooing Negroes in the North while simultaneously building an organizational framework in the South did not seem to bother Republican National Committee staff members," one contemporary scholar observed. After all, "the Democratic Party had encompassed both regions and races for years."[127] Such "both-and" strategic straddling was becoming increasingly untenable, however, in the face of a movement determined to force its party to choose sides.

The 1964 Goldwater insurgency is a story that movement conservatives and their chroniclers have long reveled in detailing. From the organizational spadework of F. Clifton White's "Syndicate" of Young Republican allies, to the parliamentary maneuvering by which Goldwaterites swept the local party offices in charge of delegate selection in one state after another, to the serially faltering efforts by established Republican moderates to beat Goldwater to the nomination, the tale makes for an irresistible origin story for the modern right. The Goldwater takeover was all the more remarkable for having been carried out through opaque and unreformed party nomination procedures. Its success provided a potent demonstration of the practical power of ideological zeal when effectively mobilized.

It also marked an end of the straddling between contradictory demographic strategies for party expansion, resolved in favor of a southern strategy that merged conservative movement-making with white racial politicking in the South. In the early 1960s, prior to any active management by Goldwater personnel, the RNC's Operation Dixie had already drifted far from its Eisenhower-era mandate to build operations and staff among racially moderate whites and African Americans in the peripheral South. Those activists who proved most interested in taking up the RNC's recruitment pitch as candidates and local party officials turned out to be both staunch ideological conservatives and opponents of federal civil rights efforts.[128] John Tower's historic victory in the 1961 Senate race in Texas, orchestrated by one such new-guard southern GOP conservative operative, Peter O'Donnell, typified the cast of southern Republicanism that Eisenhower's initiative had inadvertently mobilized.[129] Officials like O'Donnell, Mississippi's Wirt Yerger, and South Carolina's Greg Shorey proved, unsurprisingly, to be staunch Goldwater supporters as well, going so far as to threaten an ouster campaign against RNC chair William E. Miller in 1963 when he vetoed a rally of southern GOP officials who supported the Arizona senator.[130] With the prodding of Goldwater allies, the RNC ramped up investment in Operation Dixie to a full third of total committee expenditures in 1964, while leaving divisions aimed at minorities and cities comparatively cash-strapped.[131]

By the time of the convention in San Francisco in July 1964, southern delegations that had in the past lived up to their reputations as rotten-borough practitioners of nomination wheeler-dealing were now at the vanguard of Goldwater's ideological insurgency. The racial dynamics of this kind of party activism were hard to mistake. Georgia sent its first all-white delegation to the GOP convention in over a half century. The state chairman explained to a reporter that the delegates were "people who believe in the philosophy expressed by Senator Goldwater," and it just so happened that no "Negroes were in the forefront of this effort."[132] A political scientist surveying southern delegates at the convention reported disproportionately hard-right issue positions among them, on civil rights as much as foreign policy and social welfare.[133] I. Lee Potter, the Virginia party chair who had overseen Operation Dixie from 1957 until he was fired by Goldwater aides in 1964, told a reporter in the bleak aftermath of the election that the southern party organization he had spent years developing "were ruined by extremists who moved in, took over, and preached white supremacy."[134] But in reducing the logic of Goldwaterite Republicanism in the South to simple racism, Potter elided the ideological work that had served to incorporate hostility to civil rights into a broader, national conservative agenda.

Potter's lament also made use of a rhetoric of hijacking—of organizational takeover by foreign elements—that permeated the language of Republicans opposed to conservatives' factional efforts in the early 1960s. They frequently cast such efforts as illegitimate and unfair play. "These groups are attempting to take over Republican committees and clubs in an effort to move the party to the right by internal force," one complained, "rather than create a climate of opinion which would make such a move profitable in terms of votes."[135] Nelson Rockefeller similarly warned of "subversion from the radical right," which was currently "boring from within."[136] The general election returns in 1964 would vindicate the notion that activists had excelled at the inside game of party capture without laying a public groundwork for electoral success.

As we have seen, however, the activists working on Goldwater's behalf were hardly foreign entities or interlopers in GOP affairs, and the 1964 campaign itself was not actually the origin story of legend. Rather, it represented a culmination of organizational and ideological work that had been shaped by two decades of factional debate within the Republican Party. In this sense it was appropriate that *A Choice Not an Echo*, the surprise bestselling campaign book by the extraordinary grassroots organizer Phyllis Schlafly, framed its case for Goldwater conservatism with an account of a quarter century of intraparty betrayal, extending back even farther than the Dewey-Taft wars. Schlafly's book offered a conspiratorial vision of party irresponsibility, depicting the marginalization of the Republican Party's conservative majority as the work of a cabal of "secret kingmakers."[137]

The long factional struggle to which Schlafly alluded had, over time, taken on more fully elaborated ideological content. By 1964 Goldwater delegates were startling longtime students of American politics by espousing a conception of partisanship that seemed downright foreign. "Even if the party loses," one told a political scientist, "at least we have presented a clear alternative to the people. At least we'll have a strong party." What did he mean by strong?

"Cohesive, united on principles." Another delegate reveled in the way that ideologically driven partisanship drew more and more issues into debate. "I think everything should be an issue," she said. "Cuba should be an issue. Civil Rights should be an issue. This is the first time a race will be on issues. I think it's wonderful."[138]

Most American voters that year found it less wonderful. Goldwater's loss was historically massive—though so were his gains in the South, six months after his Senate vote against the Civil Rights Act. He won five southern states outright and notched major Republican gains over the party's showing four years earlier in virtually every other one. The totals outside of Dixie, however, seemed to provide ample evidence for one commentator's postelection insistence that Republicans "cannot win in this era of American history" except as a "me, too" party.[139]

Others went farther, insisting that the very *kind* of party that Goldwaterites sought to forge out of the GOP—ideologically defined, relentlessly issue-driven—was bad for America. Michigan governor George Romney, who along with fellow moderates like Rockefeller and Jacob Javits had refused to endorse Goldwater, wrote a letter to the senator soon after the election that addressed the idea of a "possible realignment of the Republican and Democratic parties into 'conservative' and 'liberal' parties." Echoing the words of Thomas Dewey fourteen years earlier, Romney pointed to the baleful experience of "ideologically oriented parties in Europe" in order to defend the American tradition of two "broad-based," big-tent parties. "Dogmatic ideological parties tend to splinter the political and social fabric of a nation, lead to governmental crises and deadlock, and stymie the compromises so often necessary to preserve freedom and achieve progress," he wrote. Meanwhile, if the GOP failed to rededicate itself to the proud American tradition of pragmatic outreach in the service of electoral majority-making, "our rehash of 1964 positions may become of interest only to the historians of defunct political institutions."[140]

Another decade and a half of continual factional efforts and institutional experimentation would ensue before it became clearer which approach to party politics had come to predominate within the Republican Party—and which had, in fact, become "defunct."

4

POWER IN MOVEMENT, 1961-1968

"We are people of this generation, bred in at least modest comfort, housed now in universities, looking uncomfortably to the world we inherit."[1] So began the manifesto drafted in 1962 at a conference in Port Huron, Michigan, by Students for a Democratic Society (SDS), the organizational revamp of an obscure, union-funded social democratic outfit called the Student League for Industrial Democracy. If the soon-to-be-iconic *Port Huron Statement* could be said to have captured not only the nascent New Left's outlook but also core tendencies of so much of the movement activism that would shape the 1960s, a good deal of it was evoked just in that opening line: the generational self-consciousness, the prosperity and education undergirding the political perspective, the tone of open-ended, nondoctrinaire searching. The ensuing document outlined a critique of the major institutions of American life as sources of alienation and political enervation, and made "participatory democracy" the conceptual watchword for an alternative world of meaningful social engagement, individual self-cultivation, and morally charged politics. The statement's authors worked to render as stark as possible the contrast in emphases between their youthful articulation of a New Left vision and the outlooks they ascribed to their elders—both the doctrinal preoccupations of the Marxist Old Left as well the consensus-oriented technocratic liberalism dominating the postwar order. In doing so they harbingered the intense generational conflict that would so color the era.

Yet continuities as much as new departures could be found in a closer read of this new progressive vision, not least in its outlook

The Overflowing Cup

FIGURE 4. Herblock, *Washington Post*, August 30, 1968. A 1968 Herblock Cartoon, © The Herb Block Foundation.

on the two-party system. A familiar critique of partisan depolarization, a prescription of responsible party government, and an explicit call for ideological realignment all appeared in the text amid the more recognizably radical analyses of bureaucratization, militarism, and social conformity. "The American political system is not the democratic model of which its glorifiers speak," the statement intoned. "In actuality it frustrates democracy by confusing the individual citizen, paralyzing policy discussion." The source of the paralysis could be found in a strange fact, namely

> that greater differences are harbored within each major party than the differences existing between them. Instead of two parties presenting distinctive and significant differences of approach, what dominates the system is a natural interlocking of Democrats from Southern states with the more conservative elements of the Republican party. This arrangement of forces is blessed by the seniority system of Congress.

The "party overlap," and the rules abetting the conservative coalition's power, served as "structural obstacle[s] of democracy in politics." In language that could have just as easily appeared in the APSA Committee on Political Parties' report more than a decade earlier, the *Port Huron* authors pointed out that when "confusion and blurring is built into the formulation of issues, long-range priorities are not discussed in the rational manner needed for policymaking." Betraying the influence of Max Shachtman and other laborite proponents of realignment, the authors even championed the nascent Goldwater movement in the GOP for its potential to help drive conservatives into a single party.

That the New Left's political analysis resonated with ideas that had colored the issue-oriented Democratic activism of the previous decade should not be surprising given the lineage of the SDS's key founders. Outnumbering the red-diaper babies of Old Left parents were young people directly connected to liberal Democratic circles. (In this sense the modest, apolitical background of Tom Hayden, the *Port Huron Statement*'s primary author and the SDS's one bona fide star, was more the exception than the rule.) Alan

Haber, who founded SDS at the University of Michigan in 1960, had worked for state Democratic chief and Paul Butler ally Neil Staebler, who was himself a member of the League for Industrial Democracy.[2] Sharon Jeffrey, Haber's partner in organizing SDS's flagship Ann Arbor chapter, was the daughter of Mildred Jeffrey, the feminist United Auto Workers (UAW) organizer and Democratic national committeewoman. (The UAW itself was a financial patron of SDS in the early 1960s.) The *Port Huron Statement*'s discussion of party realignment appeared thanks largely to the influence of Steve Max, a Marxist New Yorker championing a concept that Shachtmanites had developed in part from the writings of the responsible party scholar and Democratic activist James MacGregor Burns.[3]

To recognize such continuities in reformist activism across the postwar generations is to begin to grasp the significance of the tumultuous sixties for the long-term ideological transformation of the party system. The decade's social movement activists helped to rupture the parties by amplifying preexisting demands for greater moral commitment and attention to issues in party politics. To be sure, the discussion of realignment and responsible parties in the *Port Huron Statement*—included in somewhat perfunctory fashion by Hayden—did not represent where the intellectual and political energies of the sixties left would move in the coming years. The rhetoric espoused by the political mobilizations on behalf of civil rights and later an end to the Vietnam war, consumer rights, environmentalism, feminism, and the counterculture tended toward a suspicion of institutions and advocacy of openness and decentralization, and such themes contrasted with classic responsible party emphases on discipline and organizational strength. Nevertheless, by injecting new issues and constituencies as well as a stronger insistence on ideological commitment into American politics, those movements ultimately contributed signally to the long-term project of breaking down the transactional elements of political parties and remaking them as more issue-defined and ideological institutions. Ironically, they did so through pitched conflict with a political establishment that, for a brief moment, itself proved to be an agent of bold and sweeping programmatic reform.

This chapter explores the interactions between movement and partisan politics in the 1960s. Contingent circumstances created a "liberal hour" in the middle of that decade in which a historic wave of progressive policymaking, presided over by Lyndon Baines Johnson, transformed the government.[4] Even as Johnson drove a newly bold programmatic agenda through a national legislature dominated as never before by liberal Democrats, he sought to frame the Great Society in nonideological, pragmatic terms while pursuing deliberately bipartisan strategies in Congress. As Johnson soon found out, however, the politics of principle—ideological conflict, moralized engagement with power, a new array of divisive issues—helped to make a hash of his consensus political project. Continuities extending well beyond the *Port Huron Statement* linked the era's nascent left-liberal mobilizations to the middle-class reform activism of the 1940s and 1950s. Efforts like the Mississippi Freedom Democratic Party's campaign in 1964 embodied the long-running relationship between civil rights advances and party nationalization. And the Democratic crisis of 1968 marked a culmination of postwar conflicts over the proper functions of parties and the role of issues in politics that would have lasting institutional repercussions for both parties. In all of these ways, the 1960s marked less a break with the past than an acceleration of the postwar process by which "principle" might be made the basis of partisanship.

LIBERAL HOUR, BIPARTISAN APOGEE

Paul Butler died of a heart attack in 1961. His untimely demise prevented him from witnessing what might have seemed a paradoxical political combination in the mid-1960s. Liberalism was ascendant both within the Democratic Party and in all three branches of the federal government. The legislative logjams that Butler and his allies had railed against—attributing them to the ideologically incoherent party system—soon enough broke with dramatic force. But, contrary to the responsible party vision, the wave of legislative activism that followed took place amid a pervasive public rhetoric of nonideological pragmatism and followed coalitional dynamics that made it the very apogee of the midcentury bipartisan system. For a brief moment, in other words, that system seemed at last to *work* as an engine of progressive policymaking and governance.

Such a moment would not come, however, before the last president Butler knew suffered his own untimely death in 1963. John F. Kennedy typified the era's cool disavowal of ideological politics. "The central domestic issues of our time," he told Yale's graduating class in 1962, "relate not to basic clashes of philosophy or ideology but to ways and means of reaching common goals."[5] This claim not only channeled the prevailing elite intellectual assumption of an ideological consensus, with politics boiled down to technocratic questions of technique and method; it also reflected Kennedy's own personality and outlook, demonstrated both in his notably cautious legislative record in Congress and in his tendencies toward ironic detachment and dispassion. Kennedy "never took ideology very seriously," Arthur Schlesinger wrote, while he prized the qualities of conciliation and deliberation that the country's institutions fostered, making him, in James MacGregor Burns's words, "a Madisonian at heart."[6]

In his time as president, Kennedy's approach to governance reflected but did little to meliorate the constraints on legislative action posed by the congressional conservative coalition. His policy agenda was frequently frustrated. Narrowed House majorities meant that Kennedy had even less leeway in grappling with a contingent of conservative southern committee chairmen operating at the peak of their powers in the committee-dominated, seniority-centered "textbook Congress" of midcentury.[7] Assessing the congressional terrain and mindful to avoid repeating the high-profile failures of the *last* Democratic administration's legislative push—Truman's Fair Deal agenda—the Kennedy White House prioritized legislation that would not inflame conservative coalition opposition.[8] This meant shepherding bills on infrastructure, job training, and recession relief, along with expansions in Social Security coverage and unemployment compensation. It also meant actively seeking to foster a stable bipartisan coalition of support for White House initiatives through strategic engagement with key Republicans like Senate minority leader Everett Dirksen.

Above all, Kennedy's strategy meant avoiding legislative proposals pertaining to civil rights, a commitment he sustained until mass action and congressional pressure from a bipartisan coalition finally forced his hand. Prior to that, Kennedy's approach followed the logic of an early memo by aide Harris Wofford, which urged avoiding not only direct civil rights legislation but also procedural causes like cloture reform in the Senate. "The Southern fight against this would inflict a serious wound to your other legislative prospects," Wofford warned.[9] Inaction on civil rights inflicted its own wounds, however. Two years into the president's term, Hubert Humphrey wrote to DNC chair John Bailey expressing concern that the party would be "caught napping" on the issue. "There is such conservative domination or infiltration in this Congress," he complained, "that the minute anyone brings up the issue of civil rights, he is branded as one seeking to divide the party and looked upon as a trouble maker."[10] Despite liberals' complaints, Kennedy was eager not to earn that troublemaker moniker.

Nevertheless, southern Democrats still worked to block numerous presidential initiatives. Congress rejected Kennedy's proposal to establish a Department of Urban Affairs and Housing, which was to have been led by the African American policy scholar Robert C. Weaver. The House also replaced his minimum wage hike proposal with a smaller increase excluding industries like laundry work that disproportionately employed African Americans. Even more dramatic were the congressional failures of medical insurance for the aged and federal aid to education. Both proposals joined the civil rights legislation Kennedy finally proposed in a pileup of deadlocked initiatives by the fall of 1963. With typical dry realism, Kennedy summed up the nature of the trouble he faced among congressional Democrats in a remark to speechwriter Theodore Sorensen: "Party loyalty or responsibility means damn little. They've got to take care of themselves first."[11]

The evident fatalism with which White House officials viewed prospects for advancing key goals in Congress only helped to prompt a flourishing of critiques of the legislative branch in the early and mid-1960s, typically following responsible party lines.[12] With a northern Democrat once again occupying the Oval Office and substantial party majorities in both congressional chambers, continued legislative lethargy could best be ascribed to institutional dysfunction, argued liberal groups like the Democratic Study Group (DSG) and Americans for Democratic Action (ADA). James MacGregor Burns himself drew together analyses he had published in various iterations since the Truman years for his 1963 book *The Deadlock of Democracy*, which described a "four-party" system in which Democrats and Republicans alike were riven by presidential and congressional wings mirroring intraparty ideological divides. Liberal lawmakers also jumped into the fray, with Pennsylvania senator Joseph Clark's 1964 tome *Congress, the Sapless Branch* followed a year later by DSG leader Richard Bolling's *House Out of Order*.[13]

The wave of institutional changes that would eventually transform Congress was still a decade away. But Kennedy and his congressional allies did succeed in achieving one significant reform breakthrough: an expansion of the House Rules Committee membership that diminished the conservative coalition's ability to bottle up legislation. The Rules Committee's agenda-setting and veto powers, along with the majority party leadership's total lack of influence over the panel's membership and actions, had long made it a target of institutional critique. The DSG had managed to extract a promise from Speaker Sam Rayburn in 1959 to reform the committee, either by altering its membership or reinstating the "twenty-one-day-rule" that limited how long the panel could prevent a bill from reaching the floor. Rules reform even appeared as a plank in the 1960 party platform. In his first year as president, Kennedy provided critical public support for efforts by congressional liberals and outside advocacy groups to make that rhetoric a reality. The compromise reform that eventually passed enlarged the panel by three seats (two Democrats and one Republican), which now gave liberals a narrow majority.[14] The measure squeaked through by a five-vote margin, aided by twenty-two votes from mainly liberal and moderate Republicans. The Herculean push for such a modest reform had the opposite of a galvanizing effect on the White House's legislative ambition. "It was a close and bitter business," Schlesinger recalled, "and the memory of this fight laid a restraining hand on the administration's legislative priorities for some time to come."[15] But the victory helped the DSG and the broader reform coalition feel their oats and plan for future reforms to enable majority rule in Congress.

The assassination of Kennedy in November 1963 itself pointed toward currents of ideological zeal stirring in society that caused great unease among mainstream political figures. In the immediate aftermath of the shooting, suspicion reflexively turned to the John Birch Society and other networks of conservative activism. "Was it one of the right-wing nuts?" Richard Nixon asked J. Edgar Hoover that day.[16] Even after Lee Harvey Oswald's identity and background had surfaced, media commentary and admonitions from many public officials continued to use the assassination as an illustration of the dangerous atmosphere fomented by political "extremism" and ideological zeal.[17] No one was more committed to this sentiment than Lyndon Baines Johnson. "Let us turn away from the fanatics of the far left and the far right," the new president declared in his first congressional address, "from the apostles of bitterness and bigotry . . . and those who pour venom into our nation's bloodstream."[18] His words foreshadowed the themes he would use to frame both his 1964 campaign against an explicitly ideological GOP opponent and his stewardship of the transformative wave of legislation ushering in his "Great Society."

If Kennedy's abbreviated presidency epitomized the paralysis that the bipartisan era could induce, his successor's tenure revealed that system's capacity for major policy advances, under the right circumstances. Those advances encompassed not only a lengthy back catalog of proposals developed by liberal Democrats—serious civil rights policies concerning desegregation and voting rights, federal aid to education, medical insurance for the aged and poor—but a slew of new initiatives: the panoply of War on Poverty programs; a dozen new environmental laws; publicly funded arts, research, and broadcasting; wholesale reform of the country's immigration system; and much more besides. The popular trauma of Kennedy's assassination, the exuberant boomtime economy, and a landslide electoral victory at both the presidential and congressional levels in 1964 all played roles in making the output from the 88th and especially 89th Congresses high-water marks of legislative productivity. But Johnson's own extraordinary political skills were also key. They were the skills of a leader even more averse to notions of "responsible," issue-driven partisanship than Kennedy had been.

As he had throughout his career, President Johnson exercised a personality-driven and avowedly bipartisan kind of leadership, even as external conditions and personal conviction now compelled him toward a vastly more ambitious policy agenda. His background in one-party Texas politics, his experience as a New Deal administrator who enjoyed cooperative rather than antagonistic relationships with business interests, above all his unmatched antenna for the specific *kinds* of skills—face-to-face persuasion, individualized knowledge, group brokerage—most beneficial to a power-seeker in a depolarized political environment, all shaped an outlook that was famously pragmatic but also antipartisan at its core. That this most ruthlessly political of men was also averse to open partisan and ideological conflict was an irony easily overlooked both at the time and in hindsight. But it could be seen in Johnson's approach as majority leader in the Senate, innovating tools of discipline and centralized command in pursuit of hyperincremental bipartisan legislation. Johnson's mastery of the Senate's legislative machinery bolstered a personal rather than party-oriented rule, in the service of blurring rather than sharpening partisan disagreements.[19] His presidency bore the same attributes.

Johnson saw politics as the forging of consensus through relentless bargaining—a process yielding incremental improvements while ensuring stability through big-tent inclusiveness in the dealmaking. "In time," he told his biographer Doris Kearns Goodwin, "the underlying consensus will have to emerge. . . . So long as men try conscientiously to resolve their differences by negotiation, so long as they follow the prophet Isaiah to 'come now let us reason together,' there is always a chance."[20] Goldwater, of course, provided a perfectly contrasting outlook on the place of ideological conflict in politics, and thus served as a perfect foil during the 1964 election. As the prospect of a landslide victory that year grew more likely, Johnson worked obsessively to maximize that margin of victory as a way of securing a transpartisan veneer and a seemingly universal support base for his policies. He not only disavowed rhetorical appeals to ideological and partisan conflict, but also sought actively to incorporate and implicate leadership from virtually all major institutions into his Great Society agenda, in a tableau of establishment consensus on behalf of an activist liberal state. "President Johnson," Rowland Evans and Robert Novak reported in 1964, "is attempting, with surprising success, to turn his party into a non-ideological, broad-based 'consensus' party cleansed of over-partisanship . . . the party is being moved outside the arena of political contention to become a rallying point for all controllers of power in America today."[21] Even his speech at that most intrinsically partisan of institutions—the Democratic convention— denounced "petty partisanship" and cast the Democrats as "an all-American party for all Americans."[22]

Johnson's vision of consensus politics was apparent in his legislative strategy. Though Democrats controlled more than two-thirds of congressional seats after the 1964 elections, the Great Society proved to be a bipartisan endeavor. Of all the major Great Society laws passed between 1964 and 1966, only one, the Economic Opportunity Act encompassing several War on Poverty programs, failed to garner at least 25 percent of Republican votes in both chambers. Most enjoyed significantly larger percentages than that.[23] This primarily reflected the ideologically unsorted nature of the midcentury party system and the presence of a genuine liberal faction within the GOP, not to mention the influence of a landslide election on pols sensitive to which way the wind was blowing. But it was also the result of conscious effort by Johnson and his aides. Johnson's cultivation of Everett Dirksen's support for the Civil Rights Act in 1964, pursued to the point of weakening the bill's Equal Employment Opportunity Commission at the Republican's behest, was only the most famous example. In an amusing twist on James MacGregor Burns's intended call for responsible party government, Johnson even cited *The Deadlock of Democracy* in private conversations with Dirksen and House minority leader Gerald Ford, urging them to prove Burns wrong about congressional recalcitrance by supporting *his* programs, and speculating that their party would "pick up a bunch of Senate seats" for doing so.[24] Johnson as president proved as ever a skeptic of most congressional reforms, with the important exception of his support for the reinstitution of the twenty-one-day-rule in the House Rules Committee.[25]

Johnson's vision of consensus politics also entailed a radically inclusive disposition toward interest groups, most notably the business community. As Kearns Goodwin described Johnson's ambition for his presidency, "all the forces and groups of American life must be assembled under the same huge tent: labor, management, farmers, blacks, browns, yellows, Republicans, Democrats, dirt farmers, and Wall Street brokers."[26] He saw no inherent contradiction in reconciling such disparate forces on behalf of the Great Society project because he saw no inherent zero-sum conflict between them that could not be negotiated. In practice this meant a historic mobilization of business support for administration policies that had lasting effects on the extent and nature of lobbying in Washington writ large.[27] The administration formed thirty business advisory groups to aid in policy formulation, organized business-driven campaigns on behalf of legislative pushes for trade, tax, and social legislation, utilized the CEO-powered National Independent Committee as a key component of the 1964 electoral campaign, and even considered merging the departments of Labor and Commerce to symbolize the harmonization of economic interests under the Great Society.[28] Many corporations and trade associations set up permanent government relations offices in Washington in the 1960s thanks to the administration's encouragement and support, an important progenitor of the explosive growth of lobbying in the following decade.

Finally, Johnson's views about how politics should function, as much as his famous paranoia and power lust, help explain his relentlessly hostile and predatory posture toward the national Democratic Party. Johnson marginalized and starved national party organs like no president before him, slashing the DNC's budget and staff and centralizing both financial and campaign operations in the White House.[29] He built upon Kennedy's innovation in large-dollar donations, the fundraising network known as the President's Club, and greatly expanded its use, in the process all but shuttering the grassroots-focused small-donor "Dollars for Democrats" drives once championed by Paul Butler.[30] Local and state party organizations became indirect victims of such efforts. A New York state senator complained that President's Club fundraisers "weakened state parties" by "siphoning away contributions," while a New Jersey party leader lamented the emphasis on "'big money' events. The precinct workers and related groups—labor, civil rights etc—are not a part of these shows, and in the past years they have been almost the total activity of the Party."[31]

Johnson directed President's Club funds as well as official DNC personnel and communications toward personal political tasks, such as marshaling pushback against growing criticism from Democrats over the Vietnam War and funding his write-in campaign against Eugene McCarthy in the 1968 New Hampshire primary.[32] His interest in muzzling a body that might serve as a forum for anti-administration, antiwar, and pro–Robert F. Kennedy forces was clearly central to his approach. But such behavior also reflected a sincere view of politics that saw explicit partisanship as a hindrance to forging programmatic consensus around a powerful president.

Johnson's genius at exploiting the dynamics of a clubby and depolarized political system contributed to a genuinely transformative bout of state-building. But contrary to his belief that a transpartisan consensus represented politics working as it should, Johnson's leadership quickly proved brittle and unsustainable in the face of disparate forces waving banners of moral politics and ideological conflict. Johnson had long thought, as he told Kearns Goodwin, that "the politics of principle" only served to "bring out the masses in irrational fights for unlimited goals," with chaotic results. "It is for the sake of nothing less than stability that I consider myself a consensus man."[33] But it was Johnson's own endeavor to forge such a consensus that proved, in the end, unstable.

MORAL INSURGENTS

The center that could not hold in the later 1960s collapsed at the hands of myriad and disparate movements, but a common argument among many of them was that morality could not be extricated from political choice. A conservative version of this claim, hinted at in the substantial Republican victories of the 1966 midterm elections, would ultimately reveal an unimagined potency in national politics, but in the nearer term the Johnson administration faced its most aggressive challenges to its left. The critique of consensus liberalism initially articulated in the *Port Huron Statement* and amplified by the civil rights movement soon gained a new mass of adherents thanks to the movement against the Vietnam War. For all the generational conflict on display, the new social movement activism of the later 1960s carried forward the "amateur spirit" that a previous generation of reformist activists had helped bring to postwar politics—namely, a focus on issues and ideology and a willingness to apply moralizing rhetoric to partisan conflict. It was conflict over issues, paramount among them Vietnam, that provoked the insurgent presidential campaigns of Eugene McCarthy and Robert Kennedy in 1968 and the battles at the Democratic convention that year. And the perception by insurgent activists that existing party structures were not responsive and accountable to their issue demands helped motivate the movement for institutional reform.

The civil rights movement, in this as in so many ways, set a precedent for morally charged agitation yielding tumultuous change within political institutions. Moreover, as disruptive as the movement's demands proved to established political institutions and practices, that activism also served as a catalyst for both ideological sorting within the parties and the centralization of Democratic Party authority at the national level. This could be seen at the 1964 Democratic convention, where the Mississippi Freedom Democratic Party (MFDP)'s alternative slate of party delegates challenged the credentials of the state's segregationist, Goldwater-supporting regulars.

The MFDP project was a grassroots endeavor spearheaded by

Bob Moses and backed by the Council of Federated Organizations (COFO), a coalition of the major civil rights organizations active in Mississippi.[34] The MFDP built off COFO's prior efforts on the so-called Freedom Ballot, a symbolic vote in November 1963 by thousands of Mississippians for an integrated slate of state and local candidates. Protesting African Americans' exclusion from Democratic primary elections, the only competitive races in one-party Mississippi, the MFDP now organized shadow elections at the precinct, county, district, and state levels. In the summer of 1964 COFO registered over 50,000 citizens—largely African Americans—in the party. The precinct, county, and district elections they held culminated in a state convention in Jackson that produced an alternative slate of delegates, chaired by the NAACP's Aaron Henry, to the national Democratic convention in Atlantic City.

Northern liberals with high-level connections to the Democratic Party worked with the MFDP to design a convention strategy that might maximize the group's impact. Joe Rauh, a ubiquitous activist lawyer and veteran convention mischief-maker, agreed to represent the delegation before the Credentials Committee. He worked with Eleanor Holmes and Miles Jaffe to draft the legal brief challenging the credentials of the Mississippi regulars on the dual grounds of racial discrimination in their party procedures and continued disloyalty to the platform and presidential candidacy of the national party. Neither Rauh nor the MFDP leaders expected the Credentials Committee, headed by David Lawrence and stacked with Johnson loyalists, to actually replace the regulars with the MFDP delegation. Instead, the plan was to trigger a floor fight—and perhaps to have both delegations seated, thus legitimating the MFDP's claims.

The ability of the MFDP to generate elite liberal support as well as broader public attention surprised everyone, not least the activists themselves. The discovery in early August of the bodies of three Congress of Racial Equality workers, murdered while registering people for the MFDP, lent a tragic urgency and national notoriety to the effort. Two weeks later, the Credentials Committee meeting was moved to a larger room to accommodate more television cameras and the crowd of observers. Captivating and emotionally charged testimony by Fannie Lou Hamer and other civil rights activists conveyed to television audiences the brutality and visceral terror that black Mississippians faced in the pursuit of political participation.

But, significantly, the MFDP's procedural case rested on the same questions of loyalty and party nationalization that had attended "loyalty oath"–related controversies over southern delegations for the past decade and a half. Activists emphasized the responsibility of the national party to address local infractions of party policy just as they demanded federal intervention in local civil rights disputes. "Federal support within the state and the seating of the Freedom Democratic Party at the National Convention are inseparable needs," Student Nonviolent Coordinating Committee chairman John Lewis wrote to Lyndon Johnson in the run-up to the convention."[35] The MFDP further staked its procedural claim on its substantive and political loyalty to a national party that the Mississippi regulars spurned. The MFDP's legal brief devoted more space to the Mississippi regulars' record of disloyalty than it did to their record of racial discrimination or to the legality of the MFDP itself.[36]

As civil rights leader Ella Baker had put it at the MFDP state convention, "a political party should be open to all the people who wish to subscribe to its principles."[37] This claim was as relevant to the national Democratic Party as it was to the MFDP. Shared principles both legitimized and motivated participation in the party, according to this outlook. Indulging dissident factions that openly flouted such principles, merely out of a commitment to federalism and an arid proceduralism, was not only a moral enormity but a political error. This argument connected the MFDP's fight to a broader set of forces, from both the Left and the Right, that impinged on the party system in the postwar decades. James Farmer made the connection explicit in his testimony before the Credentials Committee when he invoked Barry Goldwater's nomination, which had been secured "through intense loyalty and support. I think the Democratic Party can win the election only through a loyalty and a support which is even more intense than that which backs Goldwater." As Rauh concluded before the committee, "We are here because

we love the Democratic Party. We will work for its candidates. . . .
Are you going to throw out of here the people who want to work for
Lyndon Johnson, who are willing to be beaten in jails, to die for the
privilege of working for Lyndon Johnson?"[38]

Advocates emphasized the moral and political case for the
MFDP in part because its legal case was weak. The MFDP was
not a legally recognized body.[39] It had been able to hold precinct
and county meetings in only thirty-five of Mississippi's eighty-two
counties thanks to logistical challenges and suppressive tactics by
the state.[40] The racial discrimination practiced by the regulars gave
some credence to Martin Luther King's claim that the MFDP was
"the only Mississippi party chosen democratically," but the group
was itself as much self-appointed as elected. Rauh all but conceded
the point in his remarks to the committee, pointing out that "you
can't follow the laws of Mississippi if you are a Negro. The laws are
made to keep Negros out of everything in Mississippi. All you can
do in a legal way is to do the best you can. And we have done the
best we can." Theodore White would capture the same sentiment:
"Though the white delegation was legal, it was morally absurd; it
had been elected under laws administered in sin," he wrote, while
the MFDP's "legal case was absurd" but its "moral case was impeccable."[41] The tension between procedural and substantive liberalism that this fight highlighted would surface again and again in
Democratic conflicts to come.

Considerations of both party law and substantive justice were, in
any case, largely moot in the face of Lyndon Johnson's unyielding
determination not only to prevent the MFDP from being seated but
to stop a minority report from even making it out of the credentials
committee. Nothing better revealed the fervor of Johnson's desire
to maximize his electoral landslide and to prevent any blight on
a cross-regional and pan-ideological consensus behind his presidency than the battle he waged against the MFDP.[42] Key liberal
leaders including Hubert Humphrey, James Rowe, and Rauh's own
patron Walter Reuther were dispatched to convince Rauh to rein
in his clients and back down, while Johnson used the FBI's sur-
veillance of Martin Luther King and Bayard Rustin to monitor the
situation. In Johnson's mind, recognizing the MFDP would pro-

voke walkouts by southern delegations and, in the most pessimistic scenario, also hurt Johnson's electoral prospects in border states
and among northern whites primed for a racial backlash. Reuther
even dutifully parroted Johnson's boldest claim to Rauh that the
election itself could be lost as a result of this fight—a notion that
Rauh, and likely Reuther himself, found preposterous.[43]

Despite the full court press, the emerging groundswell of liberal
support for the MFDP at the convention and among the viewing
public forced Johnson into negotiations, which his agents pursued
in several days of closed-door meetings with MFDP leaders.
Agreement had yet to be reached when Reuther lured Rauh away
from the credentials committee room. Walter Mondale introduced
a compromise measure in his absence, which promptly passed by
voice vote.[44] The compromise seated the regulars but required
a loyalty oath from them, gave two at-large seats to the MFDP's
Aaron Henry and Ed King (denying Hamer a seat), and launched
formal efforts to ban discriminatory delegations at future conventions. When all but three Mississippi regulars refused the loyalty
oath and bolted the convention, MFDP delegates occupied the
empty seats until gingerly removed by sergeants-at-arms.[45]

The legacy of this denouement proved double-edged. The
MFDP organizers interpreted the compromise as a betrayal and
balked. "We're not here to bring politics to our morality," Bob
Moses declared in an omen of the dawning political era, "but to
bring morality to our politics."[46] This perception of a backroom
sellout fatefully soured some civil rights activists and young New
Left collaborators on the very idea of working within major political institutions.[47] Nevertheless, *within* the two-party system the
MFDP fight left a lasting institutional legacy. The Call to the 1968
Convention passed in Atlantic City included newly explicit affirmation that state delegations would have to both practice nondis-
crimination and "cast their election ballots for the Presidential and
Vice Presidential nominees selected by said Convention"—a forceful assertion of the national party's supremacy over state parties'
behavior and nominating procedures.[48] Even more significant was
the convention's vote to establish a Special Equal Rights Committee in the DNC to study racial discrimination in state parties

and make appropriate recommendations for reform. As discussed below, that panel's ultimate report would provide a key mandate for the more sweeping reform commission created in 1968.

The MFDP dispute presaged far more damaging intraparty tumult to come, centered around the Vietnam War and the broader counterculture. Johnson's military escalation in Vietnam epitomized the downside of technocratic liberal governance and personalist leadership. It damaged irrevocably his authority over the Great Society's congressional coalitions and sparked a mass antiwar movement that gravitated to the New Left's critical analysis of elite institutional power in society. For those not radicalized to the point of rejecting party politics altogether, the movement prompted a set of intraparty conflicts with transformative long-term repercussions.

Though organized resistance to the war and, eventually, to Johnson's presidency was youth-driven and suffused with radicalism, much of the movement not only resembled the amateur activism of fifties-era club Democrats but drew in a who's who of those Democrats themselves. The mid-decade crisis that gripped Americans for Democratic Action offered a microcosm of these generational dynamics. ADA's leadership remained wary about Johnson's war policy but publicly mum in the wake of the Gulf of Tonkin Resolution in 1964. But just as opposition to the war fueled a massive upsurge in the SDS's ranks across the country, so too did that sentiment swell the local and campus ADA chapters with new members and shift the organization in an antiwar direction.[49] Thanks to the extraordinary organizing efforts of the hard-charging ex-student activist Allard Lowenstein, both within the ADA and in broader left-liberal networks, a "Dump Johnson" movement targeting the 1968 election gained strength throughout 1966 and 1967.[50] By the latter year, ADA board members like Joe Rauh, Arthur Schlesinger, and John Kenneth Galbraith had followed Lowenstein, Curtis Gans, and the rest of the group's antiwar faction into breaking openly with the administration over Vietnam.[51] After Gene McCarthy entered the race in November, followed soon after by the Tet Offensive, the organization officially endorsed him.

For all the connections fostered by bridge-building figures like

Lowenstein to more radical antiwar actors, the Dump Johnson movement offered a direct continuation in style, rhetoric, and personnel of postwar liberals' issue-driven reform activism. As California congressman Donald Edwards insisted at a national meeting of the antiwar Conference of Concerned Democrats in Chicago in December 1967, "We are here today as loyal Democrats—seeking to return our party to the course of Franklin D. Roosevelt, Adlai Stevenson, and John F. Kennedy."[52] Meanwhile, the major holdouts within the ADA leadership who remained loyal to Johnson and his Vietnam policy were representatives from organized labor, several of whom left the organization in protest of its McCarthy endorsement. Their actions reflected the labor movement's emergence as a factional foil to the nascent social movement activism of the era.

Contrary to most accounts of intraliberal conflict in the 1960s and beyond, however, labor was not monolithic on these issues. The rivalry between George Meany, president of the American Federation of Labor and Congress of Industrial Organizations (AFL-CIO), and the UAW's Walter Reuther reflected the range of unions' outlooks on the changing social forces of the 1960s. The Meany wing's loyalty to Johnson stemmed in part from a substantive commitment to hardline anticommunism in general and to continued US military engagement in Vietnam in particular. Ideology also overlapped with cultural and generational tensions. The tenor of New Left and countercultural appeals antagonized many labor leaders and members, none more so than those in Meany's base among the building and skilled trades.[53] Reuther, on the other hand, not only posed a continual leadership threat to Meany on the AFL-CIO Executive Council, but also espoused a social democratic vision putting labor at the organizational core of a broader, cross-class array of progressive reform and social justice movements. By the mid-1960s, that outlook translated into independent UAW support for a wide network of causes and organizations, from teacher and farmworker unionism to antipoverty efforts to campus activism.[54]

Reuther's openness to coalitions with the New Left, new identity groups, and middle-class liberal activists put him at both substantive and strategic odds with the Meany wing. He had dovish instincts on Cold War policy and, by the mid-1960s, faced intense pressure from other UAW leaders and rank-and-file activists to break with the AFL-CIO's line on Vietnam. In 1966 he issued a wide-ranging open letter to UAW locals decrying the AFL-CIO's lack of "social vision." He pointed to the confederation's "narrow and negative" foreign policy and its failure "to develop stronger ties with labor's historic and essential allies in the liberal and intellectual academic community and among America's young people."[55] He resigned from the AFL-CIO Executive Council in 1967. The following year, the 1.4-million-member UAW formally left the confederation. The split was an omen of further divisions over political strategy, issue commitments, and institutional reform that would help shape the next decade of left-of-center politics.

The unexpected strength of the anti-Johnson insurgency within the Democratic Party, meanwhile, testified to the potency of issue-driven activism as an engine of party politics. Johnson's initial confidence about facing down an antiwar challenge dwindled as his strength in the party deteriorated, and his aides took note of the unanticipated vigor of the grassroots campaign for Gene McCarthy. The day after the March 1968 New Hampshire primary, in which the insurgent garnered a stunning 42 percent of the vote, Ben Wattenberg reported to Johnson the field observations of elections scholar Richard Scammon. "He was very impressed by the young people who worked for McCarthy," Wattenberg wrote. "Essentially, they ran a European-style campaign, canvassing door-to-door throughout the state. This, Scammon says, is rare in American politics—usually because of lack of articulate manpower that could help a candidate."[56] For his part, McCarthy justified his candidacy not only by opposition to Johnson's Vietnam policy but also by a responsible party critique of the breakdown of policy discussion within the party. "What we have is a personalized presidency," McCarthy wrote, "somewhat independent of the political party from which the president has come."[57] His candidacy, he argued, would provide the vehicle for restoring actual programmatic deliberation to party politics.

McCarthy's showing in New Hampshire, followed by Robert F. Kennedy's entrance into the race, prompted Johnson's stunning decision to drop out. Vice President Hubert Humphrey quickly emerged as the candidate of continuity for the administration, and the nomination battles of the spring and summer unfolded across a backdrop of novelistic tumult and tragedy in American public life that helped to make 1968 a watchword for years to come. But amid the chaos, in an echo of the 1964 MFDP fight, turmoil among the Democrats helped to generate a long-term process of transformative institutional change in the party system.

FROM REVOLT TO REFORM

In his memo to Johnson about McCarthy's potent showing in New Hampshire, Ben Wattenberg had made a glancing observation that revealed much about the workings of the presidential nominating system then. He pointed out that McCarthy could continue doing well in every future primary and *would still not be able to win the nomination*.[58] The prescient comment captured precisely the elements of the system that activists would target in a series of sweeping reforms in the early 1970s. The long road to those changes—the translation of insurgent social movement energies into a long-term institutional reform project—might be said to have begun on June 23, 1968. That evening 200 delegates to the Connecticut Democratic Party convention in Hartford staged a walkout.

The meeting was meant to select the forty-four state delegates to the national party convention in Chicago that August. Connecticut's Democratic Party was a traditional, tightly organized machine, and the way that the state convention had worked in years past was straightforward. The organization, under the control of longtime party boss and current DNC chairman John Bailey, would select the delegates, all officially unpledged to any presidential candidate. (This year, unofficially, the regulars were all Humphrey backers, as was Bailey.) At the national convention, the delegation would vote as a single bloc, since Connecticut, like a dozen other states, employed the "unit rule," which bound delegation minorities to majority decisions.

What made that year's state convention different were, of

course, the insurgent antiwar campaigns of McCarthy and the late Robert Kennedy, which had managed to secure almost a fourth of the delegates through victories in town caucuses, committees, and "challenge primaries" mounted via petition drive.[59] That show of strength came as a shock to Bailey, who had predicted to the White House as recently as January that, at most, "10 or 15 state delegates out of 1,000 . . . might be noisy" at the state convention, and thus "there will be no problem at all."[60] In the face of insurgent delegates numbering instead in the hundreds, Bailey felt compelled at the outset of the convention to scrap the unit rule for the first time and to offer a handful of national delegation seats to McCarthy backers. The McCarthy forces, led by ADA activist Joe Duffey and local organizer Anne Wexler, demanded twelve of the forty-four seats in proportion to their convention presence. Nine was as high as regulars would let Bailey go. Invective rained down from the stage: officials condemned the antics of the McCarthy supporters, while Kennedy confidant Richard Goodwin denounced Bailey as "the last nonelected boss in America." Finally, Duffey announced his delegates' rejection of the party's offer, rounded up the troops, and marched out of the hall to loud boos from the regulars.[61]

What the exiles did next was consequential. A steering committee of McCarthy delegates and state campaign organizers met that night in West Hartford. All of them agreed immediately that a credentials challenge to the Connecticut delegation in Chicago would be necessary, but McCarthy's state coordinator persuaded them to do more. The obstacles that they had encountered in the run-up to the state convention—not only procedural irregularities and arbitrary actions by local officials, but the closed nature of the system itself—were facing activists in other states. He argued that the credentials challenges should have the backing of a report, produced under the auspices of a party reform committee, that would catalog all state nominating procedures and make the case for systemic reform. Over the next month, activists recruited six men and one woman to a Commission on the Democratic Selection of Presidential Nominees, to be chaired by Iowa's pro-McCarthy governor, Harold Hughes. This was a staff-driven operation, however. The full commission met only once.[62]

To deflect suspicions that the reform agenda was a mere stalk-ing horse for McCarthy's candidacy, the organizers of what be-came known as the Hughes Commission took pains to include a Humphrey supporter in its ranks. Donald Fraser fit the bill. The Minneapolis congressman was a longtime Democratic-Farmer-Labor (DFL) Party activist who remained loyal to his political men-tor, Humphrey, while breaking with Johnson's administration over its Vietnam policy. His substantive sympathy for the insurgent campaigns' policy agenda was matched by a longstanding interest in party reform. Fraser had an affinity for parliamentary forms of governance featuring disciplined but permeable parties with clear policy agendas, and had assumed the chairmanship of the DSG in 1968 to push for further procedural reforms in the House.[63] His acceptance of the vice chairmanship of this new commission sig-nified, in his mind, an application of the same reform impulse to a different party arena.

The staff worked that summer on research for a report catalogu-ing inequities and inadequacies in state and territorial nominating systems as well as the national convention. The resulting report was published as *The Democratic Choice*. The commission ensured the report's practical impact at the Chicago convention in August through coordination among allied members of both the Rules Committee and Credentials Committee. This convention strategy had been shaped by the resolution of the dispute in Connecticut, where the McCarthy delegates' walkout proved short-lived, as they eventually decided to accept the nine seats offered by John Bailey along with an added sweetener: two of the delegation's committee slots.[64] Anne Wexler thus became a member of the Rules Commit-tee, organizing a whip system to coordinate proreform members of the panel. She also ensured that a copy of *The Democratic Choice* was waiting for every member of the committee when it convened.[65]

In the substance of its recommendations as well as the nature of its critique of the nominating system, the report would prove highly influential. "Events in 1968 have called into question the in-tegrity of the convention system for nominating presidential can-didates," *The Democratic Choice* declared. "Recent developments have put the future of the two-party system itself into serious jeopardy." Such developments included upheavals on campuses and in the ghettoes, which reflected growing popular alienation from the political system. The irregularities and nonresponsiveness encountered by the insurgent campaigns threatened to compound this alienation, unless the party made an effort to meet "the demand for more direct democracy and the call for an end to 'boss control' of the nominating machinery."[66]

The Commission recommended that certain actions be taken immediately in Chicago, most notably a prohibition on any delegation's enforcement of the unit rule and aggressive implementation of the new rules on racial non-discrimination. The panel also prescribed an array of state-level procedural changes for the future, starting with the outright abolition of all methods of delegate selection lacking direct popular participation.[67] Further recommendations were organized around basic principles. "Meaningful access" required an end to proxy voting, secret caucuses, and informal or unpublicized rules for delegate selection. "Clarity of purpose" implied that voters would choose delegates for that role alone, without thereby selecting the same people as state party officers, and that those delegates would be pledged to support specific candidates. The principle of timeliness meant that no delegates could be chosen more than six months prior to the national Convention, before the issues and candidates relavent to the election had emerged. (Over 600 delegates to the 1968 convention were chosen in 1966.) Finally, the report advocated proportional representation of candidate preferences at all levels of the delegate selection process except winner-take-all primaries.

Just as important was the Hughes Commission's theory of the party system and political change. *The Democratic Choice* put new calls for reform in the context of nearly two centuries of evolution toward more direct democracy in presidential politics. More recent developments in communications technology, especially radio and television, "contributed to the continuing expansion of the democratic dimension of the selection of presidents." But most important were ongoing changes in the mass electorate. African Americans were increasingly dissatisfied with a role as "junior partners" in the New Deal Democratic coalition, putting them in conflict with northern party organizations at the state and local levels. "Mean-while," the report claimed, "Negro demands for civil rights and the support of those demands by the Northern liberal wing of the Party have alienated the once Solid South and dropped the black belt from the list of states that could be counted on, or even hoped for, on the Democratic side in presidential elections."[68]

If the civil rights revolution created one stream of intra-party tensions and demands for institional reform, another stream grew out of a more gradual development the Commission labeled "the emergence of the issue-oriented independent." "The electorate is generally more affluent and more widely educated," it argued. Stable partisan attachments have eroded, while "issue-oriented individuals who rank relatively abstract ideological questions high among the criteria by which they approve or disapprove of candidates have become a substantial portion of the electorate, as the Vietnam War has shown." How did this relate to the nominating system? The proliferation of issue-oriented voters "has taken a significant portion of the electorate outside the tightly-knit groups represented by Democratic party operatives."[69] The thrust of the commission's prescriptions was to empower issue-driven party activism.

The report's drafters had in mind most immediately those voters and activists influenced by the mobilizations of the 1960s, but their description of the increasing issue orientation in US politics could also have described the "amateurs" analyzed by James Q. Wilson in 1962 and the "purists" of Nelson Polsby and Aaron Wildavsky's 1968 textbook.[70] By using the designation "issue-oriented," draft-ers implied that the key distinction between such voters and the party professionals was less a matter of differing issue positions than of differing relationships toward national issues per se. At the outset of McCarthy's candidacy in early 1968, political scientist Andrew Hacker had identified this distinction as a key obstacle to the campaign's efforts. "The typical delegate is not only not chosen or pledged by a primary," he wrote, "but he is a local party loyal-ist. Most are year-round county committeemen, quite senior in service, and accustomed to going along with the leadership. Very few, especially among the Democrats, have opinions that are in any way ideological and quite a few have no opinions at all on national issues." Hacker concluded that, while "in the best of political worlds it might be possible for the parties to reflect and incorporate the most pressing issues of the day in their candidates and platforms," such responsiveness was usually lacking. "We do not, then, have a really 'open' political system. It is smug and stolid and well-guarded by those who got into it first."[71]

That system proved less well guarded than Hacker had anticipated, given the surprising capacity of McCarthy and Kennedy to amass delegates during the spring and summer of 1968. (Following Kennedy's assassination in June, many of his delegates would eventually reassemble behind the candidacy of George McGovern.) But the insurgent forces still entered the convention on August 26 facing an essentially insurmountable delegate deficit, which shaped their dual-track strategy. First, they would wage an all-out fight over the Vietnam plank of the platform through substantive arguments for an unconditional halt to bombing as well as a political argument about the need for the two-party system to produce a viable choice for voters on such an important issue. Second, they would pursue procedural and credentials challenges that, short of shaking up the delegate counts sufficiently to give an alternative candidate to Humphrey a chance at the nomination, would at least lay the groundwork for fundamental reforms in later years.

Famously, the platform fight made it to the convention floor, where the antiwar plank went down to defeat while still garnering 40 percent of the vote. Even more famously, violence in the streets of Chicago escalated through the week as demonstrators clashed with police under the aggressive direction of Mayor Richard Daley, filling jail cells and hospitals by the hundreds. This spectacle of discord overshadowed major decisions on party reform.

Battles within the Credentials Committee illustrated connections between the longstanding reform agenda arising from the civil rights movement and the newer reform efforts. The number of credentials challenges in 1968 was unprecedented: seventeen in total, covering fifteen states.[72] Most Deep South states faced challenges over alleged violations of the Call to the Convention's strong provisions on racial discrimination. The drama of the

MFDP fight four years earlier and the subsequent work of the Special Equal Rights Committee helped ensure that both McCarthy *and* Humphrey endorsed the 1968 challenge of the Mississippi regulars, which resulted in the seating of the alternative slate led by Aaron Henry.[73] The Special Equal Rights Committee offered a model for wresting institutional reforms through dramatic on-the-ground delegation fights, one that the new reformers took to heart. The McCarthy forces, with Joe Rauh leading the credentials effort, had worked to build ties to alternative slates filing challenges in Alabama and Texas and went so far as to seize near-total control of Georgia's challenge delegation, thereby bootstrapping civil rights advocacy to the broader reform agenda they were developing at the convention.[74]

The Credentials Committee upheld the Mississippi challenge and meted out partial victories to two other southern challengers. The Georgia delegation's seats were split evenly between the regulars, hand-picked by segregationist governor Lester Maddox, and the alternative slate of "Loyal Democrats" headed by the young African American state senator Julian Bond. (The bulk of the Maddox forces walked out of the convention in protest.) The Alabama regulars were seated only on condition of signing a loyalty oath. Though the specter of George Wallace set the short-term context for this requirement, the decisions to force a pledge on one delegation and to fully or partially replace two others with self-described "loyal" Democrats marked new steps in the long-running project of nationalizing the southern parties and bolstering the authority of the national party to regulate the state organizations. This dynamic was also seen in the Special Equal Rights Committee's final report, which called for a new Commission on Party Structure "to study the relationship between the National Democratic Party and its constituent State Democratic Parties, in order that full participation of all Democrats without regard to race, color, creed or national origin may be facilitated by uniform standards."[75]

Meanwhile, the reformers' broader effort was evident in the array of credentials challenges filed against northern delegations that were *unrelated* to racial discrimination, justified instead on the basis of principles more sweeping than those typically seen in party conventions. Challengers based their cases against several delegations on the undemocratic character of the unit rule, the use of ex officio delegates, and delegate selection by unelected committees—all perfectly lawful devices. Challenges against Connecticut and Minnesota touted novel principles relating to proportional representation and adherence to the Supreme Court's "one-man, one-vote" ruling in the allocation of state delegates.[76] The McCarthy forces' strategy in making such systemic challenges—mainly based on research from *The Democratic Choice*—was pragmatic, a short-term bid to maximize their candidate's pledged support while swaying uncommitted delegates.[77] But they set in motion future reform efforts, offered as fig leaves by Humphrey backers to secure the nomination. The Credentials Committee rejected all of the northern challenges but included a resolution calling for the DNC to establish a new commission to study delegate selection practices and recommend improvements following the principles of timeliness and participation.[78]

The third and most important document giving an official mandate to party reforms emerged from the Rules Committee. There, Anne Wexler's whip system kept sympathetic members behind a series of resolutions drawn from Hughes Commission findings. Humphrey's forces successfully voted down all of the Wexler faction's resolutions. Their strategy, though, focused on limiting the reformers' short-term impact on the nomination rather than rebutting the substance of their arguments. Indeed, the Humphrey forces conceded the validity of many of those arguments.[79] In the process, they contributed to a growing consensus about pursuing reforms after the election.

While the Humphrey strategists and party regulars were satisfied to leave questions of reform to a purely advisory future commission issuing nonbinding recommendations, the reformers seized the opportunity to put the power of party law behind the mandate of a prospective reform body. Wexler helped draft a Rules Committee minority report resolving that the Call to the 1972 Democratic Convention would include language requiring state parties to make "all feasible efforts" to adopt delegate selection procedures that allow for full and timely public participation and prohibiting the use of the unit rule at all levels.[80] When the convention adopted that report on Tuesday, August 27, in a surprise 1,350–1,206 vote, few except the reform activists themselves realized its potential significance. On top of the two resolutions calling for a formal reform commission, the convention had now committed the party to implementing such reforms for 1972 and provided guiding language for them.

This origin story of the reform project that would preoccupy the Democratic Party over the next four years already anticipated its core themes, actors, and dynamics. Advocates buoyed by the decade's social mobilizations sought to remake party procedures in such a way that the influence of issue-driven activists would be enhanced at the expense of party actors who benefited from a more closed system. Doing so would also serve to institutionalize the power of the national party to regulate the procedures and actions of state parties.

REPUBLICAN DÉTENTE AND THE RISE OF THE "SOCIAL ISSUE"

Issue-driven and ideological activism was hardly a phenomenon limited to Democrats in the later 1960s, even after the GOP electoral debacle of 1964 had revealed the limits of hard-edged ideological partisanship's appeal to American voters. A significant new iteration of such para-party ideological advocacy emerged in the wake of Goldwater's defeat. Activists who blamed the loss on moderate Republicans' abandonment of their candidate organized a new satellite organization, the American Conservative Union, to sustain a coordinated conservative presence within the GOP.

There was no shortage of resistance to conservatives' efforts to retain power in the GOP after 1964, of course, though party leaders worked hard to contain the factional strife. Both moderates and many pragmatic GOP regulars waged a protracted and ultimately successful effort to force the Goldwater-picked Dean Burch's resignation as Republican National Committee (RNC) chairman.[81] The nonideological "organization man" Ray Bliss was installed at the committee's helm to refocus party efforts on campaign training, candidate recruitment, and professionalization rather than divisive ideological battles. Bliss's tenure was manifestly successful as a party-building project, and his focus on organizational development had the added benefit of sidestepping divisive questions related to ideology and national party program.[82] Similarly, the Republican Coordinating Committee, comprising the GOP congressional leadership along with a broad spectrum of eminent figures including Dwight Eisenhower, Nelson Rockefeller, and Barry Goldwater, served as a forum for unified Republican messaging and at least the superficial resolution of factional disputes.

Nevertheless, liberal and moderate Republicans made efforts to press their advantage in the wake of Goldwater's electoral repudiation. Liberal groups like the Ripon Society dismissed Bliss-style party-building in some of the same terms used by their conservative counterparts, arguing that "the 'organizational' strategy avoids the real problems" concerning party program and philosophy.[83] Ripon attacked the Right's southern and western electoral strategy and laid out an alternative vision of an urban-oriented, culturally progressive GOP program emphasizing market-friendly public-private approaches to liberal policy goals. Liberal and moderate officeholders used their base of support in the Republican Governors Association to seek greater clout in party decision-making, though they encountered resistance from congressional leaders as well as conservative forces in doing so.[84] A number of liberal Republican governors and mayors emerged as potential contenders for the 1968 presidential nomination. The various individualized mishaps and contingent events that ultimately stalled the political momentum of men like George Romney, Nelson Rockefeller, and John Lindsay, however, should not obscure some common weaknesses in the liberal Republican cause then. Forces of Republican moderation were disorganized, prone to dilettantism, and lacking in ideological coherence and passion compared to their factional foes on the right. Most important, they were top-heavy among elected officials and intellectuals and devoid of grassroots strength.[85]

Between a conservative wing unbowed but reeling from defeat

and a moderate wing crippled by ineffectuality, Richard Nixon re-established himself as a political force that could garner support from all major party factions in the 1968 presidential nomination race. A potent challenge from the right in the form of Ronald Reagan, fresh from his stunning victory in California's gubernatorial election two years earlier, was defused partly by the successful efforts of Strom Thurmond to sustain southern support for Nixon. Conversely, Nixon's candidacy proved to be sufficiently palatable to moderates to head off any late challenge on his left.

Fittingly, the ideological legacy that Nixon as both a candidate and a president would leave was complex and ambiguous. He kept conservative activists and intellectuals at arm's length, and in office demonstrated clear comfort deploying activist government in an array of policy realms.[86] But the electoral and ideological strategy that came to guide his approach to governance differed sharply from the Ripon prescription. Instead, it connected to the second major 1960s development that altered the place of issues and ideology in party politics, after the gate-crashing insurgencies of issue-driven activists themselves: namely, the emergence of a new *issue dimension* in the ideological landscape of party politics.

This dimension encompassed a disparate array of seemingly unrelated issues—from racial backlash in housing policy to fights over the counterculture, from crime control to environmental regulation—but most such issues concerned some cultural or quality-of-life element rather than bread-and-butter economic and welfare-state concerns. The centrist Johnson advisors Ben Wattenberg and Richard Scammon coined the term "the Social Issue" as a collective reference to the array of conflicts stemming from the cultural ferment of the 1960s.[87] Conservatives at the state and local level were beginning to capitalize on populist electoral appeals to voters' sociocultural grievances rather than classic doctrinal messages concerning free markets, limited government, and anticommunism.[88] For their part, a growing segment of liberals and leftists adhering to the "New Politics" label increasingly emphasized issues related to identity, antiwar policies, consumerism, and environmentalism over New Deal–vintage economic concerns. A decade earlier, Arthur Schlesinger had anticipated the emergence of such a dimension with his prediction that "qualitative liberalism" would supplant subsistence-oriented "quantitative liberalism" as the country as a whole prospered.[89] A late 1968 report by the National Committee for an Effective Congress confirmed the growth of this tendency within the Democratic caucus, describing new factional skirmishes between "emerging political modernists" and "classic, orthodox labor liberals."[90]

The potential for the Social Issue to reshuffle electoral demographics, or even to displace economic issues as the major cleavage in the party system through a wholesale realignment, invited contrasting strategies across the political spectrum. Nixon and his advisors—chief among them the electoral guru Kevin Phillips—saw in the ferment of the era a recipe for Republican domination. Though "the silent majority" served as a rhetorically effective evocation in speeches, Nixon's men typically used the shorthand "New American Majority." Demographically, the majority combined the traditional bastions of Midwestern Republicanism with middle-class suburban voters in the Sunbelt states, George Wallace supporters in the South, and disaffected white ethnics in cities across the country. Ideologically, Nixonian conservatism rejected the libertarian antistatism of Goldwater and was defined more by opposition to the cultural tumult of the 1960s than opposition to the core architecture of the welfare state and postwar economic policy. Phillips called it "consolidationist Republicanism" in his best-selling blueprint for an emerging Republican majority.[91] New Politics liberals, meanwhile, saw the potential for a coalition of racial and ethnic minorities, youth, and the educated united by progressive views on Social Issue questions to forge a durable national majority. Even leading liberal *Republican* actors like the Ripon Society advocated a New Politics strategy for electoral expansion.[92] Finally, centrist Democrats like Wattenberg and Scammon stood athwart this potential new realignment, yelling "stop." They advised Johnson to target the still predominant demographic of working- and middle-class whites—"the people who bowl regularly," as Scammon put it—with economic appeals and sensitivity to their cultural and racial grievances.[93]

The return of social and cultural issues to the forefront of politics after a period of relative abeyance had ambiguous implications for the ideological sorting of the parties.[94] On the one hand, it introduced new conflicts into the political system that were less conducive to transactional bargaining—and arguably more prone to ideological activism—than the issues of economic and welfare state policy that had dominated midcentury politics. On the other hand, the introduction of new crosscutting issues occurred at the same time that major social institutions, parties included, suffered growing levels of mistrust and illegitimacy. This contributed to a sense that parties themselves were in decline as organizing forces. It would take the pivotal political developments of the next decade—a less celebrated but no less transformative era—to clarify the long-term legacy of the "Social Issue."

5

THE AGE OF PARTY REFORM, 1968-1975

In the 1970s diagnoses of American political parties tended to sound more like eulogies. David Broder told book readers in 1971 that *The Party's Over*.[1] Political scientists' debates over partisan realignment segued into a new discussion of *de*alignment.[2] The chief electoral advisors to the decade's hapless presidents echoed the sentiment. "Realignment is less likely than the disintegration of both parties," wunderkind pollster Patrick Caddell told a journalist in 1975, predicting "the death of the two-party system" shortly prior to joining Jimmy Carter's presidential campaign.[3] "Elections have become virtually totally candidate-oriented," observed Gerald Ford's pollster Robert Teeter a year later at a Republican National Committee meeting following the president's loss to Carter. He called that election "a non-partisan media event" carried out before an electorate inexorably shedding its party ties.[4]

Later, in the aftermath of the 1978 midterm elections, veteran reporter Lance Morrow described the national scene: "Today, the parties have virtually collapsed as a force in American politics." He lamented "the draining of energy and resources away from the parties and into a sort of fragmented political free-for-all," a disintegration as evident in the behavior of elected officials—like those populating a Congress that "now has all the discipline of a five-year-old's birthday party"—as it was in the rising rates of self-declared independence, split-ticket voting, and political disaffection among the mass electorate. Institutions connecting voters with politicians, Morrow reported, no longer served to aggregate interests into stable party alignments, producing a disorderly po-

FIGURE 5. Pat Oliphant, *Four More Years* (New York: Simon and Schuster, 1973), 147.
OLIPHANT © UNIVERSAL UCLICK. Reprinted with permission.

litical world populated by entrepreneurial politicians, candidate-
centered campaigns, and ad hoc legislative coalitions. Procedural
reforms crippled parties' ability to control nominations, television
provided a direct link between office-seeking individuals and the
public, and proliferating special interest groups mobilized to push
policymaking in multiple directions simultaneously. Underlying
these changes in the organization of politics, he claimed, was a
popular disenchantment with parties that reflected the broader
"atomizing process of American culture"—a turning away from
traditional institutions of all kinds.[5]

The story of parties in the 1970s has a flip side, however. Along
various measurable dimensions of strength, coherence, and influence, American parties did indeed reach a nadir in those years. But
the *reversal* of those trend lines, and the beginning of a gradual but
uninterrupted forty-year progression toward ever-greater partisanship, is also a story of the 1970s. The proportion of "pure independent" voters, those who did not lean toward either major party,
peaked in the mid-1970s and began to decline thereafter.[6] The
prevalence of "split-ticket" voting followed the same trajectory,
while one estimate of the influence of party labels on vote choice

showed a gradual, long-term rebound of such "party effects" after 1972 for presidential voting and 1978 for congressional voting.[7] As for the behavior of elected officials in Morrow's undisciplined kindergarten Congress, it too had already begun slowly to cohere along party lines by the time of his quip. Both the frequency of votes cast in which a majority of one party voted against a majority of the other and the margins of those vote differences began to rise starting in the early 1970s.[8] And rather than reflecting mere reversions to some midcentury norm after temporary drops, these turnarounds turned out to mark the beginning of a new, decades-spanning march of ever-rising partisanship.

What accounts for the dissonance between observers' impression of party politics in the 1970s and the partisan resurgence that originated in those years? A second, related set of trends offers a clue. Trough-and-rebound arcs similar to those traced by measurements of party strength during the 1970s can also be seen in measures of ideological sorting among the two parties in Congress.[9] Within the mass electorate, meanwhile, trends in the measured association of partisan affiliation with self-described ideology and issue positions also showed long-term increases following early 1970s lows.[10] The percentage of Americans polled during presidential election years who affirmed the existence of meaningful differences between the two parties hit a nadir in 1972 and slowly, steadily increased after that.[11]

The two trends were related: the parties' ideological sorting fueled the partisan resurgence. But few contemporary observers were prepared to recognize such a relationship between partisanship and ideology. Indeed, their conception of the party system emphasized precisely its nonideological nature. If American parties were supposed to be broad-based, pragmatic coalitions incorporating diverse interests and outlooks, this thinking went, then partisan strength should be indicated in part by professionals' ability to *withstand* the pressures of "purist" and issue-driven activists. Conversely, observers took signs of ideological zeal in politics as evidence of party weakness. But to counterpose parties and ideology in this way was to misapprehend some of the changes to the political system emerging in the 1970s.

The early postwar decades had witnessed the frequently vexed efforts of activists on both the left and right to forge a national two-party politics of starker programmatic contrast—a choice rather than an echo. During the 1970s the interplay of long-term developments with the concerted action of engaged activists, reformers, and political elites helped at last to render the two major parties more conducive to ideological sorting and differentiation, restructuring party politics for decades to come. In this way the parties proved central to making the 1970s the "pivotal decade" that historians have labeled it.[12] It was an age of dynamic flux and experimentation for the parties rather than the end state of their terminal decline, and the party system that 1970s activists helped to initiate would ultimately consist of less, rather than more, fragmentation. Parties became increasingly centralized in their national organizations, increasingly defined and differentiated by issues, and increasingly capable of disciplined action. Seventies-era institutional reform of the parties proved central to such developments, even if few observers appreciated it at the time.

The first half of the 1970s saw two historic waves of party reforms initiated by Democratic activists—one aimed at the party's presidential nominating procedures and national structure, the other aimed at its organization in Congress. These were dramatic, highly contested efforts yielding far-reaching changes that affected both parties. But they were equally notable for the speed with which popular and scholarly portrayals came to lament their ill effects. Changes that proponents had initiated in the name of saving an endangered party system came soon enough to be blamed for that system's very endangerment. In 1970 the key party reform commission had declared that the alternative to opening up the Democratic Party's nominating procedures would be either fragmentation or "the anti-politics of the street."[13] But by 1977 the prevailing tendency to blame the would-be treatment for the disease was typified by one political scientist's declaration in *Fortune* that "'Reform' Is Wrecking the U.S. Party System."[14]

What did these reforms entail? Emerging from the debacle of the 1968 convention, the Commission on Party Structure and Delegate Selection—commonly referred to as the McGovern-

Fraser Commission after its two successive chairmen, South Dakota senator George McGovern and Minnesota congressman Donald Fraser—established uniform standards for state nominating systems emphasizing grassroots participation, the binding of delegates to specific candidate support, and demographic representation in convention delegations. One byproduct of states' implementation of the reforms, largely unintended by the reformers, was a rapid proliferation of state primaries as the major method of delegate selection. As for Congress, among the reforms made between 1970 and 1975 were requirements that the House Democratic caucus vote to approve committee chairs, a diffusion of authority to subcommittees, the enhancement of party leaders' institutional power, and, in the Senate, a reduction of the number of votes needed to break a filibuster.

The initial, highly influential assessments of these reforms cast them as misguided interventions that weakened the parties, fragmented political authority, and hastened the rise of candidate-centered politics. This chapter reassesses the Age of Party Reform and its connection to the subsequent emergence of a more programmatic, ideologically sorted party system. The two reform initiatives, of nomination procedures and congressional organization, were connected in both personnel and outlook, and the responsible party themes of *issue politics* and *party nationalization* guided the work of key activists. Reformers used the participatory rhetoric of 1960s social movements more often than older responsible party emphases on discipline and majority rule, leading many scholars to cast them as latter-day, antiparty Progressives.[15] But the reformers' core goal resonated powerfully with responsible party doctrine: an issue-oriented party, accountable to an activist base representing its ideological majority. Ultimately, reforms so often cast as contributors to party decline in fact helped to create a newly receptive institutional setting for programmatic activism within the parties, with consequences for future ideological sorting and polarization.

"BY THE PEOPLE RATHER THAN BY THE BOSSES"

The mandate to reform Democratic presidential nominating procedures came about thanks to savvy parliamentary work by Eugene
McCarthy and Robert F. Kennedy activists at the 1968 convention
as well as the desire of party regulars to extend an olive branch
to the insurgents. The postconvention survival of the commission idea was also supported by Democratic officials and Hubert
Humphrey's campaign largely as a means of reconciling with
McCarthy and Kennedy supporters. Moreover, the activist network
that had worked on the unofficial Hughes Commission prior to the
convention remained fully engaged with the issue both during
the desultory fall campaign and after Humphrey's loss to Richard
Nixon. A new national party chair elected in January 1969, Fred
Harris, championed thoroughgoing reform, while Humphrey, reeling from defeat and still mindful to repair relations among party
factions, reiterated his support. Harris appointed two reform commissions: a Commission on Party Structure and Delegate Selection, to focus on nominating procedures and national-state party
relations, and a Commission on Rules, focusing on the procedures
of the party conventions themselves.

To avoid exacerbating tensions with party regulars, Harris
opted not for Harold Hughes but for a more congenial compromise
choice, George McGovern, for chairman of the delegate selection
commission. Hughes would serve as vice-chairman, while two
other members of his Hughes commission, Donald Fraser and
former Kennedy aide Fred Dutton, also received appointments.
Organized labor had two representatives on the new commission;
Aaron Henry held one of two "civil rights" seats; and two moderate southern party leaders, Will Davis of Texas and LeRoy Collins
of Florida, also accepted membership. The twenty-eight-member
panel also featured two political scientists steeped in the scholarship on reform and comparative party systems: the advocate-
turned-critic of responsible party doctrine, Austin Ranney, and a
leading US scholar of British politics, Samuel Beer.

If the official membership of the Commission on Party Structure and Delegate Selection tilted toward reformers, the staff that

McGovern and Harris recruited did so even more. McGovern's longtime aide Robert Nelson headed it, while his 1968 convention coordinator Ken Bode served as research director and McCarthy campaigner Eli Segal was staff counsel. Wexler was too much of a lightning rod among party officials like John Bailey to be appointed directly to the commission, given her leading role in the Connecticut antics that had kickstarted the reform push the previous summer. But she used her position on a panel of outside consultants to maximum effect.

The McGovern-Fraser Commission's origin story embodied themes, actors, and patterns that would recur during the reform process. The constellation of forces on each side proved an important constant. From 1968 on, the most visible proponents of reform were those youthful, educated participants in McCarthy's and Kennedy's presidential campaigns and, more broadly, the era's progressive social mobilizations related to civil rights, the Vietnam War, feminism, and the counterculture. Their New Politics political outlook emphasized both procedural openness and substantive commitments on issues of peace, racial and economic justice, and identity. It also envisioned a potential majoritarian party coalition combining the progressive elements of existing New Deal constituencies, unaffiliated middle-class voters motivated by interests like consumerism, feminism, and environmentalism, and such "outgroups" as youth, minorities, and the poor.[16] The impetus was not circumscribed generationally, however. Longstanding advocacy groups like the ADA also supported reform, while collaboration between New Politics activists and the older Democratic club movement found expression in the 1968 founding of the pro-reform New Democratic Coalition (NDC).[17]

While fights over issues and candidates had set the context for reform in 1968, its deeper stakes concerned whether the party should be more issue-oriented in general and national in structure. Unsurprisingly, then, the opposition to reform coalesced as an alliance of the elements that had long undergirded the party's reputation for pragmatic and decentralized bargaining. The conservative South and the remaining urban machines constituted two of those blocs, but they lacked persuasive rationales for the legitimacy of the procedures—localized, often informal—on which they depended.[18] It would instead be left to the other major antireform constituency, the majority faction of the AFL-CIO under president George Meany, to articulate the case against reform and resist its implementation. Early in 1969, the AFL-CIO's Committee on Political Education (COPE) director Alexander Barkan met with Fred Harris to object to the preliminary list of commission members, claiming it was overly stacked with insurgents. Shortly thereafter, Meany, Barkan, and AFL-CIO secretary-treasurer Lane Kirkland agreed to institute a blanket confederation boycott of the commission.[19] As one labor figure said, the panel would only serve to "give attention to those 'New Politics' nuts who helped lose the election for us."[20]

The Meany wing's opposition to reform had multiple sources.[21] Substantive disagreement with New Politics positions on key issues, especially foreign policy, was exacerbated by cultural tensions with the style and rhetoric of New Politics activists. Just as important, however, the existing constellation of authority in the party privileged Meany and his allies. Meany had successfully positioned himself as the primary interlocutor on behalf of labor in negotiations with the Johnson White House, while the AFL-CIO exercised significant influence through its relationships with the state party officials who typically led delegations. These arrangements relied on informal, face-to-face relationships among small numbers of players. A reform project intending to regularize delegate selection and convention procedures and to greatly expand the number of participants would render moot this informal power.

But labor was no more monolithic regarding party reform than it was regarding political strategy and outlook. Walter Reuther's rival vision of a robust social unionism allied with new social movement forces constituted a contrasting approach to party reform. Reuther worked directly with Harris to organize the McGovern-Fraser Commission at the beginning of 1969 with the goal, in Reuther's words, of recruiting "people committed to bring about fundamental change in the structure and opportunity for participation in the Democratic Party."[22] The UAW's representative on the commission, Bill Dodds, was an active member. The union helped to underwrite the commission's activities on several occasions, providing facilities for regional hearings and funding the publication of the commission's report, *Mandate for Reform*.[23] Throughout this time, Paul Schrade, the UAW's California director and its chief liaison to the New Politics, lobbied for reform from the outside as NDC co-chairman.

Following an inaugural meeting in March 1969, the Commission on Party Structure and Delegate Selection held a series of seventeen regional public hearings through the spring and summer while its staff catalogued state party bylaws and procedures. The regional hearings generated publicity for the cause while activating reformist networks. Witness lists were dominated by those activists most interested in participatory reforms, while the fairly paltry turnout of representatives from the regular party organizations reflected the same combination of strategic wariness and political weakness that the AFL-CIO was demonstrating.[24]

The New Politics vision of political coalition that underlay party reformers' agenda for institutional change was a recurring subject at the hearings. "New coalitions of big-city Blacks, Youth, and suburban young to middle-aged must be brought into the party, if for no other reason than numbers," said the civil rights activist Channing Emery Phillips at one hearing.[25] "Younger voters, black citizens, and college educated suburbanites" were "three constituencies on which the Democratic Party must build as the lower middle class, blue collar vote erodes," concurred Fred Dutton, outlining the argument he would make in his book *Changing Sources of Power*.[26] The NDC echoed this sense of the emerging forces in politics in its call "to coalesce a massive constituency of the oppressed with a massive constituency of conscience"—a coalition that, it acknowledged, did "not presently compose a voting majority of politically active Americans, nor even of the Democratic Party. But it is a large and growing proportion of the voting public."[27]

Hearing witnesses drew a connection between that emerging political coalition and the growing importance of issue politics. Edmund Muskie, Humphrey's 1968 running mate and a leading contender for the 1972 presidential nomination, observed that "the electorate is becoming more educated. The grassroots Democrats are becoming more educated." What this meant was that "ideas alone"—issues and policies rather than partisan spirit or patronage—were coming to determine the political behavior of increasing numbers of Americans.[28] Muskie's argument recurred throughout the hearings, as a staff summary of testimony conveyed: "Vast numbers of intelligent and energetic Americans today . . . do not respond to the traditional inducements of party loyalty or patronage. They are issue-oriented citizens."[29] As McGovern declared at one hearing, "the real heart and soul of a political party is its policy, its philosophy, its stand on the great issues of the day. . . . Really the only purpose of party reform is to provide a vehicle through which those policies can be determined by the people rather than by the bosses."[30]

A short-term conflict catalyzed reformers' efforts. The perception that existing procedures had failed to represent the rank and file's views on Vietnam had inspired the movement. But systemic reform had implications that extended beyond transient issues and policy conflicts, and was relevant to a category of political actor a good deal more specific than "the people." Ensuring through national guidelines that party elites in the patchwork of state organizations could no longer exercise arbitrary control over delegate selection would have a permanent, structural effect: the empowerment of issue-driven activists, who had the inclination and resources to mobilize on their own. As primary systems proliferated in the years ahead, engaged activists' higher participation rates and organizational capacity did indeed give them enhanced positions in the party.[31]

Party nationalization loomed as another core theme in the panel's work. In summarizing the regional hearings, commission staff reported that "in the area of party structure, many witnesses have expressed the view that the national party should play a more significant role in the ongoing affairs of the party." "The U.S. has become more national in economic, communication, and, increasingly, social terms," Dutton pointed out, "yet the party essentially reflects a commonwealth base not true of most of the rest of American life." He advocated measures to integrate state and local parties with "presidential politics and the more inter-related policy which we really have now."[32] The most vivid demonstration of McGovern-Fraser's nationalizing thrust would be its success in prodding state and local parties to open up their nominating procedures. But since the activists that reformers sought to empower tended to be motivated by national issues, making the party more issue-oriented was itself also a way to encourage nationalization. Such activists, Beer wrote, "see themselves not so much as a faction within a state party as part of a nation-wide combination, and therefore want a system which will register their strength in the nation as a whole. . . . Our politics, in short, is becoming more 'nationalized' and the nomination system should reflect this fact."[33]

Over the course of public hearings and Executive Council sessions, commission members and staff fixed into place the key elements of the reform agenda they would mandate to states in early 1970. These elements, formalized as eighteen guidelines in *Mandate for Reform*, were remarkably consistent with the prescriptions laid out by the Hughes Commission in the summer of 1968. Most practical were requirements to make delegate selection procedures transparent, timely, and accessible to all Democrats. The participatory focus also underlay prohibitions on devices that privileged party officials and officeholders, including the automatic designation of delegate status to such officials (so-called ex-officio delegates) and proxy voting and lax quorum requirements at party meetings. Another guideline required that candidates for delegate seats declare their presidential preference or otherwise designate themselves as "uncommitted." Closely related were efforts to ensure that minority views on candidate preferences could not be snuffed out by majorities, including the abolition of the unit rule at the state level and at national conventions.[34]

Though these participatory reforms would prove to be by far the most consequential and transformative of the McGovern-Fraser Commission's actions, its provisions concerning demographic representation came unexpectedly to occupy the center of thorny controversy beginning in the fall of 1969. At the behest of members Fred Dutton and David Mixner, a guideline that had reaffirmed the Special Equal Rights Committee's provisions on racial discrimination was turned into two, the first addressing discrimination based on race, the second doing so for "age or sex." Those agreeing were quick to insist that they not amount to anything resembling numerical quotas for specific groups. But prior to codifying the guidelines, Austin Ranney noted that "our fellow black Democrats feel that something more is needed than a no-discrimination rule," and suggested adding language urging state parties to include fair representation of racial minorities in their delegations. Indiana senator Birch Bayh augmented Ranney's proposal with language referring to "some reasonable relationship between the representation of delegates and representation of the minority group to the population of the state in question."[35] After the commission narrowly voted to adopt Bayh's additions, Dutton and others pushed to apply the same language to the guideline covering women and youth. Many members blanched, including Ranney, now lamenting having "opened Pandora's box."[36] But they were unable or unwilling to push back against the extension.

The results were two reform guidelines, A-1 and A-2, whose demographic requirements covering racial minorities, women, and youth would prove to be a lightning rod of controversy in the party for the next several years. Ironically, demographic affirmative action was never a guiding priority for the reform activists on and around the commission staff. After the commission's haphazard introduction of such measures in the fall of 1969, the impetus to strengthen rather than water them down came from outside social movements. In 1971 the National Women's Political Caucus (NWPC), a new feminist organization led by Bella Abzug and Patsy Mink, managed to secure a key policy from the chairmen of both the DNC and the McGovern-Fraser Commission. They agreed to add language to A-1 and A-2 stating that failure to achieve demographic representation in proportion to the three targeted groups' presence in the population would constitute prima facie evidence of discrimination in any credentials challenges.

This confirmation in all but name that state parties now needed to meet numerical quotas sparked an intractable debate. The history of failed promises to enforce antidiscrimination provisions against African Americans rendered hollow claims that quotas were unnecessary to achieve representation.[37] The new aggressiveness of feminist activists, moreover, disinclined many officials from rolling back A-2. At the same time, reform activists faced an intellectual conflict between changes meant to empower the grass-roots in choosing the composition of delegations and those directing state parties to compose them in specific ways. That conflict also explained why, compared to the transformative effects of the participatory reforms, the significance of the demographic quotas would prove largely symbolic. In the short term, they provided the basis for a slew of credentials challenges at the 1972 convention, and thus were of some practical importance that year. But in the long term, precisely because the main thrust of the McGovern-Fraser reforms reduced the autonomy of convention delegates and bound them to the wishes of primary and caucus participants, debate over regulating the composition of delegations would dwindle.

The real significance of the A-1 and A-2 guidelines in the early 1970s lay in how they symbolized the Democratic Party's institutional posture toward the social movements that had emerged over the previous decade. The provisions for minorities, women, and youth reflected the incipient party coalition that New Politics advocates envisioned, and the very visibility of the changes in the makeup of conventions was part of the appeal. The campaign to implement the reforms itself helped to channel movement efforts into the party. "I thought I was retired from politics, partly by choice but mainly by having no playing field," longtime activist Martha Ragland of Tennessee reported in 1971. "But the 1968 convention and the McGovern Commission guidelines gave a new leverage."[38] Ragland and others' involvement in the effort to bring Tennessee into compliance with McGovern-Fraser provided a locus for state-level feminist organizing. Similar mobilizations occurred across the country. The composition of the 1972 convention testified to the reforms' effect: blacks' share of delegates rose from 5.5 percent in 1968 to 15.5 percent; women's rose from 13 to 40 percent; youth's, from 4 to 21 percent.[39] These changes embodied the party's interest in absorbing 1960s movement currents—in augmenting the labor-liberal core of the New Deal coalition with newly mobilized constituencies.

This was a political posture that would be revealed, in the catas-

trophe of McGovern's defeat that November, to be inadequate to
the task of building a national electoral majority in early 1970s
America. Indeed, it was hardly a posture that could address the
disaffection of those millions of *other* Democratic voters who had
moved in a radically different ideological direction in 1968, toward
George Wallace's campaign.[40] And it was a posture that major
Democratic elements bitterly opposed. But, in the sharp contrast it
struck with the coalitional strategy then being pursued by the GOP,
and in the way it helped keep the era's left-liberal energies channeled into a major party, it proved lastingly significant for future
party alignments.

PUSHING THROUGH AN OPEN DOOR

The McGovern-Fraser reforms that exerted the greatest long-term
effect on the party system were those that did away with methods
by which party professionals, free from activist *or* voter influence,
could determine the makeup and behavior of convention delegations. The very act of implementing those reforms, of course,
would require the cooperation of fifty-five states and territories,
each of which would need to meet the requirements either through
private changes or a combination of internal party reform and state
legislation. This would be a tall order. "You can define 'all feasible
efforts' . . . any way you like," Will Davis of Texas had pointed out at
the very first McGovern-Fraser meeting. "There are plenty of conservative Democrats, who control the legislatures in several southern states, for example, and they are not going to line up like sheep
to pass reform legislation."[41] Davis's logic was unassailable, and
applied similarly to resistant states outside the South.

Between McGovern-Fraser's promulgation of its guidelines in
the fall of 1969 and the convention in July 1972, opponents had
several opportunities to mount an effective resistance, and they
passed up each one. In October 1969 the commission distributed
draft guidelines to thousands of officials throughout the country,
soliciting their feedback. Among the responses were notably few
critiques from party regulars or their allies. The regulars' next op-

portunity came when the panel distributed its compliance letters to all state party chairmen and DNC members in February 1970. Most states replied with pro forma thanks and then took no action, while some set about immediately to pursue compliance. Reform critics at the DNC might have translated resistance into meaningful action in 1971 during the meeting to adopt the Preliminary Call to the convention. Instead, the DNC voted to incorporate the entirety of the McGovern-Fraser guidelines into the Call. Even then, state parties might *still* have opted for foot-dragging as a strategy to undermine reform. But by the eve of the convention, forty-five states and territories were deemed by the commission to have achieved full compliance with its guidelines, with the remaining ten in substantial compliance.[42]

What accounted for the curious failure of the very forces targeted by the McGovern-Fraser Commission to resist its reforms? Because existing nominating procedures varied so widely across states, and had so often been informally or casually performed by insiders, party regulars lacked coherent and identifiable standards, arguments, or alternative proposals around which they could rally.[43] Political developments also undermined the regulars' strategic decision to refrain from vocal opposition for as long as possible. Lawrence O'Brien replaced Fred Harris as DNC chairman in 1970 and, contrary to reformers' fears, the ex-Kennedy and Johnson aide proved as committed as Harris to implementing the McGovern-Fraser guidelines and more *effective* in doing so given his credibility among party leaders.[44] O'Brien secured a crucial ruling from the DNC's counsel confirming that failure to comply with the guidelines would be grounds for delegate credentials challenges in 1972.[45] The 1970 midterms, which saw the election of many pro-reform Democratic governors, bolstered the momentum of state-level implementation.

The sources of the regulars' defeat were not merely practical and political, but also intellectual. Opponents of the guidelines' emphasis on participation never became more than defenders of the status quo—and as such, they lacked a compelling case.[46] Practices in numerous states were obviously irregular, arbitrary, and closed to new entrants. The long legacy of intraparty struggles over the

South's racially discriminatory procedures delegitimized any arguments against national party incursions into state affairs. From the very outset of the reform campaign in 1968, virtually no regulars openly questioned the idea that a basic set of uniform national standards for nominating procedures would be desirable. Nor did many regulars question an emphasis on democratic participation in such standards. When Richard Daley himself appeared at a McGovern-Fraser public hearing in Chicago in 1969, he gave no full-throated defense of the famously disciplined and closed Cook County party organization he led. He instead proposed his own set of party reforms: a series of minor changes to convention practices along with the establishment of a presidential primary in every state.[47]

Opponents of reform could not articulate a plausible argument for existing arrangements, which could not be shown to effectively translate voter sentiment on policy issues into coherent and distinct party positions. Reform advocates emphasized the failure of the 1968 nominating process to provide general election voters with a meaningful choice regarding Vietnam. They attributed that result to institutional failure. Reform critics like the centrist Democratic strategists Richard Scammon and Ben Wattenberg could mount a persuasive counterargument that, in fact, the 1968 Democratic convention did produce both a nominee and a platform position on Vietnam that reflected the wishes of a rank-and-file party majority. But what even they could not do was explain how the unreformed nominating process worked systemically to ensure such outcomes. The system's "institutionalized helter-skelterism," they wrote in 1970, "is so complicated, it is hard to say exactly *why* and *how* it ends up as responsive as it is. . . . What can be said about the delegate selection system is this: Somehow it works." Delegates were either elected, selected by people who were elected, or "selected by people who were selected by people who were elected popularly at one time or another. There is then, a democratic process, if far removed, behind each delegate."[48] This was as close to a full-throated defense of the existing system as any the era produced. It left little reason to expect that the system could dependably adjudicate among and reconcile party factions divided over major issues.

What party regulars' practical inefficacy and intellectual difficulties ultimately reflected was weakness—the wages of decades
of organizational decline.[49] The current beneficiaries of organizational arrangements dating back to a previous century's partisan
era were the occupants of often-sleepy state and local party organizations. They lacked the inclination, credibility, or resources to
fight back effectively against the forces calling for long-overdue
reform. To a great extent, McGovern-Fraser–era reformers found
themselves pushing through an open door.[50]

Unlike the party regulars, the reformers benefited from the support of a national coalition of organizations featuring an interlocking network of actors. Anne Wexler consulted on the NDC's Party
Reform Task Force and headed the delegate selection reform effort
at Common Cause, a new good-government organization founded
by ex–Health, Education, and Welfare secretary John Gardner.[51]
The ADA formed a Convention Task Force to monitor states' implementation of the reforms, overseen by Wexler's fellow activist and now-husband, Joe Duffey, and co-chaired by McGovern-
Fraser staffer Ken Bode after he left the commission in 1970. The
leading staffer on the NWPCs's Task Force on Delegate Selection
was Phyllis Segal, whose husband Eli had served as McGovern-
Fraser's counsel, while the NWPC's policy council included Ar-
vonne Fraser, wife of one of the commission's namesakes. Bode
established his own independent organization, the Center for Political Reform (CPR), which coordinated pressure campaigns for
state-level implementation and devised strategy for credentials
challenges at the 1972 convention.[52]

The pattern of state adoption of the guidelines reflected not
only the effectiveness of these new efforts but also the enduring
legacy of a longer reform movement among issue-oriented Democratic activists. Those states with traditions of volunteer party
activism and robust "amateur" club activity—Minnesota, Wisconsin, Oregon—were typically the earliest and easiest states to reform, while the longest holdouts were those states—Texas, New
York, Connecticut—with surviving patronage-oriented party organizations.[53] Even the latter states could hold out for only so long.
George McGovern's insurgent presidential campaign gathered

strength in the spring of 1972, amassing hundreds of pledged delegates amid a crowded field as one opponent after another either
stumbled on the trail or failed to adjust his strategy to the new procedural landscape of proportional delegate counts and participatory contests. McGovern's frontrunner status by the convention in
Miami meant that there was little chance recalcitrant state parties
would get a sympathetic hearing there.

The saga of that most iconic political machine—Richard Daley's
Cook County organization—dramatized the shifting constellation
of power within the party in 1972. As early as 1970, activists in Illinois laid groundwork for a challenge to the delegates who would
emerge from Chicago two years later. The state's NDC chapter
launched Challenge '72 to monitor Daley's organization for reform violations and to mount a credentials challenge in Miami
if need be. "YOU just may occupy the seat next to Daley," it announced cheekily in a report to members.[54] By primary season of
1972, Cook County Democrats had given no indication of interest
in complying with the guidelines. "We'll elect our delegates as we
always have," Daley told party workers in February. "Why the hell
should we let those people in Washington tell us how we should
elect them?"[55] In Illinois's primary that May, Daley's organization
got its fifty-nine delegates elected as usual. Immediately, a group
of ten reform Democrats led by Chicago Alderman William Singer
and civil rights activist Jesse Jackson filed a challenge to "the Daley
59," on behalf of "Democrats in general, and, in particular, all
Blacks, Latin Americans, Women, and Young People."[56] Reform
networks at the state and national level supported the challenge,
which cited violations of six McGovern-Fraser guidelines.[57] The
challengers held district caucuses to elect an alternative slate of
delegates. Regulars disrupted several of them, but an alternative
delegation did come into being.

The next step in the process testified to the degree of nationalization the party was undergoing. Though the Commission on
Rules, McGovern-Fraser's counterpart panel, concerned itself
chiefly with convention logistics, one reform it implemented bore
directly on the Illinois challenge. This was the new institution of
"hearing officers"—impartial observers appointed by the DNC to

hold open hearings in states where credentials challenges were occurring. The officers would prepare reports for the Credentials Committee to help guide its decisions. Such a device was intended to bolster a rule-of-law ethos and to reduce the degree of pure candidate-driven horse-trading that afflicted the panel. The officer assigned to the Chicago challenge withstood unrelenting hostility from Daley's forces to hold a hearing and file a report. He sided with the challengers, citing "abundant and probative" evidence that the regulars carried out "deliberate, covert, and calculated" violations of McGovern-Fraser guidelines.[58] The report helped the challengers' case in the Credentials Committee, which voted 71–61 in the challengers' favor.

The regulars' last chance to keep their seats came on the first night of the convention. The mammoth array of credentials disputes pushed the floor debate on the pro-regular Illinois minority report to 2:00 a.m. Speaking for the regulars, attorney Raymond F. Simon charged that the alternative delegates "were chosen by a handful of non-elected, self-appointed usurpers."[59] Supporters of the challengers recited the litany of violations by Cook County Democrats and invoked themes of reform and New Politics coalition-building. Jesse Jackson connected the challenges against Cook County to those made against southern states in 1964 and 1968. "Mississippi was not an exception," he declared. "Georgia was not an exception. Chicago can't be an exception. We must nationalize the McGovern rules."[60]

The final vote approached like a slow-motion wreck. McGovern was fully aware of the disastrous symbolism that would accompany the ouster of fifty-eight Chicago Democrats and their iconic leader, but he also could not openly oppose the Singer-Jackson delegates, who embodied his own reforms. A final compromise proposal to seat both delegations failed. The convention voted narrowly to uphold the Credentials Committee decision to seat the reformers. The visceral nature of the hostilities in this drama could hardly be overstated, and was captured in the gendered language ascribed to a party official by columnists Rowland Evans and Robert Novak: "They urinated right in the face of all those people. They insulted Daley's political manhood."[61]

The intramural warfare continued throughout the general election and in the aftermath of McGovern's landslide loss—and institutional reform was never far from the center of the factional strife. In the summer of 1972 meetings among operators in Meany's orbit lay the groundwork for a counterrevolution in the aftermath of the anticipated loss in November.[62] Central to the plan would be replacing the McGovern-backed DNC chair, Jean Westwood, with the party's former treasurer, Texas attorney Robert Strauss. The plan commenced after the election, and Strauss was duly elected in December. His first decision was to hire an AFL-CIO staffer as the party's executive director. Strauss, a close friend of ex-governor and Nixon cabinet member John Connally, had a reputation as a southern conservative. Meany's patronage of Strauss captured well the alliances that had emerged out of shared opposition to New Politics reform.

A related antireform organization similarly originated in pre-election meetings. Ben Wattenberg began consulting in September with a dozen other New Politics opponents about the need to form an anti–New Politics outfit. In the weeks after McGovern's loss, the Coalition for a Democratic Majority (CDM) launched with a newspaper ad campaign featuring the headline, "Come Home, Democrats."[63] The major indictments CDM laid out against the New Politics were substantive rather than procedural, including its adherents' alleged belief "that the United States must withdraw from its international responsibilities and effect a serious diminution of its own power."[64] Despite the incipient neoconservatism of the group's outlook and its leaders' penchant for rhetorical attacks, CDM's agenda concerning McGovern-Fraser was fairly modest. The coalition recommended repealing the demographic targets in A-1 and A-2 and curbing regulations of slate-making and ex-officio delegates.[65] But it did not challenge fundamentally the core of the reforms.

That same dynamic could be seen in the deliberations of McGovern-Fraser's successor panel, the Commission on Delegate Selection and Party Structure, tasked by the 1972 convention with reviewing and reassessing the guidelines in light of that year's election.[66] Chaired by Baltimore councilwoman Barbara Mikulski in symbolic reflection of the need for the party to repair relations with white ethnic constituencies, the new commission served during the year of its operations as an arena for chronic factional squabbling but little in the way of major rollbacks of reform. At commission meetings that year, reform critics made their case for nixing the demographic targets and restoring ex officio delegates. Despite the pressure, Strauss generally worked to ameliorate divisions. The commission's final report offered a compromise reform to A-1 and A-2 along with a new Compliance Review Commission expanding on the role of hearing officers.[67] Ultimately, the Mikulski Commission entrenched McGovern-Fraser's participatory and nationalizing elements. Despite McGovern's election loss, the reforms' intellectual and political underpinnings proved durable.

REFORM'S FORGOTTEN TURN: THE PARTY CHARTER AND MIDTERM CONVENTIONS

By the time the Mikulski Commission issued its report, the focus of debate over institutional change within the party, and the attention of wary leaders like Robert Strauss, had largely shifted away from nominating procedures. The new focus concerned the party's organization and mechanisms for enhancing issue-based deliberation and ideological cohesion within it. The "Party Structure" component of the Commission on Party Structure and Delegate Selection's mandate, in other words, was more than empty verbiage. A Charter Commission would carry out this element of the reform project in 1973 and 1974.

If the issue focus and nationalizing thrust of McGovern-Fraser's delegate-selection reforms drew from responsible party doctrine, the panel's forgotten structural agenda bore even clearer connections to that outlook. Though these efforts proved less enduring and easily entrenched than the nominating reforms, they undermine portrayals of the reformers as antiparty zealots. And in the near term, such reforms—particularly the institution of midterm conventions—exerted a real political impact.

From the beginning, McGovern-Fraser's reformers considered addressing structural issues in the national party to be a component of their mandate, and an answer to the Special Equal Rights Committee's call in 1968 for a panel "to study the relationship between the National Democratic Party and its constituent State Democratic Parties." The commission temporarily narrowed its focus to delegate selection, as that topic faced the most pressing timetable. But Fraser in particular remained committed to structural reform and made suggestions in 1969 and 1970 to his own panel and to James O'Hara's Commission on Rules on reforming the DNC, establishing a Democratic Advisory Council–style research arm, and drafting a party constitution.[68]

The latter proposal, to write the first-ever charter for a major US party with codified rules and procedures governing the national organization and its relationship to local and state counterparts, garnered renewed interest in 1971. Fraser and O'Hara agreed early in the year to work jointly on those topics. They built an informal network of correspondents that included Sam Beer, James MacGregor Burns, and Michigan's Neil Staebler, the advocate of programmatic party-building who had worked with Paul Butler at the DNC.[69] The group considered longstanding responsible party proposals, from biennial party conferences to political education arms to national policy councils. Other proposals connected organizational reform to the participatory ethos of the delegate selection reforms then underway, including a national dues-paying party membership system that could enhance grassroots participation while building a financial base.

The discussions culminated in a joint meeting of the McGovern-Fraser and O'Hara commissions in the fall of 1971, where party nationalization and issue activism recurred as central themes.[70] Anne Wexler praised the 1964 and 1968 conventions for seeking "to adopt binding standards on constituent state Democratic parties" and for finally enabling "the national convention to become the party's national policy maker." Emphasizing programmatic party-building, Sam Beer situated his proposal for issue conferences in an analysis of broad changes among voters. "The electorate as a whole is showing a great and growing interest in issues and public policy," he asserted, attributing the development to "the rising level of education among voters." He insisted that "there are votes in issues. This is a heretical remark among some political scientists even today," given the influence of works like *The American Voter* that emphasized affective affiliations over ideology or issue positions.[71] But Beer drew on new findings from scholars grappling with the tumult of the 1960s to claim "it's finally getting around to political scientists that people in the millions choose the candidate they vote for and the party they identify with . . . on issues. That's the thing we haven't allowed for in the structure of our party." James MacGregor Burns went further by connecting programmatic reform to an eventual ideological sorting of the party system itself. A reformed party "would welcome and recruit members on the basis of one test and one test alone—belief in the principles and goals of the party as defined in the national platform," and so, soon enough, "those who do not share its goals would see no point in joining it, or staying in it."

The presence of another participant at the 1971 meeting, David Anderson of Canada's Liberal Party, reflected a notable theme of the era's reform efforts: a transnational engagement with party systems in other democracies. Fraser, whose congressional work focused on international affairs, frequently took advantage of his travels and interactions with foreign officials to discuss parties. In 1971 he organized a meeting on party organization and reform with a British Conservative Party member, alongside O'Hara and Bob Nelson.[72] And when considering proposals for a dues-paying Democratic membership, Fraser drew on Beer's expertise to gather data on British Labor Party finances and dues' role in it.[73] The difficulty of attempting to adopt elements of foreign systems that US parties lacked for historical and constitutional reasons was not lost on the reformers. "The British example has been very much in my mind," Neil Staebler told Fraser, "but I do not find it possible to jump very far to their organizational forms because of our geographical diversity and federated character."[74] Despite such obstacles, they still sought to heighten national party supremacy and to foster issue activism within the parties.

Biennial national conferences stood at the center of structural reformers' proposals. Such meetings' international ubiquity was an argument in the idea's favor. "Such a conference would take on the character less of the quadrennial national convention," Burns argued, "than of the kinds of annual national policy-making conferences that are held by scores of political parties . . . throughout the world."[75] As Fraser later framed his case, Democrats rarely made an "effort to think about the party and its role in society," while "Western European political parties concern themselves with political education on an ongoing basis."[76] The late 1960s had seen renewed interest in this longstanding responsible party proposal as a channel for the seemingly explosive issue activism of the period, one less divisive than nomination challenges. Gene McCarthy had proposed biennial conventions during the campaign, as did officials ranging from Al Lowenstein to Jesse Unruh to Ed Muskie at the McGovern-Fraser field hearings the following year.[77]

Fraser, O'Hara, and several of their staffers produced a draft charter in the spring of 1972 that was striking in its sweep and ambition.[78] The proposal called for a new national party membership system requiring annual enrollment, with a nominal fee "strongly urged." The state-based structure of the DNC would be replaced by a new system of seven regional organizations and a national executive committee composed of the national and regional chairmen, congressional leaders, and various at-large members. Finally, the draft charter called for regional party conferences to be held on odd years and a national policy conference of 3,000 delegates to take place on even years between the conventions.

Support for the proposal came not only from avowed responsible party advocates but also from New Politics activists better known for their focus on grassroots participation and demographic representativeness. "Party responsibility, a stillborn concept in many sections of this country, now stands a chance of becoming the foundation of party organization and policy," wrote one political scientist.[79] New Politics activists endorsed the draft charter as well, voicing support at a CPR meeting featuring representatives from the NWPC, the Youth Caucus, and other groups.[80] Such support showed how a participatory reform vision could be compatible with responsible party prescriptions.

The political implications were just as apparent in the array of forces opposed to the proposal. Democratic state chairmen re-acted with outrage to the regional party organizations that would supplant much of their power. (Fraser and O'Hara eventually jetti-soned them.)[81] A mass membership system, meanwhile, struck many officials as a radical and foreign concept—"reprehensible and dangerous," according to South Carolina's Donald Fowler, privi-leging "those who are highly motivated because of special inter-ests or extreme ideological commitments."[82] A dues fee's resem-blance to a poll tax gave even some pro-reform liberals pause. The drafters thus watered down the provision to a vague call for "peri-odic, personal enrollment in a manner specified by the Democratic National Committee," with dues explicitly prohibited.[83] Even in modified form, the charter proposal provoked intense opposition from elements who had long resisted responsible party reforms, from southern conservatives to machine pols to congressional leaders.

When Fraser appeared before a Democratic House caucus meeting to present the draft charter, Chicago representative Frank Annunzio, a loyal member of Daley's machine, was outraged. He began rounding up the required signatures to call another meet-ing of the caucus to discuss the charter exclusively. Annunzio's co-signers were disproportionately "southern and old-line con-gressmen," according to the *Washington Post*. Wayne Hays of Ohio pointed to the activists who would dominate delegations at the proposed midterm conferences. "These people shouldn't run the party, elected officials should," he said. "I was elected by the people of my district. Not by some packed caucus."[84] Florida's Robert Sikes connected the charter's attempt "to mold the Demo-cratic Party into a liberal party in the hands of a narrow ideologi-cal elite" to a longer-range and dangerous agenda to transform the party system itself, defined by "a new division of the American party structure into liberal and conservative camps."[85] The emer-gency meeting of the caucus, held two weeks before the national party convention, turned into a raucous shouting match between representatives angry about the whole sweep of institutional re-forms and defenders of the charter. The former outnumbered the latter there, resulting in a 105–50 vote for a resolution that formally opposed a convention vote on the charter and called instead for further study.[86]

Fraser lobbied to win over skeptics in the weeks leading up the convention, supported by Common Cause and Democratic Study Group campaigns.[87] But he could not ignore the many voices arguing that a charter was too complicated a project to tackle at an already overscheduled convention. These voices included the McGovern campaign, wary of raising novel reform issues just when it needed to secure victory.[88] Fraser and O'Hara eventually agreed to refrain from advocating a floor vote on the charter, opting instead for a resolution that called for a commission to pursue the charter-writing process and a midterm conference in 1974 to amend and ratify that commission's work.[89]

The proposed charter of 1972 marked a peak for centralizing, programmatic party reform during this period. The eventual product of the commission mandated by the Miami convention would be a much more modest set of bylaws and structures, though the limited changes they embodied all still ran in the direction of greater nationalization and issue focus. From the outset, Robert Strauss worked to retain tight control over the Charter Commission's work, with the overriding goal of patching up factional disputes over institutional issues.[90] Strauss, an ostentatiously pragmatic backslapper, was averse to any forums that might occasion public party squabbling. He thus vehemently opposed the very concept of party-wide issue conferences. The Miami convention had mandated that a Conference on Democratic Party Organization and Policy take place in 1974 to ratify the charter, but Strauss did all he could to control the planning of that meeting—and to keep discussion of public policy issues out of its purview altogether. He was never less than candid about his view: "I am not the father" of the midterm conference, he told a reporter. "And I would admit to you that I'm not Catholic and I would have practiced a little more birth control if I were father to this child."[91]

Strauss's outlook put him in direct conflict with reform advocates like Fraser, who worked throughout 1973 to build support within the DNC for including issue seminars and platform discussion in the midterm conference. In response to one critical missive from Fraser, Strauss emphasized his intention to "heal the wounds of the past, to bring Democrats together," a goal he said would be jeopardized by introducing "ideological debate" into the mini-convention.[92] "Your faith," he wrote to Fraser, "that opening up the 1974 conference to questions of public policy will serve to unite the party is not shared by all other Democrats across the nation." He then took a detour into academic disquisition that did much to illustrate the intellectual and political stakes driving structural reform:

> You cite the American Political Science Association Committee on Political Parties' 1951 work, "Toward a More Responsible Two-Party System," as a guide to political reform in the Democratic party. You should be aware that the APSA report has been criticized by some over the last several years as being ill-conceived and contradictory. ... Political scientists have concluded that many of the suggestions employed in this document are inappropriate and dysfunctional to the American political system.[93]

Over the course of public hearings and commission meetings in 1973 and 1974, the charter debate pitted those seeking cohesion and programmatic commitment against those touting the pragmatic functions of parties. As notes from one of the meetings summarized, "the broadest division in the Party is between those who feel the purpose of the Party is to elect Democrats, and those who feel the Party must represent some point of view."[94] Fraser and Staebler led the second camp, supported by most of the major New Politics and liberal advocacy groups. The anti-reform coalition on the commission was led by the same elements that had fought McGovern-Fraser: southerners, machine pols, and the Meany wing of labor. In July 1973 that coalition demonstrated its strength by passing resolutions to schedule the midterm party conference for after the 1974 elections and to restrict conference discussion to the charter. As a member put it, Democrats had recently "gotten into trouble by talking about the environment and Vietnam and things like that. . . . The way to win elections is to get people to vote for Democrats because they're Democrats."[95]

Such arguments received their most articulate expression in a 1973 position paper prepared by the Coalition for a Democratic Majority called "Unity out of Diversity." The paper criticized the 1972 draft charter as well as newer proposals by Fraser and Staebler for seeking "to centralize, ideologize, and 'Europeanize' the Party in ways which run against the grain of American political tradition and the unique coalitional character of the Democratic Party."[96] CDM described the responsible party doctrine underlying the proposals as "an approach to the role and structure of political parties which is suited to parliamentary systems of government—not our own." The paper acknowledged that the national parties had a stronger role to play, but called proposals to inject issue-based activism into party institutions dangerous and ill-timed. New issue cleavages, from Vietnam to law and order to the counterculture, divided Democrats among themselves. "It is unrealistic to talk of the desirability—or even the possibility—of a united, liberal 'national' party driving out the impure and arousing new converts" while such divides remained.

The CDM advanced a coherent, tempered argument against the tide of reform efforts. But such intellectual engagement did not quite match the intensity and vitriol with which the anti-reform coalition, led as always by the aggressive Al Barkan of COPE, moved against factional enemies in 1973 and 1974. Barkan had pushed to replace Jean Westwood with Strauss after the 1972 election, waged anti-reform battles in the Mikulski Commission, and mobilized opposition to midterm party conferences. His combativeness ran counter to the themes of comity and pragmatic compromise that other reform critics emphasizes. A DNC staffer later recalled that Barkan and Meany "wanted not only to defeat the McGovern wing of the party but to castrate them and throw them to the sharks."[97] Overreaching, Barkan's forces attempted to use a Charter Commission meeting in August 1974 to muscle through major rollbacks of McGovern-Fraser reforms, prompting a walkout by the commission's black members and most of their allies.[98] The meeting dissolved for lack of a quorum, the anti-reformers drew condemnation, and Strauss subsequently kept his distance from the counterrevolutionaries.

No similar fireworks accompanied the actual midterm conference, formally titled the Conference on Democratic Party Organization and Policy. A month after the party's massive, Watergate-fueled congressional victories had produced a net gain of 3 seats in the Senate and 49 in the House, 2,035 delegates convened in Kansas City. The afterglow of those victories, combined with wariness over the infighting of the August commission meeting, bolstered the position of those seeking a conflict-free conference. Strauss pursued unity at all costs by micromanaging the proceedings. Those participants not engaged by the technical aspects of reform were caustic. "Never in the history of human boredom," Texas representative Jim Wright declared, "have so many traveled so far to be stirred by such matters of immeasurable triviality."[99]

Fittingly for such a controlled conference, the charter that emerged was a modest document.[100] It included a carefully worded requirement for state-level affirmative action programs to "provide for representation as nearly as practicable" of minorities, youth, and women in proportion to their Democratic presence—but it forbade mandatory quotas. It created a Judicial Council "to adjudicate disputes arising from the interpretation and application of national Party law"—but it stipulated that the national convention and the DNC retained control over their own credentialing disputes. It created a National Education and Training Council that gestured toward the kind of political education functions prized by Staebler and Fraser—but it remained vague about the nature and scope of the new entity's responsibilities. As for midterm issue conferences, a narrow floor vote ensured that future meetings would not be required, only permitted. Modest though it was, the charter signified a new step in party nationalization while inscribing the core elements of the era's procedural reforms into stable party law. It institutionalized a party model that was highly permeable and driven increasingly by volunteers and issue activists.

No actor was more central to the structural reform process than Fraser, designated by Neil Staebler as "the Thomas Jefferson of the New Democratic Party."[101] After the charter's passage, Fraser established a new organization, The Democratic Conference, underwritten by unions, feminist groups, and reform lobbies, which worked to defend the reforms and monitor the party's institutional health.[102] As the Age of Party Reform dwindled, Fraser remained engaged in the service of both participatory and responsible party principles. Simultaneously, he served as a leader in another reform project with direct bearing on the party system: the transformation of committee organization and partisan institutions in Congress.

CONGRESSIONAL REFORM AND PARTY GOVERNMENT

During the joint meeting of the McGovern-Fraser and O'Hara commissions in 1971, the question had been raised whether the party charter should mention congressional organization or not. Sam Beer cautioned against it on the grounds that the DNC lacked any formal ability to compel changes in the workings of the congressional party. Aaron Henry, the Mississippi civil rights activist and party organizer, responded to Beer in frustration. "Unless, Sam, we take a position somewhere that there is going to be a modicum of conduct that we demand by people who call themselves Democrats, or be willing to exclude them, you give me a great fear," he said. "The racist element that permeates the Democratic Party, it permeates it in terms of committee assignments." James Mac-Gregor Burns chimed in to support Henry, calling the congressional party "a separate power base" whose southern contingent amounted to an "opposition party" that reformers would need to "confront and overcome." Fraser responded that this could happen only "by getting a congressional party that will refuse these people chairmanships." As another member put it, "Congress is going to have to reform itself."[103]

It is not coincidental that a transformative period of reform in Congress took place alongside the McGovern-Fraser reforms. The two movements shared key personnel, motivations, and theoretical premises about the function of parties. Responsible party doctrine was central to the movement for congressional reform. Key items eventually achieved in the 1970s, from eliminating the sanctity of seniority to empowering the caucus and party leadership to reforming the filibuster, had all appeared in APSA's 1950 report.[104] From its founding in 1959, the leading force for institutional reform in the House, the Democratic Study Group (DSG), peppered its reports and memos with explicit references to *Toward a More Responsible Two-Party System*.[105] Moreover, the key responsible party themes informing the McGovern-Fraser reforms—nationalization and programmatic partisanship—also underlay the major elements of congressional reform. "The strength of the Democratic Party is in its national characteristics and broad-based responsibilities," the DSG wrote in 1964, "not narrow regional interests." The party must "provide the necessary legislative machinery and internal party unity to guarantee action on the Democratic programs pledged in our platform."[106]

Efforts in the 1960s to challenge seniority and to discipline recalcitrant congressional Democrats connected directly to reform developments in the *non*-congressional party. An early demonstration of the House Democratic caucus's capacity to punish dissident members came in 1965, when the DSG organized a successful campaign to strip the seniority of congressmen John Bell Williams of Mississippi and Albert Watson of South Carolina for their support of Goldwater in the recent presidential election. The DSG, referencing the MFDP delegate challenge the previous year, argued that stripping Williams's and Watson's privileges would reaffirm "the sound and historic role of the caucus in the achievement of party responsibility."[107] Four years later, the DSG persuaded the caucus to strip the seniority of Louisiana's John Rarick, a founding supporter of George Wallace's 1968 campaign.[108]

But such actions were sporadic and targeted rather than systemic. At the mid-1960s high tide of Great Society legislative productivity, the concern for procedural reform had been tempered by the evident capacity of Lyndon Johnson and liberal congressional majorities to break through institutional logjams. This capacity proved fleeting, however, largely stalling after Democrats' 1966 midterm losses. As reformers began sweeping efforts at presidential nomination reforms late in the decade, the executive leadership within the DSG coalesced around a new strategy to reform the congressional party, focusing on party procedures and the committee system. In December 1968 Don Fraser suggested that the DSG should lobby to achieve, as a matter of party policy, an up-or-down secret ballot vote in the Democratic caucus for all committee chairmanships at the start of each new Congress.[109] His approach won unanimous support from his colleagues.

The DSG's campaign began with a successful effort in 1969 to pass a new rule requiring caucus ratification of the Committee on Committees' nominations before they proceeded to a full House floor vote. (The Committee on Committees consisted of the Democratic members of the Ways and Means Committee, and controlled committee appointments for the caucus.) The same year, the caucus also reinstated the practice of holding regular monthly meetings. Under Fraser's chairmanship, the DSG ramped up its communications and lobbying capacities and released two major reports related to seniority and the committee system. The first compiled data on key votes in 1967 and 1968. Over a third of all Democratic committee and subcommittee chairmen were found to have voted against the majority of their party more often than with it. Thirty-four exceeded the *Republicans'* overall record of voting with the Democrats. The second report laid out the stakes of the fight over seniority, articulating critics' charges that it "fragmented and diffused power in the House, thereby crippling effective leadership and making it impossible to present and pursue a coherent national program." Congressional liberals grew increasingly open in attacking "the dead hand of seniority," as one member put it. "Even societies that worship their ancestors," Al Lowenstein quipped, "don't automatically put their ancestors in charge of the Armed Services Committee."[110]

A political dynamic familiar to veterans of the Eisenhower years aided the reform push. Once again, the ascension of a Republican president—this time Richard Nixon—soon led to liberal criticisms that the Democratic congressional leadership and committee chairs were failing to offer effective opposition. A DSG-proposed resolution noted in 1969 that "although we Democrats are in control of both Houses of Congress as a result of last year's elections, we have no overall legislative program, and seemingly no prospect of developing one." The resolution called on all House committee chairmen to review the 1968 party platform and develop a plan to bring its provisions to the floor in legislative form.[111] Though the resolution failed by caucus vote, increasing numbers shared its critique. Speaker John McCormack, seventy-eight at the start of Nixon's presidency and noted for his passive leadership style and deference to committee barons, came in for particular criticism for enabling the conservative coalition and resisting reform.[112]

Just as party leaders during and after the 1968 Democratic convention had sought to appease insurgents by appointing a commission to study future nominating reforms, so did Speaker McCormack and Majority Leader Carl Albert agree in 1970, at the DSG's suggestion, to appoint a Democratic Organization, Study, and Review Committee as a means of tempering their critics.[113] This committee's output proved modest but consequential. It recommended allowing the caucus to vote up or down on specific chairmanship nominations made by the Committee on Committees if at least ten members made the request. The proposal also noted that seniority need not be the only criterion used in selecting chairmen. The Democratic Caucus's adoption of these recommendations at the beginning of the 92nd Congress in 1971 marked a fundamental break with party practices that had helped to structure House lawmaking for the previous several decades. At least as a matter of formal procedure, committee assignments were now subject to the sanction of the Democratic caucus.

The mere existence of formal powers hardly guaranteed they would be utilized in ways antagonistic to congressional elites, however. To do that, reformers depended on a major mobilization of outside advocacy and pressure in the early 1970s, carried out by many of the same organizations and activist networks pushing the McGovern-Fraser reforms. These included ADA, which began in 1970 to give congressional reform "the highest possible priority," in the words of its chairman.[114] The same year, Common Cause initiated intensive lobbying efforts related to congressional reform. It organized letter-writing campaigns challenging the seniority privileges of specific House members as well as advocating system-wide reforms.[115] In January of 1971 it advocated that the Democratic caucus strip the chairmanships of three southerners known for both conservatism and autocratic leadership styles: William Colmer of the Rules Committee, W. R. Poage of the Agriculture Committee, and John McMillan of the District of Columbia Committee.[116] Letter-writing campaigns generated thousands of constituent messages urging Democrats to block those three chairmen's renomination.[117] All three survived, but the precedent of open votes on senior chairmen had been set.

A broader network of groups coalesced in 1972 as the Committee on Congressional Reform, representing over forty member organizations ranging from ADA and the National Committee for an Effective Congress to the League of Women Voters and the United Methodist Church Board of Christian Concerns.[118] The liberal philanthropist Stewart Mott financed the committee at the same time he was underwriting activism related to party nomination reforms.[119] Common Cause launched a new campaign of electoral pressure called Operation Open Up the System, urging members to submit to congressional candidates a questionnaire covering key reform issues.[120] Such efforts not only helped make reform a salient issue in the 1972 congressional elections, but also popularized a specific *kind* of reform agenda, focused centrally on curbing the power of committee chairs—"the feudal barons of Congress," in John Gardner's words.[121]

The reform network, which consisted mainly of legally nonpartisan organizations, tended not to emphasize explicit responsible party themes concerning discipline, party centralization, or ideological cohesion. Instead, like that of the McGovern-Fraser activists, the discourse surrounding congressional reform was steeped in the New Politics–tinged language of participation and transparency. Generational turnover in Congress and among the lobbyists and advocacy groups in Washington amplified this participatory rhetoric.[122] And several of the reformers' prescriptions did seek to diffuse power and enhance procedural regularity and transparency. In 1970, for example, the DSG and Common Cause alike lobbied to require publishing roll call votes within committees as well as so-called teller votes on legislative amendments in the Committee of the Whole (a device for marking up bills by the full chamber that has lower quorum requirements than official activity on the House floor).[123] They also successfully lobbied for the caucus's passage of a ban on any member chairing more than one subcommittee, which had the effect of spreading chairmanships among lower-ranking members. These reform goals were also supported by a cohort of junior Republicans.[124] Such decentralizing and nonpartisan aspects of the congressional reform movement would color its reputation in later accounts that emphasized reforms' fragmenting effects.[125]

Most of the decentralizing and anti-secrecy reforms that were justified on grounds of participation and transparency, however, also served the substantive and partisan goals of liberal reformers. Unrecorded teller votes in the Committee of the Whole, for example, advantaged senior Democrats who participated disproportionately in the activity of that "committee." Requiring that those votes be recorded reduced such officials' influence over the process, in part by encouraging participation from the party's liberal majority. Limiting members' ability to chair multiple subcommittees, meanwhile, eliminated a widely used tool that committee chairmen had employed to agglomerate power. Expansions of subcommittees' numbers and resources similarly served both to boost rank-and-file participation and to provide the party's middle tier with end-runs around conservative chairmen.

Virtually all key outside reformers were themselves liberals acutely aware of the connection between institutional reform, partisan behavior, and policy outcomes. Even the most avowedly nonpartisan groups endorsed a normative commitment to intraparty majority rule. When Common Cause distributed rankings of committee chairmen in 1975, one of its criteria was conveyed by the question, "Does he use [power] to further the programs and policies favored by the Democratic majority or does he use power to undercut such programs?"[126]

This push for party cohesion and internal majority rule found notable if comparably limited expression in the other chamber of Congress in the early 1970s. The Senate, with its extraordinarily open legislative procedures and limited capacity for centralized control, inevitably encouraged greater individualism than the House ever did, pre- or post-reform. Neither committee chairmen *nor* party leaders in the Senate could aspire to exercise the kind of power over members' behavior that they could within the House. Nevertheless, the outside reform coalition worked with Democratic liberals in the Senate to moderately strengthen the party caucus (known in this chamber as the Conference) and its leadership and to diminish the autonomy of conservative committee chairmen. Majority Leader Mike Mansfield agreed in 1970 to let the Democratic Policy Committee make policy recommendations to the Conference. A year later, he agreed to hold Conference meetings automatically at the request of members and to appoint a committee to study seniority reform.[127]

The incremental movement for party-enhancing reforms proceeded in the wake of the 1972 elections. Retirements, redistricting, and the electoral efforts of the reform coalition all helped to produce a younger and more pro-reform Democratic caucus in both chambers. House Democrats passed a new requirement for automatic votes on all committee chairmanships at the beginning of each new Congress. The year 1973 also saw the establishment of the Democratic Steering and Policy Committee, which would serve as a kind of executive committee for the Democratic caucus, pursuing legislative coordination and making appointment recommendations to the Committee on Committees. The caucus voted to make the Speaker, majority leader, and whip all *ex officio* members of the Committee on Committees. "We have made committee chairmen more accountable to the Democratic Caucus," Fraser summarized to his constituents in March. "We have also moved to strengthen the House leadership and centralize its decision-making capability."[128]

Procedural strikes against the committee barons' power still did not translate into the direct removal of individual chairmen by the caucus, however. The highest number of votes cast in 1973 to remove a sitting chairman was forty-nine against Richard Ichord of the Internal Security (formerly Un-American Activities) Committee, followed by forty-eight against W. R. Poage of the Agriculture Committee.[129] One factor contributing to the caucus's continual reluctance to exercise its newfound powers was progress on the very electoral realignment in the South and elsewhere that reformers sought. The top target for reformers seeking a chairman's scalp in previous Congresses had been South Carolina representative John McMillan of the District of Columbia Committee, but a liberal primary challenge in 1972 removed McMillan from the race. In the general election, a conservative Republican candidate defeated that liberal Democrat, in a preview of the basic partisan and ideological dynamic that would come to define congressional races in the South in later decades.

The breakthrough for reformers came in 1974 when the first congressional elections since the Watergate crisis and Nixon's resignation ushered in an enormous crop of freshman Democrats. Many of these new members, soon termed the "Watergate Babies," had run on congressional reform platforms in coordination with the reform coalition and, in the case of House candidates, with financial support from the DSG. Common Cause had expanded its Open Up the System electoral campaign that year, while the umbrella Committee on Congressional Reform promoted a comprehensive reform package covering issues related to seniority, party leadership, and committee structure.[130] The public atmosphere created by Watergate, the generational replacement underway among members of Congress, and the concerted mobilization of outside advocacy at last gave reformers an opening to enact truly sweeping change.

At its organizational meeting in December of 1974, the numerically expanded and demographically younger House Democratic caucus enacted a new slew of reforms. Two of the boldest provisions directly enhanced the power of the party leadership while indirectly empowering the caucus's liberal majority. First, the caucus voted to give the Speaker the power to appoint all Democratic members of the Rules Committee. Second, the caucus did away entirely with the Committee on Committees, removing the authority over committee appointments from its longstanding home at Ways and Means to the Speaker-dominated Steering and Policy Committee.

A month later, reformers seized the opportunity to make

precedent-setting examples out of key committee barons targeted for ouster. The DSG, Ralph Nader's Congress Watch, and Common Cause had all collaborated on a formal report assessing the record of fourteen House chairmen on rule compliance, fairness, and fealty to caucus wishes.[131] Common Cause distributed the report to congressional Democrats just days before the meeting of the Steering and Policy Committee. Simultaneously, the seventy-five-member freshman caucus flexed its institutional muscle by inviting every committee chairman to meet with it for what many perceived to be implicit auditions to retain their jobs. One longstanding chairman got off on the wrong foot by referring to the freshmen as "boys and girls," while Agriculture Committee chairman W. R. Poage reported encountering hostility from his disproportionately liberal and nonrural interlocutors.[132] Such chairmen found themselves in the unfamiliar position of needing to defend their records and actively campaign to retain their power.[133] Following the meetings with the freshmen, the Steering and Policy Committee voted to oust two chairmen for the first time: Wright Patman of Banking and Wayne Hays of House Administration. Then, at the full caucus meeting the following day, Democrats voted to uphold the Steering Committee's ouster of Patman, narrowly rejected its decision on Hays, and, most stunning of all, also rejected its recommendations to retain Poage and F. Edward Hebert as chairmen.[134] The caucus had exercised its power to oust three sitting chairmen, an unprecedented overturning of longstanding norms and practices.

The response from the reformers' targets mirrored the alarm that party professionals had conveyed in their reactions to McGovern-Fraser, castigating the barbarians at the gate. "Common Cause is running Congress," Hebert declared in February. "Who elected them?"[135] Others made explicit comparisons between the reformers in Congress and McGovernites. As the embattled chairman Richard Ichord declared at a caucus meeting, "what we are doing here is conducting another Miami Convention."[136] One twelve-term incumbent's reaction to the developments constituted his own small contribution to the process of ideological sorting that would soon transform the party system itself. "In the last few days," Oklahoma congressman John Jarman announced in January, "I have seen the caucus taken over by some of the same elements which took the party over in 1972." To Jarman, their intent was clear: "to do everything possible to force their liberal views on this Congress and on this country by nullifying the seniority system and punishing those who do not adhere to the liberal party line." Refusing "to serve under this kind of party control," Jarman announced his intention to switch to the GOP. House Minority Leader John Rhodes applauded Jarman's move, and reflected on reform's implications for realignment. "For many years it has been speculated that moderate and conservative Democrats might find sufficient justification to cross party lines," he said. Seniority perks had long posed a "roadblock in this scenario," but the reforms now removed the "incentive for many Democrats to maintain their affiliation with a party whose general philosophy is not reflective of their views."[137]

The same reformist surge rocking the House after the 1974 elections did not fail to affect the Senate. That chamber's Democratic Steering Committee appointed several new liberals to key committees while blocking the return of segregationist James Allen to Judiciary. The Democratic Conference also passed a rule requiring automatic secret-ballot votes on all committee chairmen at the beginning of each Congress.[138] Senate liberals also launched a new campaign against a longstanding target of responsible party reformers: the filibuster. For nearly three decades, activists had sought to change the requirements for cloture, arguing that the threshold of two-thirds of the chamber needed to break a filibuster mocked majority rule and empowered conservatives. Newer reform advocates in the early 1970s, led by Common Cause, endorsed cloture reform.[139] The 1974 election results combined with the ascension of liberal Republican Nelson Rockefeller to the vice presidency (the presiding officer of the Senate) to provide a window of opportunity. In January 1975 the Senate voted to lower the threshold for invoking cloture from two-thirds to three-fifths of the chamber, marking only the third time in the twentieth century that the chamber had managed to modify its most potent countermajoritarian procedure.

When the dust settled in early 1975 following the tumultuous organizational meetings of House Democrats and the hard-fought achievement of a modest reform of the Senate filibuster, only the startling extent of the reformers' victories was evident. A vision of just how policymaking might change for the long term in the wake of those victories was still far from clear. The beginning of the 94th Congress would prove the highwater mark for deliberate institutional change there. Occurring just after Democrats' ratification of a party charter, it might also be said to have marked the beginning of the end of the Age of Party Reform that had, starting in 1968, seen so many elements of the party system transformed.

FROM DISARRAY TO CENTRALIZATION

It was not merely the impetus toward further institutional reform that dissipated quickly in the mid-1970s. Optimism over the consequences of the new reforms seemed to vanish just as fast. Invocations of reform's unintended consequences soon became a rote accompaniment to ceaseless commentary on political fracture and party decline. This focus on political disarray had multiple causes. On one hand, the later 1970s saw developments that exacerbated the fragmentation and paralysis in the political system. Stagflation presented novel, seemingly intractable policy dilemmas. Successive presidents working in rocky terrain weakened their position by setting priorities at odds with key allies. More subtly, tectonic shifts of party allegiance among various voter blocs intensified the impression of disarray. On the other hand, party reforms themselves did produce some initially decentralizing effects. The number of primary systems proliferated, for example, as states found them to be cheaper and logistically easier to establish in conformity with the new guidelines than conventions or caucuses.[140] Since primaries were the most direct, unmediated system of delegate selection, their rise to predominance meant a relative marginalization of formal party organizations in favor of campaign armies amassed by individual office-seekers. This occasioned an explosion of commentary on the rise of "candidate-centered" politics. The commentary also encompassed members of Congress, for whom reforms had created new opportunities for individualistic behavior thanks to transparency rules and the proliferation of subcommittees.[141]

On both fronts, a critical literature on reform emerged quickly. The first influential work on presidential nominating reform came from political scientists within the orbit of the CDM, most notably Jeane Kirkpatrick and the regretful McGovern-Fraser veteran, Austin Ranney. They were soon joined by a panoply of centrist and neoconservative scholars, including Everett Carll Ladd, James Ceasar, Nelson Polsby, and Polsby's doctoral student Byron Shafer.[142] To these critics, reform was not merely an antiparty, neo-Progressive venture. It was also a mechanism for transferring power from party professionals and traditional constituency leaders—cast now as representative stewards of group interests rather than out-of-touch bosses and hacks—to a new group. In 1977 DNC testimony, Kirkpatrick termed reform's benefactors "a verbalist elite" holding "a much greater interest in what might be called style and symbol issues, ideological issues . . . environmentalism and foreign policy and so forth, and much less interest in the bread and butter questions." Alarm over this ideological coloring compelled critics to make arguments similar to those lodged against responsible party doctrine. Noting that delegates in 1972 were distinguished "by their zeal," O'Hara argued that reform produced "a system that was open to capture by an aroused minority." Lost were "the views of the non-participating Democrats, the casual Democrats . . . whose support we need in November."[143]

Concern over the reforms was not limited to centrist and neoconservative critics, however. Some of the most devoted proponents of responsible party doctrine worked throughout the later 1970s to organize a collective response to developments in party politics. Starting with informal correspondence led by James MacGregor Burns in 1975, these scholars eventually organized themselves as the Committee on Party Renewal. In roundtables at APSA meetings and testimony before party commissions, members generally endorsed the participatory thrust of the McGovern-Fraser reforms and directed their concerns instead at fragmenting developments like the proliferation of primaries.[144] They advocated measures to strengthen the national party organizations and bolster issue-based party activism while protecting intraparty democracy. But they were hardly confident about the prospects of achieving such goals.

At the same time that fragmentation seemed to dominate party politics, however, moves to shore up and strengthen the parties commenced. Some of these developments stemmed directly from changes made by party organizations. The next two DNC reform panels to form after the McGovern-Fraser, Mikulski, and Charter commissions took as their goals a modest curbing of their predecessors' participatory reforms and a restoration of the role of elected officials. In 1978 the Commission on Presidential Nomination and Party Structure called for "add-on" ex-officio delegates numbering 10 percent of each state's delegation.[145] Four years later, a new Commission on Presidential Nomination expanded that concept with the introduction of so-called superdelegates to Democratic conventions—several hundred unpledged delegate slots reserved for public and party officials.[146] The easing of factional tensions reduced opposition to such proposals. In a self-reinforcing process, increasing party cohesion enabled the adoption of reforms to empower majorities and curb dissidents.

That dynamic would be far more forcefully, if less visibly, manifested in the *informal* ways that engaged activists, politicians, and interests came to coordinate nomination races after the 1970s. In 1975 Fraser had lamented the proliferation of primaries and speculated on what the most feasible way might be to produce some degree of stability without jettisoning voter participation. What might work, he said, would be to treat the primaries as "the one place down the track for the public to intervene in the process. Then we could try to move one step earlier to get some kind of ad hoc or informal coalitions across the country which can try to reach an agreement on one or two or three candidates."[147] Something resembling that very system emerged by decade's end. Party actors would now seek through meetings, endorsements, and informal agreements to coalesce behind acceptable candidates prior to the race's public phase—a process labeled the "invisible primary."[148] Increasing ideological cohesion within the parties enhanced the ease and effectiveness of this coordination.

The same gradual move from fragmentation to centralization commenced in Congress by the later 1970s. As with the nominating process, the first wave of commentary on the transformed Congress emphasized the unintended consequences of reforms that dispersed power.[149] "On many days," a reporter wrote, "Congress has all the earmarks of a Southern state legislature where, in the absence of party influence, a new coalition has to be put together for every roll-call."[150] The southern comparison was ironic, since the transformation of that region proved so central to the revival of congressional party discipline. Conservative southern Democrats were increasingly replaced by conservative Republicans, moderate Democrats representing biracial coalitions, or liberal Democrats in largely African American districts. Remaining conservative Democrats began to liberalize their own voting, a result of electoral trends and new incentives for party loyalty brought by reform.[151]

Growing ideological cohesion was not only an effect of reform. It also helped compel party leaders to use reform's centralizing tools more aggressively, as increasingly likeminded partisans became inclined to allow leaders to exercise coordinating and agenda-setting power.[152] Beginning with Tip O'Neill's Speakership in 1977, Democratic leaders flexed the institutional muscles afforded by reform. They expanded the whip system and used the Steering and Policy and Rules committees to set the legislative agenda, and had Party Task Forces handle initiatives across multiple committee jurisdictions.[153] The combination of ideological sorting and tighter control by party leaders led to a rebound in voting cohesion in the late 1970s that continues to this day.

Leaders in the Age of Party Reform shared two responsible party goals: programmatic politics and party nationalization. They were well aware that achieving them would catalyze the ideological realignment of the two parties. In the initial wake of reform, many political observers grew more pessimistic, fearing that the institutional disruptions caused by reform might not be alleviated. "What would take the place of parties?" the Committee on Party Renewal asked in 1977. "A politics of celebrities, of excessive media influence, of political fad-of-the-month clubs . . . of heightened interest in 'personalities' and lowered interest in policy."[154] The logic of ideological partisanship is what kept this vision from coming to pass—at least for several more decades. Far from being either issueless or partyless, politics in the post-reform era became increasingly partisan as a result of being increasingly ideological. Democrat-authored reforms were hardly the only driver of this process. But institutional changes did matter, and not only in ways *un*intended by their architects.

6

THE MAKING OF A VANGUARD PARTY, 1969–1980

To understand what happened to the Republican Party in the 1970s, ponder for a moment a realignment that might have been. Past figures as disparate as Franklin Roosevelt, Karl Mundt, and Paul Butler had each discovered that the task of remapping American parties along ideological lines was difficult to achieve in a top-down manner. But that did not stop several aides of Richard Nixon as well as House leaders from pursuing one more bid for an instant realignment of the congressional parties, in 1972 and early 1973.

Gerald Ford, the House minority leader, called the gambit "Operation Switch Over." Early in the summer of 1972, he sensed that George McGovern's impending presidential nomination provided the best opportunity yet to make an argument to the remaining southern Democratic congressional barons—conservatives like Joe Waggonner, George Smathers, and Jamie Whitten—that their party was truly lost to them.[1] He sought to convince a sufficient number to switch parties en masse for control of the House to shift to the GOP. Nixon, however, discouraged Ford's pursuit of this plan until after the November elections, calculating that his personal electoral majority would be maximized by the symbolism of *bi*partisan support.

A new effort proceeded in the winter following Nixon's landslide victory. Vice President Spiro Agnew publicly exhorted southern audiences to switch their party allegiance from Democratic to Republican, describing modern Democratic Party as a crew of "exotics, elitists, and philosophical abstractionists" whose new chairman had just "read George Wallace and John Connally out

'It became necessary to destroy the party to save it'

FIGURE 6. Paul Conrad, *Los Angeles Times*, May 4, 1976. Used by permission of the Conrad estate.

of the party."[2] Simultaneously, backdoor talks took place between southern Democrats and Ford and Nixon aides, with Waggoner serving as a liaison. Nixon's lack of down-ticket coattails in the 1972 election, however, meant that the Democrats' majority did not shrink sufficiently to enable willing switchers to give the GOP control of the House.[3] Scattered reports claim that, during the wintertime negotiations, upwards of thirty-five Democrats contemplated switching, though other sources put the realistic number at half that.[4] Whatever the count, discussion of a mass conversion ground to a halt in March, as the Senate Select Committee on Presidential Campaign Activities began its Watergate investigation.

The fact that, at such a late date as 1972—a moment of maximal Republican electoral dominance at the presidential level—senior southern Democrats still either could or would not coordinate a mass conversion owed to a mix of personal and institutional factors. The inertia borne of career-long affiliation to the party of Dixie affected not only officeholders but many of their constituents, who would continue to vote Democratic in down-ballot races for years to come. The institutional perquisites of seniority also mattered, and Ford encountered stiff resistance from GOP colleagues to the notion of transferring the converts' seniority in the event of a switch. Nevertheless, the evident effort put into orchestrating this congressional realignment lends it at least a modicum of plausibility in spite of its failure. It poses a counterfactual that helps set into relief the nature of important changes that the GOP underwent in subsequent years.

"Operation Switch Over" was of a piece with the vision of partisan realignment that animated Nixon's presidency and shaped his most ambitious political efforts.[5] Such efforts—some implemented, others merely discussed—included the administration's attempts to nationalize the 1970 midterm elections around a backlash against social unrest; its intensive courting of southern Democrats like Virginia's Harry Byrd; and Nixon's grooming of the ex-Democrat John Connally of Texas as his heir apparent, who would head a Republican Party reconstructed, and perhaps even renamed, as a result of Nixon's transformative leadership.[6] All of these efforts revolved around a particular conception of the party system's changing electoral landscape and issue terrain. Nixon sought a new partisan alignment, oriented around "the Social Issue" rather than economics, that might usher in a New American Majority backing a particular kind of culturally oriented conservatism. This conservatism rejected the libertarian antistatism of Goldwater and would prove, in power, able to accommodate wage and price controls, turbo-charged Keynesianism, Social Security expansion, and a proposed guaranteed income. Realignment theory bolstered the idea among Nixon strategists that a sociocultural issue dimension would displace rather than augment the economic one as the basis for partisan conflict.[7] The wooing of southern officeholders through Operation Switch Over and of Wallace populists in the electorate fit a plan to construct a party alignment largely around racialized social issues, cultural "permissiveness," and foreign policy.

To imagine Operation Switch Over succeeding in 1973 is to imagine a trajectory for American conservatism and party politics different from that which eventually occurred. The aging Democrats targeted for conversion certainly held conservative positions on issues ranging from labor to civil rights to foreign affairs. But they were not shaped by a conservative intellectual and institutional milieu that was only beginning to form as of 1973, one that included congressional caucuses, think tanks, and advocacy organizations, and was defined by ideologically driven partisanship and a movement orientation. These Democrats were in fact the last master practitioners of committed *bi*partisanship in American politics, and of an instrumental kind of partisan maneuvering to maintain the South's clout within the system. The question of whether Nixon's New American Majority would have taken political root had not Watergate destroyed his presidency is speculative. What matters is that the actual post-Watergate trajectory of both GOP and conservative politics differed from his vision in key ways.

The years following Watergate saw experimentation in conservatives' approach to partisan politics, featuring arguments about the potential viability of a third party and the proper relationship between issues and partisanship. Ronald Reagan's primary challenge to Ford in 1976 signaled a new strategic convergence on pursuing ideological activism through the GOP. Conservatives built new organizations within and around the party and took advantage of changing institutional contexts to maximize their leverage. Their efforts gained momentum during the Carter years, thanks partly to ideological business mobilization and an influx of "amateur" activism from the Christian Right. The result by decade's end was a reconfiguration of the GOP agenda, in which moderate elements on both social and economic issues were marginalized and the "fusionism" of the modern Right became the programmatic core of the party. In this reconfiguration, contrary to realignment theorists' predictions, party divides on cultural issues *supplemented* rather than supplanted those on economic and welfare state issues.

In the explosion of historical literature on postwar American conservatism and, in particular, the Right's mobilizations during the 1970s, the partisan context of that movement-building has often been underemphasized. This is in keeping with contemporary commentary during that decade that cast ideological politics as symptomatic of system-wide party decline. But analyzing the conservative movement as a kind of partisan project helps to bring the Right into a broader story of party development, one it shared with liberal activists and reformers who also sought to forge a more ideologically sorted, issue-based system. Conservative actors and political elites made some of the same responsible party arguments as liberal reformers—against "unprincipled," transactional partisan organizations, in favor of issue politics and programmatically distinct parties. They also took advantage of the very institutional reforms that were rendering the party system more permeable to activist influence. That new institutional context and the coalitional efforts made by conservative activists in turn help explain why the party polarization that began at the elite level in the 1970s occurred along multiple issue dimensions at once.[8]

From the 1970s onward, conservatives within the GOP would occupy the vanguard of efforts to inscribe a firmer line of ideological division into the party system, to marry partisan team spirit to substantive and philosophical zeal in pursuit of a politics of permanent combat. The congressional realignment of the white South that Operation Switch Over had symbolized would eventually occur, though its unfolding spanned decades rather than months. But the southern Republicans who eventually came to power would operate differently from their Dixiecrat predecessors— conservative across more dimensions of policy, more steeped in the ethos of a well-defined national conservative movement, and far more partisan in orientation. The conservative story of the Ford

and Carter years is the story of how that combination of characteristics came to predominate within the GOP and, in so doing,
changed American politics.

CONSERVATIVE REVOLT AND THE NEW-PARTY PATH

Gerald Ford had been president of the United States for all of two
weeks when he began receiving warnings of the collapse of conservative Republican support. "There is a mini-revolt among congressional conservatives over some of the week's activities," legislative
aide William Timmons wrote him on August 22, 1974.[9] Those activities, which had taken on symbolic significance as the new president's first, tone-setting batch of directives, included a new policy
regarding clemency for Vietnam War draft evaders, Ford's reaffirmation of support for the Equal Rights Amendment (ERA), and
Nelson Rockefeller's nomination as vice president.[10] "The House
funny-farm rumors are that you will come out soon for busing, gun
control, and abortion," Timmons reported. To calm right-wing
nerves, he recommended holding meetings with both chambers'
conservative-dominated Republican steering committees: "If you
approve, we'll prepare some conservative issues to discuss at these
meetings." Ford did not approve, checking off the "Do Not Schedule" option at the bottom of the memo.

That checkmark well captured both the new administration's
disposition toward movement conservatives and the latter's marginal position in national politics as of 1974. Ford's presidency,
borne of crisis and forced into a harried midstream transition,
lacked the kind of overarching agenda that typically emerges out
of a campaign and lengthy preparation for office. In a climate of
crisis management, with national reconciliation and reassurance
the basic orienting goals, Ford's team drifted in the direction of
prevailing policy currents. In 1974 that direction ran toward the
Center and away from the Right. Most decisions made during the
early months of the administration reflected an inclination to shore
up Ford's left flank.

This inclination revealed the degree to which conservatives

lacked intraparty leverage after years serving as fitful junior partners to Nixon. The weakness was evident, for example, in the ad-
ministration deliberations regarding Ford's vice-presidential pick.
It was not surprising that his moderate aide Bob Hartmann thought
it wise to choose Rockefeller as a genuflection to the party's moderate wing.[11] More striking was the fact that Pat Buchanan, the old
Nixon staff's token hard-right voice, echoed the recommendation.
"If I were speaking of the President's interest alone," he wrote
Ford, "regrettably, Rockefeller is the one." Picking Reagan or Barry
Goldwater would "cause a mighty rupture in the liberal establishment and tear up the pea patch with the national press corps"—and
that establishment was something Buchanan evidently considered
a force that still required accommodation.[12] Similarly, Ford's new
policy for Vietnam draft evaders was conceived as a conciliatory
gesture, a break from Nixon-era divisions, with little thought given
to a conservative backlash.[13]

But the dam of conservative frustration, which had strained
against Nixon's ideological transgressions, burst in the wake of his
fall, with the newcomer to the presidency immediately becoming
the target of factional dissent. The swiftness of the "mini-revolt"
that Timmons noted was striking. Tennessee Senator Bill Brock
remarked that his constituent calls and wires were "running 50-1
against [Rockefeller] already." Idaho's reliably blunt Jim McClure
asked, "How many times do you have to kick a guy in the groin before you let up?"[14] Conservative grumbling from the Senate cloak-
room soon turned into public criticism and streams of mail from
GOP voters and officials. Looking to the midterm elections, Georgia congressman Ben Blackburn warned Ford that he threatened to
"force many of our Republican candidates into a 'me too' posture
when in confrontation with a liberal Democratic opposition."[15]

This latest round of conservative grousing about me too-ism
helped inspired a new era of activism. The Ford years would mark a
productive and experimental period for conservatives who sought
a new, closer alignment of party and principle and who perceived
in the tangled thicket of public opinion, demographics, and changing institutions an increasingly hospitable environment for such
a project. That experimentation entailed a quixotic inquiry into

third-party politics and, eventually, a direct intraparty challenge to the president.

Prior to Ford's ascension to the White House, during the stormy endgame of Nixon's presidency, some conservatives were already envisioning the eventual transformation, if not outright replacement, of the Republican Party. For most of them, such a possibility stemmed less from the short-term Watergate crisis than from long-term political changes to which the GOP had proven institutionally incapable of responding. Clif White, for example, speculated in January 1974 to *National Review*'s publisher William Rusher and editor William F. Buckley about the coming breakup of the GOP and "the development of a new political grouping after 1976."[16] That new grouping would likely still be the coalition of Republicans and Wallace Democrats, aligned around the Social Issue. But with Watergate having cut short Nixon's fitful efforts to forge a new majority, and with public identification with the Republican Party at an all-time low, it was increasingly possible to imagine the coalition taking a different form and name.

A few months later, at a dinner honoring conservative movement hero Clarence Manion, North Carolina senator Jesse Helms gave a speech suggesting just such a possibility.[17] His argument deftly rendered Watergate a symptom of a different, deeper-seated malady—namely, the American party system's anachronistic ideological incoherence. Helms asked his audience, "Could it be that it is time to forge new political parties, fashioned along the lines that the people are thinking, not along the existing lines of political power-seeking? If we are going to have honesty in government today, we must have honesty in the basic philosophies of our political parties." "Honesty" recurred throughout Helms's call for realignment, which rendered Watergate an apotheosis of the grubby, "power-seeking" default mode of American politics. The party system "must give an honest choice, and it must furnish the mechanism for politicians to carry out honestly the principles they set before the people." For now, though, Americans remained "locked into two major political parties by geography, by tradition, by sentiment," in an outdated alignment that obscured rather than facilitated the expression of philosophical disagreement. A

formal project of ideological party-building could ameliorate public disillusionment and cynicism. Helms, a television commentator
turned politician whose well-earned reputation for scabrous hard-
ball masked a serious intellectual engagement with American political history, made sure in his speech to tip his hat to the conservative pioneer of realignment arguments, Karl Mundt. Like Mundt,
Helms was equivocal about whether this realignment should involve the existing parties or new entities with new names. "I intend
to remain a Republican," he said, "unless there is a general realignment into Conservative and Liberal parties, by whatever names."

That Helms would be the one to emphasize this distinction
between party and principle was fitting, since, as a recent party-
switching southerner, he embodied the core transformation on
which realignment hinged. Indeed, the North Carolina scene in
which Helms won election to the Senate in 1972 was a cauldron
of shifting alliances and incipient sorting—American polarization
writ small. That election warrants attention for dynamics therein
that proved prophetic.

Both of North Carolina's parties in 1972 were riven by internal
divisions and transforming rapidly. Helms had anticipated challenging the conservative elder statesman Everett Jordan that year,
but in the Democratic primary Jordan fell to a moderately liberal,
pro-civil rights challenger, Nick Galifinakis, thanks to the support
of African American and younger voters. As for the Republicans,
Helm's campaign kickstarted a protracted effort by conservatives
to wrest control of the state GOP machinery from a party establishment led by moderate governor Jim Holshouser. The governor's
faction, based in the historical strongholds of Republicanism in the
state's western mountain and Piedmont regions, was a vigorous but
largely nonideological network of party professionals tied together
by patronage and tradition rather than national issues. Helms's
base of support skewed east, was overwhelmingly conservative,
and included a large number of Democrats disaffected by the very
forces of partisan change enabling someone like Nick Galifinakis
to defeat someone like Everett Jordan.[18] Thus the general election
contest in 1972 pit a staunchly conservative Republican against a
liberal Democrat, an alignment that had only occasional precedent

in the state but whose logic would become increasingly obvious in decades to come.

Helms's come-from-behind victory over Galifinakis that November had several sources. He employed brutally negative, race-laden campaign tactics. Numerous Democratic officials in the state crossed lines to support Helms, a dynamic exacerbated by the unpopularity of George McGovern at the top of the ticket. Most significant was the nature of the Helms campaign itself. Run by a visionary attorney named Tom Ellis, Helms's operation was manned by movement activists recruited out of Young Americans for Freedom (YAF) and College Republicans. Helms and Ellis brought in nationally known conservative consultants like Clif White and managed to outraise Galifinakis 4-to-1. They spent the largesse on a sophisticated television and radio campaign tying the Democrat to his national party and its beleaguered presidential candidate.[19]

What Helms and Ellis did with their operation after the election proved to have lasting national implications. Ellis started the North Carolina Congressional Club as a fundraising committee to pay down Helms's campaign debt. Soon, the membership-based club expanded its operations to dinner events featuring conservative speakers as well as pathbreaking direct-mail efforts carried out by Richard Viguerie that brought in out-of-state revenue. Over the course of the decade, the North Carolina Congressional Club turned into the National Congressional Club, one of the most powerful ideological political action committees (PACs) in the country. The club would recruit and fund conservative candidates for office in elections nationwide, in the process building computer files of donor lists to be utilized by other conservative organizations.[20]

What Helms sought to advance in his 1974 Manion speech was a nationalized version of the politics he had helped bring to North Carolina. It was a system in which ideological activism, rather than the transactional, "power-seeking" politics epitomized by Holshouser's faction, undergirded partisan campaigns. It was a politics that emphasized sophisticated media appeals and direct mail over the pragmatic precinct work of older party organizations. It was an approach colored by a slash-and-burn, polarizing style of attack precisely *because* the binary lines of ideological conflict would align so closely with the partisan lines of campaigns. For conservative activists seething at the timidity of Republican officeholders, Helms's vision resonated powerfully. A few began working with Helms to explore options for realizing it.

One participant, *National Review*'s William Rusher, had less trouble than most writing off the GOP and contemplating an effort to replace it.[21] Helms's speech, coming soon after Rusher's discussion with Buckley and Clif White about the prospects for new party formations, inspired Rusher to write about the subject in his syndicated column and to find allies among newly disillusioned leaders in institutions like YAF and the American Conservative Union (ACU).[22] The awesome Republican electoral defeats in 1974—forty-three House seats, six Senate seats, fifteen statehouses, six governorships—further emboldened conservatives to conceive of a final break with the decrepit party. At a board meeting in December, the ACU initiated plans to explore state-by-state technical considerations for building a new party. In an indication of the coalition this new formation was to embody, ACU president M. Stanton Evans agreed to reach out to George Wallace "to discuss political cooperation with his constituency and organization."[23] Meanwhile, Rusher drafted a book-length manifesto for the project.

The Making of the New Majority Party, hurried into publication in the spring of 1975, hinged its case on a talismanic statistical ratio and a tantalizing historical analogy. The ratio was 60-40. Since the 1930s Gallup had occasionally surveyed Americans about party realignment, asking which side they would prefer if the two-party system rearranged itself into ideologically sorted conservative and liberal parties. Rusher opened his book by pointing to the Gallup result of spring 1974, which found that 26 percent of respondents chose the liberal party, 38 percent chose the conservative party, and 36 percent were undecided.[24] By either ignoring the undecided block or splitting it by the same proportions as the affirmative answers, Rusher concluded that "59 percent of the American people considered themselves 'conservative' and only 41 percent 'liberal.'" This rough 60-40 conservative-liberal split had arguably been approximated in both the 1968 and 1972 presidential re-sults. In the former, 57 percent voted for either Nixon or Wallace versus 43 percent for Humphrey; in the latter, 61 percent voted for Nixon versus 38 percent for McGovern. This was the ideological alignment that Rusher claimed now defined American politics, awaiting conservatives' achievement of a new partisan apparatus to take advantage of it. The conservative majority combined tra-ditional GOP economic conservatives with Wallacite populists. But the Social Issue's congeries of cultural conflicts provided the main line of cleavage, pitting, in Rusher's conception, producers of all stripes ("businessmen, manufacturers, hard-hats, blue-collar workers and farmers") against the anticapitalist coalition of edu-cated liberal elites and welfare constituencies.[25]

The historical analogy, which would pop up constantly during the next two years in journalistic discussions of the GOP's fate, reached back to the mid-nineteenth century. The modern Republi-can Party, so the argument went, was experiencing the same de-composition that befell the very Whig Party it had supplanted in the 1850s.[26] The Whigs' depleting leadership and organization, built around a cross-sectional agenda, proved incapable of sur-viving the onset of slavery as a primary political issue, and thus it found itself preempted and swiftly replaced by a fledgling party organized for the antislavery cause. Rusher argued that the mod-ern GOP faced the same imminent fate. His proposed new group-ing, organized around the Social Issue, would not be a minor third party but rather a new major one, swiftly replacing the GOP up and down its ranks and representing a broad-based political coali-tion. Indeed, Rusher's argument was not quite a case for consistent ideological conservatism in a new party vessel. He endorsed the classic scholarly critiques of responsible party theory and stressed that a coalition with the Wallacite Democratic tendency would necessarily mean accommodating a greater degree of statism than conservative orthodoxy normally allowed.

Why could the Republican Party not be transformed from within, through the absorption of the social conservative impulse? Rusher conceded that this was the normal course of American party poli-tics and the most desirable possibility, but he saw both immedi-

ate and longer-term obstacles to conservatives' changing and uti-
lizing the GOP. The immediate problem was the post-Watergate
trough of party strength and popularity. Gallup polls showed public
identification with the GOP vacillating between a fifth and a quarter of the population.[27] Meanwhile, "the leadership and organization of the Republican party are today at an all-time low. In state
after state it scarcely exists at all." But even this organizational de-
composition was less a temporary result of Watergate than a byproduct of the key longer-term problem—"the party's essential
meaninglessness. No one can effectively lead or even work for the
Republican party today, because no one can possibly say what it
stands for." The structural source of that incoherence was the in-
extinguishable presence of a "liberal-Republican minority whose
only real function is to prevent any effective coalition with formerly
Democratic social conservatives." Though conservatives outnumbered liberals two-to-one among party convention delegates and
enjoyed majorities in the congressional caucuses, Rusher saw the
minority bloc as "ineradicable" and permanently capable of compelling programmatic adjustment in the wrong direction.[28]

The book's argument became ubiquitous among conservatives
in Rusher's orbit. The second Conservative Political Action Conference (CPAC), jointly sponsored by YAF and the ACU in 1975,
showcased the new party project. Congressman and ACU official
Bob Bauman cited the Gallup poll on conservative-party support
in his speech, likening it to election outcomes in 1968 and 1972.[29]
Senator James Buckley advocated a "philosophy of political alternatives . . . Republicanism of the kind that accepts, in the name of
moderation, half the Liberal Democratic program holds no appeal
to those Conservative-minded independents and Democrats who
were essential to the victorious Presidential election in 1972."[30]
Buckley refrained from endorsing the new-majority party project,
but advocated that it be wielded as a threat to compel GOP mili-
tancy.

As for the man who had introduced the idea the previous year,
Jesse Helms now added an important new line of analysis in his
own CPAC speech.[31] Though he still invoked the Whigs, Helms no
longer made a straightforward case for coalition based on realign-

ment theory and historical analogy. Instead, he saw in the contemporary scene a historically novel departure from how American parties formerly operated, and used it to herald "the realignment of political action into philosophically consistent parties." American parties had traditionally been based on sectional interests, Helms explained, which, given the "homogeneity of the social systems in the various sections," meant that "voters did not have to think about issues very deeply to get a man and a party generally representative of their interests." But when the Great Depression brought economic issues to the fore, Roosevelt used them to mobilize massive support in the North and the West, "combining it with the geographic tradition of the South" to form a powerful coalition. The latter "geographic element in the coalition" began to break down in 1964, however. In the 1960s voters were growing "aware that their personal interests and the interests promoted by politicians were beginning to diverge. People began to get interested in issues." What was historically new, Helms implied, was that *white southerners* began to connect issues and voting. In 1968 "both Nixon and Wallace attracted voters because of their stands on specific issues; the Democratic candidate was a creature of party structure and organization, and that structure could no longer deliver." In the 1972 election "issues emerged as more important than party," said Helms, pointing to a study showing that voters' likelihood to back Nixon increased in proportion to their conservatism. "The party which is based on geographic or social division is dead," he declared. Issue-based politics meant issue-based parties—and thus the parties' ideological sorting-out.

Though Helms marshaled this argument to claim that a specifically conservative majority in the United States was ripe for mobilization, the argument itself resonated with major new findings among political scientists with no such agenda. After the political tumult of the preceding decade, scholars in the 1970s began to challenge the dominant "Michigan School" view of mass political behavior laid out in 1960's *The American Voter*.[32] That study had deemphasized the role of issues and ideology in guiding voters' behavior. The authors identified partisanship, determined by "affective" ties that bore little connection to policy positions, as the overwhelming factor in voter choice. A new view emerging in the early 1970s suggested that the Michigan School's findings reflected the seeming quiescence and ideologically scrambled partisan lines characterizing the 1950s more than any fundamental law of American voting behavior. The *American Political Science Review* published a symposium on the subject of issue voting in 1972, led by Gerald M. Pomper's argument that voters had moved a good deal of the way "from confusion to clarity" during the conflictive sixties.[33] Pomper used survey data to show both a tightening correlation over time between respondents' party affiliation and issue positions as well as their increasing ability to differentiate between the two parties' respective positions. The 1972 McGovern-Nixon contest only served to heighten the salience of issues and ideology in voting, just as Helms would note in his CPAC speech.[34] In 1974 two other scholars reported "major increases in the levels of attitude consistency in the mass public" since the 1950s, with New Deal–vintage issues as well as "new issues as they emerged in the 60s" becoming increasingly "incorporated by the mass public into what now appears to be a broad liberal/conservative ideology."[35]

Seeking a new partisan vehicle for that conservative ideology, CPAC participants authorized the formation of a Committee on Conservative Alternatives (COCA) in 1975 to provide "a formal mechanism to review and assess the current political situation and to develop future opportunities."[36] The fifteen members included Rusher, Evans, New Hampshire governor Meldrim Thomson, Phyllis Schlafly, and George Wallace's aide Eli Howell. Jesse Helms chaired. The language Helms used in a statement following COCA's inaugural meeting sounded themes of alienation and renewal that could easily have come from the McGovern-Fraser Commission. "A time of profound change is upon our nation," Helms intoned, "and old systems of political organization are passing." Helms decried "the American people's headlong slide into alienation from the present system of parties." COCA would explore ways to remedy that alienation, including the option of forming "a major new party if the present political system fails to respond to the need for philosophical realignment."[37] Staffers in Helms's Senate office performed most of the spadework for COCA, including detailed research of state election laws.[38]

Knowledge of ballot line procedures would amount to little without a plausible candidate. Conservatives had no doubt who that should be. Six weeks after stepping down as governor of California, Ronald Reagan delivered a closely watched speech at CPAC.[39] "I don't know about you," he related, "but I am impatient with those Republicans who after the last election rushed into print saying, 'We must broaden the base of our party'—when what they meant was to fuzz up and blur even more the differences between ourselves and our opponents." He coyly raised the subject of the new majority party through a rhetorical question: "Is it a third party we need, or is it a new and revitalized second party, raising a banner of no pale pastels, but bold colors which make it unmistakably clear where we stand on all of the issues troubling the people?" A new party project would sink or swim largely based on Reagan's answer to that question.

Third-party advocates made their case directly and repeatedly to Reagan. Rusher dined at his Pacific Palisades home, a copy of *The Making of the New Majority Party* in hand.[40] Stan Evans followed up with a letter arguing on pragmatic grounds against Reagan's chances as a GOP challenger to Ford, pointing out that the latter's advantage was "unusually large in the heartland of organizational Republicanism—the North Central states." The primary calendar would force Reagan "to run a gauntlet of 'pragmatic' bosses and Republican loyalists of the type who tend . . . to be swayed by arguments about backing-our-President and not dividing the party."[41] A panoply of leaders of the nascent populist "New Right"—Joseph Coors, Richard Viguerie, Paul Weyrich, Howard Phillips—along with Kevin Phillips, Pat Buchanan, and two Wallace aides made one final effort to woo Reagan to a third party at a DC meeting in June 1975.[42] They were all too late. In the previous fall, Reagan had, in fact, considered a third-party run for 1976, but his California financial backers and aides swatted the idea down.[43] Ford's missteps with Republicans bolstered Reagan's confidence that he could topple the president through a nomination challenge. His skepticism of the third party plan in turn fueled conservative reluctance to back it.[44]

Rusher, for his part, felt committed to the project regardless of Reagan's decision. Convinced that Reagan's intraparty effort would fail, he proceeded with a state-by-state plan to ensure that, following this inevitable failure, the ex-governor would have the option of pursuing a third-party candidacy in the general election via ballot lines secured in as many states as possible. Rusher formed the Committee for the New Majority (CNM) in the summer of 1975 with financial support from Viguerie.[45] With Reagan's nascent campaign drawing away mainstream conservatives, however, the pool of available CNM supporters was dominated by a certain type of activist: insular, conspiracy-minded, and extreme. Rusher realized that the route to achieving state-level ballot access lay in merging the CNM project with the network of organizers and entities left over from Wallace's third-party bid in 1968, some of which already had ballot lines in many states. But the activities of that network in the aftermath of Wallace's reentry into Democratic politics had been marked by byzantine infighting.[46] As William F. Buckley warned Rusher, the "situation sounds to me awfully close to the kooks, and I am troubled by it. In the last analysis, if you have to deal with people of that sort, a) you're not going to get anywhere and b) you are simply going to besmirch yourself."[47]

The comic-opera denouement of the CNM effort fulfilled Buckley's prediction. By June 1976 the committee had secured ballot lines in at least thirty states. But, as its executive director reported to the board, "the diverted attention of the Reagan types" jeopardized the prospects of securing a credible candidate for those lines.[48] Reagan's campaign had gained momentum in the spring, leading eventually to a convention that saw Ford win renomination through one of the smallest delegate margins in history. The fact that conservative forces proved so capable of near-victory within the GOP undermined the idea that structural barriers would always prevent activists from ideologizing the party. Meanwhile, the Democrats' nomination of the southern evangelical Jimmy Carter seemed to moot the possibility that 1976 would see a breakthrough for a New American Majority electoral coalition. These factors made Rusher and Viguerie's efforts to recruit a plausible CNM candidate futile. When they traveled to Chicago for the Wallacite American Independent Party convention in August, the best they could propose was a ticket consisting of an ex-congressional staffer and Viguerie himself. The delegates, for their part, revolted against these northern carpetbaggers' machinations and opted instead to nominate the racist ex-governor of Georgia, Lester Maddox. The band played "Dixie," crowds waved "This is Maddox country" signs, the keynote speaker railed against "Atheistic political Zionism"—and Rusher and Viguerie walked out in disgust.[49]

The CNM was the Right's last notable third-party effort in the twentieth century. After the election—in which Maddox garnered 170,531 votes—Rusher decided his "inclination to attempt to cooperate any further with the people who run the American Independent Party approaches zero" and shuttered the CNM.[50] The ACU circulated a strategic working paper after the election that argued against further third-party adventures, emphasizing the clear potential for conservative strengthening within the GOP.[51] In its short life, the CNM revealed a bit about the potentialities of new ideological coalitions in the 1970s and much about the enduring difficulties of challenging the US two-party duopoly. The real action for the rest of the decade would take place inside the GOP.

"NO PALE PASTELS": CHANGING THE REPUBLICAN PARTY FROM WITHIN

Congress provided one locus for this intraparty activity. During the Nixon years, Paul Weyrich, a Wisconsin-raised journalist turned Senate staffer, was a key organizer of congressional conservative opposition. Through these efforts, he also became the Hill liaison for Colorado beer magnate Joe Coors, advising him about worthwhile conservative projects to fund and facilitating contact with relevant parties.[52] Two of the most important Nixon-era initiatives funded by Coors—the advocacy think tank Heritage Foundation and conservatives' answer to the Democratic Study Group, the Republican Study Committee—had reflected the inside-outside advocacy strategy and penchant for aping the Left that would become hallmarks of the Right's institution-building. The focus of Weyrich's energies for the rest of the decade originated in the summer of 1974. Facing the impending disaster of the midterm elections, Jesse Helms and three other officials formed an emergency PAC to protect conservative incumbents. Weyrich headed the outfit and secured Coors's financing. The Committee for the Survival of a Free Congress (CSFC) gave contributions to seventy-one candidates in November, and in the ensuing years Weyrich expanded the operation, in emulation of the liberal National Committee for an Effective Congress, to engage in fundraising, technical support, and candidate recruitment.[53]

Though Weyrich was, like his New Right compatriots Viguerie and Howard Phillips, a reliable font of colorful press quotes heralding the destruction and replacement of the GOP, the CSFC in practice was almost entirely focused on intraparty activism. Weyrich described in a 1975 memo the importance of distinguishing the CSFC from "just another Republican committee," suggesting that "it would help our credibility were we to back a conservative challenger to a liberal Republican."[54] The greater its success at promoting conservative Republicanism, the less necessary any new-party effort would be.

While the practical results of its activity made the New Right's network a largely intra-Republican force, a circle of conservative leaders worked more explicitly to keep political energies channeled through the GOP during the Ford years. In early 1975 Clif White and James Buckley organized the first meeting of twenty-eight conservative luminaries known as "the St. Michael's Group," after the Maryland resort town that hosted them. Attendees included senators and congressmen, leading conservative journalists, GOP officials like Clarke Reed of Mississippi and Karl Rove of Texas, and financiers Coors and Roger Milliken.[55] The opening sessions assessed politics with "an emphasis on the Republican Party—the position of conservatism within it and its viability as a continuing vehicle for the realization of conservative goals."[56] Though new-party advocates like Helms and Rusher made pitches, the majority of the attendees opposed them and steered the group toward intra-

GOP work over the next two years.[57] This included advocacy of an open convention in 1976 as well as explorations of "ways in which conservatives can maximize their influence within the Republican Party organizational structure."[58] Clif White suggested an audit of the existing conservative institutional infrastructure in journalism, policy development, and electoral work.[59] Staffer David Keene, meanwhile, proposed a funded effort to target states in which moderate and liberal Republican National Committee members were stepping down in 1976 and ensure that conservatives replaced them. "If we, as conservatives, are going to argue that the Republican Party is a vehicle through which we can achieve some specific political and policy goals," he told Buckley, "we will have to have some impact at the National Committee level."[60]

Though such stirrings put gradual conservative pressure on the Ford administration, the most important point of ideological leverage over administration behavior remained the threat of a credible nomination challenge. Thus, Ronald Reagan loomed as a specter over the Ford White House to the same extant that he came to dominate the organizational energies of American conservatism in 1975 and 1976. His potential candidacy exerted a meaningful rightward pull on an administration that also faced more than a typical share of political and institutional burdens to its *left*.

Indeed, Ford's essentially untenable political balancing act during his two and a half years in office was a symptom of the partisan flux and institutional transformations that defined the 1970s politically. "President Ford is fighting hard these days to hold the middle ground of American politics," wrote James Reston early in 1975, "but he's getting into serious trouble with the huge Democratic Congressional majorities on the left and with an increasingly critical Republican minority on the right."[61] The economic context—recession coinciding with rising inflation—narrowed his range of options at the same time it guaranteed that his policy priority of inflation-fighting would clash directly with the congressional majority's focus on measures to end the recession. In a fateful early confrontation with the swollen Democratic ranks of the 94th Congress over a deficit-increasing tax cut, one White House aide made the case for vetoing the measure as a way to "make the President somewhat more popular with the right wing of the GOP and other conservatives as well. We have been looking for some broad action that would accomplish this."[62] The impetus to secure compromise and legislative agreement outweighed such considerations, and Ford signed the bill.

The subsequent flood of spending initiatives that emboldened congressional Democrats sent to Ford's desk, however, soon prompted an unprecedented number of presidential vetoes. Given the hand it was dealt, Ford's legislative operation performed well, making deft use of the remaining conservative coalition led by Waggoner to sustain fifty-four of the sixty-six vetoes issued.[63] Still, the exigencies of policymaking in a divided government inevitably caused frustration among conservatives, particularly when veto threats and presidential brinksmanship proved hollow. "He draws one line," a *Human Events* editor complained, "and when Congress steps across, he falls back and draws another. How can we accept that?"[64] Jim McClure led a band of right-wing senators who periodically demanded meetings with Ford to remind him that their support could not be taken for granted. "This is a two-way street," he warned the president.[65]

Reagan's threat gave teeth to such conservative complaints, and over the course of 1975 the administration acted accordingly, shifting rightward.[66] That summer Ford tapped Howard "Bo" Calloway, a conservative Georgian who had bolted the Democratic Party to support Goldwater in 1964, to chair the President Ford Committee for Reelection. The pick reflected the need to reach out to New American Majority constituencies and challenge Reagan in the Sunbelt. More dramatic was the unceremonious dumping of Nelson Rockefeller from the reelection ticket in October 1975, in an obvious sop to conservatives. On the legislative front, meanwhile, Ford followed months of steadily proliferating vetoes with a fall proposal for a dramatic new package of steep federal spending cuts and tax reductions. He then reversed course on a bill that his own labor secretary had drafted permitting the picketing of entire construction projects by unions in dispute with specific contractors—so-called common situs picketing. Conservative activists and a resurgent business lobby blindsided the administration with a lobbying effort against the bill that generated more constituent mail than any other issue in Ford's entire presidency.[67] The blitz, waged through Viguerie's direct-mail efforts, not only demonstrated how little the New Right's self-styled populism actually deviated in practice from conservative economic orthodoxy.[68] It also signaled to Ford another issue that Reagan could use against him. After bluntly telling Labor Secretary John Dunlop, "if I sign the bill I won't get nominated," Ford issued a veto—and Dunlop resigned.[69] "The Gerald Ford of November, 1975," Pat Buchanan concluded, "is a more conservative President than the Gerald Ford of November, 1974."[70] This was unmistakably true, and unmistakably the result of concerted organization and advocacy.

Ford's efforts to shore up his right flank even provoked a threat from the GOP's beleaguered moderates and liberals. In September of 1975 a dozen Republican senators expressed written alarm to Ford about his rightward drift, while one of them, Maryland's Charles Mathias, gave a major speech decrying the Right's effect on the party system.[71] Mathias laid on the rhetoric of party declinism and echoed critics on the left and right in calling for an issue-based politics. But he turned this call into an argument for reversing the exodus of "thoughtful, serious, concerned and moderate women and men" from the GOP due to right-wing ascendance. That winter, Mathias pressed Ford for a meeting while speculating publicly about launching his own primary challenge or third-party presidential bid.[72] Mathias's behavior, which came to naught, reflected the general maladies of liberal Republicanism in the 1970s—a motley collection of individual personalities and uncoordinated gestures of independence.[73] The organization and initiative were all on the right by 1976.

Still, when Mathias warned a Ford aide that "should the Republican Party become a purely conservative party in 1976, the GOP may well lose its very claim to existence," he was offering an idiosyncratic version of an argument echoed by others—one that cast Ronald Reagan's challenge as a symptom of broader party decline.[74] According to this argument, the post-reform proliferation of primaries rendered the system more porous to challengers and weakened party leaders' control over nominations. Reagan's decision, egged on by a cult of zealous supporters, to spurn his own famous 11th Commandment against GOP infighting and challenge a president was seen as a reflection of the incentives the new system offered during an era of continual party decomposition. But Reagan's failed challenge actually succeeded as a programmatic effort. The price of Ford's renomination was conservative ideological consolidation of the party itself. This could be interpreted as "weakening" the party under a theory in which ideology and partisanship are inherently conflicting forces. But the political world that Reagan helped to build would undermine such dichotomies.

The ups and downs of Reagan's primary battles with Ford have been well told before, from his early, near-fatal stumbles in New Hampshire and Florida to his recovery and spectacular late-season surge of victories heading into the Kansas City convention.[75] What matters about the campaign for an analysis of American political realignment and polarization is the extent to which it constituted an ideological and movement-oriented rather than personalized campaign. It is in that light that the recurring clashes over strategy between the campaign's resolutely nonideological director, John Sears, who sought to emphasize Reagan's personal presidential qualities, and its more conservative staffers took on broader significance. The turning point in the campaign's fortunes coincided with a change in strategy from character-based appeals to an issue-driven, ideological approach. That change took place in North Carolina, at the behest of Jesse Helms and Tom Ellis.

North Carolina's March 1976 primary was a make-or-break proposition for Reagan after having lost five state contests in a row, and Ellis insisted on complete control over the effort, independent of Sears and his staff. With Helms's factional rival Jim Holshouser chairing Ford's campaign in the state, the contest took on added stakes as a new round in the long-running battle for control of the state GOP. Helms and Ellis activated the statewide network of movement-conservative volunteers and donors they had been building since 1972, brought in veteran consultant Art Finkelstein to help with an unprecedented GOP primary voter identification effort, and utilized massive direct-mail, television, and radio advertising.[76] Most important, they pushed Reagan's red-meat ideological material to the fore, emphasizing hardline, nationalist, and caustically critical appeals, particularly concerning détente and the administration's support for ceding US control over the Panama Canal. Augmenting this approach was an independent campaign effort on Reagan's behalf in North Carolina by the ACU.[77] When Reagan defied pre-election polls to garner a shocking 53–47 percent victory in North Carolina, the win reenergized his campaign and set him on a winning streak across the South and West that featured more ideological than character-based appeals. Crossover voting in open-primary states by Democrats whose chosen candidate, George Wallace, steadily lost to Carter in their party's primaries provided notable support for the GOP insurgent.[78]

The Reagan campaign's transformation into an ideological crusade culminated in a party convention in Kansas City that its activists dominated even as Reagan himself narrowly lost the nomination. Heading into the convention, Reagan trailed Ford by about 100 pledged delegates. Surveys of the delegates recorded 77 percent of Ford's supporters describing themselves as moderate and 8 percent liberal, compared to the 85 percent of Reagan's backers describing themselves as conservative.[79] Sears's gambit to shake up the race in early August by having his candidate announce his running mate—moderate Pennsylvania senator Richard Schweiker— managed to alarm conservative supporters without noticeably changing the dynamic of the contest. Helms and Ellis, for their part, resolved to pursue a different, platform-based strategy for picking off Ford delegates. In late July they convened a meeting in Atlanta with forty conservative members of the Resolutions Committee, along with Reagan aide Lyn Nofziger, to hatch their plan.[80] As Ellis explained, conservatives should provoke a platform fight that would polarize the convention ideologically, with Reagan picking up some of Ford's conservative delegates in the ensuing scramble.[81] For Helms and Ellis, success in defining the party platform would be its own reward even if it failed to garner Reagan new delegates, an outlook that set them apart even from sympathetic members of Reagan's campaign staff.[82] As Nofziger remarked to a reporter, there were three forces at work at the convention: Ford's camp, Reagan's camp, and "those crazy SOBs from North Carolina."[83] What gave the North Carolina group its power was the degree to which Reagan's delegates shared its view of the platform. Three-quarters of his delegates reported in a survey that, if forced to choose, they would rather have a "correct" platform than party unity.[84]

The Ford campaign was well aware of "the determination on the part of the conservative delegates to get a very strongly worded conservative platform," as one aide put it.[85] Reflecting the administration's rightward shift, the draft document already jettisoned certain moderate positions, like support for a Consumer Protection Agency, that had appeared in the 1972 platform. But Ford's team knew more was to come. Conservatives demonstrated their strength early in the process, voting to prevent the platform committee chairman from personally appointing the seven subcommittee chairs.[86] This enabled a conservative revolt on the Subcommittee on Human Rights and Responsibilities, covering abortion and women's rights. The subcommittee appointed a Reaganite chairman, added a new plank supporting a constitutional ban on abortion, and *removed* the existing GOP platform plank endorsing the ERA.[87] Through organized efforts by the Republican Women's Task Force and the Ford camp, the ERA plank was narrowly reinstated in the full committee. But it was an ominous development for GOP feminists, whose ranks were both thinning and concentrated at the elite rather than grassroots level. The antiabortion plank, meanwhile, survived the committee, securing a place as party doctrine for decades to come.[88]

The centerpiece of the conservative challenge to Ford's preferred platform language lay in foreign policy. Reagan owed his resurgence in the spring to a relentless focus on a string of related issues tapping into deep-seated popular discontent with détente and with other diplomatic initiatives, like the cessation of US control over the Panama Canal, that seemed to encapsulate a self-imposed American weakness.[89] At Helms and Ellis's behest, political scientist John East drew up an alternative plank entitled "Morality in Foreign Policy." The document singled out Soviet dissident Alexander Solzhenitsyn as "that great beacon of human courage and morality," an obvious swipe at the Ford administration's snubbing of the émigré during a 1975 visit.[90] The Helsinki Accords, the administration's Taiwan policy, the Panama Canal handover, and Ford's opposition to importing Rhodesian chrome all came in for criticism in East-penned amendments.[91] In subcommittee, the "Morality in Foreign Policy" plank failed narrowly. But Helms and Ellis rallied their forces for a floor vote at the general convention. The Ford camp, fearing a roll call that would reflect majority opposition to the administration, opted instead to accept the "Morality" plank without a fight, though with some last-minute dilutions.[92]

The platform that emerged from the convention was a distinctly conservative document filled with implicit criticisms of the administration. It was the most vivid illustration of the degree to which ideological activists dominated a convention that did, after all, eventually choose to renominate the incumbent president. The "paradox in Kansas City," journalist Tom Wicker wrote, lay precisely in the fact that Gerald Ford, entering with a two-digit delegate lead, had so little control over its unfolding. "Even after he had withdrawn as a candidate for renomination," Wicker observed, "Lyndon Johnson had greater command of the Democratic convention [in 1968] than Mr. Ford does of the Republicans today."[93] Everywhere the sense of right-wing momentum and initiative was palpable. Liberals and moderates closed ranks around Ford and, with the exception of the fights over abortion and the ERA, deliberately eschewed any policy demands or platform advocacy of their own, knowing how weak their hand had become. Speeches by liberal officials, such as Jacob Javits, were drowned out by the blown horns of Reagan supporters.[94] Even after strategically ceding major ground to conservatives regarding platform language, the Ford camp found itself forced to use valuable time shoring up the support of Helms and Ellis by reaffirming the president's commitment to the platform.[95]

The most notable achievement of conservative activists at the 1976 convention may have been to turn the platform into a manifesto emphasizing contrasts with the opposition party rather than a glorified campaign brochure for a specific candidate. In the convention's final day, when Reagan conceded after falling short by 108 delegates, his impromptu speech hailed the platform as "a banner of bold, unmistakable colors with no pale pastel shades. We have just heard a call to arms."[96] That call to arms had not been the sole work of Reagan's campaign. It was the product of extensive conservative experimentation during a period in which existing partisan arrangements seemed in flux. What Reagan's presidential challenge helped to reveal was that a changing GOP was, indeed, a hospitable vessel for conservative programmatic politics.

MOVEMENT AND PARTY: A NEW SYMBIOSIS

"Perhaps a little more emphasis on the ticket and a little less on the platform would have been helpful." That was how Ford's running mate Bob Dole later described Reagan's tardy and tepid campaign support during the 1976 race against Jimmy Carter.[97] Reagan's pointed decision to focus on the platform rather than Ford's candidacy that fall reflected not only sour grapes, but also broader conservative disaffection with the president's determinedly non-ideological campaign. Facing an opponent who was himself an ideological cipher, Ford shied away from conservative programmatic appeals, demobilizing movement activists in the process. Dole's frustration with Reagan captured the tension, inherent and to some degree ever-present, between party leaders seeking electoral majorities and ideological purists waving a banner of bold colors.

The story of the Right in the ensuing Carter years, however, is the story of a time in which that tension between party-building and ideological activism diminished meaningfully—a time when revitalizing the GOP went hand in hand with efforts to consolidate conservative control over the party. This was partly the result of a troubled presidential administration that responded to a difficult environment in ways that alienated its allies while mobilizing partisan opponents. But it was also a product of the very process of ideological sorting that activists had managed to initiate in the American system by the 1970s as, first, elite party actors and then electoral constituencies began to more firmly align their partisan allegiance with their issue positions. The Carter-era context opened up space for conservatives to make ideological appeals to a larger potential electorate, and the ongoing transformation of the party system helped to ensure that those appeals would redound to the GOP's benefit. The Carter years saw not only such ideological work on the right but also the activist tenure of an RNC chairman, Bill Brock, who would join Paul Butler and Ray Bliss in the small echelon of historically significant postwar party chiefs. In a reflection of the changing political scene, Brock managed to *combine* Butler's programmatic orientation with Bliss's commitment to nuts-and-bolts organizing, which helped make the GOP a finely tuned and well-resourced vessel for the Reagan revolution to come.

In the immediate aftermath of the 1976 election, the second electoral setback in a row for the Republican Party, few were predicting such a fast and dynamic rebound. It was a time of soul searching and prescriptive debate typical of parties under duress. Ford plunged into efforts to renew, if not reorient, the party institutionally after the election. He held a White House meeting in December with three party eminences—Reagan the conservative standard-bearer, Connally the southern Democratic convert, and Rockefeller the icon of the beleaguered moderates—to discuss the GOP's future and the viability of the two-party system.[98] Proposals from other party quarters struck notes of experimentation and renewal. A Kansas congressman wrote to Ford about the idea of "holding a Mini-Convention, similar to the one held by the Democrats" in 1974, gathering party regulars as well as "conservative and independent groups."[99] Soon after, the RNC passed a resolution to investigate the possibility of changing the party's name so as to help overcome lingering resistance to the party brand. Reagan and Ford, meanwhile, continued to espouse contrasting visions for the GOP's future, helping to sustain their factional rivalry. When Ford told GOP state legislators that "a contest within our ranks to prove who is purer of ideology will not attract the American people," the target of his argument was obvious.[100] The rivalry informed the race to succeed Mary Louise Smith as RNC chairman in early 1977.[101] Ford and Reagan were each aligned with a candidate in the run-up to the vote—James Baker and Richard Richards, respectively—while ex-Tennessee senator Bill Brock, solidly conservative but a Ford supporter the previous year, slipped through on the third ballot of voting as something of a compromise choice.

Little in Brock's career would have indicated the dynamism with which he tackled his new job, though an engagement with the mechanics of party-building and sensitivity to changing political dynamics had long been evident. A Young Republican activist in the early 1960s, Brock had helped to organize the local GOP in Chattanooga just as the Democrats' statewide lock on power began to break.[102] He served three terms in the US House before successfully defeating the Democratic incumbent Al Gore Sr. in a 1970 Senate race that heavily emphasized the social and cultural issues Nixon's strategists sought to amplify that year. In the Senate he amassed a conservative voting record while showing a talent for party work during his stint running the National Republican Senatorial Committee in 1974. Brock lost his 1976 reelection bid to a moderate Democrat who forged a biracial coalition with the help of Carter's coattails.[103] When Brock next turned to the RNC chairmanship, he campaigned on a message of party unity and nuts-and-bolts organizing.

He made good on that message through aggressive efforts to rebuild the party organizationally, with a focus on grassroots and local levels of activity. "We have become too dependent on the presidency," Brock told the RNC in his acceptance speech, "oriented too much to the top of the ticket."[104] He launched a hiring spree at the RNC, recruiting fifteen regional political directors and four regional finance directors to work with state chairmen on their party organizations and electoral needs at the local and state levels. Most aggressive of all was a program to place a salaried field organizer in every state—a plan described by David Broder as "far more ambitious, not just in cost but in its redefinition of state and national party responsibilities, than anything that has been attempted previously."[105]

Noting that the GOP enjoyed unified control over the legislatures of only four out of fifty states, Brock initiated an unprecedented RNC project called the Local Elections Campaign Division, which concentrated on recruiting and training state legislative candidates. Between 1977 and 1981 its efforts helped boost the number of GOP-held legislative seats by over 20 percent and the number of GOP-controlled legislatures from four to fifteen—fateful gains given legislatures' control over congressional redistricting every new decade.[106] Such efforts also expanded the pool of trained and competent candidates for future higher office. Brock's emphasis on the RNC's Campaign Management College, candidate training seminars, and national conferences for party volunteer and professional education all similarly reflected an interest in cultivating sustained labor at the grassroots level for party activities.

Harnessing grassroots energies only worked, of course, if there was energy on the ground to be harnessed—and in this as in many other areas, Brock's organizational approach came at a fortuitous time for the prospects of Republican Party growth. Most significantly, the mobilization of evangelical Protestants to political activism in the late 1970s signified a massive infusion of new personnel to fill the cadres of Republican Party volunteers, campaign staff, and candidates.[107] As an influx of new, predominantly middle-class actors to partisan politics embodying an issue-driven "amateur" approach, the emergence of the Christian Right invited comparison to the rise of club Democrats in the 1950s and the electoral efforts of 1960s social movement activists. It marked a new step in the long-running replacement by ideological activists of the old party workers at the grassroots of American politics.

GOP leaders like Brock hardly instigated this activism. Rather, political brokers capitalized on both tectonic demographic developments and short-term events, forging issue-based attachments among politicized Christians that soon became durable partisan ties.[108] Conservative evangelicals mobilized to enhance their power within American Protestant institutions during the 1970s while shedding their aversion to political engagement.[109] Catholic activists like Phyllis Schlafly drew Protestants into antifeminist and other conservative causes, while key Protestant theologians like Francis Schaeffer helped to mobilize evangelical support for the formally Catholic-dominated antiabortion movement. Richard Viguerie's mailing lists brought together motivated small donors across an array of issues, and from the early 1970s he observed the crosscutting predominance of evangelicals on his lists, notably among George Wallace supporters. He and other New Right architects like Weyrich worked to connect nascent evangelical political interests with existing conservative organizations and support. They took fateful advantage of the controversy over the Internal Revenue Service's 1978 effort to revoke the tax-exempt status of Christian schools deemed in violation of the Civil Rights Act. That conflict drew evangelicals into a fight that touched on the core post-1960s political flashpoints of race and taxes, and New Right brokers and evangelical leaders like Jerry Falwell helped derive from it a coherent antigovernment ideological basis for evangelical coalition with conservatives.

Such elite linkages and issue mobilizations channeled conservative evangelical party activism almost exclusively into the GOP. Brock's training and recruitment efforts at the RNC took place at the beginning of this process and did not involve explicit targeting of evangelicals. But he encouraged rather than resisted Christian conservative inroads into the GOP. As the RNC's counsel later put it, Brock and his team viewed evangelical churches as both vehicles for mobilization and a "distribution system" for GOP appeals.[110] He invited top leaders including Falwell, Bob Jones, Pat Robertson, and Tim LaHaye to meetings to forge ties with the party and to provide input on the 1980 Republican platform.[111] This party posture toward the nascent Christian Right in the late 1970s, mirroring that of both Reaganites and the conservative GOP congressional factions, came at a pivotal developmental stage. It helped ensure the movement's lasting primacy as a source for party volunteers and candidates.

To finance the RNC's extensive party-building efforts, meanwhile, Brock became as much of a pathbreaker in party fundraising as he proved to be in organizing, and similarly capitalized on contemporary developments in ideological activism. Brock viewed direct-mail fundraising in much the same way Viguerie did, as both an advantageous adaptation to the donor limits imposed by the Federal Election Campaign Act (FECA) and a tool for engaging potential volunteers on given issue and electoral campaigns. Brock invested the $2.6-million surplus the RNC enjoyed as of spring 1977 into expanding the parties' direct-mail donor base. The result of this investment was an increase in that base from 250,000 to 1.2 million people in the next three years.[112] In 1980 net revenues garnered by direct mail accounted for fully 73 percent of all the money raised by the RNC.[113]

To a more limited extent, Brock also sought to reap partisan gains from the political mobilization of business in the 1970s—a broad social development that, under FECA's campaign finance regime, partially took the form of an explosive proliferation of corporate PACs, from 89 in 1974 to 1,204 in 1980.[114] Brock appointed a coordinator "to lobby Corporate and Association Political Action Committees for the benefit of the Republican Party" and provided RNC consultation to businesses interested in establishing PACs and seeking advice on where to direct funds.[115] His efforts ensured that the RNC became a financial juggernaut by 1980, dwarfing its cash-strapped Democratic counterpart.

What Brock's organizational work amounted to was not just the strengthening of the RNC's capacities and the expansion of its campaign efforts but the relative *nationalization* of Republican activity—a centralization of technical support, candidate recruitment, and campaign-service functions in the national party. This structural shift took place, ironically, as the very result of Brock's focus on building up the party's ranks at the grassroots and lower levels of public office, since these new training and recruitment initiatives were centrally administered by the RNC. They were not without controversy. "Your program of State Organization Directors would be worthy of the most liberal Democrat alive," an Oklahoma committeeman wrote to Brock, calling the initiative "a concentration of power, authority, and responsibility at the national level."[116] State chairmen occasionally complained about RNC organizers failing to coordinate with the state parties, while others expressed consternation with the committee's willingness under Brock to intervene in GOP primary contests.[117] The GOP's organizationally focused nationalization during the 1970s contrasted with the Democrats' procedural, reformist approach to expanding their national party's authority. Both approaches, however, made the US party system more national in orientation, just as responsible party tenets prescribed.[118]

Another prescriptive tenet of responsible party doctrine was programmatic partisanship. To an extent unusual for most party chairmen, Brock also attended to matters of issue development and ideological branding as RNC chair. His interest in party policy work was shared by other GOP leaders facing exile from national power after the 1976 election[119] In his bid for the RNC chairmanship, Brock ran on a proposed policy council to be housed in the national committee.[120] Once elected, Brock spent months operationalizing the plan in the form of five advisory issue councils, each to be governed by a small policy board and incorporating the work of 50–100 members. Reminiscent of the structure of Paul Butler's Democratic Advisory Council of the late 1950s, the five RNC Issue Councils were intended, as Brock put it, "to restate with some clarity our own values, policies, and programs."[121]

Brock retained substantial cooperation and participation from congressional Republican leaders as well as major national figures in the party while pursuing this initiative. This was a contrast to Butler's experience, reflecting the relative programmatic cohesion Republicans were beginning to experience by the late 1970s. Between 1978 and 1980, the councils produced roughly two dozen position papers focusing on economic and foreign policy issues. Their aim was to develop positions that united the party and "distinguish[ed] the Republican philosophy and approach from that of the Democrats," as Republican Senatorial Campaign Committee chairman Bob Packwood put it.[122]

By far the most consequential work done by the councils and by Brock's related programmatic initiatives concerned tax policy. The rapid triumph of supply-side economics in American conservatism is a tale oft told.[123] The sketchy doctrine of an obscure business economist named Arthur Laffer, the supply-side argument for federal income tax rate cuts that would *raise* rather than lower federal revenue found well-placed and energetic champions in the media, most notably the *Wall Street Journal*'s Robert Bartley and Jude Wanniski. Irving Kristol, the most politically strategic of the neoconservative intellectuals, helped to bring both the idea and its chief evangelist, Wanniski, to the attention of officials in Washington, including Republican congressman Jack Kemp. Kemp adopted supply-side economics as his cause and in June 1977 introduced a Tax Relief Act, co-sponsored by Delaware Republican William Roth in the Senate, which reduced income tax rates across the board by 30 percent. The coordinated effort inside and outside of Congress to put income tax cuts at the center of the GOP agenda benefited immensely from the great "tax revolt" of 1978, a wave of state-level reactions against property taxes that peaked with California's Proposition 13. The front-runner for the 1980 nomination, Reagan, would come under the supply-siders' spell, putting Kemp-Roth at the center of his campaign and, eventually, shepherding it to passage in what became the cornerstone of his domestic policy legacy, 1981's Economic Recovery Tax Act.

Less often noted is the unusually central role played by the RNC in promulgating Kemp-Roth as a consensus GOP policy and a new key to the party's brand during Brock's tenure.[124] At an RNC meeting in September 1977, Brock first succeeded in passing a party resolution formally endorsing the bill.[125] During the same period, he and the Issue Councils' director set about bringing key supply-side advocates and sympathizers onto the Economic Affairs advisory council, including Kemp, David Stockman, Murray Weidenbaum, and Lew Lehrman.[126] That council's tax subcommittee helped to develop an issue network in Washington conversant in and supportive of aggressive income tax cuts as a supply-side growth strategy.[127] The advisory council unanimously endorsed Kemp-Roth in the summer of 1978. Brock held a news conference with the bill's sponsors to announce the RNC's plan to fund a series of workshops and training programs educating Republican candidates across the country about the proposal and the theory behind it.[128] Such work helped explain how supply-side economics became, in Rowland Evans and Robert Novak's words, "the GOP's first universally recognized economic theology since the protective tariff."[129]

Beyond the Issue Councils, Brock waged an aggressive political campaign in 1978 to make Kemp-Roth "the cornerstone of this year's Republican campaign and communications efforts."[130] In July he announced a multistate "Tax Blitz" tour on behalf of Kemp-

Roth, underscoring his intension to nationalize the midterm elections around the tax issue and touting the unanimity of Republican candidates' position on it. "This is a major, significant issue, a clear division between our parties," he said. "We want to have our party and all our candidates speaking with one voice."[131] For the three-day Tax Blitz in September, the RNC chartered a plane it christened the Republican Tax Clipper and took major Republican figures, including Ford and Reagan, to press events in eight cities.[132] After the election, during the 96th Congress, Republicans demonstrated growing cohesion in a succession of votes on Kemp-Roth, each of which lost to Democratic opposition but helped to pull the debate over tax policy notably rightward. By the time that supply-side devotee Ronald Reagan had ascended to the Republican nomination in 1980, forestalling last-ditch attempts by his moderate rival George Bush to tarnish the theory as "voodoo economics," Brock's policy apparatus at the RNC, including key Issues Council staffers, were well placed to channel the Kemp-Roth proposal directly into the Republican platform. The final document endorsed Kemp-Roth by name, devoted two lengthy sections to the tax-cutting cause, and mentioned the word "tax" 145 times.[133]

That the GOP could achieve such programmatic unity around this or any other issue is notable in itself. The lasting significance of the party's embrace of supply-side tax-cutting went beyond that, however, touching on key dynamics of electoral coalition-building that would allow for party polarization along multiple issue dimensions in the coming decades. Simply put, a theory that severed a direct correlation between taxes rates and revenues—and disputed the zero-sum logic of conventional budget politics—amounted to a claim that tax-cutting did not necessarily require welfare state retrenchment. That claim in turn held the potential to appeal to constituencies beyond traditional small-government conservatives.

In this way, supply-side economics offered a solution of sorts to the Right's longstanding challenge of sustaining a coalition between anti-statists and Wallacite social conservatives. Back in 1975, when Robert Novak had considered Bill Rusher's plan for a new majority party, he had described the tension this way: "Whereas

Mr. Rusher sees give-and-take between economic and social conservatives, I see the necessity of all give and no take on economic grounds if a national party embracing the blue-collar vote is to be founded."[134] Now, three years later, Novak and his partner Rowland Evans could see the potential of supply-side theory to dissolve that tension. "Whereas Republicans for the past half-century have tried pouring the castor oil of balanced budgets and reduced government services down the throats of resisting Americans," they wrote, "Laffer has a prescription that makes them feel good."[135] As one consultant marveled to a reporter in 1978, supply side arguments meant that the GOP "suddenly could become the party of *more*."[136] Little wonder that one ambitious Republican, running for a House seat in a suburban Georgia district, centered his 1978 campaign on Kemp-Roth. The issue, Newt Gingrich declared that spring, "exceeds anything I have seen in 18 years of politics and 5 years campaigning in its potential to create a conservative majority in this country."[137] That potential stemmed from the fiscal promise of a free lunch. The tax cuts appealed to traditional conservatives, while their disconnection from specified spending cuts avoided alienating broader middle- and working-class constituencies ripe for Republican outreach through cultural appeals.

In line with basic responsible party tenets prizing the clarification of partisan differences over bipartisan cooperation, Brock generally espoused a parliamentary approach to party opposition. He received his share of complaints from Republican voters decrying the GOP as "a party of no conviction *whatsoever!*" and calling for "a clear cut choice when we go to the polls, not a me-too party."[138] In response, he could point to the Kemp-Roth campaign and the growing voting cohesion of congressional Republicans as evidence that the GOP was offering a genuine alternative.[139] Fittingly, he traveled to Great Britain to watch the Conservative Party's historic electoral victory in the spring of 1979 under party leader Margaret Thatcher, and presented reports on that campaign's themes and strategies to the RNC and Republican congressional leaders. When he argued to conservative critics that "Republicans have been ideologically consistent, coherent, and committed" during the Carter years, Brock was appealing to a growing sentiment at the time that political victory for Republicans required disciplined opposition and programmatic line-drawing.[140]

Though Brock's programmatic initiatives emulated British opposition-party practice, their ultimate fate underscored enduring differences between the American and British systems. Brock was the latest in a succession of party leaders who attempted to institutionalize an American version of the kind of in-house policy research, program development, and issue work that British and other European parties had long practiced. But despite their impact in the run-up to the 1980 convention, the Issue Councils did not survive the end of Brock's tenure that year. Similarly, Brock's venture into substantive policy journalism, a quarterly journal called *Commonsense* he intended as an RNC-funded version of *Public Interest*, survived for only a few more issues after Reagan's inauguration. What accounts for the short half-life of Brock's programmatic initiatives? Part of the answer is that, compared to parliamentary systems, the fragmentation built into the US system still hindered top-down efforts to establish party policy. But timing also mattered.

Brock served as party chairman during the exact period that witnessed the great flourishing of intellectual and policy activity carried out by the conservative movement's interlocking network of corporate and foundation-backed think tanks, advocacy organizations, and lobbies.[141] Between 1970 and 1980, to take one example, the American Enterprise Institute's budget jumped from $1 million to $10.4 million and its staff increased sixfold.[142] The Heritage Foundation, launched in 1973 with a $250,000 Coors grant, saw its budget surpass $7 million by the beginning of the next decade, when it mobilized as the right-wing advance guard of the Reagan revolution.[143] Developments in the 1960s had helped to challenge the legitimacy of disinterested, ostensibly nonideological technocratic expertise and to inject ideology into the politics of policy knowledge. Subsequently, the Right's long march through the institutions in the 1970s had resulted in a great proliferation of new, politicized centers of issue expertise. These avowedly ideological organizations lacked official partisan ties but, given the ideological sorting underway among the parties, their alliance with the GOP was clear. This, rather than institutionalized research arms within the formal parties, became the model for partisan policy development.

In matters organizational, financial, and ideological, the formal Republican Party experienced a revitalization in tandem with conservative ascendancy during the late 1970s. In a party system that was only starting to sort ideologically, the relationship between the party and right-wing activists was hardly conflict-free in these years. But, despite tensions, partisans and ideologues were increasingly pulling in the same direction. This dynamic could also be seen electorally; 1978 and 1980 proved to be important election cycles both for the GOP and for conservatism—and, especially, for conservatism's position within the GOP.

As early as the fall of 1977, aides in the Carter White House were sounding warnings about the ill winds blowing for Democrats in the next year's midterm elections.[144] Matters only darkened for the administration and its party in the ensuing months, as a confluence of events prompted a conservative breakthrough. The policy battles of the Carter presidency were one key to the developments rendering 1978 a watershed year in the history of American conservatism. Just as important were conservative activists' efforts to leverage those battles into effective pressure on Republicans inclined to cooperate with Democrats.

This was done through primary challenges, lobbying, and issue-based mailing campaigns. "I want a massive assault on Congress in 1978," Viguerie boasted to a journalist in the summer of 1977. "I don't want any token efforts. We now have the talent and resources to move in a bold, massive way."[145] New Right leaders personally lobbied conservative senators to abandon their reelection support for liberal colleagues.[146] Candidate-oriented PACs, led by Reagan's juggernaut Citizens for the Republic, distributed millions of dollars in 1978 in campaign donations, and their choices often hewed to an ideological logic in ways the official party organs could not. Reagan's PAC gave support in races at the Senate, House, gubernatorial, state legislative, and even state party chairmanship levels that systematically ignored liberal incumbents. It also intervened in GOP primary contests for open seats.[147] New Right activists went a step further than this, waging strong primary challenges against incumbent liberal Republican senators over the opposition of party officials like Brock. Edward Brooke of Massachusetts barely survived a potent nomination challenge by a right-wing talk radio host, while New Jersey's Clifford Case shockingly failed to beat back a challenge by ex-Reagan aide Jeffrey Bell.

The dichotomy between party politics and ideological politics was often presumed in the late 1970s discourse about the New Right. Whether it was the letter sent to Brock in 1977 from eight Republican senators warning of GOP "cannibalism" over the Panama Canal treaties or the comments that Brock himself made in 1978 describing single-issue activism as "hazardous to our political system," the fear that issue-driven politics was both a symptom and a cause of party decline grew in these years.[148] But in a system where two parties structured political conflict, even a consciously unpartisan strategy of political coalition through single-issue mobilizations had the practical effect of driving ideological sorting and increased partisanship.[149]

The 1978 and 1980 elections demonstrated that ideological politics could, in fact, deliver pragmatic partisan victories. Republicans gained three Senate and fifteen House seats in 1978, and Brock was quick to point out that the RNC's party-building investments at the local and state level paid off in a gain of 300 state legislators and seven governors. The chairman also emphasized the ideological victory: "The 96th Congress, by all accounts, will be decidedly more conservative than the 95th," he told one Republican.[150] Brock's occasional antagonist Paul Weyrich sounded the same theme in a postelection report to one of his major philanthropic backers, Richard Mellon Scaife. He reported the CSFC's calculations that seventeen House races saw outcomes reflecting modest leftward shifts in the seat holder, compared to thirty-two races that produced strong rightward shifts. "Not only did we gain in districts," he wrote, "but we gained in intensity to the conservative cause."[151] In the Senate, ten new members represented a rightward shift from their predecessors, compared to four who reflected a move left.[152]

The behavior of Republicans in and out of Congress in 1979 and

1980 reflected a new cohesion and aggressiveness, borne of ideological zeal and favorable political winds. "There's a new passion
running beneath the impassive exterior of the House Republicans,"
the *Wall Street Journal* reported in April 1979. "It's a new feistiness,
a stick-'em-in-the-eye combativeness toward the Democratic majority."[153] Outside of Congress, the same marriage of ideological
combativeness and political effectiveness was evident as the conservative standard-bearer Ronald Reagan sustained his dominant
position in the race for the GOP presidential nomination against a
slew of rivals. Once Reagan sewed up the nomination, the official
party operation and independent conservative efforts mobilized on
behalf of the same goal—a stark contrast with 1976. Though Brock,
in his capacity as leader of the official party organization, still expressed reservations during the race about the "divisive" role that
such independent campaigns might play, the $10.6 million that the
National Conservative Political Action Committee and other out-
fits ultimately spent on Reagan's behalf proved a help rather than
a hindrance.[154]

The election results of 1980 marked a Republican sweep that
was also a conservative rout. The GOP gained twelve Senate seats
and thirty-three House seats. As James Sundquist noted, eleven of
the sixteen new GOP senators "had campaigned as ultraconserva-
tives on social, military, and foreign, as well as economic, policy."
The electorate also conveyed an increasing ideological logic to
their partisan alignments. Democratic Reagan supporters came
from disproportionately conservative ranks, and a higher percentage of respondents in one survey reported seeing "important
differences" in what the two parties stood for than in the last six
presidential-year surveys.[155]

Statistics help to frame what was happening to the party system—its shifting elite alignments, the changing relationship between partisanship and ideology. But these changes were also lived
experiences for men and women who had spent their careers in the
parties, and those stories do their own kind of work to convey the
dynamics involved. To take the measure of the GOP's transformation in the 1970s, consider one last story—a coda on a bygone era.

THE SAGA OF MARY CRISP: FACTIONAL STRUGGLE AND
THE PARTISAN POLARIZATION OF SOCIAL ISSUES

By June 1980 RNC co-chairman Mary Dent Crisp had begun to suspect that her Washington, DC, office was bugged. For weeks she had wondered why sensitive information appeared to be leaking from her office to the press, and she noticed a beeping sound on the line during calls. Eventually she called in a private investigator to conduct a countersurveillance sweep of the office.[156] The investigator found no direct evidence of bugging but noted "two suspicious situations": a wire running from a neighboring office through Crisp's room to an unknown destination, and an electromagnetic "energy/radio field" detectable at a window near her desk.[157] Crisp reported this to fellow RNC officials, and three days later—an excessively long time, in her opinion—they called in another firm to investigate.[158] Eventually the police themselves took over the investigation, finally concluding that no bugging had taken place.[159]

Though this case was deemed a false alarm, the idea that espionage might take place in a party committee's headquarters would have hardly seemed farfetched just two presidential election cycles after the Watergate break-in. What was more notable was the fact that Crisp suspected the culprits to be fellow members of her own party.

The story of an RNC co-chairman whose gradual professional isolation brought her to the point of suspecting skullduggery by factional enemies captures in a vivid way a broader process that activists on the left and right helped to hasten during the 1970s: the partisan sorting of cultural and social issues. Positions on issues relating to gender, religion, identity, and ecology that had come to the fore thanks to 1960s movements did not, as of the early 1970s, have clear partisan valences. That had begun to change by decade's end, and nowhere was the dynamic more evident than in the politics of women's rights. The untenable position in which Mary Crisp found herself in June 1980 resulted from the parties' polarization in the preceding years.

Crisp was a career-long GOP party worker and a feminist, and

during her rise within party ranks, few perceived such a combination to be contradictory. Originally a precinct captain in Maricopa
County, Arizona, Crisp served as a Republican national committeewoman during the Ford years and the national convention secretary in 1976.[160] Despite her support for Ford in the nomination
contest that year, she encountered little opposition from Reaganites when Bill Brock chose her as party co-chairman in January 1977
as part of a Sunbelt-heavy leadership team. Within months, however, Crisp's penchant for candid press quotes drew their ire, beginning with her public criticism of Reagan's "idea of purism" and
her insistence that the GOP had to be able to encompass figures as
ideologically disparate as Barry Goldwater and Jacob Javits.[161] The
main focus of conservatives' opposition to Crisp was her outspoken
feminism. Her patron, Mary Louise Smith, had managed to serve
as the party's first female chairman without controversy despite a
reputation as, in one profiler's words, an "ardent feminist."[162] But
in the years since Smith first took the reins in 1974, a powerful antifeminist movement had grown in coalition with other elements of
the New Right. When Crisp spoke out on behalf of abortion rights,
federal support for childcare, redressing gender inequities in Social
Security, and attacking job discrimination, those movement activists listened.

The ERA was the key symbolic issue around which feminist and
antifeminist forces mobilized for a fight in the mid to late 1970s,
and Crisp's pro-ERA advocacy galvanized intense conservative
opposition to a degree that Smith's had not done just a few years
earlier. The National Women's Conference, set to take place in
honor of International Women's Year (IWY) in Houston in 1977,
became a proving ground for anti-ERA and antiabortion forces.[163]
That March, Phyllis Schlafly, the shrewd leader of STOP ERA and
the Eagle Forum, launched a new initiative called the IWY Citizens' Review Committee. The project mobilized social and religious conservatives to participate in state delegate-selection conferences and to work to elect their own as delegates. Such action,
taken relatively late in the process, resulted in conservative representation of a quarter of the Houston delegates. A startled fellow
GOP feminist described the mobilization to Crisp. "The IWY at

Nebraska was a disaster last weekend," she reported in July. "The 'Pro-Lifers' rallied hundreds of people to drive into Lincoln on Sunday, register, and vote for their slate. That was the end of a balanced slate. Their slate was 500 votes ahead of the next names."[164] Schlafly's committee also led letter-writing campaigns concerning the National IWY Commission's draft resolutions, which featured a panoply of liberal feminist planks including not only endorsement of the ERA and abortion rights but also federal aid for childcare, universal health care, and an end to discrimination based on sexual orientation. In the run-up to Houston, conservatives deluged public officials and convention delegates alike with outraged letters.

Crisp, as both an Arizona delegate to the conference and an RNC official, hardly escaped the deluge. "I was appalled at the manner in which the Arizona IWY Convention was conducted," one woman wrote to her, "and I am ashamed to know that you are a delegate of the IWY (at the same time as National Co-Chairman of the National Republican Party—*my* party)." Crisp was undaunted, pointing out in response that support for ERA ratification was included in the 1976 Republican Platform, as it had been for decades before.[165] The following year, she wrote to every GOP member of Congress to urge support for the bill extending the ERA ratification deadline.[166] These efforts outraged conservatives anew and sent more streams of mail both to her office and to Brock's. One ex-senator articulated to Brock the partisan case against Crisp's lobbying effort: "It is quite obvious that [the ERA] is a liberal Democrat sponsored effort at best, and therefore, not in the Republican area for activity."[167]

Brock would dutifully point out in response, just as Crisp did, that support for ERA ratification was a current Republican platform position. But the center of gravity on gender issues was shifting so rapidly within the party by 1978 that the letter-writer's arguments for what did and did not constitute a legitimate "Republican area for activity" were plausible. The polarization of the parties on gender was underway in Congress. Since 1972 the percentage of House Democrats co-sponsoring legislation related to women's rights had begun to exceed the figure for Republicans, with the margin expanding with each Congress. The same interparty gap began to open in the Senate by 1978. Also starting in 1978, the difference in the National Women's Political Caucus voting scores earned by the median members of the two parties began to skyrocket—with Democrats scoring ever higher and Republican scores plummeting.[168]

As Crisp ran into such crosswinds, she became a source of growing irritation for Brock and his staff. In early 1979 Jimmy Carter removed Bella Abzug as head of the National Advisory Committee on Women after Abzug openly criticized the president's proposed budget cuts. The entire membership of the committee resigned in protest of the firing, Crisp among them. Conservative Republicans expressed befuddlement. "Why oh why did you resign just because that dreadful Bella was removed?" a Virginia woman asked her. A group of ten congressmen wrote Brock asking him to "please help us explain to Republicans in our Districts why the removal of Bella Abzug from any governmental body is not cause for rejoicing rather than regret and resignation."[169] Brock began to keep her at arm's length at the RNC.[170]

Tensions mounted between Crisp and Brock during the primary election season of 1980. As the Reagan campaign marched forcefully from state victory to state victory against his Republican competitors, Crisp grew increasingly vocal about the threat his candidacy would pose to the survival of the platform's pro-ERA plank. Engagement with issues like ERA and abortion rights helped pique Crisp's interest in John Anderson's campaign. The Illinois congressman had run as a maverick social liberal in GOP primary contests with little success; in March, he relaunched his bid as an Independent. Three months later, with Reagan having all but secured the GOP nomination, Crisp shared her thoughts to a *Chicago Sun-Times* reporter. Supporting Anderson might pose a solution to the "big dilemma" pro-ERA women faced heading into a convention dominated by Reagan, Crisp said. She deemed Anderson's chances of winning "not so far-fetched" and referred to his GOP credentials as "impeccable—he only refuses to say he's content with Reagan's way of looking at problems."[171]

Within a day of the publication of Crisp's interview, Brock sent her a blistering memo that called her comments "wrong and totally inappropriate for a major party official." So as to ensure that she "adopt the lowest profile possible" to avoid exacerbating the damage she had caused, Brock informed Crisp that he would eliminate her from the convention program and cancel the two events she had been scheduled to host. Four days later, she informed her colleagues that she would not be seeking re-election.[172] A week after that came the intrigue surrounding the bugging scare in Crisp's office. Brock made it clear that he thought Crisp's suspicions were unwarranted. Members of Reagan's camp were happy to go farther, offering sexist mockery to reporters through a veil of anonymity. When a reporter asked one Reagan aide why Crisp might suspect that she was being surveilled, he responded, "I have no way of judging the reaction of frustrated middle-aged women."[173]

Crisp's professional crisis coincided with the crisis of feminist Republicanism now culminating in the platform meetings that preceded the national convention in Detroit. In early July conservative delegates succeeded in routing the last-ditch efforts of the Republican Women's Task Force (RWTF) to save the ERA plank. The committee passed a draft resolution that scrapped the party's forty-year-old endorsement of the amendment and included language condemning White House–directed pressure on anti-ERA states. It also sharpened the antiabortion plank that conservatives had managed to first get adopted in 1976. Gone were the previous platform's acknowledgment of party differences on the issue and call for "continuance of the public dialogue on abortion." What was left was an unequivocal endorsement of a constitutional ban and a call for the legislative prohibition of taxpayer-funded abortions.[174]

At the final RNC meeting that she would attend as co-chair, Mary Crisp reacted to these developments with a tearful but defiant speech that startled her colleagues.[175] She declared that the new ERA and abortion language would "bury the rights of 100 million American women under a heap of platitudes. . . . I cannot turn my back on these issues, and I feel compelled to do whatever is within my power to prevent these two tragedies from occurring." She finished her speech to silence from most committee officials—Brock included—along with a smattering of applause from the pro-ERA minority.[176] But Crisp's vow to reverse the platform committee's actions proved futile. The RWTF lacked the votes for a minority report on either plank, and both made it into the final platform.[177] The denouement of Crisp's Republican career, meanwhile, was swift. Her term ended on July 18. Less than a month later, she took a new position: co-chairman of John Anderson's independent campaign.

The journey of Mary Crisp from party co-chairman to party dissident to party outcast in a few years played out as a one-woman dramatization of the ideological sorting that transformed the party system during the 1970s. Two implicit questions would recur every time a new controversy flared up over her tenure: what was the proper Republican position on a given issue, and how *should* a given issue position relate to one's bona fides as a Republican? Revealingly, when a reporter told Reagan about Crisp's blistering farewell speech in early July, he couched his combative response in the language of partisan loyalty: "Mary Crisp should look to herself and find out how loyal she's been to the Republican Party for quite some time."[178] Reagan's remark implied not only that conservative positions on social issues were the proper "Republican" positions, but that a sufficient degree of apostasy on those or other policy issues amounted to partisan disloyalty. For those, like Crisp, on the losing end of such factional conflict, the newly emerging ideological cast of American partisanship seemed synonymous with the breakdown of the party system itself. "Establishing purity tests for political views is contrary to the basic assumptions underlying our two-party system," she wrote in a post-convention statement she never released.[179] Crisp was correct that such tests were contrary to basic assumptions that had underlay the American system for decades. But those assumptions were no longer tenable.

The changing politics of women's rights within the Democratic Party in 1980 highlighted the same dynamic. Feminist activists were an ascendant force within that party, one whose organizational clout had been on full display during the 1978 midterm issue convention mandated by party reformers. At the 1980 Democratic Convention, a few weeks after conservatives reversed the GOP's ERA position, feminists demonstrated anew their mastery of issue politics within a reformed party structure. Though most members and leaders within the feminist Coalition for Women's Rights supported Ted Kennedy's nomination challenge against Carter, their policy agenda survived the collapse of Kennedy's candidacy. Thanks to an effective whipping operation at the convention, the coalition not only secured the reaffirmation of existing planks supporting ERA ratification and opposing a constitutional amendment to ban abortion, but also managed to win convention floor votes on two planks opposed by Carter.[180] The first explicitly opposed restrictions on federal funding for abortions. The second stated that the "Democratic Party shall withhold financial support and technical campaign assistance from candidates who do not support the ERA."[181] The latter item was, of course, just the kind of "purity test" that Crisp decried, on the very issue that had compelled her to exit her own party.

The simultaneous ascendance of feminist forces within the Democratic Party and antifeminist forces within the GOP illustrated the dynamic logic of issue sorting in a two-party system. One party's position change affected the other party's approach, along with the strategic arguments that internal factions might make. As Gloria Steinem pointed out to fellow activists in the summer of 1980, the Republicans' decision to stake out the right wing on women's issues bolstered the electoral rationale for the Democrats to speak forthrightly on them as a way of mobilizing female voters.[182] And the further such sorting proceeded on a given issue, the more obvious was the necessity of choosing a side—of joining one party's coalitional team or the other. That logic, combined with the iron laws of first-past-the-post electoral systems from which all third-party bids suffered, crippled Anderson's ability to win the support of more feminist activists. A National Organization for Women (NOW) official who personally supported Anderson wrote to Crisp in the fall of 1980 to explain why the organization itself had chosen not to endorse him, opting instead only to emphasize "total opposition" to Reagan: "The labor-feminist alliance is important, and there are hopes that it will thrive and expand," she wrote. "John Anderson was viewed by many to be against labor reforms and was an unacceptable choice for the labor union advocates."[183] In other words, the logic of a labor-liberal coalition inclined NOW toward continued advocacy within the Democratic Party rather than to third-party adventures or a pose of bipartisanship. The mirror of that coalition and logic was the GOP's alliance of social and economic conservatives.

Seen this way, the great churn of sociocultural conflict that the 1960s produced had not, by the end of the 1970s, established a new issue dimension to replace economic issues as the defining cleavage of the party system, as many realignment theorists had predicted. Instead, these new "postmaterialist" issues augmented the economic divisions. Once the conditions were in place for such additive polarization to occur—permeable party institutions, the ascendance of issue-based and ideological activism as the predominant basis for partisan activity, and a clearly dominant faction within each party—the logic of its unfolding proved irresistible. Thus, by the end of the 1970s, party divergence on issues from economics to race to gender to the environment began to become visible.[184] The trick was establishing such conditions in the first place, and that was the accomplishment of political activists in the 1970s. In this work, Left and Right both played a part, but the Right was at the vanguard. By using the GOP effectively as a vessel for ideological politics, by capitalizing on a changing institutional landscape to devise new mechanisms of discipline, and by pushing the boundaries of party norms concerning the aggravation of conflict and the politics of line-drawing, conservatives in the 1970s managed to do more than anyone else to usher in the dynamics that still define American party politics.

7

LIBERAL ALLIANCE-BUILDING
FOR LEAN TIMES, 1972-1980

For good reason, the 1970s has never been seen as a time of liberal ascendance. Beyond the active contributions made by conservatives to liberals' troubles, an array of external developments set an increasingly difficult context for liberal progress over the course of the decade. Stagflation produced a policy environment of zero-sum material conflict between groups, diminishing the political prospects for expansive social, economic, and regulatory policies. Businesses, aided by a newly porous institutional environment in Washington, engaged in new forms of both coordinated and narrowly tailored political mobilization, resulting in an explosive proliferation of corporate lobbyists and advocacy groups.[1] The ranks of liberal issue advocacy organizations, meanwhile, also exploded in the wake of the 1960s but came swiftly to be defined by an elite, professionally staffed, DC-based organizational model that eschewed cross-class mass membership and participation.[2] A similar absence of grassroots energy also came to characterize organized labor, as union density continued its long-running decline throughout the 1970s while businesses adopted a newly hostile posture toward workplace organizing.

All these factors stood as obstacles to liberal political initiative from the 1970s onward and, unsurprisingly, they are central to a narrative that dominates understanding of later-twentieth-century American politics nearly as much as the rise of the Right: the breakdown of the New Deal political order. But the partisan context for such ideological developments matters. A narrative of liberal fragmentation and decline connects ambiguously to the resurgence of

By McNelly for The Richmond News Leader

FIGURE 7. Jeff MacNelly, *Washington Post*, August 16, 1980. © MacNelly King Features Syndicate, Inc.

partisanship and ideological polarization that occurred in the last decades of the twentieth century. Indeed, unless that polarization could be said to have been entirely the byproduct of conservative ascendance within the Republican Party, such a narrative exists in some tension with it. As we have seen, conservatives in the Republican Party were at the vanguard of the transformation of American party politics in the 1970s. But this chapter argues that, within the defensive parameters for liberalism set by the context of the era, changes occurred in both the structure and personnel of the Democratic Party and its allied activists that contributed meaningfully to the long-run transformation of the party system along more programmatic lines.

Some of the same forces for change rendering the GOP more open to conservative takeover—most significantly the atrophying of the conservative southern Democratic wing and its gradual replacement by Republicans—helped make the ranks of the Democratic Party more generally liberal via attrition. But liberal activists, like their counterparts on the right, also worked consciously to bring about changes to the internal balance of power in their allied party. For liberals, the 1970s featured fracture and disarray at the governing level but a gradual process of coalitional reformation at the activist level. And that process of alliance-building was carried out by actors who shared the responsible party vision of cohesive, programmatic partisanship that had motivated reformers of previous decades. By decade's end, in contrast to conservatives, activists on the left had succeeded neither in attaining national power nor in shifting the national policy discussion of major issues in a leftward direction. What they had succeeded in doing, however, was consolidating a new coalition of groups, interests, and movements as *the* grassroots organizational base of the Democratic Party as well as its dominant national faction. In doing this, they helped to drive forward the ideological sorting of the parties and the tightening of the alignment between issue position and party affiliation. An important substantive implication of the coalitional work carried out by liberal activists in the 1970s paralleled that of activists on the right: the bases of each party grew respectively liberal and conservative on multiple issue dimensions simultaneously.

Liberal activists and strategists played a crucial role in this process by consciously facilitating the reconciliation of elements of the liberal coalition that had fallen into conflict during the 1960s. George McGovern's landslide election defeat in 1972 convinced many liberal activists drawn from or sympathetic to sixties cultural politics that they had to more effectively appeal to working-class elements of the old New Deal coalition on an economic basis. The work of such activists helped to produce an important and undernoted political development of the 1970s: the reemergence of a labor-liberal alliance uniting progressive unions with 1960s-inspired social movements and advocacy groups in a series of formal organizations.[3] Thanks in part to the effects of the decade's institutional reforms in empowering issue-driven activists in Democratic Party affairs, this labor-liberal coalitional work had a partisan impact. Reform-mandated midterm Democratic conventions, for example, provided forums for activists to tighten coalitional ties, a key background factor in the decade's second potent intraparty challenge to a sitting president, Ted Kennedy's 1980 bid for the Democratic nomination.

Ultimately, a changing issue context, the effects of institutional reform, and the concerted activism of labor-liberal coalition partners all combined over the course of the 1970s to facilitate the absorption of "New Politics" cultural and social movement energies into a Democratic Party that was simultaneously losing its most conservative faction. It is this contribution to the making of an ideologically sorted party system that the declensionist narrative of post-1960s liberalism obscures. Right and Left alike participated in redrawing the lines of issues, ideology, and partisanship in the 1970s. Both stories are necessary to understand the dynamics of the Reagan years that followed.

"TO MAKE THEM CONSCIOUS OF THEIR COMMON NEED"

As on the right, the major efforts of liberal issue and party activists in the 1970s to foster new, lasting political formations began with intellectual work, in the search for potential new coalitions latent in the world that the 1960s had helped to produce. Surprisingly enough, one project that would exert a meaningful impact on the mainstream Democratic Party sprung from the intense internal conflicts of a tiny political sect—the Socialist Party.

Michael Harrington, a party member who had gained mainstream fame with his 1960 work *The Other America*, was an activist-intellectual haunted by regret over a missed opportunity. He had famously clashed with the young activists of Students for a Democratic Society (SDS) at its founding meeting in 1962, in the process filling the paternal role in a generational Old Left-vs.-New Left psychodrama. In the wake of Vietnam, however, Harrington came to appreciate both the substantive contribution he saw the antiwar and new social movements making to American politics and the coalitional potential of such middle-class activism. By 1968 he was declaring the "youthful reform surge" of the McCarthy and Kennedy movements "the most exciting, and perhaps most significant, thing to have happened in American politics since the industrial workers of the CIO became an electoral force in the thirties." He hoped that the movement might "reflect the growth of a college-educated constituency in which quantitative expansion may well have turned into something qualitatively new: a mass base for 'conscience politics.'"[4]

During the Nixon years, Harrington's increasing openness to the New Politics and new social movement activism placed him at odds with fellow acolytes in Max Shachtman's wing of the Socialist Party. His intraparty antagonists, including the ailing Shachtman himself as well as younger activists like Tom Kahn and Penn Kemble, retained influence within mainstream Democratic Party politics through extensive personal and professional connections to the labor movement, civil rights organizations, congressional staffs, and journalists. Kahn and Kemble formed the nucleus of the hawkish, anti–New Politics Democratic faction that became the Coalition for a Democratic Majority (CDM) in 1972, reflecting the outlook of George Meany and his AFL-CIO allies. Harrington battled them within the Socialist Party, breaking openly with their support for the Vietnam War in 1970 and arguing the next year that the emergence of an educated stratum inclined toward reform and potentially open to socialist appeals made it imperative for the Labor Left to ally with New Politics constituencies. As he saw it, even if the growing ranks of service and professional workers were to be organized, "it is likely that these college educated unionists are going to be open to a 'New Politics,' issue-oriented approach."[5]

But as the McGovern's landslide loss approached in 1972, the Shachtmanites moved to consolidate their control of the Socialist Party in tandem with new preparations to battle McGovern supporters for postelection influence within the Democratic Party. Harrington tendered his resignation as Socialist Party co-chairman, and in December 1972 the Shachtmanites rechristened the organization as Social Democrats, USA. Soon after, they distributed an exhaustive report detailing Harrington's years-spanning "attempt to split the socialist movement" through apostasy on anticommunism and cultivation of "the affluent, educated elite making up the so-called New Politics movement."[6] The *Wall Street Journal* was not alone in seeing Harrington's ouster as a microcosm of conflicts in the Democratic mainstream, terming it "the successful first skirmish of a mounting attack against the New Politics, which is now underway on such traditional liberal fronts as the intellectual community, the labor movement, and the Democratic Party itself."[7]

While Meany's allies and such likeminded strategists as *The Real Majority* authors Ben Wattenberg and Richard Scammon mobilized to lead a counterinsurgency against New Politics activists in the Democratic Party, many of those very activists used McGovern's loss as an occasion to reevaluate. Even prior to the defeat, numerous McGovern supporters had shared a perception that the New Politics coalition of professionals and various "out-groups" could not in itself constitute a viable electoral majority. McGovern's shattering loss in November, in which he failed to win even a majority of union voters among his 37.5 percent overall share of the popular vote, painfully vindicated such concerns. It provoked new attention to repairing the breaches of the last half decade in the name of coalition politics. "We have always been a minority," Joe Rauh told a postelection meeting of liberals. "We made the mistake in 1972 of thinking we were a majority. We really are a minority in search of a coalition."[8]

Harrington's next move after his Socialist ouster signified just such a search—an effort to build ties between the labor left and 1960s-borne social movements. At a small conference in early 1973 at NYU, Harrington convened a hundred compatriots to discuss "The Future of the Democratic Left," out of which came a new organization, the Democratic Socialist Organizing Committee (DSOC). Its founding manifesto described a nonsectarian vision of "coalition politics" and an ambition "to link together the various movements for reform and protest and to make them conscious of their common need."[9] Over the course of the year, a nucleus of organizers and intellectuals including older socialists like Debbie Meier, Irving Howe, and Bogdan Denitch as well as the youth activists Jack Clark and Frank Llewellyn organized a shoestring office and monthly periodical called the *Newsletter of the Democratic Left*.[10] By the time of DSOC's inaugural convention in October of 1973, it counted about 200 members from Social Democrats, USA and another 300 from the broader liberal left in the country.[11]

That the United Auto Worker (UAW)'s Victor Reuther and the American Federation of Teachers president David Seldon served as founding board members, soon to be joined by International Association of Machinists (IAM) chief William Winpisinger, reflected in miniature a fateful development within the labor movement at the time. The crucible of the 1960s had helped to provoke a split between Meany's ruling faction within the AFL-CIO and a collection of dissident left-liberal unions, and the 1972 election helped to bring that conflict to the surface. The federation's decision to remain neutral in the general election for the first time that year, muscled through an executive council vote by Meany, prompted an unprecedented independent political effort for McGovern by liberal AFL-CIO unions.[12] Over thirty-three such unions plus two major nonaffiliated ones, the UAW and the National Education Association (NEA), representing about 8 million workers, endorsed and campaigned for McGovern that fall.[13] In the process, some AFL-CIO unions also developed new organizational capacities for independent political action. The American Federation of State, County and Municipal Employees (AFSCME) devised its own political outfit, Public Employees Organized to Promote Legislative Equality.[14] Frustration over the neutrality decision prompted Bill Lucy and other African Americans to form the Coalition of Black Trade Unionists. Soon afterward, 58 unions formed the Coalition of Labor Union Women, reflecting a growing feminist-labor alliance.[15] The Communications Workers of America (CWA), meanwhile, set up regional political directorships engaged in grassroots electoral activities that expanded in scope after the election. For CWA's Glen Watts, breaking politically with the federation was revelatory. As a participant in a later labor meeting paraphrased him, Watts "didn't realize what the Communication Workers were capable of doing in community action at least until they stumbled into it during the McGovern campaign and their CAP Councils really flowered."[16]

Contrasting social and institutional bases underlay the two labor factions' contrasting political outlooks, and conflict stemming from these differences would have important implications for party politics in the 1970s and beyond. Substantively, the anti-Meany labor officials followed in the tradition of Walter Reuther (who died in 1970) in advocating an expansive social democratic political vision, a skeptical view of the Vietnam War in particular and hardline anticommunism in general, and an interest in forging coalitional ties to reformist and New Politics constituencies. These officials were disproportionately likely to be leading either industrial unions originally affiliated with the CIO or the growing ranks of service, professional, and public-sector unions, while Meany supporters were concentrated among building trades and craft unions.[17] This meant that, in addition to the lingering legacy of Depression-era conflicts between the AFL and CIO, ethnic and gender disparities also informed the federation's factional split. The female and minority proportion of the rank and file grew more rapidly in the 1970s in the dissident service and public-sector unions, just as those sectors' share of the overall organized population grew.[18]

The dissident wing of the labor movement, in other words, was changing demographically and intellectually in ways similar to the activist ranks of the Democratic Party, a phenomenon that Harrington had noted in his losing arguments with the Shachtmanites. Liberal union leaders supported party reform efforts that would empower issue-based activists in the broader political arena, as a way of forging coalitional ties with left-of-center groups whose primary policy goals were not labor-related. Three such leaders in particular would prove to be pivotal players in every major organized effort to strengthen a new left-liberal political and partisan alliance in the 1970s, beginning with DSOC: Doug Fraser, the Scottish-born secretary treasurer and eventual president of the UAW; the IAM's William "Wimpy" Winpisinger; and Jerry Wurf of the rapidly growing public employees union AFSCME. All three men shared a socialist ideological background and a basic comfort with the new social and cultural currents that 1960s activism had brought to the political surface.

Harrington had little trouble sustaining the support and engagement of such labor officials over the course of DSOC's work in the next decade. But fulfilling his organizational goal of bridge-building within the polyglot mass Left would require an ability to engage with *non*-labor activists that proved easier in theory than in practice. DSOC's white male–dominated leadership experienced growing pains and occasionally strained relations with feminist and minority activists.[19] The group eventually secured more stable coalitional relations with feminist organizations and leaders, but its efforts to develop African American and Hispanic memberships bore little fruit save for significant relationships with black congressional leaders Ron Dellums and John Conyers.

Among the remnants of the New Left, meanwhile, DSOC gradually forged ties with the SDS's organizational heir, the New American Movement (NAM). Surveying the scene in a 1975 article, NAM leader Harry Boyte echoed Harrington's optimism about the potential of the largely subterranean, nonelectoral currents of left-liberal activism in the country—"a large-scale resurgence and expansion of grassroots insurgencies *off* college campuses" that included the growth of "women's groups and projects of many sorts, consumer organizations, civil rights groups, environmental and health and safety campaigns, [and] public interest and advocacy projects."[20] DSOC was one elite-level effort to connect such localized, organizationally diffuse activism with sympathetic labor leadership and a national agenda.

An important ally in Harrington's outreach to feminist, public interest, and community groups was the Chicago-based Heather Booth, herself a consummate bridge-builder. Booth's activist résumé was comprehensive: a student organizer, SNCC activist, and SDSer in college, she participated in a string of labor and tenant organizing projects in Chicago in the mid- and late 1960s, established the Chicago Women's Liberation Union in 1969 and the Action Committee for Decent Childcare in 1970, and attended Saul Alinsky's Industrial Areas Foundation Training Institute to learn new community organizing techniques in 1972.[21] In 1973 Booth founded the Midwest Academy, a training center for radical and liberal organizers of all stripes that brought her into contact with a national array of neighborhood groups, state-level citizen organizations, unions, and religious activists.[22] The academy's annual summer retreat became an institutionalized gathering for liberal activists to socialize and collaborate in the 1970s and 1980s.

Booth was in regular professional acquaintance with Harrington, and soon enough would embark on her own major collaborative venture with liberal labor leaders.

If Harrington conceived of DSOC as a meeting ground for disparate elements of the activist left, he also intended to direct that collaboration toward a *partisan* agenda within the Democratic Party. In this DSOC reflected the orientation of much of the broader liberal left. In contrast to conservatives in the early and mid-1970s, liberal activists had only occasionally considered pursuing new-party ventures since the battles of 1968, and the party reforms, McGovern's insurgent nomination, and his subsequent defeat in 1972 had all served to push such notions further to the margins.[23] DSOC's founding statement made it clear that it retained the old Shachtmanite commitment to coalitional politics—to achieving ideological realignment through direct factional engagement within the Democratic Party—even as it extended this principle to support for the minority groups, feminists, environmentalists, peace activists, and public interest advocates that Shachtmanites disdained.[24] "The organizational focus for bringing together these disparate forces in the foreseeable future is, for better or worse, the Democratic Party," the statement declared. In the 1974 and 1976 elections, "the serious choice between Left and Right will counterpose liberal Democrats to Reactionary Republicans and the latter's Dixiecrat Fifth Column in the Democratic Party."[25]

The statement went on to articulate a responsible party critique of the Democrats' lack of cohesion and ideological coherence. The fact that DSOC would work within the Democratic Party does "not mean that we regard the amorphousness of American party politics, or of the Democratic Party in particular, as good." Contrary to those, "including some liberals, who celebrate the unprincipled and unprogrammatic character of the American party system as a bulwark against 'extremism,'" DSOC believed that "the problems before America today cannot be solved on an ad hoc basis." The group envisioned a future in which "trade unionists, the minorities, the poor, and the middle class liberals and radicals would not simply vote for a party which is also heavily influenced by the Dixiecrat South and Big Business," but instead "would turn it into their own party with their priorities." Not surprisingly, the *Boston Globe* reported that at DSOC's founding convention, "Walter Mondale was mentioned more often than Karl Marx."[26]

DSOC would come to focus on platform and program work within the Democratic Party for a number of reasons. Practically, it was an area that the post-reform institutional environment had rendered conducive to the efforts of committed elite activists—allowing DSOC, in Harrington's words, to play "a role quite out of proportion to our very modest numbers."[27] Normatively, DSOC leaders shared a commitment to ideological partisanship that had longstanding roots in the labor movement and among socialist intellectuals. And strategically, Harrington perceived in the 1960s growth of middle-class activism an emergent mass constituency for specifically *issue*-oriented politics. He saw in these liberals something similar to what Jesse Helms saw in southern white ticket-splitters and new conservative activists: potential agents in the transformation of the party system along ideological lines.

DSOC's first, modest effort in this vein occurred in late 1974, on the occasion of the Conference on Democratic Party Organization and Policy in Kansas City. The Kansas City "mini-conference" was intended to ratify a party charter as well as inaugurate a new institution long advocated by responsible party reformers: regular midterm party conferences. In the language of a 1972 convention resolution, such conferences were meant to "increase communication between disparate segments of the Party and to discuss and adopt Democratic statements of policy on various issues."[28] Reformers led by Minnesota congressman Donald Fraser had conceived of such meetings as both a means for enhancing the programmatic function of the party and, in James MacGregor Burns's words, "a transmission belt between movement politics and party politics."[29] Though DNC chairman Robert Strauss largely neutered the 1974 mini-conference's programmatic function, it still served as a gathering place for issue and party activists, and DSOC sought to take advantage. At the conference, Harrington, his colleague Marjorie Phyfe, and other DSOC-affiliated delegates found socializing with activists and party officials encouraging. "We were amazed at how open the Party is to its left," Harrington reported, "we were amazed at how many unorganized socialists were there, and we were amazed by the warm reception our ideas received."[30]

Those ideas, which remained the core substantive agenda of DSOC's efforts for the rest of the decade, emphasized bedrock economic and domestic policies as a common ground for left-of-center interests divided by cultural and foreign policy issues. Top policy items included a commitment to full employment, universal health care, nationalization of energy industries, and progressive tax reform. This class-focused policy approach was shared by mainstream elements of the Democratic Party in the mid-1970s, both in Congress and among core party interest groups seeking to coalesce around a universalistic agenda. The clearest expression of this strategy was the mobilization behind the Humphrey-Hawkins full employment bill, first drafted by Congressional Black Caucus leader Gus Hawkins and Hubert Humphrey in 1974. In its original form, the bill proposed expansive federal planning measures to achieve a mandated target of 3 percent unemployment along with a legally enforceable right to work for every American.[31] Humphrey-Hawkins, as well as a series of universal health insurance plans backed by Ted Kennedy, would provide core points of programmatic focus for DSOC in the next several years.

Following the 1974 mini-conference, Harrington and his colleagues decided to make a more intensive effort at factional politicking inside the Democratic Party, with a focus on the 1976 platform process. Harrington, Phyfe, and Jack Clark met in late 1975 to devise a campaign to "build a programmatic tendency of the democratic Left in the Democratic Party and related constituent organizations (women's movement, trade unions, etc.)" and "create a presence for that tendency at the Convention."[32] The platform project, which received funding from the UAW, the IAM, and AFSCME, came to be called Democracy '76, with a declared purpose "to help redefine the political and programmatic debate in the 1976 presidential election."[33] Harrington circulated a draft economic manifesto for feedback from intellectuals and activists in his orbit, including Heather Booth and her husband Paul, then working for AFSCME.[34] The resulting Democracy '76 statement took aim at neoconservative critiques of Great Society social policy and called for more aggressive action by Democrats. "Far from being too radical, our liberal policy makers have not been liberal enough," it read.[35]

This focus on the platform as opposed to a candidate campaign was deliberate. The 1976 Democratic nomination contest featured an unusually open field with a shifting array of plausible candidates. Though Harrington personally supported liberal congressman Morris Udall, his commitment to a coalitional effort cautioned against becoming enmeshed in the race. This outlook was shared by the nine liberal unions who formed the Labor Coalition Clearinghouse to coordinate endorsement and convention strategy apart from Meany's influence. They agreed to eschew efforts to produce a single collective endorsement and instead to focus on boosting their members' presence in the convention delegations and influencing platform policy.[36] Key actors within the Clearinghouse, however, did demonstrate an affinity for the dark horse candidate from Georgia, Jimmy Carter, both for his ability to cut into George Wallace's support from southern white Democrats and for his seeming malleability on major issue positions.[37]

Indeed, that malleability was the flip side of Carter's central campaign strategy both in the nomination contest and the ensuing general election race: to deemphasize issues and run on his own personal appeal as a Washington outsider. A relative cipher on policy, Carter drew some liberal support through his apparent willingness to accede to policy demands. In April 1976, for example, he delivered a speech unveiling his national health insurance plan that was drafted in close collaboration with the UAW. Carter, having capitalized on early caucus and primary wins to build momentum in the media, secured the nomination long before the convention in July. But a priority for his campaign remained shoring up support on his left to avoid the kind of visible intraparty strife that had characterized the last two Democratic conventions. It motivated both his choice for a running mate—the stalwart labor liberal Walter Mondale—and his approach to the platform.

While Carter forces remained in control of the process, they deliberately acceded to liberal demands on most of the platform's substance.[38] The result was a strongly liberal platform whose

centerpiece was a modified version of Humphrey-Hawkins—
legislation about which Carter had grave personal misgivings.
When Harrington testified before the resolutions committee on
behalf of Democracy '76, he laid out an agenda that, in his words,
"united leaders of the major progressive constituencies of the
Democratic Party" and provided "a central policy core for the
Democratic Administration which the nation will inaugurate in
January."[39] To a striking degree, the platform document resulting
from the committee reflected the substance of that agenda. Its very
first plank addressed full employment, while later ones included
"a comprehensive national health insurance system with universal and mandatory coverage," "opposition to the undue concentration of wealth and power," and urban policies justified with explicit
reference to the Kerner Commission on Civil Disorders.[40] Beyond
the platform, Carter's campaign also fatefully agreed to support
liberals' resolution calling for another midterm party conference
in 1978.

Carter's acquiescence to liberal platform priorities ensured, as
intended, that no policy fights would occur during the convention. His team also tightened control to keep a lid on potential conflicts. Strauss pushed a rule through the platform committee that
increased the threshold requirement for petition signatures calling for a floor vote on minority reports.[41] Later, when a Wisconsin committeeman proposed twenty-minute televised debates on
three policy issues of the convention's choosing, Carter's team mobilized to defeat his resolution.[42]

Ultimately, the outcome of the convention consisted of a full-
throated liberal party platform and a nominee whose commitment
to either the platform or the activist ranks of his own party was
highly questionable. In his testimony to the platform committee,
Harrington had urged the nominee to avoid the perennial American temptation to "finesse the issues" and win a personal rather
than agenda-based victory. UAW president Leonard Woodcock
had gone further, sounding a classic responsible party theme in
calling on the committee to "declare, explicitly, that the national
platform is supreme and preemptive with respect to general principles and broad national issues."[43] Such a notion was, of course,

foreign to American party traditions. But it hinted at what would become a recurring argument of Carter's liberal critics during his presidency: that he betrayed a platform to which he was morally bound. This critique would eventually lead key actors to mount the decade's second major intraparty nomination challenge to a president. Fittingly, as early as May 1976, Ted Kennedy criticized Carter's platform testimony for "intentionally [making] his position on some issues indefinite and imprecise."[44]

DISILLUSION AND DISSENT IN THE CARTER YEARS

Intentional imprecision could well describe *both* presidential candidates' approach to issues in the general election contest that fall, to the chagrin of activists left and right. "In 1976," campaign chronicler Kandy Stroud would later write, "issues were no more important than the price of hoopskirts."[45] The limited programmatic stakes emphasized in the general election race reflected the circumstances that had led to the parties' respective nominations. A southern moderate, having capitalized on a fragmented liberal opposition in the Democratic primaries and committed to a personality-based campaign approach, squared off against a GOP incumbent whose own nomination had depended on the support of moderate party regulars and whose general election campaign would depend on an exceedingly cautious Rose Garden strategy. This match-up ensured that the emerging fault lines of American politics that had been visible during Gerald Ford's presidency would be obscured rather than deepened by the general election.

Carter's southernness and apparent centrism, for example, made an appeal to southern conservatives a tougher proposition for the Ford campaign, and left open the possibility of ideologically scrambled entreaties to other constituencies. With the South foreclosed, one aide wrote in a June memo, Ford's path to victory would run through the industrial North, a region where GOP politicians project "a generally progressive image." At the same time, given continued liberal skepticism about Carter, the memo argued that Ford "can—and must—win a proportion of the liberal vote," along with that of smaller targeted groups like environmentalists and teachers.[46] Ford did, in fact, campaign in the South to diminish Carter's advantage. Indeed, in a sign of the continuing force of the partisan realignment at work in the South, Ford would actually win a majority of the white southern vote, even as Carter won the Confederate states themselves thanks to strong support from African Americans.[47] But Ford's campaign shied away from explicitly conservative programmatic appeals, while conservative movement activists generally refrained from mobilizing electorally on his behalf.

If Ford's and Carter's campaign strategies ensured that 1976 would not see a repeat of the programmatic contrasts characterizing the election of 1972, this fact gibed well with a view of the electorate shared by both campaigns' pollsters. "The notion that this country is made up of people who identify themselves as conservatives or liberals is just not correct," Bob Teeter told a reporter in 1975. "To the great majority of Americans, the whole idea of conservatism and liberalism is not useful." Pat Caddell agreed: "We just don't have an ideological country now. We just have small groups on each side who take these things very seriously."[48] The swamp of mass opinion on major issues provided some support for this contention. But to draw from Americans' professed aversion to ideology a prediction that politics was moving in a nonideological direction was a questionable leap. For "small groups on each side" had an outsized capacity to affect the behavior of the parties and their politicians. Their influence was enhanced both by the new permeability of the reformed parties and Congress as well as by the diminishment of cross-pressures that ideologically dissident factions within both parties—conservative southern Democrats, liberal northern Republicans—had traditionally exerted.

It was thus all the more consequential that the narrow victor of the 1976 presidential contest, a loner resting his popular appeal on a kind of outsider antipolitics, would show a knack in office for choosing political battles that simultaneously mobilized right-wing opposition while alienating liberal Democrats. In so doing, Jimmy Carter would help accelerate the process of partisan ideological sorting while, like his predecessor, nearly losing control of his own party. If he proved in office to be, like Ford, a victim of the political times, his own political profile differed from his predecessor's in ways that only compounded the difficulties. Though Ford had been ill-equipped to respond to conservative mobilization, he was a stalwart party man with longstanding relationships in the national GOP and a commitment to party-building.[49] Carter, by contrast, came of age in a largely one-party state where political competition lacked an explicitly partisan dynamic. He framed his political appeal as both a Washington and partisan outsider, and approached governance with a Progressive's conception of public "trusteeship" that eschewed pragmatic bargaining and intra-party negotiation.[50] It was a governing approach calibrated to alienate allies and worsen political dilemmas.

In his first two years in office, Carter continually failed to set legislative priorities, sending an array of initiatives to Congress without a strategy for building and sustaining support.[51] Modest stimulus measures and an increasingly austere approach to economic policy alienated liberals. Amnesty for draft evaders, IRS scrutiny of Christian schools' tax status, and a protracted renegotiation of the Panama Canal Treaty that Carter chose to attempt early in his tenure against the judgment of advisors all served to unite and mobilize right-wing opposition. Simultaneously, the president stoked bipartisan outrage in Congress through repeated targeting of parochial interests embedded in the appropriations process, from water projects to B-1 bombers. Carter's presidency occasioned continued right-wing ascendance within the GOP thanks partly to the influx of new streams of conservative activism. But liberal activists and their Democratic allies in Congress also mobilized to assert programmatic pressure on a titular leader of their party who seemed openly contemptuous of them.

Harrington revamped Democracy '76 as Democratic Agenda, again with the financial backing of the UAW, AFSCME, and the IAM. Harrington and executive director Marjorie Phyfe initiated the project in November 1977 through a major conference in DC, which focused substantively on full-employment policies and politically on resistance to Democratic waywardness in Congress and the White House. On the second day of the conference, participants marched to the Democratic National Committee to demand accountability to that platform.[52] One day was dedicated to a series of panels on policy issues that emphasized the coalitional potential of the Left's diverse constituencies.

This attention to building organizational and intellectual alliances among historically leery movements typified liberal activities during the Carter years, which saw a great proliferation of acronym-happy coalitions. The Full Employment Action Council (FEAC), co-chaired by Coretta Scott King and union chief Murray Finley, followed rallies across the country in the summer of 1977 with a Capitol Hill lobbying effort on behalf of Humphrey-Hawkins.[53] A coalition of consumer and labor activists organized the Campaign on Inflation and Necessities (COIN) to advocate targeted, sectoral anti-inflation policies as a substitute for austerity measures.[54] Unions across the board, meanwhile, had reversed their opposition to the Equal Rights Amendment (ERA) by the mid-1970s, and many of them would provide support for the campaign when the conservative counter-mobilization intensified. On the fault line dividing environmental activists and labor, several important initiatives emerged in the late 1970s, including Environmentalists for Full Employment as well as a major project launched by Heather Booth and William Winpisinger, the Citizen Labor Energy Coalition (CLEC).[55]

One legacy of the decade's party reforms was that activists disgruntled with Carter and seeking to forge new organizational ties had a focus for their efforts: the midterm party conference mandated by the 1976 convention. Carter's aides recognized that the 1978 conference posed a political danger and urged that the president "pay special attention" to strategizing for it.[56] The White House instructed the national committee to schedule it, like the 1974 mini-conference, after the congressional elections in November to diminish the gathering's impact.[57] At the administration's behest, the DNC Executive Council required the signatures of 25 percent of conference delegates to propose a resolution—and stipulated that the signatures be presented to the DNC at least three days prior to the conference.[58] The clear intent of both requirements was to make the introduction of floor resolutions logistically infeasible. But Democratic Agenda utilized information about the conference's requirements it acquired through consultation with Donald Fraser's reform organization, the Democratic Conference. Three days before the conference, the group was able to present to a shocked staff at DNC headquarters 409 delegate signatures for four policy planks, which exceeded the 25 percent threshold.[59]

The move revealed the degree to which years of networking among party and issue activists had rendered Democratic Agenda, in Harrington's words, "a communication center of the liberal-labor wing of the Democratic Party."[60] The organization's efforts were sufficiently notable for Carter's spokesman to name it as the administration's chief conference antagonist in a press conference prior to the gathering.[61] Over 500 of 1,625 delegates to the conference attended a caucus meeting jointly held by Democratic Agenda and the Democratic Conference the day before, some sporting "Still 4/76" buttons in phonetic honor of the 1976 platform.[62] Once the conference convened, Doug Fraser and UAW legislative director Howard Paster led the effort to whip support for the resolutions while negotiating with DNC chairman John White.

At the midterm conference itself, held in Memphis, the pro-Carter forces repeated the strategy they had used during the nominating convention two years earlier, combining tight organizational control with a concessionary posture regarding policy planks. The official proceedings of the first two days accorded with the anodyne script devised by the administration. Off the floor, meanwhile, negotiations on resolutions proceeded between White and various liberal forces—chiefly Doug Fraser regarding the Democratic Agenda–sponsored economic planks and Mildred Jeffrey and the National Women's Political Caucus over resolutions related to the ERA, abortion, and gender representation in the party. White agreed to Fraser's demand that the health care resolution include language calling on Democrats and the president to pass national insurance legislation during the 96th Congress. In exchange for feminists' backing down on a resolution forbidding the party from providing financial support for anti-ERA candidates, White also agreed to a guarantee of 50 percent female delegate representation at the 1980 convention and a pledge to work toward electing fifty women to Congress in 1980.[63] Finally, administration forces did not resist Democratic Agenda's efforts to dominate the twenty-four issue workshops, each of which was to choose "platform advisors" for the 1980 platform drafting process.[64]

Despite their concessions, the Carter forces were unable to avoid a public confrontation. The point of opposition around which liberal activists coalesced was a resolution on the federal budget that had emerged out of a conference-eve meeting between labor leaders, the ADA, the Democratic Agenda, and the Democratic Conference. Carter had announced in October that, as part of his anti-inflation agenda, he was committed to keeping the 1980 deficit below $30 billion. Given a previous commitment to increase defense spending by 3 percent above inflation, this pledge guaranteed painful austerity for domestic social programs. The liberals in Memphis drafted a resolution condemning Carter's budget priorities and insisting that social programs not face overall reductions.[65] As one strategist explained to a reporter, the budget offered "an issue that unites the progressive community, such as it is here—labor, the black caucus, the women's caucus, the city people. There are a lot of special-interest resolutions floating around. . . . The budget is the one that pulls the progressives together."[66] The resolution's direct criticism of administration policies was a bridge too far for Carter, but Doug Fraser refused to back down in negotiations. It became clear that the vote on this resolution, to be held on the final day of the meeting, would be the key test of strength between the contending forces.

The administration deputized 200 loyal delegates to act as floor whips and sent out nearly every senior White House official to lobby against the resolution. Ultimately, the roll call on Saturday counted 521 in favor of the resolution, 872 against. Carter's victory owed to the large number of ex officio delegates at the conference, staunch southern support, and an effective effort to woo black delegates by Detroit mayor Coleman Young, who argued pragmatically against antagonizing a president on whom urban interests depended.[67]

But the president's victory was partial. The conference had confirmed rather than obscured the reality of party disunity on core matters of program and policy. That a conference under the administration's own tight control would feature an open rebuke by 40 percent of its delegates to a president halfway through his term spoke volumes about his perilous position as well as the clout of the party's dissident faction.[68] "There is no doubt that the left was the dominant force at the Democrats' midterm conference," the *Congressional Quarterly* concluded. "It managed to set the agenda for discussion, do nearly all the talking, and force the Administration to make serious concessions on resolution-writing and new party rules."[69] As a *Nation* editorial put it, "the midterm convention had been rigged, but poorly rigged."[70] It proved particularly significant in demonstrating a base of potential support for a nomination challenge to Carter in 1980—which had been very much part of Harrington and Doug Fraser's intentions.[71]

Indeed, the conference provided an occasion for the most likely such contender to articulate liberals' discontent and rally them to his side. The Saturday workshop on health care featured a panel (chaired by Arkansas governor Bill Clinton) comprising White House aide Stuart Eizenstat, Health, Education, and Welfare Secretary Joseph Califano, Doug Fraser, and Senator Ted Kennedy. After the Carter officials spoke staidly about the administration's hospital cost containment bill, the senator rose to his feet and offered a hoarse-voiced stump speech that electrified the auditorium's crowd of 2,500. Kennedy veered away from the topic of his own national health-insurance bill to offer an expansive warning about the president's policy direction and the Democratic Party's fate. "The party that tore itself apart over Vietnam in the 1960s cannot afford to tear itself apart today over basic cuts in social programs," he shouted, prompting the audience to stand and applaud.[72] To White House strategists, activists, and journalists alike, Kennedy's performance looked unmistakably like the opening salvo of a nomination challenge.[73]

Before Kennedy felt sufficiently persuaded about the existence of a plausible path to the nomination to launch a formal campaign, however, liberals pursued further efforts at institution-building in 1978 and 1979. Two major initiatives in that vein, both launched partly in imitation of New Right organizational successes, represented efforts to go beyond single-issue coalitions like COIN,

CLEC, and FEAC and to establish more durable political formations on behalf of a broad-based agenda. The first, Doug Fraser's
Progressive Alliance, was ballyhooed but short-lived. The second,
Heather Booth's Citizen Action, began more modestly but would
grow greatly in size and significance over the next decade.

LABOR LIBERALISM IN LEAN TIMES

The UAW president's initiative originated in the breakdown of
the decade's last remaining effort to address stagflation through
corporatist bargaining among business, labor, and government
officials.[74] The Labor-Management Group was an informal committee, organized by former Labor secretary John Dunlop and co-
chaired by Meany and the chairman of General Electric. It met
periodically during the Nixon, Ford, and Carter years in an effort to
address issues of mutual concern to unions and management. But
from the point of view of one of its most important labor-affiliated
members, Doug Fraser, the unprecedented corporate political
mobilization during Carter's first two years belied the group's assumed context of consensual relations.[75] The struggle over a labor
law reform bill in 1977 and 1978 was a case in point. After passing
easily in the House in October 1977, the bill stalled in the Senate
due to a filibuster. Months of fierce lobbying to break the logjam
failed in the face of a massive effort by business. Emboldened by
their earlier victory over common-situs picketing and organized in
an array of coordinated fronts, from the Business Roundtable and
Chamber of Commerce to advocacy groups like the Right-to-Work
Committee, business interests teamed with conservative activists
to wage a Capitol Hill "holy war," in the words of the AFL-CIO's
chief lobbyist.[76] This successful effort to block a modest reform
bill, coming on the heels of similar mobilizations against a minimum wage hike, Humphrey-Hawkins, and the establishment of
a Consumer Protection Agency, prompted Fraser to take a public
stand.

On July 18, 1978, Fraser sent a letter to the Labor-Management

Group's membership as well as the press announcing his resig-nation.[77] "I believe that leaders of the business community, with few exceptions, have chosen to wage a one-sided class war in this country," Fraser contended, describing an across-the-board stra-tegic shift among business elites "toward confrontation, rather than cooperation." Rather than legitimize the new posture by con-tinuing to participate in an enterprise predicated on good-faith negotiation, Fraser announced, in a clarion call for militant social unionism, that the UAW would seek to make "new alliances" and "new coalitions"—to "reforge the links with those who believe in struggle: the kind of people who sat-down in the factories in the 1930s and who marched in Selma in the 1960s." Fraser's resigna-tion letter caused a stir in the press and electrified liberals. What resonated was not only Fraser's identification of an ascendant, militant corporate-conservative alliance in the political arena, but also his commitment to reengaging the labor movement in coali-tion building with other left-liberal activists and interests.

In the months following his resignation, Fraser worked with top UAW political staff to outline plans for a new national umbrella organization for activists from labor, antipoverty, feminist, civil rights, consumer, and environmental backgrounds.[78] In September of 1978, Fraser formally invited leaders from over 100 such groups to attend a conference in Detroit "to consider formation of a new alliance aimed at transforming the American political system."[79] He framed the meeting as a response to conservative ideological initiative—"the tremendous power of a newly sophisticated right-wing corporate alliance." He warned that "corporate reactionaries and their ideologues for the first time in years have taken the mo-mentum from progressives in the arena of ideas," and advocated a united front of left-leaning activist organizations to mobilize a response. The organization itself was incorporated that winter as the Progressive Alliance, with the UAW's Bill Dodds installed as executive director. A roster of unions from labor's progressive wing served as the Alliance's funding base outside of the UAW.[80] The group drafted a statement of principles acknowledging the diver-sity of its membership but sounding a theme of solidarity: "While we each bring our own separate concerns to this alliance, we share a common belief that our individual problems can only be solved through collective action."[81]

Fraser intended the Alliance to focus on reforming the political *system*, and his conception of such reform bore the mark of responsible party doctrine. His invitation to the 1978 exploratory meeting outlined an agenda that included abolishing the filibuster and pursuing reforms "aimed at creating a stronger, more accountable, more ideological Democratic Party." The Alliance's statement of principles similarly connected substantive progress with the transformation of party politics. "We need political parties that are accountable, issue-oriented and disciplined to abide by their platform commitments," it read. "Revitalized parties and issue-based politics are tools through which the struggle of the 1980s can be waged."[82] A working paper on the Alliance's reform program detailed a theory of partisanship that E. E. Schattschneider would have recognized. "Democratic theory links the effective political participation of citizens to the effective performance of governments," it declared. Rather than exploiting "the politics of personality" or pursuing merely the "spoils of office," political contenders "must obtain office on the basis of coherent, clearly specified principles and policies" and must try to enact those policies in office. "If they fail to do so, or, if in practice, their policies fail to serve the common good, citizens must be able to: 1.) identify who failed; 2.) hold them accountable for their failures; 3.) replace them."[83]

Motivating Fraser's focus on political transformation was not just alarm at the gains being achieved by an ascendant alliance of business interests and conservatives, but also a perception of pervasive, systemic party decline and political fragmentation that he shared with most journalists and scholars in the 1970s. Fraser took pains to emphasize Congress's culpability in the failures and frustrations of the Carter years. "It has no cohesion," he told a reporter in 1978. "There's no discipline."[84] That same year *Time* ran a cover story on the "bold and balky" post-reform Congress that summarized the emerging consensus about the atomization and disarray of the institution and its parties. "Many political scientists fear that Congress may eventually become unmanageable by its leaders," it reported.[85] For Fraser, the indiscipline and fragmentation of Democratic legislative behavior was directly connected to the party's faltering commitment to labor-liberal policies.[86] He singled out a younger group of Democratic freshmen and sophomores from suburban districts for particular condemnation, as neoliberal apostates dissenting from key progressive tenets related to taxes, regulation, and social provision.[87] For Fraser as for many liberals during the Carter years, the fact that Democratic domination of both the executive and legislative branches could produce so little in the way of liberal policy achievements was a source of frustration and puzzlement. "We had a big victory in '76," one of his aides put it, "and wound up with a pile of shit."[88]

The legislative disarray of the Carter presidency that contemporaries like Fraser so often bemoaned has lived on as a touchstone in histories of post-1960s liberal collapse. It is worth qualifying the assessment. The frustration of liberal policy goals during the Carter years was very real. Moreover, some of the new and increasingly suburban Democrats arriving to Congress in this period, beginning with the massive influx of "Watergate babies" in 1974 and continuing in 1976 and 1978, did indeed embody the new issue orientation that Fraser lamented. They were liberal on social and cultural issues, while fiscally conservative and skeptical of redistributive state activism.[89] Their influence combined with stagflation, resurgent conservative and antigovernment energies, and a trend toward retrenchment across the industrial world in the late 1970s to put new constraints on liberal policy progress. Measures of the congressional Democrats' overall voting patterns on issues relating to business regulation and fiscal policy did show a slight rightward shift in the middle and late 1970s.[90]

The conservative trend within the Democratic Party of the 1970s is, however, easily overstated. The same measurements showing a rightward shift in the congressional caucus's economic positions showed *leftward* shifts on issues ranging from civil rights to foreign and military affairs to social welfare policy—and even labor legislation.[91] Scholars and commentators have tended to give the iconic Democratic congressional class of '74 a monolithic cast as a cohort of suburbanite neoliberals paving the way for Reaganism. But the

Watergate babies counted among their ranks not only the likes of Tony Coelho, Tim Wirth, and Gary Hart, but also such future liberal legislative leaders as Henry Waxman, George Miller, and Tom Harkin. By the time a Democrat returned to the White House in 1977, he faced a congressional majority party that hewed to more liberal policy priorities than his administration did. In Carter's first year in office, congressional Democrats set the pattern for intraparty relations by seeking to push him leftward on spending, the minimum wage, and public works and employment policy.[92] In a more pertinent example, the very 1978 labor law defeat that prompted Doug Fraser's formation of the Progressive Alliance did not reflect a new antilabor bias among congressional Democrats. The House passed the bill by a vote of 257 to 163 before the measure met the fate that had befallen virtually all progressive labor law bills in the postwar era: a Senate filibuster sustained by conservative coalition votes and supported by only two northern Democrats.[93]

Despite the success of the labor law filibuster, southern Democrats themselves were undergoing changes by the end of the decade. Indeed, easily the most important electoral development among congressional Democrats in the 1970s was the gradual, halting, but forceful transformation of the party's southern ranks. By removing some of Congress's most conservative lawmakers from Democratic ranks while inducing more liberal voting behavior in others, southern realignment was already rendering the party more internally coherent *and* marginally more liberal overall, even as other developments introduced countervailing influences.

The settings in which lawmakers operated were more significant contributors to the frustrations and disarray of Carter-era policymaking than any ideological changes among congressional Democrats. The congressional reforms implemented in the first half of the decade contained both centralizing and decentralizing measures. In the initial years following the reforms, the decentralizing changes predominated, as party leaders hesitated to maximize their use of new powers and individual members swamped the system in the absence of management and coordination by legislative "traffic cops." The Carter White House exacerbated such centrifugal tendencies through inept legislative leadership as well as its prioritization of the kinds of comprehensive reform packages on thorny issues like energy and welfare that Congress has difficulty tackling even under the best circumstances.[94] But the legislative frustrations of those years motivated further organizational changes that would ultimately diminish rather than perpetuate party fragmentation. Under the energetic speakership of Tip O'Neill beginning in 1977, the House leadership began pursuing the expansion of its whip system, the enhanced use of the Steering and Policy and Rules committees to manage legislation, and the deployment of task forces to develop proposals across multiple committees. Partly as a result, Democratic voting cohesion began to rise late in the decade, and never again reversed course.

These developments were latent and largely undetectable to activists like Doug Fraser amid the legislative confusion and conservative mobilizations of the Carter years. What was vividly clear was both a sense of liberal disarray as well as a Democratic president and congressional majority's obvious lack of commitment to the progressive party platform of 1976. Other liberal groups were thinking in terms similar to Fraser during Carter's presidency, whether seen in Democratic Agenda's claim that the "drive for a more responsible Political Party structure never been more attractive than it is now" or in ADA officials' insistence that "the 1976 platform is not obsolete, and those who are elected under it should stay with it."[95]

Beyond political reform, the Alliance had long-term organizational goals that typified the outlook of left-liberal activists in the late 1970s. Included in an internally distributed "Long-Range road map" in early 1979, for example, were plans for the "establishment of a more or less formal caucus within the Democratic Party," the forging of a "media network" of progressive communications efforts, the "creation of an 'AEI' on the left," and the building of a 25,000-name mailing list to be overseen by "a 'Viguerie' on our side."[96] The latter two items, in their explicit mimicry of recent conservative efforts, reflected liberals' growing fascination with the ascendant New Right and their desire to emulate its organizational approaches. Mike Miller of the CWA gave presentations on the New Right's mobilizations in 1978 to liberal and Democratic audiences, including the DNC, while the NEA prepared a national conference on the new conservative threat to education.[97] In April 1978 270 liberal organizations formed the network Interchange as a communications hub exchanging "alerts on the New Right's actions."[98] The ADA distributed 250,000 copies of its report "A Citizen's Guide to the Right Wing" that same year.[99] In 1979 NOW workshops were held on "Reproductive Rights and the Right Wing" and a National Conference on Right-Wing Strategy was organized by Democratic activist Midge Miller.[100]

By the end of the decade, liberal calls abounded for the explicit emulation of conservative organizational innovations from the 1960s and 1970s. This marked an ironic new turn in a long-running cycle among ideological activists, since so many of those very innovations on the right had begun as answers to organizations on the left. The American Conservative Union was the Right's ADA. The Republican Study Committee was the Right's Democratic Study Group. The Committee for the Survival of a Free Congress was the Right's National Committee for an Effective Congress. The Heritage Foundation and the American Enterprise Institute were the Right's versions of the Brookings Institution. The cycle of combat and emulation turned anew during liberalism's lean years.

Liberals and conservatives were not equally successful in their respective institution-building efforts from the 1970s onward, however. The fate of the Progressive Alliance helps illuminate some of the factors underlying the Left's relative disadvantage. After a flurry of activity and ambitious planning, the Alliance buckled under its own top-heavy structure, officially disbanding in April 1981. Long prior to that official decision, the organization found itself hamstrung by the need to accommodate myriad member organizations, and its leadership struggled against the accurate perception that all the effective power remained concentrated in the UAW.[101] In a 1980 letter to Michael Harrington, one departing staffer called the Alliance "about as productive as flower tending in seventh century Byzantium. Lots of nice sprouts that keep getting stepped on."[102] But more important than any such organizational dysfunctions was the manufacturing crisis, particularly in the auto industry, that was beginning take a toll on the American labor movement at the same time that employers launched a newly aggressive mobilization against unions.[103] The long-term decline of labor would exert a crippling handicap on left-liberal mobilizations in the next few decades—not least by ensuring the Democratic Party's continued dependence on corporate financial support—while in the short term the auto crisis had a practical and devastating effect on the Progressive Alliance. From 1979 onward, Doug Fraser's attentions were increasingly concentrated on the looming bankruptcy of Chrysler and efforts to secure federal help for the company, and between 1979 and 1981 the UAW's membership declined by 20 percent amid a wave of plant closings.[104] The Alliance lost priority in the crisis. Fraser's decision to step down as the group's chair in March 1981 swiftly precipitated its disintegration.

Beyond suffering travails specific to the labor movement, meanwhile, the Progressive Alliance could be said to have shared in a deficiency common to much of the Left at the time: it lacked a mobilized grassroots constituency comparable either to those that drove the social movements of the 1960s or to the growing ranks of engaged foot soldiers for Christian right and tax-revolt causes in the 1970s. Against the loftier hopes of its organizers, the Alliance remained largely a staff-dominated coalition of letterhead organizations. This lack of real grassroots muscle played as important a role as the conflicting legal and strategic postures among member organizations in hindering the Alliance's ability to engage in such factional party efforts as candidate sponsorships and primary challenges.[105] It was not a problem unique to the Alliance. By the late 1970s, the Democratic Agenda also began to acknowledge an inability to buttress its influential elite-level party operations with a mass base or grassroots leverage. "We have had an impact on program and structure within the Democratic Party qua party," one leader pointed out at in 1979, "but we have no electoral clout."[106] A year later, DSOC's Ruth Jordan offered a similar assessment and recommended renewed efforts to build independent, locally rooted grassroots bases for Democratic Agenda.[107] But such efforts never succeeded.

Those failures reflected the general post-1960s tendency of many advocacy groups on the left to organize as elite, staff-dominated letterhead organizations lacking mobilized mass constituencies, a popular hollowing-out of movement politics that could also be seen in the increasing emphasis on legal rather than legislative strategies for pursuing political aims.[108] Indeed, the combination of continued influence and diminished grassroots muscle could characterize the position of liberal Democrats writ large at the time. *Congressional Quarterly*'s assessment of the 1978 midterm Democratic conference in Memphis noted "the ambiguous role of liberal activists in American politics—increasingly important within the nation's majority party, but isolated from public policy decisions and from national opinion itself."[109] That isolation stemmed not merely from the mistrust and conflicting priorities of the Carter administration, but from an electoral weakness that reduced liberals' leverage.

It was precisely this lack of a grassroots base that Heather Booth sought to address when she built upon the organizing efforts of the issue-based labor-liberal energy coalition CLEC to pursue a broader national initiative called Citizen Action. Through the Midwest Academy as well as her work alongside William Winpisinger at CLEC, Booth had begun to forge a national network of relationships and commitments among several state- and local-level citizens groups. In December 1979 Booth convened a three-day Citizen Action Organizing Conference in Chicago that brought together representatives from liberal unions and five of the most active and influential state-level groups: the Connecticut Citizen Action Group, Massachusetts Fair Share, Ohio Public Interest Campaign, Oregon Fair Share, and the Illinois Political Action Council.[110] The aim was to achieve "a national dimension" to the issue work being done by the state groups, and in particular to expand CLEC's state coalitions into multi-issue campaigns.[111]

To the extent that those efforts remained focused on practical, locally rooted struggles over issues like toxic waste contamination, plant closings, or the decontrol of natural gas prices, CLEC and Citizen Action were not quite innovators. They did, however, serve as important institutional connectors between labor's progressive wing and the community organizing, public interest, and consumer groups that had emerged as an activist legacy of the 1960s. This alliance was vividly embodied in the oddball public teamwork of Booth the veteran New Left feminist and William "Wimpy" Winpisinger the gruff, fifty-something Machinists union boss. George Meany had advised Winpisinger against working with Booth given her New Left background, but Winpisinger saw an alliance with such forces as the only hope for revitalizing progressive politics in America.[112] Booth and her partners in state-level citizen groups felt the same way.

Moreover, Citizen Action did *not* ultimately confine itself to issue campaigns that avoided electoral entanglements. CLEC's lobbying efforts on oil deregulation, both at the state level and in Washington, helped serve as a model for formal political engagement as well as an inducement to consider electoral activity a component of Citizen Action's approach. By the end of the decade, Booth and fellow leaders in the organization like Michael Ansara of Massachusetts Fair Share and Robert Creamer of Illinois Public Action had begun the process of coaxing community and consumer activists who had resisted partisan politics to take the plunge.[113] The goal should be to "seize control of the Democratic Party," Ansara insisted, and to do that, "winning office" was key.[114] The model of the Republican right remained paramount. Michael Harrington told Citizen Action conference attendees in 1980 to recall Barry Goldwater's famous landslide defeat. "What did the Goldwaterites do?" he asked. "They did what we should do. They got up and they started organizing. They doubled and redoubled their efforts. They have now totally and completely taken over the Republican Party."[115] "If we want a majority constituency," Booth declared in 1980, "we need alliances with people who have organized primarily in an electoral direction. . . . We need to build a political machine." Citizen Action's efforts soon included the provision of training, resources, and personnel for groups working on over a hundred local, state, and federal election campaigns in 1982.[116]

The "ground game" undergirding such electoral efforts marked a signature contribution of the public interest and community organizations to progressive politics in the last decades of the twentieth century: the large-scale revival of canvassing. Though door-to-door recruitment and mobilizing campaigns had been mainstays in urban electoral politics and in the voter registration drives of the civil rights movement, the advent of television, phone-banking, and large-scale direct mail practices reduced the incentives for such canvassing efforts during the mid-twentieth century. But the innovations of encyclopedia salesman-turned-environmental activist Marc Anderson and an ex-Nader's Raider named David Zwick during the 1970s led to the rapid spread and professionalization of the canvass as a fundraising and recruitment tool for a full array of consumer, feminist, environmental, civil rights, and economic justice groups.[117] The turn toward electoral politics that organizers like Booth began to take by the end of the decade thus marked the introduction of a new stream of canvassing resources and operations to the Democratic Party.

All of this activity contributed to an important, underappreciated political development that had begun with the explosion of social movement activism in the 1960s. Particularly in the wake of 1968's insurgent campaigns and George McGovern's defeat in 1972, these activists had demonstrated occasional antagonism toward, and frequent wariness of, mainstream party politics. But the work of leaders like Heather Booth succeeded in helping not only to midwife a reconfigured labor-liberal alliance but also to foster the gradual reentrance of a generation of movement activists into Democratic politics. This network of activists and organizations ultimately contributed to the ideological sorting and structuring of the two-party system by enlisting on one side for battle. Inducing them to enlist was a contested, fitful process requiring intellectual and organizational work, but it had largely occurred by the dawn of the Reagan era.

SAILING AGAINST THE WIND

Before those years commenced, liberal activists mounted one more significant partisan effort that, though a failure in the short term, forged vital coalitional ties that endured into the Reagan era.

The successful platform work done by Democratic Agenda and feminist organizations at the Democratic convention in 1976 and the midterm conference in 1978 had failed to affect the Carter administration's behavior. This failure helped to convince such activists that a credible nomination challenge was required for 1980. "A serious issue challenge has to also be a candidate challenge," Harrington wrote his colleagues in early 1979, just as a Progressive Alliance official emphasized to Doug Fraser "the necessity of considering the building of a left challenge (EMK) within the Democratic Party so that Carter cannot play general-election, right wing politics from now through '80."[118] The initials specified the candidate activists had in mind. At least since his barn-burning speech at the party conference in Memphis, activists had been "waiting for Teddy."

Long cast as a quixotic effort by a political celebrity whose ideological appeal was a relic of bygone times, Edward M. Kennedy's 1980 nomination challenge against Jimmy Carter has recently come under renewed scholarly appreciation, as a venture stemming directly from the significant coalitional work carried out by liberals in the 1970s.[119] As with Reagan's challenge to Ford four years earlier, Kennedy's campaign appeared to many contemporaries as symptomatic of a party system rapidly fragmenting into a candidate-centered free-for-all.[120] But the programmatic cast of both of these challenges in fact made them signposts of nascent polarization.

Certainly by the time Kennedy began to seriously contemplate the run that so many Democratic officials and activists urged him to make, beleaguered Jimmy Carter was feeling the pinch of this polarization. Stagflation, soaring energy prices, and right-wing resurgence put the president in a crippling position that was bound to exacerbate conflict with liberals in his party. "It is damn hard to be in a Democratic administration in Republican times," one Carter administration official told David Broder at the 1978 Memphis conference.[121] In May 1979 Carter's domestic policy advisor Stuart Eizenstat sent a memo to senior White House officials signaling the danger signs on Carter's left. "I am increasingly concerned that the President is moving further and further from his

Democratic Party base by a number of actions," he wrote, including "his economic policy, which is widely viewed as Republican in thrust," as well as his austerity budget and support for decontrol of oil prices. "Can we get together on this to develop ways to reach out to our *badly* estranged friends?"[122]

Eizenstat's pleas, along with those of his liberal ally in the administration, Vice President Walter Mondale, fell on deaf ears, as Carter became convinced by advisor Pat Caddell that a deeper problem than mere party politics beset the country—a psychic crisis of confidence and faith in public institutions that had to be addressed openly. The result was Carter's famous Camp David summit of citizens and civic leaders in July 1979, followed by a televised address to which posterity would lend the moniker "the malaise speech."[123] Carter's analysis of the nation's ills tapped directly into the prevailing sense among political observers of a system crumbling in the face of dissensus, mistrust, and apathy—"fragmentation and self-interest," as he put it. The speech was initially well received by the public, but it did little to assuage committed liberals convinced that viable programmatic solutions to the nation's problems were, in fact, readily available, only to be rejected by an ideologically compromised president.

Kennedy certainly thought this, and his proto-candidacy was closely connected, in both program and personnel, to the Left's new coalitional network in civil society. His hiring of Carl Wagner as a political advisor in late 1978 typified such connections—Wagner was both an ex-McGovern activist and current staffer at AFSCME—as did the intensive legislative and lobbying work Kennedy did with Doug Fraser through the Coalition for National Health Insurance.[124] In July 1979 William Winpisinger lent his signature to the first major national direct-mail effort to raise funds for a "Draft Kennedy" movement, an operation overseen by the "Viguerie of the left," Tom Matthews.[125] The ADA voted to endorse a Kennedy challenge that summer, while NOW announced opposition to Carter's reelection in December.[126]

To be sure, some of the leading lights of labor-liberal coalitional politics in this period remained loyal to Carter due to specific ties of interest and policy. Most significant was the NEA's decision to endorse the president for reelection in 1979. The teachers' union, under Terry Herndon's aggressive leadership, was at the vanguard of left-liberal activism within the Democratic Party at the time. Its endorsement, rewarding Carter's fulfillment of campaign commitments to raise federal education spending and establish a Department of Education, ultimately provided Carter with important electoral muscle to complement the inherent advantages of incumbency in his fight against Kennedy.[127] Such conflicting positions among allied organizations, meanwhile, persuaded the leaders of coalitions like Democratic Agenda and Progressive Alliance to eschew official organizational involvement in the race in favor of continued work on platform and issue advocacy.[128] Countless individual leaders in these groups, however, from Harrington and Doug Fraser on down, became active Kennedy supporters.

The details of Kennedy's vexed primary campaign, formally launched in November 1979, have been well chronicled by journalists and historians.[129] Less noted is the striking parallel in trajectory and form between his campaign and the Reagan insurgency of 1976. In both cases, an initial campaign strategy deemphasizing ideology and issues in favor of gauzier, candidate-centered appeals appeared to contribute to losses in early caucuses and primaries. Mid-campaign changes of course then turned the respective efforts into programmatic crusades on behalf of ideological party activists—crusades that failed to make up for early delegate losses but that carried the fights to the conventions and to alterations in the party platforms, demonstrating the vitality of the majority factions within each respective party.

The Kennedy men who devised an initial campaign strategy eschewing ideological appeal included campaign manager Steven Smith, pollster Peter Hart, and political advisor Paul Kirk.[130] There was a clear logic to their thinking. As of fall 1979, Kennedy's lead over both Carter (whose approval rating frequently fell below 30 percent) and various prospective Republican presidential candidates in public opinion polls was consistently large. Given the evident wishes of the public and of broad swathes of the party, Kennedy's advisors deemed it sensible to pursue a general election-style campaign from the outset, heavy on platitudes about "leadership" and light on the substance of his already well-known liberalism.[131] But the cautious strategy confused and demobilized Kennedy's supporters while helping to render him an uncomfortable, inarticulate campaigner. The first months of the campaign, meanwhile, coincided with an upsurge in Carter's support as a result of two crises that initially drew Americans to their commander in chief's side: Iranian militants' raid of the US embassy on November 4 and the Soviet invasion of Afghanistan a month later. In the shadow of these crises, Kennedy suffered a 2-to-1 defeat in the Iowa caucus, followed by losses in New Hampshire and a string of southern primaries.

The campaign soon agreed on a course correction toward more explicit programmatic and ideological appeals, which Kennedy debuted in a major address at Georgetown University in late January. Repeating a phrase he had used in his triumphant speech at the 1978 midterm party conference—"sometimes a party must sail against the wind"—Kennedy articulated a classic case for hewing to the core programmatic traditions of Democratic liberalism so as to offer a stark contrast with the opposition.[132] "We cannot permit the Democratic Party to remain captive to those who have been so confused about its ideals," he declared, making the same case to Democratic primary voters that Reagan had made to Republicans four years earlier when calling for a party banner of "bold colors" rather than "pale pastels." The program Kennedy laid out was liberal across the board, encompassing national health insurance, wage and price controls to tackle inflation, increased environmental protections, new arms-control efforts, curbs on wasteful military spending, and even cautionary notes about the danger of an overly belligerent Cold War posture. The speech electrified his supporters and helped refuel his campaign's fundraising. Reenergized on the stump now that he felt freer to launch issue critiques of Carter from the left, Kennedy began to make headway in primary contests, particularly in the industrial north. Compared to Reagan's late-primary surge in 1976, Kennedy's comeback was fitful and uneven, and he ultimately entered the 1980 party convention trailing Carter's delegate count 1,239 to 1,964. But his support .

was substantial enough to give him leverage in major convention decisions in August.

The characteristics of the supporters that Kennedy drew over the course of his campaign reflected just the coalition that left-liberal activists like Michael Harrington, Doug Fraser, and Heather Booth had sought to construct in the 1970s. As the agenda laid out in his Georgetown speech indicated, Kennedy's issue appeal mirrored those activists' *additive* approach to coalition-building, in which cultural and foreign policy liberalism augmented rather than supplanted New Deal economic appeals. Kennedy's campaign rested on mobilized support from a large portion of the labor movement, feminists, environmentalists, consumer groups, African American organizations (including the Congressional Black Caucus), Hispanic activists, and the nascent gay rights movement. The class base of this support did not skew upwards in the manner of McGovern in 1972, and the programmatic core of the campaign—the common ground for all of these groups—was a liberal agenda on economics and the welfare state.[133] By pursuing this additive approach, liberal Democrats paralleled their conservative counterparts in the GOP, who worked in the late 1970s to sustain New Right and Christian conservative mobilizations on social issues without trimming conservative positions on the economy.

The campaign's final echo of Reagan's 1976 insurgency occurred at the Democratic convention in August. By the end of the primary season, Kennedy's delegate deficit was essentially prohibitive. But after Carter rebuffed an offer to hold a televised policy debate with Kennedy in exchange for his withdrawal and endorsement, the challenger decided to pursue a long-shot rules strategy aimed at destabilizing the alignment of delegate support. The campaign mobilized at the DNC's Rules Committee hearings in June to seek an "open convention," in which delegates pledged to Carter would be allowed to reassess their allegiances.[134] Kennedy's forces, lacking a committee majority, lost the fight. But they vowed to take a rules challenge to the convention floor in August—along with a series of minority reports on the party platform.

Liberal forces' success in dominating the platform process was the major surprise of the 1980 convention. The process could first be seen in the same Rules Committee sessions that quashed the open convention effort. The Progressive Alliance, the Democratic Conference, and Democratic Agenda worked in tandem to secure passage of two resolutions related to party reform. The first tasked the DNC with creating a new Commission on Party Accountability, which would explore measures that could "yield an effective and disciplined effort to implement the Platform of the National Democratic Party."[135] The second, mandating another midterm party conference in 1982, won in a narrow committee floor fight.[136]

Beyond process victories, the summer saw a successful push by liberals to influence the platform's substance. At the Resolutions Committee hearings in late June, Kennedy forces advocated an alternative platform called "A Rededication to Democratic Principles," which contrasted starkly with the cautious document written by Carter loyalists on the drafting subcommittee. The committee rejected most of its planks, but environmentalists and feminists allied with Kennedy delegates to successfully pass sharpened antinuclear and pro-choice resolutions.[137] These surprise votes against the administration were indications of a growing restiveness among delegates. In the month leading up to the convention in New York, the Kennedy campaign built political momentum on behalf of the minority planks, benefiting from the help of platform-focused groups like Democratic Agenda and the Progressive Alliance. On the day of the convention's platform session, the Agenda held a Town Hall rally featuring speeches from Fraser, Winpisinger, Cesar Chavez, Ruth Messinger, Eleanor Smeal, and Gloria Steinem, all advocating a bolder party platform.[138] And that evening, before a primetime television audience, Kennedy spoke on behalf of his economic planks in what became the most acclaimed speech of his career.

"I have come here tonight not to argue as a candidate but to affirm a cause," Kennedy intoned. "I am asking you to renew the commitment of the Democratic Party to economic justice." Kennedy laid out the substantive vision represented by his minority planks, that vision's connection to Democratic history, and its contrast with the Republican approach. At the concluding lines declaring that "the work goes on, the cause endures, the hope still lives, and the dream shall never die," the convention hall erupted into a near-riot of applause and chanting that lasted thirty minutes. The speech provided the final bit of persuasion to Carter strategists engaged in behind-the-scenes negotiation with Kennedy forces over the platform. Now convinced that a floor vote on Kennedy's planks would embarrass the president, they sent word to convention chair Tip O'Neill that they would accept all of them, with the exception of wage and price controls. O'Neill swiftly gaveled his way by voice vote to the passage of all of Kennedy's other proposals, including a disavowal of recessionary anti-inflation measures and a $12-billion jobs program.[139] The 1980 Democratic nomination was Carter's. But much of its platform belonged to Kennedy—and to the robust liberal coalition mobilized behind him.

ISSUES, "SINGLE ISSUES," AND THE DEMOCRATIC COALITION

Back in November 1979, Ruth Jordan of Democratic Agenda surveyed the new left-liberal coalitions that had sprouted up in the preceding years:

> There's the Full Employment Action Council, the Citizen/Labor Energy Coalition, the Leadership Conference on Civil Rights, the Democratic Agenda, Democratic Conference, COIN, CAPE and Progressive Alliance. There's Interchange, the Consumer Coalition for Health and even the Consumers' Committee for No-Fault Insurance. Too many coalitions? For the trade union leaders called upon to provide the bulk of the financial support for many of these organizations, it must certainly seem so.[140]

A reader encountering Jordan's list in the pages of DSOC's newsletter might draw contradictory conclusions. On the one hand, the array of organizations conveyed a sense of energetic and experimental alliance building. And indeed, the 1970s was a time in which many on the broad liberal left worked effectively to forge a rapprochement between the forces of 1960s-borne cultural and social activism and older elements of the New Deal coalition. Central to this work were leaders within an American labor movement that was itself undergoing important compositional and ideological change. By the end of the decade, not only had progressive unions managed to establish important and enduring ties with many left-liberal groups, but also divisions within the labor movement itself were beginning to diminish.[141]

But Jordan's list hinted at key limitations in left-liberal political activism, underlying an enduring asymmetry with conservative forces. The organizations mentioned almost all lacked mass memberships and bases, and tended to be staff-driven coalitions of coalitions. As Jordan emphasized, moreover, organized labor provided the bulk of the funding for these groups. This fact imposed a limitation on liberals' organizational prospects that would only become more acute as union density in the United States declined with increasing speed through the 1980s and 1990s. Organized labor's decline, taking place within the context of resurgent political activism by business interests, conservatives' ascendance within the Republican Party, and steady increases in the cost of political campaigns, had important implications for an enduring *partisan* asymmetry as well. The GOP's ideological agenda and its funding base reinforced one another. Both the party and its supporters shared an increasingly cohesive antiregulatory and antitax conservatism. In contrast, Democratic officeholders and activists faced cross pressures between donors from labor and other liberal ranks and the business support upon which many still depended. This produced an imbalance in the relative coherence and aggressiveness of the two major parties' respective policy agendas and programmatic appeals.

The laundry-list quality of Jordan's catalog hinted at another source of the asymmetry between conservative and liberal forces, and between the two parties into which those forces were sorting at the dawn of the Reagan era. The very process of attempting to stitch together the electoral, legislative, and partisan activity of newer movements and issue groups with older labor and civil rights interests helped to lay bare the fragmented quality of post-

1960s liberalism. Liberal coalitional work came to bear that critical moniker "single-issue politics." Activists were cognizant of the problem. At the 1978 meeting called by Doug Fraser, a sympathetic attendee told *Newsweek* that "all the one-issue people wound up in arguments about which issues were the most important," while a reporter at the Democratic midterm conference two months later compared listening to the delegates speak to "opening the morning 'mailing list' envelopes. There were dozens of different 'very special pleas.'"[142] The Progressive Alliance had pitched itself in its founding statement as a solution to balkanization: "Individual interest groups and causes have evolved in unprecedented numbers. . . . Many of us have been activists in such single-issue struggles of necessity, yet we join together recognizing the compelling need for a common program and the political vehicles to achieve it."[143] But the outfit never really managed to solve the problem.

Left-liberal fragmentation had implications for the Democratic Party. Increasingly it would be described as a mere vessel for the disparate agendas of implacable single-issue groups—a visionless and incoherent broker for particularist interests and identity groups. By contrast, though conservative movement-builders in the 1970s and 1980s had their own coalitional challenges and their own set of single-issue allies, they benefited comparatively from an overarching movement consciousness and esprit de corps. This contributed to the relative sense of programmatic cohesion and confidence among Republicans as they achieved sweeping electoral victories in 1980 and went about the task of governing in the Reagan years.[144]

That such contrasts and asymmetries existed, however, does not discount the contributions made by liberals to the ideological sorting of the party system in the 1970s. For decades, a key goal of liberal activists interested in changing partisan dynamics in the United States had been to compel the ouster of the Democratic Party's conservative faction. By the end of the 1970s that process was well underway. A related goal of party reformers, one emphasized anew by those who drove the McGovern-Fraser and congressional reforms in early 1970s, was to increase the access and influence of issue-driven activists in party affairs and to make substantive issues the basis for partisan activity. The criticism that began to attach to the party by the end of the decade—that it was a prisoner of its own single-issue and ideological client groups— was itself an indication that, for better or for worse, reformers had also achieved this goal. Finally, the coalitional work done by labor-liberal activists, like the efforts of tax-cutters and cultural conservatives on the right, contributed to the *additive* quality of the issues around which the parties sorted.

By the end of the 1970s, certain political observers were beginning to perceive the rise to prominence of issue politics and the attendant ideological sorting of the party system. Nearly two decades after producing his pathbreaking analysis of issue-oriented "amateur" activism, James Q. Wilson emphasized in 1979 "the enhanced importance of ideas and ideology" in shaping and driving political conflict in contemporary politics. A new class of educated professionals had grown as a portion of the electorate in the years since he wrote about club Democrats, and Wilson now noted that members of such a class tended to practice a more issue-oriented and ideological brand of politics on both the left and the right. "The rise of an educated, idea-oriented public," he argued, combined with the greater permeability of political institutions achieved by reformers, has produced both the "'one-issue' politics so characteristic of the present era" and growing polarization of the two major political parties at the national level. Within Congress, "the Republican party seems to have become more consistently conservative and the Democratic party more consistently liberal." Among legislators, "the principle of affiliation" had grown to be "more clearly based on shared ideas, and to a degree those shared ideas conform to party labels.... The notion of party in Congress has been infused with more ideological meaning by its members."[145]

If Wilson and others sensed at the end of the 1970s that the notion of party was being infused with more ideological meaning in American politics, few predicted that such an infusion might bring with it a growing degree of discipline in partisan behavior. Wilson described the confluence of ideological politics and weak, fragmented political institutions as underlying "the schizophrenia of contemporary politics." But ideological sorting was making both parties less, rather than more, internally schizophrenic, and that fact would have profound effects on politics in the years to come. Liberals' contributions to this process were substantial—notwithstanding the fact that the decade ended with their most profound political defeat in the postwar era.

8

DAWN OF A NEW PARTY PERIOD, 1980-2000

The triumphs of Ronald Reagan and his party in the 1980 election were sweeping and decisive. The president-elect's claims of having earned an electoral mandate for conservatism were difficult to counter. But when political journalist James Reston assessed the meaning of the race that had just transpired, it filled him with foreboding. "The sad thing about this election," he wrote soon after the polls closed, "is that it has not clarified the nation's problems but deepened them; not unified the people but divided them." Reagan's refusal to dull the ideological edge of his message during the general election meant that, unless he and his supporters now chose "cooperation instead of confrontation," the country would continue to be wracked by division. In penning this post-mortem, Reston the centrist veteran wrote like a man without a country. The very notion that the outcome of a presidential race in a two-party system could or should leave Americans *more united* would prove an intellectual remnant of a fading political era.[1]

Once in office, and particularly during his first term, Reagan took a programmatically coherent and ambitious governing approach that served to strengthen rather than fragment partisan politics. In an intellectual climate still dominated by discussion of party decline and disarray, a few contemporary observers managed to detect how Reagan's ideological presidency might undergird partisan revival. "On a whole range of domestic economic and role-of-government questions," noted the realignment theorist James Sundquist soon after his election, "any perception that political parties do not take clear stands must have been shattered

FIGURE 8. R. J. Matson, *Ripon Forum*, May 1989. Used by permission of the Ripon Society.

by the forceful, categorical positions taken by Ronald Reagan and his party during the campaign." Because Reagan's agenda "drew clean lines between the parties," it could be expected to "create, or reinforce, the attachment of voters to the parties."[2] A few years later, Sidney Milkis would reaffirm Reagan's historic accomplishment in helping to rejuvenate the party system via ideological governance. "Reagan's firm adherence to cons〈 wrote, "contributed significantly to the emer〉 Republican party, one more national and pro〈 entation than the traditional GOP." In this anɑ ministration "marked both a restoration of the r〈 and a revitalization of partisan politics."[3]

In fact, the Reagan presidency was less the ca sult of a process of ideologically driven partisan 〈 ﹍ady underway at its inception. The construction of an ideologically sorted and defined party system is what made Reagan's approach to campaigning and governing viable. And this project was not the achievement of any individual leader, let alone a president. It was rather the product of conscious work carried out by myriad activists, reformers, and politicians on both the left and right over the course of several decades.

A new system of ideologically defined parties had not fully emerged by the 1980s. The partisan sort of conservatives and liberals among both public officials and American voters would continue for years to come, and as long as the process remained incomplete, the late-century political scene retained elements of fluidity and flexibility. Nevertheless, by the advent of Reagan's presidency, the system's advocates and architects had managed to put in place conditions that would make the dynamic logic of continuous ideological sorting between the two parties all but irreversible in the coming years, thus ushering in a new kind of "party period" in American politics.[4]

PARTISAN ARMIES

Congress led the way in manifesting resurgent polarization and partisan discipline in the 1980s—though, in the blinding light of the Reagan Revolution's initial legislative breakthroughs, such polarization was hard to detect. Reagan owed his achievements in tax and fiscal policy to a bipartisan congressional majority, with the disproportionately southern and conservative Democratic "boll weevils" led by the likes of Phil Gramm and Richard Shelby sup-

n with the margin of victory in the House. That coalition
ioned only for the first two years of his presidency, however.
The 1982 midterm elections saw the loss of Republicans' Senate
majority as well as Reagan's working bipartisan majority in the
House. Divided government and resurgent partisanship would
prove to be the twin themes of the remainder of the Reagan era
and beyond.

Scholars late in the 1980s first began to quantify the increasing rates of party-line voting in both the House and Senate, and
to connect this development to public officials' changing institutional environment.[5] By curbing the independent power centers
formally found in the major committees and empowering central
party organs to control the legislative agenda, the 1970s congressional reforms secured a link between ideological cohesion and
party discipline. During the Reagan and George H. W. Bush presi-
dencies, the Democratic House Speakerships of Tip O'Neill and
Jim Wright revealed a growth in the capacity of congressional party
leaders to coordinate legislative behavior and articulate coherent
programmatic positions that set them starkly apart from their predecessors.[6] This involved tightening their procedural grip over the
agenda on the House floor. More bills were put to a vote under rules
restricting the ability of members—including Republicans—to
offer amendments, and floor activity was reined in. Wright in particular accelerated the use of such practices, famously provoking
the ire and indignation of the Republican minority, for example,
when he kept the clock running for an extra fifteen minutes on a
vote in 1987.

Those Republicans' outrage would prove ironic, as the congressional GOP, first in the minority and then eventually in the majority, developed a highly disciplined and confrontational political strategy that would take partisan combat in both chambers to
new heights. Newt Gingrich, an ambitious House member from
the Atlanta suburbs, led the way.[7] Few national political leaders
in American history have ever proven so committed to a specific
vision for the working of the party system and, for a time, so consequential in implementing that vision. For Gingrich, responsible
party principles were paramount. In his first year as a congress-

man in 1979, Gingrich engaged in the same pilgrimage to Great Britain that Bill Brock took to study the smashing electoral victories of Margaret Thatcher's Conservative Party.[8] From the outset, he viewed the congressional minority party's role in terms akin to those found in parliamentary systems, prioritizing drawing stark programmatic contrasts over engaging the majority party as junior participants in governance.

In 1983 he organized the Conservative Opportunity Society (COS) among younger House Republicans while working with Paul Weyrich at the Free Congress Foundation to organize an ancillary contingent of conservative movement activists outside of Congress to promote the COS's agenda and strategy. As Weyrich explained the COS's rationale that year, "more than 60% of the electorate" believes in basic conservative positions, but "we don't get 60% of the representation in the Congress because people have not been forced to choose between the fruits of a liberal welfare state or the conservative opportunity society."[9] Forcing stark ideological choices would be the COS's core function, and Gingrich would lead this faction to eventual dominance within the House GOP conference on the basis of an explicit critique of bipartisan engagement with the majority. The COS's confrontational posture toward the Democrats also entailed an agenda for internal party reform that echoed liberal Democrats' achievements in the previous decade. This included proposals to revamp and amplify Republican Research and Policy committee activities, regularize meetings of the House Republican Conference (the caucus of all GOP House members), and expand party whip operations.[10] Such an agenda also included new scrutiny by the conservative GOP majority toward wayward ranking members of committees.[11]

Gingrich rose to power within the House GOP espousing a critique of alleged accommodationism among the Old Guard in the Republican leadership. That Old Guard's outlook, epitomized by minority leader Bob Michel's insistence that the congressional minority had "an obligation to the American people to be . . . responsible participants in the process," grew increasingly out of step with a Republican rank and file that, with each new election cycle, became steadily more conservative.[12] Newer members took a dim view of participation in Democrat-backed legislative initiatives and agreed with Gingrich that the surest route to winning a majority would be to combine high-profile public relations confrontations with Democrats with the articulation of a distinct alternative programmatic agenda. Growing support for such a strategy drove Gingrich's closely fought election to the House minority whip post in 1989.

A watershed moment came the following year, when Gingrich led a House Republican revolt against the 1990 budget agreement worked out between congressional leaders and George H. W. Bush. That budget raised revenues in famous violation of the president's own campaign pledge. GOP leaders Bob Dole and Bob Michel issued a joint statement defending the agreement in terms pointedly aimed at the ideological crusaders in their midst. "We believe it has been the genius of the American system," they wrote, "from the creation of the Constitution until now, that we have been able to avoid the fantasy lands of utopian, so-called 'painless' political solutions . . . by standing on the solid ground of principled compromise."[13] Gingrich's success in leading a majority of the Republican conference to reject this plea reaffirmed supply-side economics as an ideological lodestar for the GOP—a party-defining opposition to what Gingrich had years earlier termed "the pain-inducing masochism of tax increases."[14] It also signified a major shift in congressional Republicans' approach to legislative behavior.

The Republican congressional takeover in 1994 followed a nationalized midterm election centered around an explicit party manifesto. Gingrich had used the normally sleepy annual House GOP retreat in 1993 as the occasion to push for a conference-wide articulation of common policy goals and ideological tenets, resulting in a pledge to "communicate our vision of America through clearly defined themes, programs, and legislative initiatives."[15] Over the ensuing year, in conjunction with polling research conducted by Frank Luntz, Gingrich and his allies devised a set of ten conservative legislative items tailored in part to maximize electoral support from disaffected Democrats and 1992 Ross Perot supporters: the Contract with America.[16] By campaign season, the entire GOP conference and over 180 challengers had endorsed the Contract, which dominated the midterm campaigns to an unusual extent given the typically more localized election dynamics of non-presidential years. Republicans' gain of fifty-two House and nine Senate seats that November served to flip some of the last remaining holdout districts containing large numbers of conservative ticket-splitting Democrats, and provided stunning vindication of Gingrich's ideologically powered strategy for building a congressional majority.

From 1995 to 2006, Republicans in control of Congress took the centralizing and discipline-bolstering tactics pioneered by Democrats and dramatically expanded their use. As Speaker, Newt Gingrich worked to curb seniority procedures for determining committee ranks among GOP members and placed term limits on committee chairmanships. Tactics intended to bring committees under the party leadership's thumb only grew more routine and effective in the hands of Gingrich's successors in the leadership. "The job of Speaker is not to expedite legislation that runs counter to the wishes of the majority of his majority," then-Speaker Dennis Hastert declared in 2003. "On each piece of legislation, I actively seek to bring our party together. I do not feel comfortable scheduling any controversial legislation unless I know we have the votes on our side first."[17] This so-called Hastert rule, capturing in practical language the main thrust of a dynamic theorized by political scientists as "party cartel" control, epitomized the arrival of a new era of party dominance in Congress.[18] Significantly, in the same speech Hastert made passing reference to the fact that, occasionally, "we have a hard time convincing the majority of the House to vote like a majority of the House, so sometimes you will see votes stay open longer than usual." And indeed, many of the same Republicans who had cried foul at Speaker Wright's clock-extending gambit in 1987 would pursue much more extreme versions of such tactics as a matter of course while in the majority, from keeping votes open several hours past the limit to scheduling votes at midnight to shutting minority members out of conference committees altogether.[19]

The Senate, boasting (or suffering under) the most permissive rules of any legislative body on Earth, saw similar developments in partisan polarization during the last decades of the twentieth

century, but with different consequences than those observed in
the increasingly parliamentarized House. As in the House, growing partisan discipline coincided with a much-lamented decline of
civility and comity in the upper chamber—and, significantly, the
pioneers of confrontational and hyperpartisan tactics in the Senate were found generally to be Republicans who had first served
in the House during the years of Newt Gingrich's rise to party
leadership.[20] But the individualistic and countermajoritarian procedural environment in the Senate meant that partisan discipline
more easily helped to produce obstruction and paralysis than it did
party-line passage of major legislation. The post-reform story of
the Senate filibuster offers the most illustrative case in point. The
employment of filibusters became ever more partisan as ideological sorting gradually transformed the Senate. And as the filibuster
came to be seen as one more partisan tool at hand for Senate minorities, its use came to be more frequent and routine. Between
the 1960s and the 1970s—very early in the progression of ideological sorting among the parties—the average frequency of filibusters doubled. That frequency would triple again in future decades.[21]

It is in this light that the failure of reformers after 1975 to further
reduce or eliminate the supermajority threshold for cloture takes
on such significance. Ideological polarization in the House helped
to drive, and was in turn further driven by, institutional changes
that made that chamber increasingly capable of disciplined party-
line legislating along the parliamentary lines that responsible party
advocates had always envisioned. By contrast, the persistence,
even in modified fashion, of countermajoritarian procedures in
the Senate like the filibuster ensured that ideological sorting would
have the effect of intensifying rather than mitigating minority obstruction, by strengthening the minority party's cohesive will to
utilize all available tactics.[22] Defenders of the filibuster had often
warned that reform would pave the way to the Senate becoming as
partisan and nondeliberative as the House. "If this body ever goes
to majority cloture," John Stennis warned typically during the 1975
debate over reducing the threshold required for cloture, "the Senate will never be the same again."[23] The historical consequence of
the filibuster surviving the Age of Party Reform as a tool for the

steadily polarizing parties, however, was that the Senate would more than ever become a redoubt for systematic minority obstruction—the graveyard of responsible party governance even during periods of unified party control in the executive and legislature.

Party revival took hold initially and most dramatically in Congress, but it was hardly limited to that institution in the last decades of the twentieth century. A new wave of political science scholarship on the "polarized" or "partisan presidency" has challenged older notions about an inherent zero-sum conflict between strong parties and a strong presidency. As this recent scholarship has documented, presidents from Reagan onward have faced a changing institutional environment and strategic incentives that align their interests—and explicit rhetorical affiliation—with that of their own parties to a greater extent than was seen in the midcentury era.[24] The constraint posed by unified opposition from the out-party has, at the same time, only strengthened during this period, as has the tendency of a president's merely taking a position on a given issue to have the effect of polarizing both public and elite opinion along partisan lines.[25]

Party organizations themselves manifested the effects of ideologically driven partisan revival. In the wake of Bill Brock's pioneering tenure, both the Republican and Democratic national committees saw major strides in professionalization and fundraising prowess from the 1980s onward. Programmatic functions were sidelined, and neither the national committees nor the parties' congressional campaign organizations enjoyed direct control over candidate nominations. But the national organizations evolved into important "parties-in-service"—centralized and bureaucratized entities oriented toward providing campaign resources and political intelligence to state and local candidates.[26]

The world of interest group politics, fluidly bipartisan in the ideal type of midcentury pluralist theory, also polarized in tandem with the parties from the 1980s onward. Issue activists and interest groups came increasingly, and sometimes quite reluctantly, to be drawn into the zero-sum logic of two-party competition, enlisting as soldiers for one or the other major party.[27] They did this precisely as a result of the increasing degree to which the parties took

distinct and differentiated policy positions on an expanding number of issues.[28]

The relationship between the formal parties and their core group
allies came to be institutionalized and routinized. In keeping with
the broader patterns of post-1970s partisan developments, the
GOP proved to be at the vanguard of interest group mobilization
and coordination. The panoply of New Right "single-issue" groups
along with the Christian Right were quick and eager adapters to
a partisan political strategy, with the GOP operative-led Christian
Coalition (formed in 1989) epitomizing the near-complete convergence of ideological advocacy with partisan politics.

Republicans proved even more aggressive in seeking to transform the political strategy of business interests and corporate
lobbyists from one of bipartisan pluralism to a stable resource- and
personnel-sharing partnership with the GOP. Though the political
mobilization of business in the 1970s had independent impetuses
outside of Republican influence, the party's increasing conservatism in the 1980s and 1990s made it an ever more natural partner to organized capital. At the same time, Republican leaders
beginning with Gingrich actively pressured business interests to
limit their support for and employment of Democrats. Gingrich
famously warned the major business-backed political action committees on the eve of the 1994 midterm elections that, "for any-
body who's not on board now, it's going to be the two coldest years
in Washington."[29] The so-called K Street Project that he and Tom
DeLay went on to develop in the House, along with Trent Lott and
Rick Santorum in the Senate, focused on pressuring Washington-
based lobbying firms to hire GOP staffers and compelling organized business interests to limit their campaign donations to Republicans. "If you want to play in our Revolution," DeLay boasted,
"you have to live by our rules."[30]

Conservative Republicans also led the way in stimulating, and
benefiting from, a polarized policy research and media landscape.
Thanks in part to the efforts of an interlocking network of conservative foundations, the Right enjoyed a dramatic numerical advantage among the ideologically driven think tanks that began to pro-
liferate in the 1970s.[31] The same funders also helped to ensure the

growth of a powerful conservative media infrastructure in print, radio and television airwaves, and, eventually, the Internet.[32] In the case of both policy research and political media, Democrats and liberals pursued important parallel initiatives, but they generally occurred later, as reactive and imitative efforts.

"NEW DEMOCRATS" AND THE NON-DEATH OF AMERICAN LIBERALISM

Such persistent asymmetry in partisan developments between Republicans and Democrats since the 1970s raises anew a basic analytical question. Is polarization even the right frame in which to view recent political history, or is it merely the byproduct of a rightward movement of both major parties that the GOP has pursued to a greater extent? Proponents of the latter view emphasize the continued breakdown of the New Deal political order and the conservative drift of the Democratic Party into the new century, offering the "New Democrat" movement that helped to bring Bill Clinton to power as a key exemplar of the process.

That movement, with its institutional origins in the Committee on Party Effectiveness established in 1981 by House Democratic Caucus chairman Gillis Long and, starting in 1985, in the Democratic Leadership Council (DLC) outside of Congress, was indeed a historically significant factional project.[33] New Democrats argued in the wake of the GOP's victories in the 1980s that Democratic electoral survival demanded a programmatic course correction.[34] They advocated centrist positioning on cultural and foreign policy issues and neoliberal approaches to economic and fiscal policy in contrast to the liberal agenda of the party's congressional base. No such moderating force within the GOP exercised anything like New Democrats' intraparty influence during the 1980s and 1990s. Moreover, they pursued their centrist ideological project during a period that witnessed other party developments putting liberal agenda-setting under strain. Party leaders like the Democratic Congressional Campaign Committee chairman Tony Coelho, for example, sought to leverage Democrats' seemingly durable congressional majorities during the 1980s for the purposes of extracting massive new funds from corporate America.[35] And organized labor's declining fortunes only increased Democrats' financial dependence on business in ensuing decades.

But just as most observers have overlooked the endurance of left-liberal strength within the post-1960s Democratic Party, so have they overstated and misperceived the New Democrats' significance. Ideologically, New Democrats embodied the centrism of post–civil rights era southern Democrats and suburban economic moderates rather than the conservatism of the old Solid South bloc and its modern, fleeting efflorescence among the boll weevils. The ideological space separating factions within the Democratic Party of the 1980s and 1990s did not come close to matching that distance during the peak of the party's midcentury dominance, and has only shrunk further in more recent years. Politically, moreover, New Democrats consistently advocated a strong, programmatically defined partisanship rather than the bipartisan legislative practices celebrated by defenders of the prepolarized system. New Democrats pitched moderate programmatic initiatives in explicitly partisan terms, proved notably committed to party platform work, and made a point of advocating issue positions that, while more conservative than those of the liberal Democratic base, fell to the left of Republican policy. In this sense they were as shaped by the context and pressures of an ideologically sorted party system as other political interests of the period.

The same analysts have also exaggerated the New Democrats' alleged intraparty triumph and ideological "takeover" within the Democratic Party. That party has, in reality, faced the continuous task of accommodating an electoral and interest group coalition that encompasses both liberals and moderates. This certainly underlies enduring asymmetries between the Democratic and Republican parties. To the extent that the moderate Republicanism of previous eras reflected a distinct ideological tradition—one that eschewed populist politics while emphasizing public-private partnerships and state activism in pursuit of market-oriented policy solutions—it may be plausibly argued that this tradition migrated parties in the later twentieth century, to define a contemporary faction among Democrats.[36] Such a development has had contrasting implications for the behavior of the two major parties but reflects the dynamics of a party system that is itself now defined by a clear ideological division.

For all the activity among nascent centrist forces during these years, moreover, the organizational and electoral base of the party remained the very liberal coalition of labor, minority group constituencies, and social and cultural activists that the New Democrats challenged. Rumors of liberals' death within the Democratic Party have been greatly, and repeatedly, exaggerated. Left-liberalism's alleged swan song in the form of Ted Kennedy's 1980 challenge, for example, was followed in 1984 and 1988 by Jesse Jackson's potent and organizationally innovative presidential campaigns championing a program of multiracial economic populism and drawing important new activists and operatives into Democratic politics.

Outside of candidate campaigns, liberals maintained organizational clout during these years by tightening coalitional ties. Major labor unions began sharing mailing lists with the DNC early in the 1980s, increasingly coordinated their participation in the Democratic presidential nominating process, and regularized their cooperation with congressional Democratic leaders.[37] Joint labor-liberal "ground game" organizations, starting with Heather Booth's Citizen Action, fused into day-to-day Democratic electoral functions. Citizen Action grew significantly over the course of the 1980s as it became an ever more central pillar of Democratic get-out-the-vote operations and campaigns on behalf of party legislative initiatives. Indeed, that partisan association grew so tight that the organization would eventually come under legal scrutiny regarding its tax status at the same time that many member groups grumbled about cooptation.[38] Organizations like Citizen Action established themselves as the party's grassroots labor force during a seeming era of liberal decline. After a union fundraising scandal forced the group's disbandment, Heather Booth helped to found a new national body composed of many of the same affiliates in 1999 called USAction.[39] More broadly, the Citizen Action model of a national umbrella coalition uniting labor with post-'60s social movement organizations came to typify Democratic electoral and issue campaigns in the new century, from the "527" electioneering group Americans Coming Together in 2004 to the Obama-era issue coalitions Health Care for America Now and Americans for Financial Reform.

Both the presidency of New Democrat standard-bearer Bill Clinton and Democrats' twenty-first-century trajectory further belie the narrative of liberal decline within the party. Beyond pursuing traditional liberal policy goals such as universal health care, Clinton certainly advanced or supported legislation reflective of a New Democratic agenda. Notably, however, majorities of congressional Democrats opposed three of the most prominent such efforts: the North American Free Trade Agreement, the granting of fast-track authority to presidents negotiating trade deals, and 1996's welfare reform law.[40] In the new century, moreover, Democrats at the electoral, activist, and officeholding levels moved leftward, driven in part by the dynamics of polarized combat with an ideologically hard-charging GOP and aided by successive waves of Internet-era political organizing and institution-building.[41] Meanwhile, the demographic landscape that signified electoral crisis for Democrats in the 1980s changed in subsequent decades. Indeed, the old New Politics coalition of progressive labor, minorities, and liberal professionals that New Democrats pilloried would eventually become the basis for viable Democratic political majorities in the early twenty-first century thanks to favorable demographic shifts.[42] While rarely at the vanguard of ideological partisanship during the new party period in American politics, in other words, Democrats were hardly unaffected by the forces of sorting, internal coalition-making, and partisan warfare that defined the era.

PARTY DISCIPLINE, GOVERNMENTAL DYSFUNCTION

By the 1990s the interaction between an increasingly disciplined party system and the fragmented, veto-laden American constitutional structure began to reveal a growing potential for crisis.[43] Within a year of the Republican takeover of Congress, a budget standoff between Speaker Gingrich and President Clinton precipitated a government shutdown. The impeachment battle two years later embroiled the country in a conflict that, for all of the salacious atmospherics of the sex scandal that provided its pretext, was at heart a deadly serious ideological struggle. Surveying the deepening partisan divide in Washington in 1998, scholar Nelson Polsby remarked acerbically to the *New Yorker* that "the trouble began when we political scientists finally got our wish—'responsible' political parties instead of broad, non-ideological coalitions. The idea was, of course, completely nuts from the start."[44]

Such "trouble" would only intensify in the new century.

CONCLUSION

POLARIZATION WITHOUT RESPONSIBILITY, 2000-2016

From a protracted presidential election requiring judicial intervention to resolve to the charged politics of war, economic crisis, and
government default in ensuing years, the American political scene
during the first decade and a half of the twenty-first century seemed
fated by the old curse: "May you live in interesting times." For most
of this time, the volatility of political events—the "wave" elections
producing swings in partisan control followed soon after by apparent electoral backlash, the politically induced crises within and between the legislative and executive branches—disguised the stable
unidirectional trajectory of systemic political change, toward ever
stronger partisanship. Developments seeming at first to herald the
introduction of potentially destabilizing or realigning forces within
the system soon proved to be symptoms and further catalyzers of
partisan polarization.

When the Tea Party insurgency emerged in the first two years of
Barack Obama's presidency, for example, many commenters saw it
as a libertarian movement that cross-cut existing partisan divides.
But in reality it epitomized the additive, multidimensional quality
of contemporary party polarization, as Tea Party activists were
revealed to be, straightforwardly, a mobilization of the existing
GOP base, holding conservative positions across the board on economic and cultural issues and a uniform opposition to compromise
with Democrats.[1] The congressional leadership that the Tea Party
helped bring to power subsequently demonstrated its responsiveness to the wishes of these citizens by instigating not only another

government shutdown but also two separate default-threatening showdowns over the statutory debt ceiling.

By the new century, scholarly and journalistic observers had begun finally to discern the dynamics of the new system and to tease out troubling implications. Discussion of party decline and fragmentation diminished. Political scholarship on partisanship and polarization flourished—including new models of party behavior positing that "intense policy demanders" rather than pragmatic politicians were the key drivers in American politics.[2] Commentators began to revisit political scientist Juan Linz's old observation that democracies with presidential systems tend toward crisis and breakdown compared to those with parliamentary systems.[3] Linz had long cast the United States as an exception to this tendency thanks to the country's famously undisciplined political parties, but both he and others now began to reconsider that exceptionalism.[4] Fifty-four years after the American Political Science Association released *Toward a More Responsible Two-Party System in the United States*, meanwhile, the same body published a new prescriptive report on party politics. Rather than advocate the sharpening of party lines as APSA had in 1950, the new report focused on devising mechanisms to facilitate deliberation, negotiation, and compromise.[5]

All told, decades of work carried out by the activists, intellectuals, and political elites at the center of this book had finally helped to produce the nationalized and ideologically distinct parties prescribed by responsible party doctrine. But, in a Madisonian system still defined by separated powers, myriad veto points, and staggered elections that all but ensure the recurrence of divided government, party majorities now find themselves with little sustained capacity to implement their program. Hence the modern American predicament of responsible parties *without* responsible party government—a volatile ill-fit between disciplined ideological partisanship and fragmented political institutions that turns routine conflict into chronic crisis.

What might this book's account of the origins of this predicament tell us about the prospects for getting out of it? If ideologically disciplined parties are ill suited for a system of fragmented political institutions, potential solutions could involve reforming the parties, or they could involve reforming those political institutions. Much public commentary decrying the decline of civility in politics and waxing nostalgic about the midcentury era of bipartisanship focuses attention on the parties themselves as the entities in need of reform. This includes not only naive antiparty proposals of the "kumbaya" variety but also the self-consciously unromantic prescriptions offered by exponents of the "new political realism," who seek to revive the prepolarization glory of transactional, pragmatic partisanship stripped of the influence of ideological purists.[6] But despite this book's emphasis on the agency of historical actors in helping to bring about the ideological sorting of the parties in the first place, the plausibility of new actors being able to effectively reverse that process, either through force of will or procedural tweaks, seems hard to credit.

As for reforming the political system itself, the story of postwar congressional reform shows us that institutional change can be brought about when sustained effort and fortuitous circumstances allow, and that changes far less sweeping and radical than some wholesale upending of the Constitution can still prove consequential. In the contemporary era, further reforms of certain antimajoritarian elements not found in the Constitution itself, such as the Senate's supermajority requirement for cloture, might constitute a compelling new program for institutional reform. Indeed, such reform appears already underway at the hands of politicians themselves, as the very partisan polarization that had driven the proliferation of filibusters (by increasing the minority's determination to block unwanted legislation whenever possible) has begun at last to threaten the filibuster's very survival as an institution (by bolstering the majority's determination to overcome minority obstruction). This new development was first evident in the George W. Bush–era Republican threat to use the "nuclear option" to ban filibusters on judicial nominees, and culminated in Obama-era Democrats' decision to deploy that very option in 2013. The power of party polarization might very well lead to the forced disappearance of filibusters altogether in short order.

But as the filibuster example shows, reforms that are intended to allow partisan majorities to more easily implement their agenda when in power represent *accommodations* to polarized partisanship—ways to make the new partisanship "work" better in the American context—rather than efforts to mitigate it. And little evidence indicates that significant numbers of Americans support reforms that are intended to make peace with our polarized parties. American voters may be, like the Founders before them, partisans in spite of themselves.[7] To turn many of them into conscious advocates of strong party government may require particularly profound and long-term changes in American political culture. The Janus-faced quality of partisanship in the twenty-first century—simultaneously all-powerful in governing voters' behavior yet perceived as illegitimate and alien to most Americans' lived experience—stems not only from longstanding American intellectual traditions but also from the *hollowness* of modern parties.[8] Organizations that were once deeply and tangibly rooted in ordinary people's lives, even as their ideological content was fuzzy to the point of irrelevance, now exist for most Americans as abstract ideological designations and vehicles of collective antipathy. A party system consisting entirely of ideologically defined networks of activists and elites and devoid of real mass organizations may lose in popular legitimacy what it gains in coherence and rationality.

An alternative path out of the current state of affairs, eschewing process reforms altogether, seemed almost unimaginable until very recently: a wholesale realignment of the party system itself. Might it be that the "party period" between 1980 and 2016 designates a distinct historical era now coming to a close?[9] Hints of destabilization in the formerly relentless dynamics of party polarization have appeared in recent years. After decades in which the logic of polarization drove congressional organization toward ever more centralized and disciplined party rule, factional chaos broke out in the House Republican conference, eventually forcing the resignation of Speaker John Boehner in the face of a contingent of recalcitrant "Freedom Caucus" members. More spectacularly, an insurgent candidate managed to secure the presidential nomination of a major party in 2016 despite concerted opposition from party insiders and seemingly glaring ideological deviations from the party's core agenda.

Whether Donald Trump's extraordinary ascension to the presidency in 2016 was a fluke of idiosyncratic celebrity and circumstance or a harbinger of broader transformations in the party system remains to be seen. The issues that Trump chose to emphasize—and those he chose not to—in his victorious bid for the GOP nomination revealed the extent to which a profound gap had opened between the core priorities of Republican elites in government and in the conservative movement, on the one hand, and those of rank-and-file GOP voters on the other. Were Trump to accentuate that gap as president by seeking meaningfully to transform Republican priorities and constituencies, a period of crosscutting issue alliances and potential bipartisanship would be one possible byproduct. Skepticism is warranted about the prospects for imminent depolarization, however. Trump's brand of ethnonationalist populism was harder to discern in GOP races below the presidential level in 2016. The general election results showed the highest rates of partisan and straight-ticket voting yet on record. And Trump's domestic policy agenda during the early months of his presidency, as of this writing, signaled more continuity with the orthodox conservative agenda endorsed by Republican congressional leaders than a bid for intraparty disruption. Partisan warfare still defines American politics in the Trump era. Given current circumstances, moreover, any plausible alternative to the rigidities and rancor of party polarization might well prove to be something more chaotic and dangerous.

To consider any of the potential paths out of polarization is to confront a basic dilemma: the inherent tradeoffs among competing democratic goals in a political system are real and unavoidable. Pragmatic bargaining might come at the expense of coherent policymaking. Principled representation of constituents might come at the expense of moderation or compromise. Achieving a more clubby elite spirit of comity might come at the expense of democratic participation and accountability. If it has succeeded at all, this book's account of the work carried out by engaged citizens to reshape American politics has lent their efforts a degree of historical recognition and respect. The lesson that the polarizers' thought and experience hold for contemporary citizens may merely be that the pursuit of effective collective decision-making in a democracy is as difficult and unending a task as it is a vital one.

BIBLIOGRAPHIC ESSAY

This book is an attempt at intellectual bridge-building. It places purposive historical actors at the center of the story of polarization—a subject that has remained largely the purview of quantitative political science. At the same time, it seeks to restore parties to the forefront of an analysis of postwar US political history—a scholarly subfield that has experienced exciting revival in the past two decades but that has remained more focused on spatial politics and grassroots mobilizations than changes in formal political institutions.[1] Parties have structured political participation and policymaking across American history. But political participants themselves can, and have, worked to alter the structure and function of those parties. The historical origins of contemporary polarization can be traced to such actors' successful efforts to recast the relationship between partisanship and ideological activism in the later twentieth century.

Partisanship and ideology are distinct phenomena whose connection to each other changes over time. Parties need not be driven by coherent ideologies and policy programs, and a relative absence of ideology was long considered to be one of the key distinguishing features of American parties.[2] The last period of intensely disciplined partisanship in American political history, for example—the "party period" of the later nineteenth century, with its torchlight parades, patronage armies, and sky-high voting participation among white males—featured a nonideological system of strong party polarization. The parties were federated and locally embedded institutions that stitched far-flung communities together into two national coalitions. Positions on certain issues divided the parties, but many others were sidelined from partisan contestation in a federal policymaking regime dominated by the distributive politics of expansion and development.[3]

The aberrant era of bipartisanship and depolarization in the middle of the twentieth century, meanwhile, stemmed from a different interaction between ideological coalition-making and partisan politics. A broad and enduring liberal-conservative ideological division had developed at the hands of intellectuals and movement leaders in the wake of industrialization, the Great Depression, and world war. But this ideological division crosscut, rather than reinforced, the partisan alignment. Such a mismatch set the context for a historically unique period of bipartisan policymaking. It also provoked discontent among those who saw existing party arrangements as hindering the accomplishment of policy goals. The protagonists of this book translated that discontent into a critique of the party system and efforts to change it through both ideological activism and institutional reform.

Two distinct but related long-term developments provide particularly important background to the polarizers' efforts. The first is the long decline of the patronage basis of mass partisanship that began in the Progressive Era. The second is the long-term rise in the education level of the electorate during the same period. Both of these trends helped to foster the rise of issue-driven and ideological party activism, as well as a growing capacity among voters to connect candidate and parties to ideological positions.[4] It was the work of ideologically driven activists, factional fighters, and strategic party elites to make such linkages between parties and issues possible. And it was the further work of many of these same actors to reform the parties *as institutions* to render them more permeable by, and accountable to, issue- and ideology-driven activists like themselves.

A focus on the changing relationship between ideology and partisanship helps us to transcend single-issue explanations for political change. Because the fulcrum of partisan transformation in the postwar United States was in the formerly one-party South, and because political changes in that region revolved around the explosive issue of civil rights for African Americans, race has long dominated explanations for party realignment in the later twentieth century.[5] And indeed, the politics of civil rights unquestionably provided a key catalyst for factional developments and organizational changes within both parties. But those who struggled to remake the parties along ideological lines were themselves *ideological* actors, motivated by systems of belief that encompassed positions on multiple issues. A growing body of political science scholarship identifies the beginning of ideological sorting around racial issues—with economic liberals tending to advocate civil rights positions and economic conservatives tending to oppose them—as early as the late New Deal.[6] This finding complements historical scholarship on the Long Civil Rights Movement, with its emphasis on labor-oriented racial advocacy over a decade prior to the emergence of the "classical phase" of the movement.[7] The sorting of racial positions into the conservative and liberal ideological agendas prior to the flashpoints of civil rights policymaking and conflict in the 1960s make it less surprising that the parties have sorted themselves in the last several decades around a slew of issues beyond those pertaining to race.[8] They have also ideologically sorted in every region of the country, not just the South.[9]

A focus on ideological partisanship also challenges an influential account of partisan developments since the 1960s that argues that the parties have simply replaced the issues that they fight over rather than reorganized themselves into coherent ideological vehicles. In this account, the "realignment" of the later twentieth century saw the parties depolarize around one set of issues—the economic issues of the New Deal era—while polarizing around social and cultural issues pertaining to ethnic and racial identity, gender, morality, and other "postmaterialist" controversies.[10] The post-1960s period did indeed see the rise of new sociocultural issues that came to divide the parties. But political scientists now confirm that measurable partisan polarization has occurred across both the older economic issues and the newer cultural ones simultaneously.[11] Activists on both the left and right worked consciously and in the face of great obstacles to forge and sustain coalitions between, respectively, labor liberals and the cultural left and anti-statist economic interests and social conservatives.

The polarizers at the heart of this narrative occupy a broad middle range of influence between the mass voting public and the occupants of high office—a middle range that might be said to be a shared analytical subject of much of the most promising recent scholarship in both American political history and historically engaged political science. Politically minded historians of postwar urban and suburban history have highlighted the work of issue activists, grassroots partisan workers, and movement builders whose locally rooted mobilizations had national ramifications.[12] Others have chronicled the efforts of activist coalitions in formal politics to produce institutional reform and policy change.[13] And a small but growing number of scholars have begun to apply such a focus to activism within the political parties themselves.[14]

Political scientists' study of American parties, meanwhile, has undergone important changes during the contemporary era of polarized hyperpartisanship in real-world politics. Eschewing models that put either the strategic decisions of national politicians or mass political behavior at the center of explanations for party development, a diverse and growing scholarship has renewed attention to issue activists, organized interests, and ideological advocates as the prime drivers in American politics. At the broadest level, these include all "engaged citizens"—the most politically informed and active subset of American voters, who are also the most ideologically polarized.[15] A somewhat more selective stratum includes the activists both informally and formally at work within the "meso-level" of party activity, running party organizations as well as satellite advocacy groups, drafting state and national platforms, mobilizing voters, and organizing collective pressure on officeholders.[16] Outside the day-to-day work of partisan and group politics, there are also the intellectuals constructing overarching ideologies out of disparate issue positions over time.[17] These were the men and women, sometimes pursuing short-range goals, sometimes explicitly seeking long-range systemic change, who worked over the course of decades to remake the parties in their image, and ultimately succeeded.

Emphasizing the changing relationship between ideology and partisanship helps to recast twentieth-century political history. The early postwar decades are still commonly characterized as a period of liberal "consensus" despite sustained assaults on this term by historians of labor, business, and politics.[18] This book complements such revisionist scholarship's emphasis on mid-century conflict by identifying in the initial postwar decades the origins of many of the developments driving later partisan transformations. The existing political historiography of the post-1960s period, meanwhile, takes as its central narrative the breakdown of the New Deal coalition and the attendant rise of the Right.[19] The two major parties obviously feature in this literature, but their development as organizations and changing functions generally do not play significant roles.[20] This lack of engagement with partisan developments has interpretive consequences. Ironically, it causes even the rich historical literature on the rise of the Right to understate the far-reaching impact of the conservative movement. That movement was a partisan project. As such, it proved to be a significant force not only in shaping policy debates but also in hastening changes in the party system itself. The prevailing historical literature also gives analytical short shrift to post-1960s liberalism, by obscuring processes of ideological consolidation and organizational development within the Democratic Party and among its allied interest groups that paralleled—though hardly matched—developments on the right.

Political scientists have supported historians' emphasis on conservative ascendancy with an array of empirical evidence for a process of "asymmetric polarization," in which Republicans have moved much farther to the right since the 1970s than Democrats have moved left.[21] This book confirms the asymmetry of modern polarization. It also, however, offers a correction to the prevailing historiography's singular focus on liberal disarray and fragmentation, by emphasizing the significance of both decreasing ideological distance among Democratic-aligned officials, activists, and ordinary voters and increasing organizational capacity from the 1970s onward.[22] Liberals were also the chief instigators of institutional reforms to both party procedures and Congress that proved central to the emergence of a new, more programmatic party system.[23]

In contrast to historians, political scientists have produced a vast literature on contemporary polarization.[24] The common empirical story in that work holds that party elites first sorted ideologically, then prompted sorting within the mass electorate by issuing partisan cues. The process of the initial elite polarization, however, largely remains a kind of black box. By treating the construction of an ideologically sorted party system as a political project carried out by conscious historical actors, this book serves to open that box—to tell the story of who, exactly, reoriented the parties around ideology, and by what means.

Doing so yields insights into several ongoing pursuits in research on parties and polarization. The narrative here details both the institutional changes necessary for, and the active coalitional work directed toward, the sorting of the two parties on both economic and cultural issues.[25] It also reveals that the work of partisan transformation was unavoidably dialectical. Even as ideological activists struggled to transform the parties in their own image, the existing parties structured their strategic choices and outlook on the political system.[26] Finally, a focus on the interplay between ideology and party structure helps to reveal the mechanisms by which polarization contributed to the growth of well-resourced national party apparatuses in recent decades.[27]

This work also historicizes postwar political science itself, tracing scholars' internal debates about parties, their changing conceptions of power, and the influence of both on real-world politics. Two key threads of this intellectual history are the postwar political career of responsible party doctrine and the declensionist turn in public and scholarly understandings of parties from the 1960s onward.[28] Investigating the sources of such ideas as well as their impact on political developments sheds light on the role that normative ideas about the political system play in that system's development. It also helps to account for the sheer unexpectedness of late-century polarization and partisan revival from the point of view of contemporary observers.

The work of building disciplinary bridges goes on. The study of parties and partisan dynamics in American politics has arguably never been as urgent a task, and our collective understanding requires both the political scientist's institutional focus and attention to systematic patterns and the historian's emphasis on the agency of human actors. Parties matter more than ever before in shaping the dynamics and dysfunctions of modern politics and governance, but parties are also, emphatically, endogenous institutions, shaped by the work and will of historical agents.[29] Teasing out who shapes the parties and by what mechanisms, and how parties in turn shape opinion and behavior, remains a core and vital task for research.

Future avenues of inquiry extend the pursuit backward in time as well as outward from the vantage point of the middle-range actors driving partisan change in this book. The attention to activists, interest groups, and movements as party agents has inspired extraordinary research in the last decade. But has decentering the mass electorate from theories of parties come at the cost of overestimating the stability and order of contemporary American politics? Bringing the voters back into the study of parties—as agents in their own right, as the background context for behavior by party actors, or as the missing ingredient in a contemporary system defined by strong partisanship and hollowed-out party organizations—may prove more relevant than ever in the age of Trump. Similarly, historians as well as scholars of American political development would do well to engage in temporal and international comparative analysis, across both American political epochs and contemporary party systems, to better identify shared or contrasting patterns in the interplay of partisanship and ideology. And finally, this book's focus on the origins of an ideologically sorted party system leaves for future inquiry the transformation in policymaking that accompanied the emergence of this new system. Amid the vast political science literature on polarization, fine-grained archival and interview-based work assessing its impact on lawmaking and policy outcomes has just recently begun to emerge. Ongoing developments in American politics seem to promise both a continuing supply of data for such inquiries and a continuing demand for scholarship that helps to make sense of it all.

BIBLIOGRAPHY OF ARCHIVAL SOURCES

American Conservative Union. Records. Harold B. Lee Library, Brigham Young University, Provo, UT.

American Federation of Labor and Congress of Industrial Organizations. Papers. George Meany Memorial Archive, Silver Spring, MD.

Bliss, Ray C. Papers. Ohio Historical Society, Columbus, OH.

Bode, Ken. Papers. Archives of DePauw University and Indiana United Methodism, DePauw University, Greencastle, IN.

Brock, William E., III. Papers. Howard Baker Center for Public Policy, University of Tennessee, Knoxville, TN.

Buckley, William F., Jr. Papers. Archives and Manuscript Library, Yale University, New Haven, CT.

Butler, Paul M. Papers. Hesburgh Library, University of Notre Dame, Notre Dame, IN.

Jimmy Carter Library, Atlanta, GA:
   Office of Congressional Liaison. Files.
   Strauss, Robert. Files.
   White House Central Files.

Common Cause. Records, 1968–1991. Seeley G. Mudd Manuscript Library, Princeton University, Princeton, NJ.

Crisp, Mary Dent. Papers. Schlesinger Library, Harvard University, Cambridge, MA.

Democratic National Committee. Records. National Archives, Washington, DC.

Democratic Socialists of America. Papers. Tamiment Library/Robert Wagner Labor Archives, New York University, New York, NY.

Dirksen, Everett M. Papers. Dirksen Congressional Center, Pekin, IL.

Gerald R. Ford Presidential Library, Ann Arbor, MI:
 Calkins, John T. Files.
 Cheney, Richard. Files.
 Hartmann, Robert T. Files.
 Reichley, A. James. Files.
 Reichley, A. James. Interview Transcripts.
 Raoul-Duval, Michael. Files.
 Teeter, Robert. Papers.
 Timmons, William E. Files.
 White House Central Files.
Fraser, Donald M. Papers. Minnesota Historical Society, St. Paul, MN.
Fraser, Douglas A. Papers. Walter P. Reuther Library, Wayne State University, Detroit, MI.
House Democratic Caucus. Records. Library of Congress, Washington, DC.
Jeffrey, Mildred. Papers. Walter P. Reuther Library, Wayne State University, Detroit, MI.
Lyndon Baines Johnson Presidential Library, Austin, TX:
 Bohen, Fred. Files.
 McPherson, Harry. Files.
 Watson, W. Marvin. Files.
 Wattenberg, Ben. Files.
 White House Central Files—Human Rights.
 White House Central Files—Political Affairs.
John F. Kennedy Presidential Library, Boston, MA:
 Democratic National Committee. Records, 1932–1964.
 Key, V. O. Papers.
 Schlesinger, Arthur M., Jr. Papers.
 Sprecher, Drexel. Papers.
 White House Central Files.
Lowenstein, Allard K. Papers. Louis Round Wilson Special Collections Library, University of North Carolina, Chapel Hill, NC.
McEntee, Gerald. Papers. Walter P. Reuther Library, Wayne State University, Detroit, MI.
McGovern, George S. Papers. Seeley G. Mudd Manuscript Library, Princeton University, Princeton, NJ.
Michel, Robert H. Papers. Dirksen Congressional Center, Pekin, IL.

Midwest Academy. Papers. Chicago History Museum, Chicago, IL.

Mundt, Karl E. Papers. Microfilm. Karl E. Mundt Library, Dakota State University, Madison, SD.

New Democratic Coalition. Records. Western Historical Manuscript Collection, University of Missouri, St. Louis, MO.

O'Hara, James G. Papers. Bentley Historical Library, University of Michigan, Ann Arbor, MI.

O'Neill, Thomas P., Jr. Papers. John J. Burns Library, Boston College, Boston, MA.

Ragland, Martha. Papers. Schlesinger Library, Harvard University, Cambridge, MA.

Rauh, Joseph L., Jr. Papers. Library of Congress, Washington, DC.

Ronald Reagan Presidential Library, Simi Valley, CA:
    Baker III, James A. Files.

Republican Party. Papers, 1911–1980. Microfilm. University Publications of America, Frederick, MD.

Reuther, Walter P. Papers. Walter P. Reuther Library, Wayne State University, Detroit, MI.

Rosenblatt, Maurice. Papers. Library of Congress, Washington, DC.

Rusher, William. Papers. Library of Congress, Washington, DC.

Schattschneider, E. E. Papers. Olin Library, Wesleyan University, Middletown, CT.

Shachtman, Max. Papers. Microfilm. Tamiment Library/Robert Wagner Labor Archives, New York University, New York, NY.

Staebler, Neil E. Papers. Bentley Historical Library, University of Michigan, Ann Arbor, MI.

Stevenson, Adlai E. Papers. Seeley G. Mudd Manuscript Library, Princeton University, Princeton, NJ.

Harry S. Truman Presidential Library, Independence, MO:
    Finletter, Thomas K. Papers.
    Murphy, Charles S. Papers.
    Nash, Philleo. Papers.
    Truman, Harry S. Post-Presidential Files.

Weyrich, Paul. Papers. American Heritage Center, University of Wyoming, Laramie, WY.

White, F. Clinton. Papers. John Ashbrook Center for Public Affairs, Ashland University, Ashland, OH.

ACKNOWLEDGMENTS

This book would not have been written without the help of a great many people. Particular thanks go to several scholars whose involvement with the project dates back years and who generously engaged with the entire manuscript in various iterations. Lizabeth Cohen has played a crucial role from the book's inception, pairing continual and detailed substantive feedback with unceasing encouragement to *think big* in conceiving and executing the project. Along the way she has provided a model of what good scholarship, conscientious academic citizenship, and supportive and constructive mentoring looks like. She has my profound gratitude. Lisa McGirr provided incisive and challenging advice while serving as a useful interlocutor regarding the place of political history in contemporary scholarship and the directions in which it is headed. Daniel Carpenter offered much needed perspective from his vantage point within political science, bolstering my efforts to make this work speak to interdisciplinary audiences. His counsel has only grown in importance as I have made my own personal disciplinary odyssey. Julian Zelizer proved exceedingly generous with his own time in sharing thoughts and advice on my project, and his intellectual influence is evident throughout the pages that follow. Daniel Schlozman's unfailing encouragement and wise counsel, his extraordinarily detailed and rich substantive feedback, and his inspiring passion for both the study and practice of American party politics all warrant special mention. So does the profound gift of his introducing me to barbeque season at Formaggio.

Colleagues at three institutions—Hamilton College, Wesleyan

University, and Colgate University—enabled and enhanced my work on this project during my years as an iterant professor on the liberal arts circuit. Particular thanks go to Timothy Byrnes, Logan Dancey, Marc Eisner, Erica Franklin-Fowler, Michael Hayes, Gbemende Johnson, Phil Klinkner, Celeste Day Moore, Nancy Schwartz, Peter Simons, Yamil Velez, and Joel Winkleman. Many other scholars have offered constructive feedback on elements of this project over the years, including Julia Azari, Leslie Brown, Devin Caughey, Nancy Cott, Andrew Gelman, David Greenberg, Peter Hall, Meg Jacobs, Ira Katznelson, Jeremy Kessler, James Kloppenberg, Hans Noel, Celia Paris, Gary Reichard, Bruce Schulman, Jeffrey Selinger, Byron Shafer, Tim Shenk, Robert Shapiro, Jeffrey Stonecash, and James R. Stoner. I thank them all. I also thank Andrew Hartman and an anonymous reviewer for providing extensive and immensely helpful comments on the manuscript for the University of Chicago Press.

Thanks go as well to the participants in workshops and seminars at which I presented portions of this project, including the Division II Faculty Seminar at Wesleyan, the Workshop on Twentieth Century Politics and Society at Columbia University, the American Politics Research Workshop at Harvard University, and numerous conference panels over the years. A key early incubator for this project, along with so many others, was Liz Cohen's Twentieth Century Dissertation Group, an invaluable workshop and supportive community of Americanist scholars at Harvard. I thank all of its participants, and in particular, I thank my unfailingly supportive friends and colleagues, Brian Goldstein, Theresa McCulla, Elisa Minoff, and Ross Mulcare.

My interest in recent changes in the American party system dates back to the time I spent working as a writer and editor at the *American Prospect* magazine in Washington, DC. I want to thank my editors there, Michael Tomasky, Harold Meyerson, Robert Kuttner, and Paul Starr, for their intellectual and professional encouragement. I also thank Scott Lemieux for serving as a helpful early guide to political science scholarship on American politics and policy. In an email that he has no doubt long forgotten but that

I have kept for ten years, Mark Schmitt actually suggested a version of this story as a good idea for a book project. As if that alone does not deserve thanks, Mark's encyclopedic knowledge and profound insight into developments in later twentieth-century American politics have been continual sources of inspiration. Matthew Yglesias deserves special thanks for being both a great friend and a seemingly bottomless font of intellectually stimulating ideas over the years, which have influenced this project immensely.

The research for this project would not have been possible without the aid and support of many people and organizations. My sincere thanks go to the archivists, too numerous to list here by name, who demonstrated such diligence and professionalism in helping to excavate holdings and brainstorm further avenues of inquiry for me in dozens of libraries across the country. Generous financial support for work on this project came from the following sources: Harvard's Department of History; the Charles Warren Center for the Study of American History; the Center for American Political Studies; the Whiting Fellowship at Harvard's Graduate School of Arts and Sciences; the Gerald R. Ford Presidential Foundation; the Lyndon Baines Johnson Foundation; and the Harry S. Truman Library Institute. I also thank the many friends, relatives, and relatives of friends who generously hosted me free of charge on my research travels.

To my immense good fortune, Tim Mennel at the University of Chicago Press has turned out to be what I had been told was an extinct species: an academic editor who actually edits. Tim's intensive engagement with this manuscript has rendered it vastly more effective—and, one hopes, accessible and appealing—as a work of publicly engaged scholarship. Beyond that, he has served as a consistently patient, conscientious, and capable guide through the sometimes bewildering publishing process. I am truly in his debt. I also thank Rachel Kelly, Therese Boyd, Ashley Pierce, and the rest of the team at Chicago for so ably steering the book through production.

Friends and family have helped more than they can ever know to support me during my work on this project. The risk of inadvertent omissions compels me to offer a blanket expression of thanks to all who have enriched my life and sustained my energy over the last decade. My immediate family warrants special mention, however. My brother, Jake Rosenfeld, has been a constant source of inspiration, support, and grizzled wisdom from the trenches of contemporary academia. I have treasured his friendship and camaraderie, along with the influence of his own intellectual interests and political passions, which have deeply informed this project. My father, Richard Rosenfeld, has long demonstrated a level of scholarly productivity as impressive as it is downright intimidating. But his approach to a well-rounded life of intellectual inquiry balanced by nonscholarly engagement has always been an inspiration—one that I may more plausibly stand a chance of emulating. I thank him as well as Janet Lauritsen for their unfailing support, encouragement, and advice during my work on this project. My mother, Frances Hoffmann, has served as a constant source of keen academic wisdom, unconditional encouragement, and infectious optimism about my work, career, and life. I am deeply grateful for her thoughtful and considered counsel and for the daily example she sets.

Profound personal milestones dot the history of my work on this project, which was bookended on each side by my marriage to Erica De Bruin and the birth of our son, Henry. His arrival coincided conveniently with the final frenzied months of drafting the manuscript on deadline (and, soon enough, past the deadline). It is probably a testament to my odd work habits that night-shift duties tending to a newborn actually seemed to boost rather than hamper my productivity, and so I thank baby Henry for his help in wrapping the book up—and of course for the more profound gifts that his daily, smiley, gobsmacking existence has brought to my life. Henry is in no position to process and accept these thanks any time soon, but his mother is a different story. Not a day goes by that I don't marvel at my good fortune to have found a partner who so inspires me with her strength and intelligence and so comforts me with her encouragement and good humor. Erica has been an unfailing advocate and instrumental partner in the writing of this book, which is dedicated to her with love and appreciation. But, of course, her advocacy and support extend far beyond this project. Words fail to convey the debt of gratitude I owe her for being who she is and for brightening every day we're together. I look forward to spending the rest of my life paying it back.

NOTES

INTRODUCTION

1   Susan Dunn, *Roosevelt's Purge: How FDR Fought to Change the Democratic Party* (Cambridge, MA: Harvard University Press, 2010), 231–32.

2   Radio broadcast of the Commonwealth Club of California, June 11, 1959; audio accessed at http://www.commonwealthclub.org/node/82025.

3   Godfrey Hodgson, *The World Turned Right Side Up: A History of the Conservative Ascendancy in America* (Boston: Houghton Mifflin, 1996), 2.

4   Transcript of *Meet the Press*, July 6, 1969, Box 10, Folder "Commission Chronological File, August 1969," Democratic National Committee (DNC) Records, National Archives, Washington, DC.

5   Jesse Helms, "The New American Majority: Time for a Political Realignment?," May 15, 1974, American Conservative Union Papers, Brigham Young University, Provo, UT.

6   Michael Bowen, *The Roots of Modern Conservatism: Taft, Dewey, and the Battle for the Soul of the Republican Party* (Chapel Hill: University of North Carolina Press, 2011), 193.

7   This specific wording can be seen in Gallup Poll no. 394, April 9, 1947, accessed at Gallup Brain, http://brain.gallup.com.

8   Nolan McCarty, Keith T. Poole, and Howard Rosenthal, *Polarized America: The Dance of Ideology and Unequal Riches* (Cambridge, MA: MIT Press, 2006), 30–32; and see their updated data at http://voteview.com/political_polarization.asp.

9   "Polarization" is protean in meaning. Scholars emphasize a distinction between polarization as a divergence toward opposing ideological extremes and polarization as sorting, or the increased correlation between one's ideology and party affiliation; see Paul DiMaggio, John Evans, and

Bethany Bryson, "Have Americans' Social Attitudes Grown More Polarized?" *American Journal of Sociology* 102 (November 1996): 690–755; Matthew Levendusky, *The Partisan Sort: How Liberals Became Democrats and Conservatives Became Republicans* (Chicago: University of Chicago Press, 2009); and Morris P. Fiorina with Samuel J Abrams, *Disconnect: The Breakdown of Representation in American Politics* (Norman: University of Oklahoma Press, 2012). Focusing on parties as institutions, I use the term "partisan polarization" interchangeably with "sorting." For a useful exploration of polarization's multiple meanings, see Hans Noel, *Political Ideologies and Political Parties in America* (New York: Cambridge University Press, 2013), 165–70.

10 Trotsky's alleged aphorism about the dialect appears, in fact, to be itself a very loose paraphrase of a line he wrote in 1939. See Leon Trotsky, *In Defense of Marxism*, 4th ed. (New York: Pathfinder Press, 1995), 115.

CHAPTER I

1 John Bartlow Martin, *Adlai Stevenson and the World* (Garden City, NY: Doubleday, 1977), 4.

2 E. E. Schattschneider to Adlai E. Stevenson, November 9, 1952, Box 1, Folder 36, E. E. Schattschneider Papers, Olin Library, Wesleyan University, Middletown, CT (hereafter Schattschneider Papers).

3 Stevenson, letter to Schattschneider, December 19, 1952, Box 1, Folder 36, Schattschneider Papers.

4 Committee on Political Parties, *Toward a More Responsible Two-Party System*, supplement to the *American Political Science Review* 40 (September 1950): 17–18.

5 Susan Dunn, *Roosevelt's Purge: How FDR Fought to Change the Democratic Party* (Cambridge, MA: Harvard University Press, 2010), 231.

6 Sidney M. Milkis, *The President and the Parties: The Transformation of the American Party System since the New Deal* (New York: Oxford University Press, 1993), 52–97; David Plotke, *Building a Democratic Political Order: Reshaping American Liberalism in the 1930s and 1940s* (New York: Cambridge University Press, 1996), 128–61.

7 A notable example of this last trend was the 1936 abolition of the century-old requirement for a two-thirds vote of convention delegates to secure the presidential nomination; the rule had afforded the southern bloc a veto power.

8 Franklin D. Roosevelt radio address, June 28, 1938, John T. Woolley and

Gerhard Peters, *The American Presidency Project* (Santa Barbara, CA), http://www.presidency.ucsb.edu/ws/?pid=15662.

9   E. E. Schattschneider, *Party Government* (New York: Rinehart and Company, 1942), 163.

10   Milkis emphasizes the impact of the purge's failure in hastening a redirection of liberal efforts away from party politics, while Sean J. Savage attributes more significance to the purge as a moment of explicit partisan rupture that helped set in motion the long-term marginalization of the South within the party. Milkis, *The President and the Parties*, 75–99; and Sean J. Savage, *Roosevelt: The Party Leader* (Lexington: University Press of Kentucky, 1991), 153–73.

11   Alonzo L. Hamby, *Beyond the New Deal: Harry S. Truman and American Liberalism* (New York: Columbia University Press, 1973), 241–65. On the congressional races, see Julian E. Zelizer, *On Capitol Hill: The Struggle to Reform Congress and its Consequences, 1945–2000* (New York: Cambridge University Press, 2004), 36–42.

12   Jennifer A. Delton, *Making Minnesota Liberal: Civil Rights and the Transformation of the Democratic Party* (Minneapolis: University of Minnesota Press, 2002), 1–39.

13   Steven M. Gillon, *Politics and Vision: The ADA and American Liberalism, 1947–1985* (New York: Oxford University Press, 1987), 35–56.

14   Kevin Boyle, *The UAW and the Heyday of American Liberalism, 1945–1968* (Ithaca, NY: Cornell University Press, 1998), 50–51.

15   Stephen Amberg, "The CIO Political Strategy in Historical Perspective: Creating a High-Road Economy in the Postwar Era," in *Organized Labor and American Politics, 1894–1994: The Labor-Liberal Alliance*, ed. Kevin Boyle (Albany: State University of New York Press, 1998), 169–73.

16   Hamby, *Beyond the New Deal*, 311–27.

17   Austin Ranney, *The Doctrine of Responsible Party Government: Its Origins and Present State* (Urbana: University of Illinois Press, 1954), 25–110; and John Kenneth White and Jerome M. Mileur, "In the Spirit of Their Times: 'Toward a More Responsible Two-Party System' and Party Politics," in *Responsible Partisanship? The Evolution of American Political Parties since 1950*, ed. John C. Green and Paul S. Herrnson (Lawrence: University Press of Kansas, 2000), 16–20.

18   Thomas K. Finletter, *Can Representative Government Do the Job?* (New York: Reynal and Hitchcock, 1945), 92, 108, 110.

19   Leon D. Epstein, "A Persistent Quest," in *Responsible Partisanship?*, ed. Green and Herrnson, 203.

20   Harold Laski, *The American Presidency: An Interpretation* (New York: Harper and Brothers, 1940); James MacGregor Burns mentions Laski's influence on his own thought in Thomas E. Cronin, "On the American Presidency: A Conversation with James MacGregor Burns," *Presidential Studies Quarterly* 16 (Summer 1986): 530.

21   Samuel Beer, oral history interview with Vicki Daitch, November 2002, p. 14, John F. Kennedy Library (hereafter cited JFKL), Boston, MA.

22   This belief was shared by other contemporary thinkers. See, e.g., Joseph Schumpeter, *Capitalism, Socialism, and Democracy* (New York: Harper and Brothers, 1942).

23   E. E. Schattschneider, *Party Government* (New York: Rinehart and Company, 1942), 52.

24   E. E. Schattschneider, "The Functional Approach to Party Government," in *Modern Political Parties: Approaches to Comparative Politics*, ed. Sigmund Neumann (Chicago: University of Chicago Press, 1956), 215.

25   E. E. Schattschneider, *The Struggle for Party Government* (College Park: University of Maryland Press, 1948), 6.

26   Schattschneider, *Party Government*, 65–98, 129–69, and *Struggle for Party Government*, 3–5, 27–38.

27   Theodore Rosenof, *Realignment: The Theory That Changed the Way We Think about Politics* (Lanham, MD: Rowman and Littlefield, 2003), 80.

28   Austin Ranney, letter to Schattschneider, January 15, 1948, Box 1, Folder 32, Schattschneider Papers.

29   E. E. Schattschneider, "Party Government and Employment Policy," *American Political Science Review* 39 (December 1945): 147–57.

30   "Political Science and the World of Tomorrow: The Post-War Program of the American Political Science Association," draft text for pamphlet submitted to APSA Executive Council, March 31, 1945, Box 104, Folder "Committees and Organizations—APSA—Executive Council Fall 1945," V. O. Key Papers, JFKL.

31   Paul T. David, "The APSA Committee on Political Parties: Some Reconsiderations of Its Work and Significance," *Perspectives on Political Science* 21 (Spring 1992): 71.

32   "Interim Report of the Committee on National Parties and Elections," undated, Box 8, Folder 10, Schattschneider Papers; David, "The APSA Committee on Political Parties," 71–72.

33   David, "The APSA Committee on Political Parties," 72. Committee on Political Parties, *Toward a More Responsible Two-Party System*, v.

34 Committee on Political Parties, *Toward a More Responsible Two-Party System*, v, 15.

35 Ibid., 43, 56–65.

36 On the debate within the discipline, see Evron M. Kirkpatrick, "Toward a More Responsible Two-Party System: Political Science, Policy Science, or Pseudo-Science?" *American Political Science Review* 65 (1971): 965–90; John Kenneth White, "Intellectual Challenges to Party Government," in *Challenges to Party Government*, ed. John Kenneth White and Jerome M. Mileur (Carbondale: Southern Illinois University Press, 1992), 1–7; and John C. Green and Paul S. Herrnson, "The Search for Responsibility," in *Responsible Partisanship?*, ed. Green and Herrnson, 5–7.

37 Pendleton Herring, *The Politics of Democracy: American Parties in Action* (New York: W. W. Norton, 1940), 106.

38 David B. Truman, *The Governmental Process: Political Interests and Public Opinion* (New York: Alfred A. Knopf, 1951), 325.

39 Herbert Agar, *The Price of Union* (Boston: Houghton Mifflin, 1950).

40 T. William Goodman, "How Much Party Centralization Do We Want?" *Journal of Politics* 13 (November 1951): 536–61.

41 Ranney, interview with Nelson Polsby, in *Political Science in America: Oral Histories of a Discipline*, ed. Michael A. Baer, Michael E. Jewell, and Lee Sigelman (Lexington: University of Kentucky Press, 1991), 219–20.

42 Ranney, *The Doctrine of Responsible Party Government*, 162. A similar contemporary critique of the APSA report came from J. Roland Pennock in "Responsiveness, Responsibility, and Majority Rule," *American Political Science Review* 46 (September 1952): 790–807.

43 Committee on Political Parties, *Toward a More Responsible Two-Party System*, 19.

44 The Gallup Polls no. 394, April 9, 1947, and no. 451, January 6, 1950, can be accessed at Gallup Brain, http://brain.gallup.com. See also George Horsley Smith and Richard P. Davis, "Do the Voters Want the Parties Changed?," *Public Opinion Quarterly* 11 (Summer 1947): 236–43; and Austin Ranney and Willmoore Kendall, *Democracy and the American Party System* (New York: Harcourt, Brace, 1956), 499–504.

45 David, "The APSA Committee on Political Parties," 73.

46 Committee on Political Parties, *Toward a More Responsible Two-Party System*, 20.

47 Goodman, "How Much Party Centralization Do We Want?," 554.

48   Committee on Political Parties, *Toward a More Responsible Two-Party System*, 20–21.

49   Schattschneider, *Party Government*, 85–93.

50   His confidence in the beneficial effects of thoroughgoing party competition also accounted for his dismissal of the need for intraparty democracy. Ibid., 53–61.

51   Julius Turner, "Responsible Parties: A Dissent from the Floor," *American Political Science Review* 45 (March 1951): 143–52. A recent restatement of this point—as description rather than prediction—is made by Nicole Mellow in *The State of Disunion: Regional Sources of Modern American Partisanship* (Baltimore: Johns Hopkins University Press, 2008), especially 176–79.

52   John D. Morris, "Reform Is Urged in Two Major Parties," *New York Times*, October 14, 1950; "Our Limping Parties," *Washington Post*, November 8, 1950.

53   Delton, *Making Minnesota Liberal*, 157.

54   Ralph M. Goldman, *The National Party Chairmen and Committees: Factionalism at the Top* (New York: M. E. Sharpe, 1990), 432.

55   "Proposed Subjects for ADA Discussion Outlines," August 24, 1951, Box 16, Folder "Americans for Democratic Action Files—July–Sept. 1951," Joseph L. Rauh Jr. Papers, Library of Congress, Washington, DC (hereafter Rauh Papers).

CHAPTER 2

1   Cornelius P. Cotter and Bernard C. Hennessy, *Politics without Power: The National Party Committees* (New York: Atherton Press, 1964).

2   Neil Staebler, letter to George C. Roberts, July 6, 1982, Box 292, Folder "Roberts, Robert," Neil Staebler Papers, Bentley Historical Library, University of Michigan, Ann Arbor, MI (hereafter Staebler Papers).

3   Lyle W. Dorsett, *Franklin D. Roosevelt and the City Bosses* (Port Washington, NY: Kennikat Press, 1977); Alan Ware, *The Breakdown of Democratic Party Organization, 1940–1980* (New York: Clarendon Press, 1985); Savage, *Roosevelt*, 48–79.

4   John Fischer, "What Do the Democrats Do Now?" *Harper's*, March 1953.

5   Ibid.

6   Angus Campbell, Gerald Gurin, and Warren E. Miller, *The Voter Decides* (Evanston, IL: Row, Peterson and Co., 1954); and Angus Campbell,

Philip E. Converse, Warren E. Miller, and Donald E. Stokes, *The American Voter* (New York: John Wiley and Sons, 1960).

7   Jonathan Bell, "Social Democracy and the Rise of the Democratic Party in California, 1950–1964," *Historical Journal* 49 (2006): 497–524; and James Q. Wilson, *The Amateur Democrat: Club Politics in Three Cities* (Chicago: University of Chicago Press, 1962), 96–125.

8   Frank J. Sauroff, "Extra-Legal Political Parties in Wisconsin," *American Political Science Review* 48 (September 1954): 692–704.

9   Dudley W. Buffa, *Union Power and American Democracy: The UAW and the Democratic Party, 1935–72* (Ann Arbor: University of Michigan Press, 1984), 3–51; Staebler, letter to Dora Beale Polk, April 8, 1953, and Staebler, letter to Samuel Lubell, July 18, 1956, both in Box 314, Folder "Neil Staebler—Summations and Forecasts; Analyses and Plans; Statements of Principles—1952–1956," Staebler Papers.

10   Sean J. Savage, *JFK, LBJ, and the Democratic Party* (Albany: State University of New York Press, 2004), 35.

11   Stevenson described his early impression of Butler as "definitely a 'new look' type" in a letter to Arthur Schlesinger, August 16, 1954, Box 73, Folder 9, Adlai E. Stevenson Papers, Seeley G. Mudd Library, Princeton University, Princeton, NJ (hereafter Stevenson Papers). Staebler employed the "new look" term in Jim Elsman, "Staebler Attacks Republican Practices," *Michigan Daily*, January 15, 1956.

12   Wilson, *The Amateur Democrat*, 3–4, 18–19.

13   Committee on Political Parties, *Toward a More Responsible Two-Party System*, supplement to the *American Political Science Review* 40 (September 1950): 67.

14   David Adamany, "The Political Science of E. E. Schattschneider," *American Political Science Review* 66 (December 1972): 1328–30; James MacGregor Burns, "Forces for Unity and Disunity in the Democratic Party, 1954–1956," paper presented at the APSA annual meeting, September 11, 1954, Box 1, Folder 32, Schattschneider Papers.

15   James Q. Wilson, *Political Organizations* (New York: Basic Books, 1973), 45–51, 95–118.

16   Stevenson's appointments to the DNC reflected this disposition. His handpicked chairman, the reformist Stephen Mitchell, took an approach to party management that in many ways anticipated Paul Butler's succeeding tenure. See James Reston, "Stevenson Selects Political Amateur as Party Chairman," *New York Times*, August 9, 1952.

17   Butler's interest in the Draft Stevenson movement can be seen in Steven-

son, letter to Butler, April 18, 1952, Box 46, Folder 56, Paul M. Butler Papers, Hesburgh Library, University of Notre Dame, South Bend, IN (hereafter Butler Papers).

18   George C. Roberts, *Paul M. Butler: Hoosier Politician and National Political Leader* (Lanham, MD: University Press of America, 1987), 35–37.

19   Paul M. Butler, "A Democratic National Convention in 1954?," p. 1, Box 176, Folder "Nat'l Committee, 1/1/54 to 11/2/54," Staebler Papers.

20   Minutes of DNC Executive Committee meeting, April 1, 1953, Box 114, Folder "Executive Committee Meeting—March 31–April 1, 1953—Transcripts," Democratic National Committee Records, JFKL.

21   Peter Edson, "Democrats Plan 1954 'Convention,'" *Nashville Tennessean*, April 14, 1953.

22   W. H. Lawrence, "Congress' Democrats Shun '54 Convention," *Louisville Courier-Journal*, April 30, 1953.

23   Ralph M. Goldman, *The National Party Chairmen and Committees: Factionalism at the Top* (New York: M. E. Sharpe, 1990), 445–46.

24   Sidney Hyman, "The Collective Leadership of Paul Butler," *The Reporter*, December 24, 1959.

25   DNC Meeting minutes, December 4, 1954, Box 116, Folder "DNC and Subordinate Committee Meetings—DNC Meeting, December 4, 1954," DNC Records.

26   A copy of the pledge is enclosed with David Lawrence's letter to Harry Truman, August 14, 1959, Box 92, Folder "Lawrence, David L.," Truman Post-Presidential Files, Harry S. Truman Library (hereafter cited as HSTL), Independence, MO.

27   Roberts, *Paul M. Butler*, 140.

28   Recommendation No. 16-A, Report to the Democratic National Committee on Recommendations of Advisory Committee on Political Organization, April 20, 1956, Box 2, Drexel Sprecher Papers, JFKL.

29   Butler speech, Lansing, Michigan, January 1, 1959, Box 3, Folder "Butler, Paul—Speeches, 1959," Butler Papers.

30   On the Finletter group's activities between 1953 and 1956, see John Bartlow Martin, *Adlai Stevenson and the World* (Garden City, NY: Doubleday, 1977), 82–89.

31   Arthur M. Schlesinger Jr., letter to Adlai Stevenson, November 7, 1952, Box 73, Folder 8, Stevenson Papers.

32   For an example of the former, see "Volunteers in Politics: Dedicated to

Adlai Stevenson's Principles of Government" pamphlet, Box 73, Folder 8, Stevenson Papers.

33 Walter Johnson, ed., *The Papers of Adlai E. Stevenson*, vol. 4 (Boston: Little, Brown, 1974), 221; Martin, *Adlai Stevenson and the World*, 8.

34 Thomas K. Finletter, *Can Representative Government Do the Job?* (New York: Reynal and Hitchcock, 1945).

35 Martin, *Adlai Stevenson and the World*, 83-84.

36 A useful overview of the group's structure is in Finletter, letter to Schlesinger, September 28, 1954, Box P-13, Folder "Incoming Correspondence File 1945-1960—Thomas Finletter," Arthur M. Schlesinger Jr. Papers, JFKL.

37 Herbert S. Parmet, *The Democrats: The Years After FDR* (New York: Oxford University Press, 1976), 126-27.

38 Joseph C. Harsch, "How Tough Is the Elephant's Hide?," *Christian Science Monitor*, November 29, 1955.

39 Stevenson, letter to Finletter, December 12, 1954, Box 32, Folder 10, and Stevenson, letter to Butler, December 30, 1954, Box 15, Folder 16, both in Stevenson Papers.

40 Charles Murphy, letter to Stephen Mitchell, November 5, 1954, Box 7, Folder "Democratic National Committee—1954," Charles S. Murphy Papers, HSTL (hereafter Murphy Papers).

41 Murphy, letter to Butler, December 20, 1954, Box 7, Folder "Democratic National Committee," Murphy Papers.

42 Committee on Political Parties, *Toward a More Responsible Two-Party System*, 43.

43 Robert Caro, *The Years of Lyndon Johnson: Master of the Senate* (New York: Alfred A. Knopf, 2002), 598-604 (hereafter cited as *Master of the Senate*).

44 William S. White, "Democrats Reject a Harsh Approach as Congress Opens," *New York Times*, January 6, 1955.

45 Robert C. Albright, "84th Congress a Bipartisan Love Match for Ike," *Washington Post*, July 24, 1955; William S. White, "Capitol Hill Armistice Holds Despite Election," *New York Times*, May 27, 1956.

46 White, "Capitol Hill Armistice Holds Despite Election."

47 Schlesinger, "Congressional Strategy and the 1956 Elections," undated, Box 73, Folder 10, Stevenson Papers.

48 Lyndon Johnson, letter to Harry Truman, December 7, 1956, Box 22,

Folder "Johnson, Lyndon B.—corres. 1955–58," Truman Post-Presidential Files.

49 D. B. Hardeman and Donald C. Bacon, *Rayburn: A Biography* (Austin: Texas Monthly Press, 1987), 407.

50 Caro, *Master of the Senate*, 842.

51 The quote is from David Lawrence, DNC Executive Committee Meeting Minutes, November 27, 1956, p. 188, Box 119, Folder "Executive Committee Meeting—November 26–27, 1956," DNC Records.

52 Arvey and Lawrence were no fans of Butler, but they shared other northerners' alarm at the atrophying of key Democratic electoral constituencies. Moreover, both were Stevenson allies, and perceived the DAC as a platform for him. Sean J. Savage offers an analysis of Lawrence and Arvey as adaptable party bosses who had consciously aligned themselves with New Deal liberalism; *Truman and the Democratic Party* (Lexington: University Press of Kentucky, 1997), 31–36, 41–48.

53 This language and the ensuing discussion come from the DNC Executive Committee Meeting Minutes, November 27, 1956, pp. 185–239, Box 119, Folder "Executive Committee Meeting—November 26–27, 1956," DNC Records.

54 Phillip A. Klinkner, *The Losing Parties: Out-Party National Committees, 1956–1993* (New Haven, CT: Yale University Press, 1994), 23.

55 Roberts, *Paul M. Butler*, 106–7.

56 Rayburn, letter to Butler, December 8, 1956, Box 14, Folder "Comments re. Advisory Council," Butler Papers.

57 Charles S. Murphy, oral history interview with Jerry N. Hess, May 19, 1970, pp. 496–97, HSTL.

58 Minutes of Combined Meeting of the Executive Committee and Advisory Committee of the Democratic National Committee, January 4, 1956, Box 357, Folder 11, Stevenson Papers.

59 Hugh A. Bone, *Party Committees and National Politics* (Seattle: University of Washington Press, 1956), 223.

60 Mildred Jeffrey, letter to Margaret Price, May 22, 1957, Box 18, Folder 2, Mildred Jeffrey Papers, Walter P. Reuther Library, Wayne State University, Detroit, MI.

61 Statement to the press, January 3, 1957, Box 358, Folder 3, Stevenson Papers.

62 Philip Perlman, letter to William S. White, December 3, 1959, Box 35,

Folder "Demo Nat Comm Advis Council, working papers July–Dec 1959," Murphy Papers.

63 Klinkner, *The Losing Parties*, 21.

64 Kenneth Kofmehl, "The Institutionalization of a Voting Bloc," *Western Political Quarterly* 17, no. 2 (1964): 256–72; Julian E. Zelizer, *On Capitol Hill: The Struggle to Reform Congress and its Consequences, 1945–2000* (New York: Cambridge University Press, 2004), 49.

65 Committee on Political Parties, *Toward a More Responsible Two-Party System*, 51.

66 Roberts, *Paul M. Butler*, 113.

67 See the clippings collected by Charles Tyroler in Box 3, Folder 6, and Box 358, Folder 4, Stevenson Papers; and Box 34, Folder "Demo Nat Advis Council—working papers, Dec. 1958–June 1959," Murphy Papers.

68 Editors, "From Small Oaks," *Dayton Daily News*, November 11, 1957.

69 Richard L. Strout, "A Voice for the 'Out' Party," *Christian Science Monitor*, November 19, 1959.

70 "Party Responsibility in the 20th Century," July 2, 1958, Box 29, Folder "Speeches—July, 1958," Butler Papers.

71 Klinkner, *The Losing Parties*, 14.

72 Katie Louchheim, *By the Political Sea* (Garden City, NY: Doubleday, 1970), 171.

73 Hyman, "The Collective Leadership of Paul Butler."

74 Arlene Lazarowitz, *Years in Exile: The Liberal Democrats, 1950–1959* (New York: Taylor and Francis, 1988), 129–30.

75 "'Sunrise' Dawning for the Democrats," *Washington Post*, May 24, 1959.

76 The applause is reported in the *NCEC Congressional Report*, June 30, 1959, Box 8, Folder 3, Maurice Rosenblatt Papers, Library of Congress, Washington, DC (hereafter Rosenblatt Papers).

77 Edward G. Carmines and James A. Stimson, *Issue Evolution: Race and the Transformation of American Politics* (Princeton, NJ: Princeton University Press, 1989), 59–88.

78 "The Democratic Task in the Next Two Years," December 7, 1958, in Box 358, Folder 6, Stevenson Papers.

79 "Rayburn Says Thanks, But House Will Set Own Course," *Chicago Sun-Times*, December 9, 1958.

80 "How Democrats Fared in 1959 Session," *Congressional Quarterly* fact sheet, September 29, 1959, p. 1305, in Box 358, Folder 7, Stevenson Papers. Liberal frustration with the 86th Congress is discussed in Nelson Polsby, *How Congress Evolves: The Social Bases of Institutional Change* (New York: Oxford University Press, 2004), 20–30.

81 "2 Liberal Groups Score Johnson in Assessing Record of Congress," *New York Times*, June 22, 1959.

82 "The Current Legislative Situation" text, June 15, 1959, Box 358, Folder 7, Stevenson Papers.

83 George Reedy, quoted in Savage, *JFK, LBJ, and the Democratic Party*, 32.

84 Klinkner, *The Losing Party*, 23.

85 Charles L. Clapp, *The Congressman: His Work as He Sees It* (Washington, DC: Brookings Institution, 1963), 25.

86 Donald Matthews, *U.S. Senators and Their World* (Chapel Hill: University of North Carolina Press, 1960), 92–117.

87 William S. White, *Citadel: The Story of the U.S. Senate* (New York: Harper and Brothers, 1956), 84.

88 Robert C. Byrd, letter to Butler, July 10, 1959, Box 449, Folder "Chairman Butler's File—Anti-Butler Correspondence, 7/8–7/11/59," DNC Records.

89 Charles Ogden Jr., "Paul Butler, Party Theory, and the Democratic Party," in *Comparative Political Problems: Britain, United States, and Canada*, ed. John E. Kersell and Marshall W. Conley (Englewood Cliffs, NJ: Prentice-Hall, 1968), 117–25.

90 Schattschneider's disciple-turned-heretic, Austin Ranney, laid out this argument in his 1956 collaboration with conservative theorist Willmoore Kendall: *Democracy and the American Party System* (New York: Harcourt, Brace, 1956), 459–87, 500–533.

91 Clinton Rossiter, *Parties and Politics in America* (Ithaca, NY: Cornell University Press, 1960), 59. Rossiter took the term "civil-war potential" directly from Ranney and Kendall's book.

92 Wilson, *The Amateur Democrat*, 20. Edward C. Banfield's most direct statement on American parties is "In Defense of the American Party System," in *Political Parties, U.S.A.*, ed. Robert A. Goldwin (Chicago: Rand McNally, 1964), 21–39.

93 Quotes from Doris Kearns, *Lyndon Johnson and the American Dream* (New York: Harper and Row, 1976), 152, 154.

94 Daniel Bell, *The End of Ideology: On the Exhaustion of Ideas in the Fifties* (Glencoe, IL: Free Press, 1960), 110.

95 Dodd delivered his speech, "The Case against Reforming Our Political System," on November 21, 1960, in New York City. The text was reprinted in the *Congressional Record—Senate*, 87th Cong., 1st sess., 107:205-8.

96 Thomas L. Stokes, "Loyal Democrats in the South: Regulars Irked by Butler's Inclination to Forgive Those Who Deserted Fold," *Washington Star*, May 18, 1955; Roberts, *Paul M. Butler*, 91-93.

97 See, e.g., Charles Diggs, letters to Butler, August 4 and September 13, 1955, and Butler's letter to Diggs, November 15, 1955, in Box 457, Folder "NAACP—Integration," DNC Records.

98 James Doyle, memo to Adlai Stevenson, February 1956, Box 358, Folder 3, Stevenson Papers.

99 Brian D. Feinstein and Eric Schickler, "Platforms and Partners: The Civil Rights Realignment Reconsidered," *Studies in American Political Development* 22 (Spring 2008): 1-31.

100 Roberts, *Paul M. Butler*, 92.

101 Press release, September 15, 1957, Box 449, Folder "Chairman Butler's Files—Advisory Council Press Releases," DNC Records. "Possible Policy Positions," April 22, 1960, Box 100, Folder "Democratic Advisory Council—Advisory Committee on Civil Rights—Meeting, April 22, 1960 [1 of 2]," Philleo Nash Papers, HSTL.

102 Abraham Holtzman, "Party Responsibility and Loyalty: New Rules in the Democratic Party," *Journal of Politics* 22 (1960): 485-501.

103 Allan P. Sindler, "The Unsolid South: A Challenge to the Democratic Party," in *The Uses of Power: Seven Cases in American Politics*, ed. Alan F. Westin (New York: Harcourt, Brace and World, 1962), 229-82.

104 Quoted in "The Democratic Party's Approach to Its Convention Rules," *American Political Science Review* 50 (June 1956): 567.

105 Holtzman, "Party Responsibility and Loyalty," 492; Austin Ranney, *Curing the Mischiefs of Faction: Party Reform in America* (Berkeley: University of California Press, 1975), 183.

106 Zelizer, *On Capitol Hill*, 42-51.

107 *The Democratic Platform 1952*, Box 43, Folder "Subject File, U.S. Senate—Rule 22," Rauh Papers.

108 Zelizer, *On Capitol Hill*, 53-56.

109 "Suggestions for More Effective Coordination by the Liberal Democratic

Group in the House," unsigned memo, November 1957, Box 60, Folder 13, Rosenblatt Papers. See also Kofmehl, "The Institutionalization of a Voting Bloc," 258–62.

110 "Notes, Remarks, and Impressions of Democratic Study Group Meetings of September 5, 7, 8, and 9," unsigned memo, September 1959, Box 60, Folder 14; and "The Republican-Southern Democratic Coalition—1937–1959," DSG report, December 1959, Box 60, Folder 7, both in Rosenblatt Papers.

111 Roberts, *Paul M. Butler*, 109. See also Charles Tyroler, memo, "Tentative Liaison Designations," May 5, 1959, Box 14, Folder "Advisory Committee," Butler Papers.

112 James L. Sundquist, *Politics and Policy: The Eisenhower, Kennedy, and Johnson Years* (Washington, DC: Brookings Institution, 1968), 389–415.

113 "Butler Repudiates Faubus on Schools," *New York Times*, October 9, 1958.

114 L. G. Gambs, letter to Butler, October 9, 1959, and Don C. Bates, letter to Butler, October 9, 1958, in Box 453, Folder "Chairman Butler's File—Statement of Faubus Re Integration and South's Reaction to," DNC Records, JFKL.

115 James MacGregor Burns, "Republicans, Democrats: Who's Who?," *New York Times Magazine*, January 2, 1955.

116 TRB, "Two-Headed Donkey," *New Republic*, December 15, 1958.

117 Partial Report of the Resolutions Committee, 17th Constitutional Convention of the United Auto Workers, October 1959, Box 446, Folder "Chairman's Files, 1960—Chapin, Arthur," DNC Records.

118 Peter Drucker, *Max Shachtman and His Left: A Socialist's Odyssey through the "American Century"* (Atlantic Highlands, NJ: Humanities Press, 1994), 192–208, 242–44; on Burns's influence, see 268, 283. An early exposition of Shachtman's strategy is in R.M. and B.S., "Oust the South from Democratic Party," *Labor Action*, July 16, 1956.

119 Resolution on Political Action, adopted by the National Committee SP-SDF, October 24–25, 1959, Series I, Reel 28, Max Shachtman Papers, microfilm, Tamiment Library/Robert Wagner Labor Archives, New York University, New York.

120 Quoted in Roberts, *Paul M. Butler*, 94.

121 Smathers is quoted in ibid. Whitten in his letter to Butler, December 19, 1958, Box 446, Folder "Chairman Butler's Files—Whitten, Jamie," DNC Records.

122 Truman, letter to Matthew McCloskey, August 1, 1957, in Box 28, Folder

"McCloskey, Matthew H.," and Truman, letter to Jacob Arvey, September 1, 1957, in Box 47, Folder "Arvey, Jacob," Truman Post-Presidential Papers; and Philip Perlman, letter to Truman, June 19, 1957, Box 33, Folder "General Correspondence, 1953–1967—Democratic National Comm, 1956–1959," Murphy Papers. See also Roberts, *Paul M. Butler*, 159–60.

123 *Celebrity Parade* television show transcript, July 5, 1959, Box 19, Folder "Butler," Staebler Papers. The second dump-Butler effort is described in Frank McHale's letters to David Lawrence, August 21, 1959, and to Harry Truman, August 21, 1959, both in Box 98, Folder "McHale, Frank M.," Truman Post-Presidential Papers.

124 Rayburn is quoted in Allen Drury, "Congress Chiefs Reprove Butler," *New York Times*, July 7, 1959. Examples of critical letters sent to Butler can be found in Box 46, Folders 53 and "Originals Not Returned," Butler Papers.

125 Roberts, *Paul M. Butler*, 83.

126 Earl Mazo, "Butler Foes Seen Losing in Ouster Bid," *New York Herald Tribune*, September 15, 1959.

127 Supportive letters from northern congressmen can be found in Box 46, Folder 52, Butler Papers.

128 Patrick McNamara, "Criticism by Paul M. Butler of the slow pace of the 86th Congress," July 8, 1959, in *Congressional Record—Senate*, 86th Cong., 1st sess., 105:12940.

129 "The Presidency in 1960," Washington, DC, January 14, 1960, text in John T. Woolley and Gerhard Peters, *The American Presidency Project* (Santa Barbara, CA), http://www.presidency.ucsb.edu/ws/?pid=25795.

130 Louchheim, *By the Political Sea*, 140–41.

131 Press release, January 22, 1959, Box 15, Folder "Personal Memoranda," Thomas K. Finletter Papers, HSTL.

132 Roberts, *Paul M. Butler*, 79.

CHAPTER 3

1 The discussion below is in the transcript to the meeting of the Republican Committee on Program and Progress, March 14, 1959, Series 1A, Reel 17, *Papers of the Republican Party*, ed. Paul L. Kesaris, microfilm (Frederick, MD: University Publications of America, 1987) (hereafter Republican Party Papers).

2 Eisenhower's authorship of the original idea for the committee is confirmed in Daniel J. Galvin, *Presidential Party Building: Dwight D. Eisenhower to George W. Bush* (Princeton, NJ: Princeton University Press, 2010), 60.

3   "Text of Goldwater's Announcement of Candidacy for GOP Nomination," *Washington Post*, January 4, 1964.

4   Robert Mason, *The Republican Party and American Politics from Hoover to Reagan* (New York: Cambridge University Press, 2012).

5   The emergence of a "fusionist" conservative intellectual movement in the early postwar decades has received extensive scholarly attention since the publication of George Nash's landmark *The Conservative Intellectual Movement in America since 1945* (New York: Basic Books, 1976). But only recently have scholars begun to attend to elite intra-Republican developments in the early postwar decades and their long-run significance. See Lara Jane Gifford, *The Center Cannot Hold: The 1960 Presidential Election and the Rise of Modern Conservatism* (DeKalb: Northern Illinois University Press, 2009); Michael Bowen, *The Roots of Modern Conservatism: Taft, Dewey, and the Battle for the Soul of the Republican Party* (Chapel Hill: University of North Carolina Press, 2011); and Mason, *The Republican Party and American Politics*, 112–82.

6   Nicol C. Rae, *The Decline and Fall of the Liberal Republicans: From 1952 to the Present* (New York: Oxford University Press, 1988), 25–30; Kimberly Phillips-Fein, *Invisible Hands: The Making of the Conservative Movement from the New Deal to Reagan* (New York: W. W. Norton, 2009), 33.

7   Malcolm Moos, *The Republicans: A History of Their Party* (New York: Random House, 1956), 420, 422.

8   Editorial, "Fashions in Politics," *New York Times*, March 17, 1945.

9   Anthony Badger, "Republican Rule in the 80th Congress," in *The Republican Takeover of Congress*, ed. Dean McSweeney and John E. Owens (New York: St. Martin's Press, 1998), 165–84.

10   James T. Patterson, *Mr. Republican: A Biography of Robert A. Taft* (Boston: Houghton Mifflin, 1972), 354–61.

11   "Republican Party Platform of 1948," June 21, 1948, accessed online at John T. Woolley and Gerhard Peters, *The American Presidency Project* (Santa Barbara, CA), http://www.presidency.ucsb.edu/ws/?pid=25836.#axzz2fYSK7VDZ.

12   H. L. Mencken, "Truman's Election: Mencken Says Country Jolly Well Deserves It," *Baltimore Sun*, November 7, 1948.

13   Charles O. Jones, *Party and Policy-Making: The House Republican Policy Committee* (New Brunswick, NJ: Rutgers University Press, 1964), 25.

14 Clarence E. Wunderland Jr., ed., *The Papers of Robert A. Taft*, vol. 3, *1945–1948* (Kent, OH: Kent State University Press, 2003), 471.

15 Mason, *The Republican Party and American Politics*, 126.

16 Kenneth Wherry, comments in the transcript of RNC meeting, Omaha, NE, January 26–27, 1949, Series 1A, Reel 9, Republican Party Papers.

17 The Republican Strategy Committee, under the control of conservatives, maintained close collaboration with McCarthy's operation before being disbanded within the RNC. Bowen, *The Roots of Modern Conservatism*, 92–94.

18 Alfred Friendly, "7 Senate Republicans Assail 'Smearing,' Exploiting 'Fear,'" *Washington Post*, June 2, 1950.

19 The importance of anticommunism and the early 1950s fight over McCarthyism in drawing future leaders of the postwar conservative movement into political and intellectual affairs has long been emphasized by those leaders themselves as well as their scholarly chroniclers. L. Brent Bozell Jr. and William F. Buckley Jr., *McCarthy and His Enemies: The Record and Its Meaning* (New York: Regnery, 1954); Nash, *The Conservative Intellectual Movement in America*, 84–130; Godfrey Hodgson, *The World Turned Right Side Up: A History of the Conservative Ascendancy in America* (Boston: Houghton Mifflin, 1996), 50–81. Carl T. Bogus, *Buckley: William F. Buckley Jr. and the Rise of American Conservatism* (New York: Bloomsbury Press, 2011), 222–56.

20 Bowen argues that the Dewey-Taft rift originated in nonideological conflicts and personal allegiances but acquired ideological content over time. Bowen, *The Roots of Modern Conservatism*, 45–55, 84–85, 182, 201–6.

21 Anderson, Scott, and Harden's quotes all found in the transcript of RNC meeting, Omaha, NE, January 26–27, 1949, Series 1A, Reel 9, Republican Party Papers.

22 John A. Wells, ed., *Thomas E. Dewey on the Two-Party System* (New York: Doubleday, 1966).

23 Ibid., 21–26.

24 Ibid., 7–9, 13.

25 James Burnham, *Congress and the American Political Tradition* (Chicago: Henry Regnery, 1959); Austin Ranney and Willmoore Kendall, *Democracy and the American Party System* (New York: Harcourt, Brace, 1956); Kendall, *The Conservative Affirmation* (Chicago: Henry Regnery, 1963), 1–49.

26 Henry Hazlitt, *A New Constitution Now* (New York: McGraw-Hill, 1942);

"Text of Hoover's Address to Publishers Here Proposing a Reorganization of U.N.," *New York Times*, April 28, 1950.

27 Clarence E. Wunderland Jr., ed., *The Papers of Robert A. Taft*, vol. 4, *1949-1953* (Kent, OH: Kent State University Press, 2006), 25.

28 Felix Morley, "A New Political Element," *Barron's*, September 24, 1951.

29 Everett Dirksen, telegram to Henry Cabot Lodge, April 8, 1952, Folder "000433 EMD Politics," Everett M. Dirksen Papers, Dirksen Congressional Center, Pekin, IL.

30 Bowen, *The Roots of Modern Conservatism*, 116.

31 Moos, *The Republicans*, 468-79, and Bowen, *The Roots of Modern Conservatism*, 123-29, 140-44.

32 Moos, *The Republicans*, 158.

33 Herbert Brownlee, quoted in Bowen, *The Roots of Modern Conservatism*, 123.

34 G. Wartham Ages to Guy Gabrielson, December 31, 1949, Reel 180, Karl E. Mundt Papers, microfilm, Karl E. Mundt Library, Dakota State University, Madison, SD (hereafter Mundt Papers).

35 Mason, *The Republican Party and American Politics*, 57, 68-70, 87-88.

36 Wunderland, ed., *Papers of Robert A. Taft*, 3:465.

37 Keri Frederickson, *The Dixiecrat Revolt and the End of the Solid South, 1932-1968* (Chapel Hill: University of North Carolina Press, 2001), 11-66.

38 Charles Wallace Collins, *Whither Solid South? A Study in Politics and Race Relations* (New Orleans: Pelican Publishing, 1947), 19.

39 Ibid., 255-56.

40 On Mundt's militant anticommunism, see Scott N. Heidepriem, *A Fair Chance for a Free People: The Biography of Karl E. Mundt, United States Senator* (Madison, SD: Leader Printing, 1988), 150-57, 166-94.

41 Karl Mundt, "Is There Need for a Southern Democrat-Northern Republican Political Alliance?," October 3, 1951, in *Congressional Record*, 82nd Cong. 1st sess., A6241.

42 Karl Mundt and Clifford Case, "Should the GOP Merge with the Dixiecrats?," *Collier's*, July 28, 1951.

43 J. Harvie Williams, letters to Albert Hawkes, Robert Dresser, and Karl Mundt, all dated July 7, 1949, Reel 180, Mundt Papers.

44 J. Harvie Williams, "Plan and Program for Political Realignment,"

undated, enclosed in letter to Karl Mundt, October 8, 1949, Reel 180, Mundt Papers.

45 Mundt, letters to Williams, April 15, 1950, and December 27, 1951, Reel 180, Mundt Papers.

46 Karl Mundt, speech in Jackson, MS, April 8, 1952, Reel 180, Mundt Papers.

47 The genesis and personnel of the group are described by Mundt, "Is There Need for a Southern Democrat–Northern Republican Political Alliance?," A6241.

48 J. Harvie Williams and John Underhill, "Liberty and the Republic: The Case for Party Realignment," December 1951, Reel 181, Mundt Papers.

49 Even the major existing southern organization pursuing the question of realignment, the Mississippi-based National Coalition Committee, had been organized by a Taftite Republican from Illinois. Spencer McCulloch, "A New Party A-Comin'?," *The Progressive*, May 1951.

50 Heidepriem, *A Fair Chance for a Free People*, 159.

51 Charles Wallace Collins, letter to Karl Mundt, June 13, 1951, Reel 181, Mundt Papers.

52 Heidepriem, *A Fair Chance for a Free People*, 159; Morley, "A New Political Element"; Editorial, "GOP-Southern Alliance," *Manchester Union Leader*, August 8, 1951.

53 Quoted in Raymond Moley, *How to Keep Our Liberty: A Program for Political Action* (New York: Alfred A. Knopf, 1952), 243.

54 "Some thought" passage from "New Political Alliance: An Interview with Karl E. Mundt," *U.S. News and World Report*, August 3, 1951; "any of the planks" passage from the radio transcript of *The Eleanor Roosevelt Show*, March 16, 1951, accessed at http://www.gwu.edu/~erpapers/documents /displaydoc.cfm?_t=radio&_docid=rad020.

55 Raymond Moley, "A '52 Coalition Budding in South," *Omaha World*, March 25, 1951.

56 Wunderland, ed., *Papers of Robert A. Taft*, 3:46–47.

57 Quoted in Mason, *The Republican Party and American Politics*, 139.

58 Charles Wallace Collins made a point of noting conservative Republican opposition to civil rights measures in *Whither Solid South?*, 154–55.

59 John Temple Graves, "The Birth of a Party," *Human Events*, May 11, 1949.

60 Quoted in Joseph E. Lowndes, *From the New Deal to the New Right: Race*

and the Southern Origins of Modern Conservatism (New Haven, CT: Yale University Press, 2008), 37.

61 Ibid., 36.

62 "New Political Alliance: An Interview with Karl E. Mundt."

63 Mundt and Case, "Should the GOP Merge with the Dixiecrats?"

64 The senators appeared on *American Forum of the Air*. Heidepreim, *A Fair Chance for a Free People*, 161–62.

65 Radio transcript of the *Eleanor Roosevelt Show*, March 16, 1951.

66 Minutes of the meeting of the Executive Committee of the Committee to Explore Political Realignment, November 30, 1951, Reel 180, Mundt Papers.

67 Albert Hawkes, letter to Karl Mundt, November 15, 1951, Reel 180, Mundt Papers.

68 Murray Snyder, "Cold Shoulder for Mundt," *New York Herald Tribune*, July 8, 1951; Drew Pearson, "Coalition Move Shunned," *Washington Post*, October 7, 1951.

69 P. B. Young, "The 'Solid South' Is Now a Political Myth," *Norfolk Journal and Guide*, July 28, 1951.

70 Albert Hawkes, letter to Karl Mundt, November 2, 1951, and J. Harvie Williams, letter to Mundt, December 1951, both in Reel 180, Mundt Papers.

71 Clayton Knowles, "Southern Democrats Wary of the North-South Alliance," *New York Times*, September 23, 1951.

72 For southern "conservatives to join the Republican party," one contemporary scholarly observer noted, "would increase rather than decrease the political potentialities of the Negro." O. Douglas Weeks, "Republicanism and Conservatism in the South," *Southwestern Social Science Quarterly* 36 (December 1955): 254.

73 Earl Black and Merle Black, *The Rise of Southern Republicans* (Cambridge, MA: Harvard University Press, 2002), 61–64.

74 Lowndes, *From the New Deal to the New Right*, 37–38; Bowen, *The Roots of Modern Conservatism*, 124–26; Raymond Moley, "A Political Revolution," *Newsweek*, December 15, 1952.

75 Shamira M. Gelbman and Jesse H. Rhodes, "Party Organization and the Origins of the Republicans' Belated Southern Strategy," paper presented at the Policy History Conference, Columbus, OH, June 2010.

76 Fred I. Greenstein, *The Hidden Hand Presidency: Eisenhower as Leader*

(New York: Basic Books, 1982). See also Gary W. Reichard, *The Reaffirmation of Republicanism: Eisenhower and the Eighty-Third Congress* (Knoxville: University of Tennessee Press, 1975); Cornelius P. Cotter, "Eisenhower as Party Leader," *Political Science Quarterly* 98 (Summer 1983): 255–83; and Galvin, *Presidential Party Building*, 41–69.

77 Dwight Eisenhower, letter to Bradford Chynoweth, July 13, 1954, in *The Papers of Dwight David Eisenhower*, ed. Lewis Galambos and Daun van Ee, vol. 15 (Baltimore: Johns Hopkins University Press, 1996), 1220. On Eisenhower's outlook on domestic policy, see Steven Wagner, *Eisenhower Republicanism: Pursuing the Middle Way* (DeKalb: Northern Illinois University Press, 2006), 7–87.

78 The Bricker amendment would prove to be the last gasp of postwar isolationist political activity among Republican conservatives. Reichard, *Reaffirmation of Republicanism*, 51–98.

79 Mason, *The Republican Party and American Politics*, 152–53.

80 Wagner, *Eisenhower Republicanism*, 114.

81 "The Week," *National Review*, September 8, 1956.

82 David L. Stebenne, *Modern Republican: Arthur Larson and the Eisenhower Years* (Bloomington: Indiana University Press, 2006), 130–35.

83 William F. Buckley Jr., *Up from Liberalism* (New York: McDowell, Obolensky, 1959), 189.

84 Arthur Larson, *A Republican Looks at His Party* (New York: Harper and Brothers, 1956), vii.

85 Ibid., 10.

86 Ibid., 12, 16, 18.

87 Wagner, *Eisenhower Republicanism*, 121.

88 "The Magazine's Credenda," *National Review*, November 19, 1955.

89 ". . . When Half-Gods Go," *National Review*, September 27, 1958.

90 L. Brent Bozell, "The 1958 Elections: Coroner's Report," *National Review*, November 22, 1958.

91 Buckley, *Up from Liberalism*, xxi, 189, 191.

92 Ibid., 221, 189.

93 Nash, *The Conservative Intellectual Movement in America*. Subsequent historical scholarship has tended to tilt the balance of the postwar conservative fusion further in the direction of the economic side than Nash did.

See, e.g., Phillips-Fein, *Invisible Hands*; Jennifer Burns, *Goddess of the Market: Ayn Rand and the American Right* (New York: Oxford University Press, 2009); and Angus Burgin, *The Great Persuasion: Reinventing Free Markets since the Great Depression* (Cambridge, MA: Harvard University Press, 2012).

94 Buckley, *Up from Liberalism*, 218–20.

95 Mason, *The Republican Party and American Politics*, 161.

96 Lisa McGirr, *Suburban Warriors: The Origins of the New American Right* (Princeton, NJ: Princeton University Press, 2001).

97 Heather Hendershot, *What's Fair on the Air? Cold War Right-Wing Broadcasting and the Public Interest* (Chicago: University of Chicago Press, 2011); Nicole Hemmer, *Messengers of the Right: Conservative Media and the Transformation of American Politics* (Philadelphia: University of Pennsylvania Press, 2016).

98 Phillips-Fein, *Invisible Hands*, 68–86; Darren Dochuk, *From Bible Belt to Sunbelt: Plain-Folk Religion, Grassroots Politics, and the Rise of Evangelical Conservatism* (New York: W. W. Norton, 2011).

99 McGirr, *Suburban Warriors*; Donald T. Critchlow, *Phyllis Schlafly and Grassroots Conservatism: A Woman's Crusade* (Princeton, NJ: Princeton University Press, 2005); Catherine E. Rymph, *Republican Women: Feminism and Conservatism from Suffrage to the Rise of the New Right* (Chapel Hill: University of North Carolina Press, 2006); Michelle M. Nickerson, *Mothers of Conservatism: Women and the Postwar Right* (Princeton, NJ: Princeton University Press, 2012).

100 Rick Perlstein, *Before the Storm: Barry Goldwater and the Unmaking of the American Consensus* (New York: Hill and Wang, 2001), 165–66; Kurt Schuppara, *Triumph of the Right: The Rise of the California Conservative Movement, 1945–1966* (New York: M. E. Sharpe, 1998); Edward H. Miller, *Nut Country: Right-Wing Dallas and the Birth of the Southern Strategy* (Chicago: University of Chicago Press, 2015).

101 The fact that they had belonged to a Dewey-aligned faction underscored the degree to which youth GOP activism took on increasing ideological coloring as the 1950s progressed.

102 John A. Andrew III, *The Other Side of the Sixties: Young Americans for Freedom and the Rise of Conservative Politics* (New Brunswick, NJ: Rutgers University Press, 1996), 25.

103 Galvin, *Presidential Party Building*, 57.

104 Eisenhower speech, June 7, 1957, transcript of the Republican National Conference, in Series 1A, Reel 17, Republican Party Papers.

105 Quoted in the Republican Committee on Program and Progress, *Decisions for a Better America* (Garden City, NY: Doubleday, 1960), 17.

106 Alcorn described the decision to appoint a number of party outsiders among the forty-four members of the committee—including a Farmer of the Year, a Teacher of the Year, a recent head of the American Nurses' Association, and the vice president of the boilermakers union—at an RNC Executive Committee meeting, April 9, 1959, Series 1A, Reel 17, Republican Party Papers.

107 Session transcript of the Republican Committee on Program and Progress, March 13, 1959, Series 1A, Reel 17, Republican Party Papers.

108 Elizabeth Tandy Shermer, "Origins of the Conservative Ascendancy: Barry Goldwater's Early Senate Career and the De-Legitimization of Organized Labor," *Journal of American History* 95 (December 2008): 678-709.

109 Session transcript of the Republican Committee onr Program and Progress, March 13, 1959, Series 1A, Reel 17, Republican Party Papers.

110 Karl Hess, *In a Cause that Will Triumph: The Goldwater Campaign and the Future of Conservatism* (New York: Doubleday, 1967), 59-60; Barry Goldwater, *The Conscience of a Conservative* (New York: Victor Publishing, 1960), 7-8; Perlstein, *Before the Storm*, 63.

111 Frank Meyer, memo to William F. Buckley Jr., L. Brent Bozell, Priscilla Buckley Bozell, William Rusher, James Burnham, May 10, 1960, in Series I, Box 10, Folder "Inter-Office Memos (1960)," William F. Buckley Jr. Papers, Archives and Manuscript Library, Yale University, New Haven, CT (hereafter Buckley Papers).

112 Gifford, *The Center Cannot Hold*, 143.

113 F. Clifton White, *Suite 3505: The Story of the Draft Goldwater Movement* (New Rochelle, NY: Arlington House, 1967), 19.

114 As illustrated by William F. Buckley's notorious 1957 editorial explicitly defending southern racial voting restrictions on the grounds that "the white community in the South" was "the advanced race," the task of deracializing opposition to civil rights legislation was a difficult one, achieved haltingly but concertedly by conservative ideologists in ensuing years. William F. Buckley Jr., "Why the South Must Prevail," *National Review*, August 24, 1957. Lowndes, *From the New Deal to the New Right*, 45-76; William P. Hustwit, *James J. Kilpatrick: Salesman for Segregation* (Chapel Hill: University of North Carolina Press, 2013), 41-142; and Stephanie R. Rolph, "Courting Conservatism: White Resistance and the Ideology of Race in the 1960s," in *The Right Side of the Sixties: Reexamin-*

ing Conservatism's Decade of Transformation, ed. Laura Jane Gifford and Daniel K. Williams (New York: Palgrave Macmillan, 2012), 21-40.

115 Goldwater, *Conscience of a Conservative*, 17, 27.

116 Galvin, *Presidential Party Building*, 63-66.

117 Perlstein, *Before the Storm*, 46-49, 76; Gifford, *The Center Cannot Hold*, 146-67, and Joseph Crespino, *Strom Thurmond's America* (New York: Hill and Wang, 2012), 128-30.

118 Gifford, *The Center Cannot Hold*, 151.

119 Robert T. Hartmann, "Nixon, Rockefeller OK Platform in Secret Talk," *Los Angeles Times*, July 26, 1960.

120 David A. Nichols, *A Matter of Justice: Eisenhower and the Beginning of the Civil Rights Revolution* (New York: Simon and Schuster, 2007); Timothy Thurber, *Republicans and Race: The GOP's Frayed Relationship with African Americans* (Lawrence: University Press of Kansas, 2013).

121 Both White and the RNC official are quoted in Mason, *The Republican Party and American Politics*, 175.

122 Leah Wright Rigueur, *The Loneliness of the Black Republican: Pragmatic Politics and the Pursuit of Power* (Princeton, NJ: Princeton University Press, 2015), 35.

123 Gifford, *The Center Cannot Hold*, 83; Wright Rigueur, *The Loneliness of the Black Republican*, 36-38.

124 Jack Bass and Walter De Vries, *The Transformation of Southern Politics: Social Change and Political Consequence since 1945* (New York: Basic Books, 1976), 26.

125 William Rusher, memo to William F. Buckley Jr., October 10, 1960, Series I, Box 10, Folder "Inter-Office Memos (1960)," Buckley Papers.

126 Phillip A. Klinkner, *The Losing Parties: Out-Party National Committees, 1956-1993* (New Haven, CT: Yale University Press, 1994), 45.

127 Karl Lamb, "Under One Roof: Barry Goldwater's Campaign Staff," in *Republican Politics: The 1964 Campaign and Its Aftermath for the Party*, ed. Bernard Cosman and Robert J. Huckshorn (New York: Frederick A. Praeger, 1968),15.

128 Klinkner, *The Losing Parties*, 51-53.

129 Miller, *Nut Country*, 115-19.

130 Lamb, "Under One Roof," 15.

131 Galvin, *Presidential Party Building*, 66; Wright Rigueur, *The Loneliness of the Black Republican*, 49.

132 Bernard Cosman, "Deep South Republicans: Profiles and Positions," in *Republican Politics: The 1964 Campaign and Its Aftermath for the Party*, ed. Cosman and Huckshorn, 109.

133 Ibid., 90–105.

134 Vera Glaser, "GOP's Dixie Architect Returns to the Fold," *Columbia Record*, October 16, 1965.

135 "Right Wing Upsurge," *Civic Affairs Monthly*, November/December 1961, in Box 15, Folder "1961," F. Clifton White Papers, Ashland University, Ashland, OH (hereafter White Papers).

136 Andrew, *The Other Side of the Sixties*, 178.

137 Phyllis Schlafly, *A Choice Not an Echo: The Inside Story of How American Presidents Are Chosen* (Alton, IL: Pere Marquette Press, 1964).

138 Aaron Wildavsky, "The Goldwater Phenomenon: Partisans, Purists, and the Two-Party System," *Review of Politics* 27 (July 1965): 397–98.

139 Perlstein, *Before the Storm*, 513.

140 George Romney, letter to Barry Goldwater, December 21, 1964, reprinted in the *New York Times*, November 29, 1966.

CHAPTER 4

1 Students for a Democratic Society, *Port Huron Statement*, accessed at http://coursesa.matrix.msu.edu/~hst306/documents/huron.html. All quotes are from this source.

2 James Miller, *Democracy Is in the Streets: From Port Huron to the Siege of Chicago* (Cambridge, MA: Harvard University Press, 1987), 30.

3 Ibid., 73–75, 102–5. Sociologist C. Wright Mills, a central intellectual inspiration for SDS's founders, had also championed "nationally responsible parties that debate openly and clearly the issues" alongside his better-known critiques of centralized technocratic power in American institutions. C. Wright Mills, "The Structure of Power in American Society," *British Journal of Sociology* 9, no. 1 (March 1958): 29–41.

4 G. Calvin Mackenzie and Robert Weisbrot, *The Liberal Hour: Washington and the Politics of Change in the 1960s* (New York: Penguin Press, 2008).

5 John F. Kennedy commencement address, Yale University, June 11, 1962, accessed online at http://millercenter.org/president/speeches/detail /3370.

6   Arthur M. Schlesinger Jr., *A Thousand Days: John F. Kennedy in the White House* (New York: Houghton Mifflin, 1965), 111; James MacGregor Burns, *The Deadlock of Democracy: Four-Party Politics in America* (New York: Prentice-Hall, 1963), 309.

7   The term comes from Kenneth A. Shepsle, "The Changing Textbook Congress," in *Can the Government Govern?*, ed. John E. Chubb and Paul Peterson (Washington, DC: Brookings Institution, 1989), 238–66.

8   Sean J. Savage, *JFK, LBJ, and the Democratic Party* (Albany: State University of New York Press, 2004), 92.

9   Julian E. Zelizer, *The Fierce Urgency of Now: Lyndon Johnson, Congress, and the Battle for the Great Society* (New York: Penguin Press, 2015), 35.

10   Hubert Humphrey, letter to John Bailey, February 16, 1963, Box 680, Folder "PL 9/1/62–2/28/63," White House Central Files (WHCF), JFKL.

11   Savage, *JFK, LBJ, and the Democratic Party*, 105.

12   Julian E. Zelizer, *On Capitol Hill: The Struggle to Reform Congress and its Consequences, 1945–2000* (New York: Cambridge University Press, 2004), 85–91.

13   Joseph S. Clark, *Congress, the Sapless Branch* (New York: Harper and Row, 1964); Richard Bolling, *House Out of Order* (New York: Dutton, 1965).

14   Savage, *JFK, LBJ, and the Democratic Party*, 94–95.

15   Schlesinger, *A Thousand Days*, 709.

16   Rick Perlstein, *Before the Storm: Barry Goldwater and the Unmaking of the American Consensus* (New York: Hill and Wang, 2001), 247.

17   Ibid., 247–49.

18   Lyndon Johnson, address before Congress, November 27, 1963, accessed at http://millercenter.org/president/lbjohnson/speeches/speech-3381.

19   Robert Caro, *The Years of Lyndon Johnson: Master of the Senate* (New York: Alfred A. Knopf, 2002), 488–515, 572–78; Doris Kearns, *Lyndon Johnson and the American Dream* (New York: Harper and Row, 1976), 382–83; Lewis Gould, *The Most Exclusive Club: A History of the Modern United States Senate* (New York: Basic Books, 2005), 132.

20   Kearns, *Lyndon Johnson and the American Dream*, 152–53.

21   Rowland Evans and Robert Novak, "LBJ's Consensus Party," *Washington Post*, July 24, 1964.

22 Lyndon Johnson, speech at the Democratic National Convention, August 27, 1964, accessed online at John T. Woolley and Gerhard Peters, *The American Presidency Project* (Santa Barbara, CA), http://www.presidency.ucsb.edu/ws/?pid=26467.

23 Voting figures for the Civil Rights Act, the Equal Opportunity Act, the Elementary and Secondary Education Act, the Voting Rights Act, the establishment of Medicare and Medicaid, and the Immigration and Nationality Act are derived from Zelizer, *The Fierce Urgency of Now*, 101, 127–28, 136, 140, 145, 181–82; the online Legislative History page of the Social Security Administration, accessed at https://www.ssa.gov/history/tally65.html; and GovTrack.us, accessed at https://www.govtrack.us/congress/votes/89-1965/h177 and https://www.govtrack.us/congress/votes/89-1965/s232.

24 Savage, *JFK, LBJ, and the Democratic Party*, 118–19.

25 Intriguingly, in 1966 Johnson also expressed support for a radical reform with roots in responsible party doctrine: a constitutional amendment that would have extended House terms to four years and synchronized them with presidential elections. He never expended any effort in pursuit of this goal, however. See the January 20, 1966, press release, Box 40, Folder "Four Year Term," Harry McPherson Files, Lyndon Baines Johnson Library (LBJL), Austin, TX.

26 Kearns, *Lyndon Johnson and the American Dream*, 244–45.

27 Cathie Jo Martin, "Business and the New Economic Activism: The Growth of Corporate Lobbies in the Sixties," *Polity* 27, no. 1 (1994): 49–76.

28 Savage, *JFK, LBJ, and the Democratic Party*, 151.

29 Daniel J. Galvin, *Presidential Party Building: Dwight D. Eisenhower to George W. Bush* (Princeton, NJ: Princeton University Press, 2010), 182–203.

30 Savage, *JFK, LBJ, and the Democratic Party*, 155.

31 Galvin, *Presidential Party Building*, 187; Edward G. Wilks, letter to Fred Bohen, undated, Box 1, Folder "Democratic Campaign of 1968," Fred Bohen Files, LBJL.

32 Savage, *JFK, LBJ, and the Democratic Party*, 165–66; Galvin, *Presidential Party Building*, 187.

33 Kearns, *Lyndon Johnson and the American Dream*, 154.

34 A detailed account of the MFDP's origins and operations in Mississippi is in Lisa Anderson Todd's memoir, *For a Voice and the Vote: My Journey with the Mississippi Freedom Democratic Party* (Lexington: University Press of Kentucky, 2014); on the state-level organizing, see 183–203.

35 John Lewis, letter to Lyndon Johnson, August 19, 1964, Box 27, Folder "Hu 2 / ST 24—7/17/64–11/30/64," WHCF-Human Rights, LBJL.

36 "Brief Submitted by the Mississippi Freedom Democratic Party," pp. 21-52, Box 86, Folder "LEGAL FILE—Mississippi Freedom Democratic Party briefs, 1964, 1965," Rauh Papers.

37 Ella Baker, speech, Mississippi Freedom Democratic Party Convention, Jackson, MS, August 6, 1964, passage included in "Mississippi: Is This America? (1962-1964)," *Eyes on the Prize: America's Civil Rights Years (1954-1965)*, 6, Blackside, 1987 (PBS DVD, 2010).

38 James Farmer and Joe Rauh, comments to the Credentials Committee of the Democratic National Convention, August 22, 1964, both found in Box 86, Folder "Legal File—MFDP: General Jul-Aug 1964," Rauh Papers.

39 The secretary of state refused to register the party, preventing it from filing a certificate of understanding with the DNC attesting that it had met state requirements to send a delegation. Todd, *For a Voice and the Vote*, 211.

40 Ibid., 197.

41 Martin Luther King Jr., telegram to Lyndon Johnson, August 24, 1964, Box 52, Folder "PL/ST 24," WHCF-Political Affairs, LBJL; Rauh, comments to the Credentials Committee, Box 86, Folder "Legal File—MFDP: General Jul-Aug 1964," Rauh Papers; Theodore White, *The Making of the President 1964* (New York: Athenaeum, 1965), 243.

42 Robert Dallek characterizes Johnson's disposition toward the MFDP as "hysterical" in his account of the convention fight in *Flawed Giant: Lyndon Johnson and His Times, 1961-1973* (New York: Oxford University Press, 1998), 162-64.

43 Ibid., 163.

44 Michael E. Parrish, *Citizen Rauh: An American Liberal's Life in Law and Politics* (Ann Arbor: University of Michigan Press, 2010), 171-74.

45 "My objective," recalled one of those convention volunteers, "was to offend neither the Southern TV viewer who may have favored forceful action nor the Northern audience which may have favored seating the FDP delegation." Walter Adams, letter to Walter Jenkins, September 1, 1964, in Box 81, Folder "PL/1 ST 24 Seating Mississippi Delegation at Democratic Convention," WHCF-Political Affairs, LBJL.

46 Parrish, *Citizen Rauh*, 173-74.

47 For an illustration of the radicalizing effect of such an interpretation, see Kwame Ture and Charles V. Hamilton, *Black Power: The Politics of Liberation* (New York: Random House, 1967), 86-97.

48 Reprinted in report by Joe Rauh and Mildred Jeffrey to the Special Equal Rights Committee, February 1, 1967, Box 19, Folder "DNC/Equal Rights Committee—Gov. Hughes," W. Marvin Watson Office Files, LBJL.

49 Miller, *Democracy Is in the Streets*, 218–59; Steven M. Gillon, *Politics and Vision: The ADA and American Liberalism, 1947–1985* (New York: Oxford University Press, 1987), 191.

50 William H. Chafe, *Never Stop Running: Allard Lowenstein and the Struggle to Save American Liberalism* (New York: Basic Books, 1993), 262–75.

51 Joseph L. Rauh Jr., "A Proposal to Maximize Political Support for an End to the War in Vietnam," Box 30, Folder "Subject File, Democratic Party: Democratic Peace Caucus," Rauh Papers.

52 Donald Edwards, address to the Conference of Concerned Democrats, December 2, 1967, Box 54, Folder 2113, Allard K. Lowenstein Papers, Louis Round Wilson Special Collections Library, University of North Carolina, Chapel Hill, NC (hereafter Lowenstein Papers).

53 Peter B. Levy, *The New Left and Labor in the 1960s* (Urbana: University of Illinois Press, 1994), 52–53.

54 Nelson Lichtenstein, *The Most Dangerous Man in Detroit: Walter Reuther and the Fate of American Labor* (New York: Basic Books, 1995), 396–415.

55 "Excerpts from a U.A.W. Letter on Union Dispute," *New York Times*, December 30, 1966.

56 Ben Wattenberg, memo to Lyndon Johnson, March 13, 1968, Box 22, Folder "Memos to the President Sent and Returned," Ben Wattenberg Office Files, LBJL.

57 Eugene McCarthy, "Why I'm Battling JFK," *Look*, February 6, 1968.

58 Wattenberg, memo to Johnson, March 13, 1968.

59 William Borders, "Connecticut Vote Buoys McCarthy," *New York Times*, April 11, 1968.

60 John Bailey, memo to W. Marvin Watson and The White House, January 5, 1968, Box 1, Folder "New England," Watson Files, LBJL.

61 Christopher Lydon, "McCarthy People Quit Ct. Convention, Frustrated over Delegates to Chicago," *Boston Globe*, June 23, 1968.

62 Byron E. Shafer, *Quiet Revolution: The Struggle for the Democratic Party and the Shape of Post-Reform Politics* (New York: Russell Sage Foundation, 1983), 14–17.

63 Nicholas Lemann, "Can a DFL Statesman Defeat Senator Anderson?," *Metropolis*, date unknown, 1977.

64 William Borders, "Connecticut McCarthy Backers Take Bailey's Offer of 9 Votes," *New York Times*, July 3, 1968.

65 Shafer, *Quiet Revolution*, 26.

66 Commission on the Democratic Selection of Presidential Nominees, *The Democratic Choice* (New York, 1968), 1, 13.

67 Thirteen states and territories in 1968 chose their delegates entirely on the basis of appointments by state party executives or officials, and ten chose part of their delegations through such methods. Commission on Party Structure and Delegate Selection, *Mandate for Reform* (Washington, DC: Democratic National Committee, 1970), 17–20.

68 Commission on the Democratic Selection of Presidential Nominees, *The Democratic Choice*, 12, 13.

69 Ibid., 14.

70 James Q. Wilson, *The Amateur Democrat: Club Politics in Three Cities* (Chicago: University of Chicago Press, 1962); Nelson W. Polsby and Aaron B. Wildavsky, *Presidential Politics: Strategies of American Electoral Politics*, 2nd ed. (New York: Scribner's, 1968).

71 Andrew Hacker, "The McCarthy Candidacy," *Commentary*, February 1968.

72 *The Presidential Nominating Conventions, 1968* (Washington, DC: Congressional Quarterly, 1968), 88, 96–131.

73 Aaron Henry, letter to John Bailey, July 17, 1968, Box 29, Folder "Democratic Party: Democratic Convention, 1968: Credentials Contest: Mississippi," Rauh Papers.

74 Humphrey supporters argued that this amounted to a hijacking of civil rights efforts in Georgia for candidate-centered campaign purposes. See, e.g., E. T. Kehrer, memo to Al Barkan, August 12, 1968, in Box 44, Folder "Political 1968 Democratic National Convention Credentials Committee," James O'Hara Papers, Bentley Historical Library, University of Michigan, Ann Arbor, MI (hereafter O'Hara Papers).

75 *The Presidential Nominating Conventions*, 196, 198.

76 To be sure, challengers also frequently cited procedural irregularities and abuses, including rampant use of proxy voting, unpublished meeting times, and arbitrary enforcement of quorum requirements. The informality of many state parties served to foster such irregularities; in at least twenty states, written rules covering the delegate selection process were either nonexistent or inaccessible to those wishing to participate. Commission on Party Structure and Delegate Selection, *Mandate for Reform*, 21.

77 Lawyers for McCarthy, memo to Eugene McCarthy, July 17, 1968, Box 29, Folder "Democratic Party: Democratic Convention, 1968: Credentials Contest," Rauh Papers.

78 *The Presidential Nominating Conventions*, 199–200.

79 Jim O'Hara, memo to Lawrence O'Brien, Walter Mondale, Jim Wright, and Fred Harris, August 25, 1968, Box 44, Folder "1968 Democratic National Convention Credentials Committee," O'Hara Papers.

80 *The Presidential Nominating Conventions*, 198.

81 Phillip A. Klinkner, *The Losing Parties: Out-Party National Committees, 1956–1993* (New Haven, CT: Yale University Press, 1994), 71–77.

82 Brian M. Conley, "Route to '66: Ray Bliss, the 1966 Election, and the Development of the Republican Service Party," *American Review of Politics* 31 (Summer 2010): 70–89; Conley, "The Politics of Party Renewal: The 'Service Party' and the Origins of the Post-Goldwater Republican Right," *Studies in American Political Development* 27 (April 2013): 51–67.

83 Lee W. Huebner and Thomas E. Petri, eds., *The Ripon Papers: 1963–1968* (Washington, DC: National Press, 1968), 48.

84 Ernest B. Ferguson, "Bid by Liberals in GOP Falters," *Baltimore Sun*, December 12, 1967.

85 Geoffrey Kabaservice, *Rule and Ruin: The Downfall of Moderation and the Destruction of the Republican Party, From Eisenhower to the Tea Party* (New York: Oxford University Press, 2012).

86 Sarah Katherine Mergel, *Conservative Intellectuals and Richard Nixon: Rethinking the Rise of the Right* (New York: Palgrave Macmillan, 2010).

87 Richard M. Scammon and Ben Wattenberg, *The Real Majority: An Extraordinary Examination of the American Electorate* (New York: Coward-McCann, 1970), 35–44.

88 Lisa McGirr, *Suburban Warriors: The Origins of the New American Right* (Princeton, NJ: Princeton University Press, 2001), 187–261; Matthew Dallek, *The Right Moment: Ronald Reagan's First Victory and the Decisive Turning Point in American Politics* (New York: Oxford University Press, 2004).

89 Arthur M. Schlesinger Jr., "The Challenge of Abundance," *The Reporter*, May 3, 1956.

90 National Coalition for an Effective Congress, "Underlying Cause of Democrats' Agony Revealed by NCEC Survey of Profound Liberal Split in House," Box 30, Folder "Politics [Folder 1 of 2]," McPherson Files, LBJL.

91   Kevin P. Phillips, *The Emerging Republican Majority* (New Rochelle, NY: Arlington House, 1969), 36.

92   Huebner and Petri, eds., *Ripon Papers*, 46–63; Howard L. Reiter, "The Collapsing Coalitions," *The Ripon Forum* (October 1968), Box 104, Folder "Ripon Society," Ray C. Bliss Papers, Columbus, OH.

93   Scammon, quoted in Douglass Cater, Ben Wattenberg, and Ervin Duggan, memo to Lyndon Johnson, August 19, 1967, Box 22, Folder "Memos to the President Sent and Returned," Wattenberg Files, LBJL.

94   Of course, cultural issues were hardly new phenomena in the longer sweep of American political history. James Morone, *Hellfire Nation: The Politics of Sin in American History* (New Haven, CT: Yale University Press, 2003).

CHAPTER 5

1   David S. Broder, *The Party's Over: The Failure of Politics in America* (New York: Harper and Row, 1971).

2   Walter Dean Burnham, *Critical Elections and the Mainsprings of American Politics* (New York: W. W. Norton, 1970), 91–134; Everett Carll Ladd Jr. and Charles D. Hadley, *Transformations of the American Party System: Political Coalitions from the New Deal to the 1970s* (New York: W. W. Norton, 1975).

3   Michael J. Malbin, "Party System Approaching Crossroads in 1976 Election," *National Journal*, May 23, 1975.

4   Robert Teeter, "The Present National Political Attitude as Determined by Pre-Election Polls," November 1976, Box 62, Folder "Post-Election Analysis—Speeches and Reports (2)," Robert Teeter Papers, Gerald R. Ford Presidential Library (GRFL), Ann Arbor, MI.

5   Lance Morrow, "The Decline of the Parties," *Time*, November 20, 1978.

6   Bruce E. Keith et al., *The Myth of the Independent Voter* (Berkeley: University of California Press, 1992).

7   Barry C. Burden and David C. Kimball, *Why Americans Split Their Tickets: Campaigns, Competition, and Divided Government* (Ann Arbor: University of Michigan Press, 2002), 5, 66; Larry Bartels, "Partisanship and Voting Behavior," *American Journal of Political Science* 44 (2000): 42.

8   Barbara Sinclair, *Party Wars: Polarization and the Politics of National Policy Making* (Norman: University of Oklahoma Press, 2004), 6–7.

9   One such measurement tracking the difference in voting behavior between mean members of the two parties over time is known by the

acronym DW-NOMINATE. McCarty, Poole, and Rosenthal, *Polarized America*, 6.

10   Richard Fleisher and Jon R. Bond, "Evidence of Increasing Polarization among Ordinary Citizens," in *American Political Parties: Decline or Resurgence?*, ed. Jeffrey E. Cohen, Richard Fleisher, and Paul Kantor (Washington, DC: CQ Press, 2001), 55–79; Levendusky, *The Partisan Sort*, 38–77; Alan I. Abramowitz, *The Disappearing Center: Engaged Citizens, Polarization, and American Democracy* (New Haven, CT: Yale University Press, 2010), 45.

11   See table 2B.4 in the American National Election Studies, *Guide to Public Opinion and Electoral Behavior*, http://www.electionstudies.org/nesguide /toptable/tab2b_4.htm.

12   Bruce J. Schulman, *The Seventies: The Great Shift in American Culture, Society, and Politics* (New York: Da Capo, 2001); Schulman and Julian E. Zelizer, eds., *Rightward Bound: Making America Conservative in the 1970s* (Cambridge, MA: Harvard University Press, 2008); Judith Stein, *Pivotal Decade: How the United States Traded Factories for Finance in the 1970s* (New Haven, CT: Yale University Press, 2010); and Daniel T. Rodgers, *Age of Fracture* (Cambridge, MA: Harvard University Press, 2011).

13   Commission on Party Structure and Delegate Selection, *Mandate for Reform* (Washington, DC: Democratic National Committee, 1970), 49.

14   Everett Carll Ladd Jr., "'Reform' Is Wrecking the U.S. Party System," *Fortune* (November 1977).

15   Assessments emphasizing a contrast between responsible party and McGovern-Fraser tenets include Austin Ranney, *Curing the Mischiefs of Faction: Party Reform in America* (Berkeley: University of California Press, 1975), 42–48; Jeane Kirkpatrick, *The New Presidential Elite: Men and Women in National Politics* (New York: Russell Sage Foundation, 1976), 354–55; James W. Ceaser, "Political Change and Party Reform," in *Political Parties in the Eighties*, ed. Robert Goldwin (Washington, DC: American Enterprise Institute, 1980), 97–115; William J. Crotty, "The Philosophies of Party Reform," in *Party Renewal in America: Theory and Practice*, ed. Gerald M. Pomper (New York: Praeger, 1980), 31–50; Morris Fiorina, "The Decline of Collective Responsibility in American Politics," *Daedalus* 109 (1980): 25–45; and Byron E. Shafer, *Quiet Revolution: The Struggle for the Democratic Party and the Shape of Post-Reform Politics* (New York: Russell Sage Foundation, 1983), 98–100. On the reformers as latter-day, anti-party Progressives, see James Ceaser, "Direct Participation in Politics," *Proceedings of the Academy of Political Science* 34 (1981): 121–37; and Kirkpatrick, *The New Presidential Elite*, 355.

16   Three works by activists sympathetic to the New Politics would describe

this vision: Frederick Dutton, *Changing Sources of Power: American Politics in the 1970s* (New York: McGraw-Hill, 1971); Lanny J. Davis, *The Emerging Democratic Majority: Lessons and Legacies From the New Politics* (New York: Stein and Day, 1974); and Stephen C. Schlesinger, *The New Reformers: Forces for Change in American Politics* (Boston: Houghton Mifflin, 1975).

17   On the NDC, see Schlesinger, *The New Reformers*, 109–36, and R. Bruce Allison, *Democrats in Exile, 1968–1972: The Political Confessions of a New England Liberal* (Hinsdale, IL: Sol Press, 1974).

18   David Plotke, "Party Reform as Failed Democratic Renewal in the United States, 1968–1972," *Studies in American Political Development* 10 (Fall 1996): esp. 237–48.

19   Shafer, *Quiet Revolution*, 55.

20   "Labor Boycotting McGovern Reforms," *Washington Post*, September 21, 1969.

21   Taylor Dark, *The Unions and the Democrats: An Enduring Alliance* (Ithaca, NY: Cornell University Press, 1999), 77–92.

22   Walter Reuther, letter to Kenneth O'Donnell, January 31, 1969, Box 437, Folder 9, Walter P. Reuther Papers, Walter P. Reuther Library, Wayne State University, Detroit, MI.

23   The UAW, the Communications Workers of America, the American Federation of State, County, and Municipal Employees, and the International Association of Machinists also lobbied for states to comply with the McGovern-Fraser guidelines in 1971 and 1972. Schlesinger, *The New Reformers*, 84.

24   Shafer, *Quiet Revolution*, 129–31, and Plotke, "Party Reform as Failed Democratic Renewal," 257–59.

25   Channing Emery Phillips, testimony at Commission on Party Structure and Delegate Selection hearing, Washington, DC, April 25, 1969, in Box 21, Folder "Hearings: Special Testimony," Democratic National Committee Records, National Archives, Washington, DC.

26   Dutton to Leroy Collins, April 22, 1969, Box 149.C.12.3(B), Folder "Democratic Party Reform—Commission on Party Structure and Delegate Selection—1969," Donald M. Fraser Papers, Minnesota Historical Society, St. Paul (hereafter Donald M. Fraser Papers).

27   New Democratic Coalition, "Statement of Purpose," February 1970, Box 2, Folder 25, New Democratic Coalition (NDC) Records, Western Historical Manuscript Collection, University of Missouri–St. Louis, St. Louis, MO.

28 Transcript of the proceedings, Commission on Party Structure and Delegate Selection hearing, Washington DC, April 25, 1969, Box 21, Folder
"VII 14A Washington DC," DNC Records.

29 Staff memo to commission members re. "Task Force Hearing Themes,"
May 27, 1969, Box 12, Folder "Commission on Party Structure and Delegate Selection," DNC Records.

30 Transcript of the proceedings, Commission on Party Structure and
Delegate Selection hearing, New York, NY, May 3, 1969, Box 22, Folder
"3A New York Hearing," DNC Records.

31 John H. Aldrich, *Why Parties? A Second Look* (Chicago: University of Chicago Press, 2005), 178–92; "Party Polarization in American Politics: Characteristics, Causes, Consequences," *Annual Review of Political Science*
(2006): 96; Marty Cohen et al., *The Party Decides: Presidential Nominations
Before and After Reform* (Chicago: University of Chicago Press, 2008), 14,
159, 171–72; and Geoffrey C. Layman et al., "Activists and Conflict Extension in American Party Politics," *American Political Science Review* 104
(May 2010): 326.

32 Staff memo to commission members re: "Task Force Hearing Themes";
Dutton to Collins, April 22, 1969.

33 Beer, letter to McGovern, November 4, 1969, Box 18, Folder "Responses
to the Guidelines II," DNC Records.

34 A majority of the staff and membership also sought repeatedly to extend
this principle to a ban on winner-take-all primary systems. But the relentless internal lobbying of Californian Fred Dutton prevented such a prohibition from being included in the commission's guidelines. Shafer, *Quiet
Revolution*, 142–44, 173–75.

35 Ibid., 166–67.

36 Ranney, *Curing the Mischiefs of Faction*, 190.

37 Plotke, "Party Reform as Failed Democratic Renewal," 275.

38 Martha Ragland, letter to Joseph L. Rauh Jr., August 19, 1971, Box 9,
Folder 119, Martha Ragland Papers, Schlesinger Library, Harvard University, Cambridge, MA.

39 William J. Crotty, *Decision for the Democrats: Reforming the Party Structure*
(Baltimore, MD: Johns Hopkins University Press, 1978), 72–79.

40 Phillip A. Klinkner, *The Losing Parties: Out-Party National Committees,
1956–1993* (New Haven, CT: Yale University Press, 1994), 102–3.

41 Shafer, *Quiet Revolution*, 89–90.

42 "The Party Reformed: The Final Report of the Commission on Party Structure and Delegate Selection," July 7, 1972, Box 1061, Folder "McGovern-Fraser," DNC Records.

43 Plotke, "Party Reform as Failed Democratic Renewal," 257.

44 Klinkner, *The Losing Parties*, 98.

45 Joseph Califano, memo to Lawrence O'Brien, May 18, 1970, Box 29, Folder "Democratic Party: Delegate Selection and Party Organizations, 1969–1971," Rauh Papers.

46 Plotke emphasizes the regulars' intellectual bind in "Party Reform as Failed Democratic Renewal," 260–69.

47 Arthur Siddon, "Plea for 'Soft Stand' by McGovern Is Refused by Daley," *Chicago Tribune*, June 8, 1969.

48 Richard M. Scammon and Ben Wattenberg, *The Real Majority: An Extraordinary Examination of the American Electorate* (New York: Coward-McCann, 1970), 142–43.

49 Plotke, "Party Reform as Failed Democratic Renewal," 254–61.

50 A similar analysis can be found in Samuel Beer's notes for a commission presentation he delivered on May 10, 1969, Box 11, Folder "Response: Intellectuals," DNC Records.

51 Shafer, *Quiet Revolution*, 54; Minutes, NDC National Steering Committee meeting, March 14, 1970, Box 1, Folder, 2, NDC Records.

52 Kenneth Bode and LaVerne Newton, "Center—Original Proposal," Box 2807, Ken Bode Papers, Archives of DePauw University and Indiana United Methodism, DePauw University, Greencastle, IN (hereafter Bode Papers).

53 Shafer, *Quiet Revolution*, 281–86, 328–29.

54 "Report of the IDC Executive Committee Meeting," April 21, 1970, Box 1, Folder 2, NDC Records.

55 William J. Crotty, "Anatomy of a Challenge: The Chicago Delegation to the Democratic National Convention," in *Cases in American Politics*, ed. Robert L. Peabody (New York: Praeger, 1976), 113. Except where noted, the following narrative of the Chicago challenge comes from this account (111–58).

56 Ibid., 120.

57 For CPR's activities related to the Illinois challenge, see Box 2831, Folder "Chicago," Bode Papers.

58   Philip Warden, "Challenge to Daley's Slate Upheld," *Chicago Tribune*, June 28, 1972.

59   *Official Proceedings of the Democratic National Convention, 1972*, ed. Shelia Hixson and Ruth Rose (Washington, DC: Library of Congress, 1972), microfilm, 206. The mayor himself chose to avoid the convention.

60   Ibid., 207–8.

61   Rowland Evans and Robert Novak, "The Dethroning of Daley," *Washington Post*, July 12, 1972.

62   David E. Broder, "Labor Exerting New Muscle in Democratic Party," *Washington Post*, September 2, 1973.

63   Jules Witcover, "Democratic Coalition Formed to Curb 'New Politics' Wing," *International Herald Tribune*, December 8, 1972.

64   Text of ad in Series RG9-003, Box 42, Folder 8, George Meany Memorial Archive, Silver Spring, MD. The roster of neoconservatives sponsoring CDM included Jeane and Evron Kirkpatrick, Max Kampelman, Richard Pipes, Midge Decter, Norman Podhoretz, and Seymour Martin Lipset.

65   CDM Task Force on Democratic Party Rules and Structure, *Toward Fairness and Unity for '76*, pp. 1 and 26, April 1973, Series RG9-003, Box 42, Folder 9, Meany Archives.

66   Crotty, *Decision for the Democrats*, 231–39.

67   See Commission on Delegate Selection and Party Structure, *Democrats All*, December 1973, Box 1061, Folder "Mikulski Commission Report," DNC Records.

68   Donald Fraser, letter to George McGovern, March 19, 1969, Folder "Comm. on Party Structure Correspondence, 1969," and Fraser statement, O'Hara Commission hearing, January 15, 1970, Folder "Democratic Party Reform—Commission on Party Structure and Delegate Selection, 1969," both in Box 149.C.12.3(B), Donald M. Fraser Papers.

69   For samples of this 1971 correspondence, see the letters in Box 79, Folder "Charter," DNC Records.

70   All of the papers, as well as minutes to the November 19 meeting itself, can be found in Box 46, Folder "Dem. Party, O'Hara Rules Commission, Meetings, Nov. 19, 1971," O'Hara Papers.

71   Angus Campbell, Philip E. Converse, Warren E. Miller, and Donald E. Stokes, *The American Voter* (New York: John Wiley and Sons, 1960).

72   Notes to ad hoc meeting with Barney Hayhoe at the 7th Anglo-American

Conference on Africa, Baltimore, MD, June 18, 1971, Box 12, Folder "National Committee Reform," DNC Records.

73   Sam Beer, letter to Donald Fraser, May 22, 1972, Box 44, Folder "Democratic Party, O'Hara Rules Commission, Charter Proposal 2," O'Hara Papers.

74   Neil Staebler, letter to Donald Fraser, July 1, 1971, Box 12, Folder "National Committee Reform," DNC Records.

75   James MacGregor Burns, presentation, joint commission meeting, November 19, 1971, Box 46, Folder "Dem. Party, O'Hara Rules Commission, Meetings, Nov. 19, 1971," O'Hara Papers.

76   Donald M. Fraser, memo, "The Case for a 1974 Democratic National Party Conference," March 3, 1974, Box 152.K.10.5(B), Folder "Democratic National Policy Conference," Donald M. Fraser Papers. Fraser's piece was soon published in op-ed form as "The Democratic Party Still Needs Reform," *Washington Post*, April 5, 1973.

77   E. W. Kenworthy, "McCarthy Bids Party Hold Convention Every 2 Years to Map Policy on Key Issue," *New York Times*, August 12, 1968. Lowenstein's testimony is in the transcript for the Commission on Party Structure and Delegate Selection's hearing in New York, NY, May 3, 1969, in Box 22, Folder "3B New York Hearing," DNC Records. Muskie's testimony at the April 25, 1969, hearing in Washington, DC, and Unruh's testimony at the June 21, 1969, hearing in Los Angeles, CA, are both in Box 21, Folder "Hearings: Special Testimony," DNC Records.

78   "A New Charter for the Democratic Party of the United States: A Draft Proposal," March 24, 1972, Box 44, Folder "Democratic Party, O'Hara Rules Commission, Charter Proposal 2," O'Hara Papers.

79   Ken Kerle, letter to Fraser and O'Hara, March 27, 1972, Box 12, Folder "National Committee Reform," DNC Records. See also Jonathan Cottin, "Reform Units Propose New DNC Structure," *National Journal*, April 1, 1972.

80   "Notes on the meeting arranged by Ken Bode," June 6, 1972, Box 44, Folder "Democratic Party, O'Hara Rules Commission, Charter Proposal 3," O'Hara Papers.

81   Transcript, Box 149.G.11.10(F), Folder "Draft of Interview of Fraser by Jim and Iric Nathanson," Donald M. Fraser Papers.

82   Donald Fowler, memo to Democratic State Chairmen, May 4, 1972, Box 44, Folder "Democratic Party, O'Hara Rules Commission, Charter Proposal 2," O'Hara Papers.

83 The final version of the proposed charter was included as an appendix in the O'Hara Commission's *Call to Order: A Narrative Report by the Commission on Rules of the Democratic National Committee* (Washington, DC: Democratic National Committee, 1972), 133–43; the quoted passage is on p. 139.

84 Mary Russell, "Special Caucus Called in Anger by Democrats," *Washington Post*, June 23, 1972.

85 Robert Sikes, remarks, *Congressional Record—House*, 92nd Cong., 2nd sess., Vol. 118: 23023.

86 Mary Russell, "Democrats Vote to Delay Some Reforms," *Washington Post*, June 29, 1972.

87 "Democratic Charter: Action Delayed for Two Years," *Congressional Quarterly*, July 15, 1972.

88 Marjorie Hunter, "Established Democrats Opposed Reforms," *New York Times*, July 11, 1972.

89 Resolution text, July 13, 1972, Box 44, Folder "Democratic Party, O'Hara Rules Commission, Charter Proposal 3," O'Hara Papers. As a first step in reform, the resolution also expanded the size of the DNC more than twofold.

90 "Democrats Plan Warily for 1974 National Conference," *Congressional Quarterly*, June 16, 1973.

91 Kathryn J. McGarr, *The Whole Damn Deal: Robert Strauss and the Art of Politics* (New York: PublicAffairs, 2011), 153.

92 Robert Strauss, letter to Fraser, March 14, 1973, Box 152.K.10.5(B), Folder "Democratic National Policy Conference," Donald M. Fraser Papers.

93 He referenced two: Kirkpatrick, "Toward a More Responsible Two-Party System," 965–90; and Gerald Pomper, "Toward a More Responsible Two-Party System? What, Again?" *Journal of Politics* 33 (1971): 916–40.

94 Charter Commission meeting, Fort Collins, CO, July 21–23, 1973, Box 185, Folder "DNC Charter Commission Oct. 1973–12/31/73," Staebler Papers.

95 Quoted in the Democratic Planning Group Newsletter, August 6, 1973, in Box 149.G.8.6(F), Folder "Dem Planning Group," Donald M. Fraser Papers.

96 Coalition for a Democratic Majority, "Unity Out of Diversity: A Draft Position Paper on a New Charter for the Democratic Party of the United States," July 1973, Series RG9-003, Box 42, Folder 9, Meany Archives.

97 McGarr, *The Whole Damn Deal*, 160.

98 Loye Miller Jr., "Reformers Walk Out of Dem Parley," *Detroit Free-Press*, August 19, 1974.

99 David S. Broder, "Discipline Among the Democrats," *Washington Post*, December 11, 1974.

100 "The Charter and By-Laws of the Democratic Party of the United States," Box 1073, Folder "Hunt Commission," DNC Records.

101 Staebler, letter to Fraser, Box 284, Folder "Donald M. Fraser (misc)," Staebler Papers.

102 "The Democratic Conference: A Report on the Past Year's Activities," July 30, 1976, and "Briefing Paper—Democratic Party Organizational Issues, 1977," Box 152.L.10.5(B), Folder "Democratic Conference," Donald M. Fraser Papers.

103 Minutes, joint commission meeting, November 19, 1971, Box 46, Folder "Dem. Party, O'Hara Rules Commission, Meetings, Nov. 19, 1971," O'Hara Papers.

104 Committee on Political Parties, *Toward a More Responsible Two-Party System*, supplement to the *American Political Science Review* 40 (September 1950): 56–65.

105 See, e.g., DSG background paper, "The House Rules Committee—Its History and a Creative Proposal for the Future," 1966, Box 48, Folder "Democratic Study Group—Congressional Reform, 1964–1968," O'Hara Papers; and the DSG report, "The Seniority System in the U.S. House of Representatives," February 20, 1970, Box 149.G.12.1(B), Folder "Seniority," Donald M. Fraser Papers.

106 DSG background paper, "The Case for House Democratic Caucus Action against Rep. John Bell Williams and Rep. Albert W. Watson," December 1964, Box 48, Folder "Democratic Study Group—Congressional Reform, 1964–1968," O'Hara Papers.

107 DSG, "The Case for House Democratic Caucus Action against Rep. John Bell Williams and Rep. Albert W. Watson," Box 48, O'Hara Papers.

108 Donald Fraser, memo to DSG, January 28, 1969, Box 151.I.11.8 (F), Folder "Rarick Ouster," Donald M. Fraser Papers.

109 Burton D. Sheppard, *Rethinking Congressional Reform: The Reform Roots of the Special Interest Congress* (Cambridge, MA: Schenkman Books, 1985), 40.

110 DSG report, "Voting in the House," March 10, 1969, Box 151.I.11.8(F), Folder "DSG—1969," Donald M. Fraser Papers; DSG, "The Seniority System in the U.S. House of Representatives," Donald M. Fraser Papers;

Michael J. Harrington, "The Dead Hand of Seniority," *The Nation*, September 21, 1970; *Meet the Press* transcript, February 15, 1970, Box 149.G.11.10 (F), Folder "Gen'l Reform," Donald M. Fraser Papers.

111 "Dear Colleague" letter from Sam Gibbons, John Culver, John Bingham, and Claude Pepper, September 11, 1969, Box 141.H.2.6(F), Folder "Demo. Caucus 1970," Donald M. Fraser Papers.

112 Norman C. Miller, "John McCormick: Speaker Under Fire," *Wall Street Journal*, February 17, 1970.

113 Sheppard, *Rethinking Congressional Reform*, 70–71.

114 Julian E. Zelizer, *On Capitol Hill: The Struggle to Reform Congress and its Consequences, 1945–2000* (New York: Cambridge University Press, 2004), 104; Leon Shull, memo to ADA officers, board, and chapters, November 27, 1972, Box 34, Folder 1240, Lowenstein Papers.

115 "New Lobby Fights 'Special Interests,'" *New York Times*, February 3, 1971.

116 "Common Cause Urges Defeat of Three Hill Chairmen," *Washington Post*, January 3, 1971.

117 See, e.g., Dianne D. Wheatley, letter to Tip O'Neill, January 16, 1971, Box 21, Folder 5, Thomas P. O'Neill Jr. Papers, John J. Burns Library, Boston College, Boston, MA.

118 Sheppard, *Rethinking Congressional Reform*, 80–83; Zelizer, *On Capitol Hill*, 132–33.

119 "Congressional Reform: The Tortoise Lumbers Forward," *ADA Legislative Newsletter*, vol. 2.2, February 1, 1973, Box 149.G.8.3(B), Folder "Congressional Reform," Donald M. Fraser Papers.

120 "A Common Cause Manual for the 1972 Congressional Elections," Box 114, Common Cause Records, 1968–1991, Seeley G. Mudd Manuscript Library, Princeton University, Princeton, NJ.

121 John W. Gardner, testimony before the Mathias-Stevenson Ad Hoc Hearings on Congressional Reorganization, December 5, 1972, Box 146, Common Cause Records.

122 Wes Barthelmes, "The Greening of Congress," *The Nation*, November 30, 1970.

123 Sheppard, *Rethinking Congressional Reform*, 47–57.

124 Eric Schickler, Eric McGhee, and John Sides, "Remaking the House and Senate: Personal Power, Ideology, and the 1970s Reforms," *Legislative Studies Quarterly* 28 (August 2003): 297–331.

125 Sheppard, *Rethinking Congressional Reform*, 21–22, 95–102.

126 Common Cause, "Report on House Committee Chairmen," January 13, 1975, Box 126, Common Cause Records.

127 Zelizer, *On Capitol Hill*, 131.

128 Fraser, "Special Report," March 26, 1973, Box 149 G.8.3 (B), Folder "Congressional Reform," Donald M. Fraser Papers.

129 Transcript, "Democratic Caucus for the Organization of the 93rd Congress," January 22, 1973, Box 4, Folder 1, Records of the House Democratic Caucus, Library of Congress, Washington, DC.

130 *In Common* 3, no. 1 (February 1974), and 3, no. 9 (June 1974), Box 127, Common Cause Records; DSG Special Report, "94th Congress Reform Proposals," December 1, 1974, Box 149 G.8.3 (B), Folder "Congressional Reform," Donald M. Fraser Papers.

131 Common Cause, "Report on House Committee Chairmen."

132 Sheppard, *Rethinking Congressional Reform*, 200; W. R. Poage, *My First 85 Years* (Waco, TX: Baylor University Press, 1985), 147.

133 For examples, see the "Dear Colleague" letters from Edward Hebert, January 14, 1975, and Jamie Whitten, January 21, 1975, both in Box 151.H.2.6(F), Folder "Democratic Caucus—1975," Donald M. Fraser Papers.

134 "Hearings before the Committee on Early Democratic Caucus for the Organization of the 94th Congress," p. 529, Box 5, Records of the Democratic Caucus.

135 Zelizer, *On Capitol Hill*, 171.

136 "Hearings before the Committee on Early Democratic Caucus," 535s.

137 Mary Russell, "Rep. Jarman Switches to Republican Party," *Washington Post*, January 25, 1975.

138 Zelizer, *On Capitol Hill*, 172.

139 See, e.g., Common Cause, "Editorial Memorandum: Senate Considers Adjustment of Filibuster Rule," February 1975, Box 137, Common Cause Records.

140 Their number more than doubled between 1968 and 1980, reaching thirty-five. Elaine Kamarck, *Primary Politics: How Presidential Candidates Have Shaped the Nominating System* (Washington, DC: Brookings Institution, 2009), 18.

141 Sheppard, *Rethinking Congressional Reform*, 219–54; David W. Rohde, *Parties and Leaders in the Postreform House* (Chicago: University of Chicago Press, 1991), 34–39, 82–93. In a separate but related scholarly development, David Mayhew's highly influential work, *Congress: The Electoral Connection* (New Haven, CT: Yale University Press, 1974), though not itself focused on institutional reform or party decline, at once embodied and helped to catalyze a disciplinary movement away from party-centered research with its declaration that "no theoretical treatment of the United States Congress that posits parties as analytical units will go very far"(27).

142 Lawrence B. Joseph, "Neoconservatism in Contemporary Political Science: Democratic Theory and the Party System," *Journal of Politics* 44 (November 1982): 955–82; Robert T. Nokamura and Denis G. Sullivan, "Neo-Conservatism and the Presidential Nomination Reforms: A Critique," *Congress and the Presidency* 9 (1982): 79–97.

143 Proceedings of the League of Industrial Democracy Conference, May 2–3, 1975, in the pamphlet "The Challenge of Change and Conflict in American Society," p. 2, Box 149.C.13.4(F), Folder "Fraser Articles," Donald M. Fraser Papers.

144 See the letters in Box 149.C.12.7(B), Folder "Committee for Party Renewal," Donald M. Fraser Papers.

145 Commission on Presidential Nomination and Party Structure, *Openness, Participation, and Party-Building: Reforms for a Stronger Democratic Party*, pp. 99–105, Box 1074, Folder unlabeled, DNC Records.

146 Commission on Presidential Nomination, *The Report of the Commission on Presidential Nomination*, Box 1073, Folder unlabeled, DNC Records.

147 "Challenge of Change and Conflict in American Society."

148 Barbara Norrander, "Presidential Nomination Politics in the Post-Reform Era," *Political Research Quarterly* 49 (December 1996): 875–915; Wayne P. Steger, "Do Primary Voters Draw from a Stacked Deck? Presidential Nominations in an Era of Candidate-Centered Campaigns," *Presidential Studies Quarterly* 30 (December 2000): 727–53; Cohen et al., *The Party Decides*, 159–234.

149 Sheppard, *Rethinking Congressional Reform*, 302–62; Anthony King, ed., *The New American Political System* (Washington, DC: American Enterprise Institute, 1978); and Thomas Mann and Norman Ornstein, eds., *The New Congress* (Washington, DC: American Enterprise Institute, 1981).

150 John Herbers, "The Party's Over for the Political Parties," *New York Times*, December 8, 1979.

151 Charles S. Bullock III, "Congressional Voting and the Mobilization of a Black Electorate in the South," *Journal of Politics* 43 (August 1981): 662–82; Sara Brandes Crook and John Hibbing, "Congressional Reform and Party

Discipline: The Effects of Changes in the Seniority System on Party Loyalty in the U.S. House of Representatives," *British Journal of Political Science* 15 (1985): 207–26.

152 This is the central argument of Rohde, *Parties and Leaders in the Postreform House*, and the key dynamic of the "Conditional Party Government" theory developed by Rohde and John H. Aldrich.

153 Barbara Sinclair, *Majority Leadership in the U.S. House* (Baltimore: Johns Hopkins University Press, 1983), 55–56, 67–85, and 138–46; and Zelizer, *On Capitol Hill*, 234–38.

154 "Professional Notes," *PS* 10 (Autumn 1977): 494.

CHAPTER 6

1   Robert Mason, "'I Was Going to Build a New Republican Party and a New Majority': Richard Nixon as Party Leader, 1969–73," *Journal of American Studies* 39 (December 2005): 476–77.

2   Nick Thimmesch, "Spiro Has Not Really Gone Underground," *Chicago Tribune*, January 7, 1973; "Agnew Opens Drive," *Washington Post*, December 13, 1972.

3   Nixon's legislative aide William E. Timmons estimated that seventeen Democrats stood ready to make the switch if it gave the GOP control, but the election left a need for twenty-six Democratic defections to bring that about; Congressman Bud Shuster endorsed these numbers. See A. James Reichley, interviews, November 29, 1977, Box 1, Folder "Nixon White House—Timmons, William," and October 6, 1977, Box 2, Folder "Congress—Shuster, Bud," both in A. James Reichley Interview Transcripts, GRFL.

4   The high-end estimate is provided by Godfrey Hodgson in *The World Turned Right Side Up: A History of the Conservative Ascendancy in America* (Boston: Houghton Mifflin, 1996), 123–27, and is backed up by William Rusher, *The Rise of the Right* (New York: William Morrow, 1984).

5   The most comprehensive assessment of Nixon's various approaches to reshaping partisan politics is Robert Mason, *Richard Nixon and the Quest for a New Majority* (Chapel Hill: University of North Carolina Press, 2004).

6   On the 1970 midterm strategy, see Matthew D. Lassiter, *The Silent Majority: Suburban Politics in the Sunbelt South* (Princeton, NJ: Princeton University Press, 2006), 251–75. On Nixon and Harry Byrd, see James R. Sweeney, "Southern Strategies: The 1970 Election for the United States Senate in Virginia," *Virginia Magazine of History and Biography* 106 (1998):

165–200. Nixon's post-reelection discussions with his aides about John Connally's future leadership is documented by H. R. Haldeman in diary entries dated December 1 and December 5, 1972; see *The Haldeman Diaries: Inside the Nixon White House* (New York: G. P. Putnam's Sons, 1994), 546, 548–49.

7   On "conflict displacement" as the hallmark of realignment, see James L. Sundquist, *Dynamics of the Party System: Alignment and Realignment of Political Parties in the United States*, rev. ed. (Washington, DC: Brookings Institution, 1983), 13.

8   Geoffrey C. Layman et al., "Activists and Conflict Extension in American Party Politics," *American Political Science Review* 104 (May 2010): 324–46.

9   William E. Timmons, memo to Gerald R. Ford, August 22, 1974, in Box 5, Folder "Memoranda—Timmons to the President August 1974 (2)," William E. Timmons Files, GRFL (hereafter Timmons Files).

10   Lou Cannon, "Amnesty and Health Plan Stir Disenchantment: Ford's Early Moves Ire Conservatives," *Washington Post*, August 26, 1974.

11   A. James Reichley, interview with Robert Hartmann, December 3, 1977, Box 1, Folder "Ford White House—Hartmann, Robert," Reichley Interview Transcripts, GRFL.

12   Pat Buchanan, memo to Ford, August 12, 1974, Box 21, Folder "Vice Presidential White House Staff Suggestions," Robert T. Hartmann Files, GRFL.

13   John Robert Greene, *The Presidency of Gerald R. Ford* (Lawrence: University of Kansas Press, 1995), 37–52.

14   Tom Korogolos, memo to William Timmons, August 21, 1974, Box 5, Folder "Memoranda–Timmons to the President, August 1974 (2)," Timmons Files.

15   Ben Blackburn, letter to Ford, August 23, 1974, Box 5, Folder "Memoranda to the President," Timmons Files.

16   Quote from William Rusher's description in a letter to William F. Buckley, February 21, 1974, Box 121, Folder 7, William Rusher Papers, Library of Congress, Washington, DC (hereafter Rusher Papers).

17   Jesse Helms, "The New American Majority: Time for a Political Realignment?," May 15, 1974, American Conservative Union Papers, Brigham Young University, Provo, UT.

18   William Link, *Righteous Warrior: Jesse Helms and the Making of Modern Conservatism* (New York: St. Martin's Press, 2008), 149–51.

19   Ibid., 111–29.

20   Associated Press, "Helms Group Helps Conservative Cause," *New York Times*, November 13, 1979.

21   On Rusher's career-spanning skepticism of the GOP, see David B. Frisk, *If Not Us, Who? William Rusher,* National Review, *and the Conservative Movement* (Wilmington, DE: Intercollegiate Studies Institute, 2011).

22   Rusher, *The Rise of the Right*, 266; ACU board meeting minutes, September 22, 1974, Box 21, Folder 10, American Conservative Union (ACU) Records, Harold B. Lee Library, Brigham Young University, Provo, UT.

23   ACU board meeting minutes, December 15, 1974, Box 21, Folder 11, ACU Records.

24   More precise figures were 25.57, 38.52, and 35.91, respectively. The Gallup Poll no. 899, April, 9, 1974.

25   William Rusher, *The Making of the New Majority Party* (New York: Sheed and Ward, 1975), xiii, xxi.

26   Ibid., 12–16.

27   The Gallup Polls no. 889, April 9, 1974; no. 908, June 18, 1974; and no. 920, December 2, 1974.

28   Rusher, *Making of the New Majority Party*, 103–4, xx, xxii.

29   Robert Bauman, CPAC speech, February 17, 1975, Box 3, Folder 27, ACU Records.

30   James Buckley, CPAC speech, February 15, 1975, in ibid.

31   Jesse Helms, CPAC speech, February 14, 1975, in ibid.

32   Angus Campbell, Philip E. Converse, Warren E. Miller, and Donald E. Stokes, *The American Voter* (New York: John Wiley and Sons, 1960).

33   Gerald M. Pomper, "From Confusion to Clarity: Issues and American Voters, 1956–1968," *American Political Science Review* 66 (June 1972): 415–28. Pomper expanded his argument in *Voters' Choice: Varieties of American Electoral Behavior* (New York: Dodd and Mead, 1975).

34   Arthur H. Miller and Warren E. Miller, "Issues, Candidates and Partisan Divisions in the 1972 Presidential Election," *British Journal of Political Science* 4 (1975): 393–434; and Arthur H. Miller et al., "A Majority Party in Disarray: Policy Polarization in the 1972 Election," *American Political Science Review* 70 (1976): 753–78.

35   Norman H. Nie and Kristi Anderson, "Mass Belief Systems Revisited: Political Change and Attitude Structure," *Journal of Politics* 36 (August 1974): 544. See also Nie, Sidney Verba, and John R. Petrocik, *The Changing*

American Voter (Cambridge, MA: Harvard University Press, 1976), with its explicitly referential title.

36 Text of CPAC resolution, February 16, 1975, Box 3, Folder 26, ACU Records.

37 Jesse Helms statement, March 7, 1975, Box 142, Folder 6, Rusher Papers.

38 John Fialka, "Arch-Conservative's Crusade: Abolish the Republican Party," *Washington Star*, June 24, 1975.

39 Reagan speech, February 15, 1975, at http://www.conservative.org/cpac/archives/cpac-1975-ronald-reagan/.

40 Rusher, *The Rise of the Right*, 273.

41 M. Stanton Evans, letter to Ronald Reagan, May 1975, Box 133, Folder 3, Rusher Papers.

42 Craig Shirley, *Reagan's Revolution: The Untold Story of the Campaign that Started It All* (New York: Nelson Current, 2005), 37.

43 Lou Cannon, *Reagan* (New York: G. P. Putnam's Sons, 1982), 197.

44 See, for examples, the Minutes to ACU board meeting, September 27, 1975, Box 21, Folder 14, ACU Records; Rusher's form letter to would-be volunteers, Box 142, Folder 12, and Howard Phillips, letter to Lester Logue, April 29, 1976, Box 141, Folder 9, Rusher Papers.

45 Alan Crawford, "A New Option for Conservatives in 1976," *Conservative Digest*, December 1975.

46 "Atlanta Statement" report, January 1, 1976; Alex Hugins, letter to William Rusher, December 10, 1975, and Ronald Docksai, memo to Rusher, January 15, 1976—all in Box 141, Folder 9, Rusher Papers.

47 William F. Buckley, letter to William Rusher, March 4, 1976, Box 121, Folder 8, Rusher Papers.

48 Ken Rast, memo to CNM board, June 16, 1976, Box 141, Folder 10, Rusher Papers.

49 Karen Elliott House, "American Independents Select Maddox," *Wall Street Journal*, August 30, 1976.

50 William Rusher, letter to Alex Hudgins, January 31, 1977, Box 141, Folder 11, Rusher Papers.

51 ACU working paper, presented at November 6, 1976 meeting, reprinted in *Human Events*, November 20, 1976.

52 Stephen Isaacs, "Coors Beer—and Politics—Move East," *Washington Post*, May 4, 1975.

53 Jake Garn, undated report to W. D. Coyne, "Committee for the Survival of a Free Congress," Box 16, Folder 3, Paul Weyrich Papers, American Heritage Center, University of Wyoming, Laramie (hereafter Weyrich Papers).

54 Paul Weyrich, memo to James McClure and Dick Thompson, May 26, 1975, Box 19, Folder 4, Weyrich Papers.

55 James Buckley, letter to William Rusher, March 11, 1975, Box 141, Folder 11, Rusher Papers.

56 David Keene, memo to James Buckley, February 13, 1975, Box 31, Folder "St. Michael's Conference, 1975," White Papers.

57 Fred Slight, memo to Jerry Jones, June 6, 1975, Box 16, Folder "Conservative Third Party," Cheney Files, GRFL.

58 Keene, memo to James Buckley, March 27, 1975, Box 31, Folder "St. Michael's Conference, 1975," White Papers.

59 F. Clifton White, memo to James Buckley, May 26, 1975, Box 31, Folder "St. Michael's Conference, 1975," White Papers.

60 Keene, memo to Buckley, March 27, 1975.

61 James Reston, "Thunder on the Right," *New York Times*, March 5, 1975.

62 John T. Calkins, memo to Hartmann, March 28, 1975, Box 2, Folder "Policy Memos," Calkins Files, GLFR.

63 A. James Reichley's interview with Max Freidersdorf, October 27, 1977, in Box 1, Folder "Ford White House—Freidersdorf, Max," Reichley Interview Transcripts, GRFL; see also Greene, *The Presidency of Gerald R. Ford*, 77.

64 Nick Thimmesch, "What the Right Thinks of Mr. Ford," *New York Times*, April 13, 1975.

65 Peter Goldman, "Ready on the Right," *Newsweek*, March 24, 1975.

66 On Reagan precipitating that rightward shift, see A. James Reichley, interview with John Marsh, September 2, 1977, Box 1, Folder "Ford White House—Marsh, John," A. James Reichley Interview Transcripts, GRFL.

67 Greene, *The Presidency of Gerald R. Ford*, 97; Laura Kalman, *Right Star Rising: A New Politics, 1974–1980* (New York: W. W. Norton, 2010), 162–63.

68 On the New Right and economics, see Kimberly Phillips-Fein, *Invisible Hands: The Making of the Conservative Movement from the New Deal to Reagan* (New York: W. W. Norton, 2009), 213–21.

69 Greene, *The Presidency of Gerald R. Ford*, 98.

70 Patrick Buchanan, "Ronald Reagan Enters from Right," *Chicago Tribune*, November 20, 1975.

71 David S. Broder, "Ford Drift to Right Alarms Center," *Washington Post*, October 30, 1975. Charles Mathias, "Can the Political Parties Survive?" *Washington Post*, November 8, 1975.

72 Max Freidersdorf, memo to Bill Nicholson, December 5, 1975, Box 2, Folder "Political Affairs 10/1/75–12/31/75," White House Central Files (WHCF) PL (Exec.), GRFL; Charles Mohr, "Senator Mathias Is Exploring Possibility of 3rd Political Party," *New York Times*, November 26, 1975.

73 Rae, *The Decline and Fall of the Liberal Republicans*, 114–16.

74 William Kendall and Patrick O'Donnell, memo to Max Freidersdorf, November 1, 1975, Box 2, Folder "Political Affairs 10/1/75–12/31/75," WHCF PL (Exec.), GRFL.

75 The most thorough account is Shirley, *Reagan's Revolution*.

76 Link, *Righteous Warrior*, 153.

77 The ACU effort is described by Stan Evans in the Manion Forum weekly radio broadcast, February 27, 1977, transcript in Box 1, Folder 13, ACU Papers.

78 Jules Witcover, *Marathon: The Pursuit of the Presidency, 1972–1976* (New York: Viking Press, 1977), 419–20.

79 Denis Sullivan, "Party Unity: Appearance and Reality," *Political Science Quarterly* 92 (Winter 1977–78): 638.

80 Martha Weinberg, "Writing the Republican Platform," *Political Science Quarterly* 92 (Winter 1977–1978): 658.

81 Link, *Righteous Warrior*, 158–59.

82 Jules Witcover, "Reagan Forces and Helms' 'Rebels' Get Together," *Washington Post*, August 12, 1976.

83 Link, *Righteous Warrior*, 161.

84 Sullivan, "Party Unity," 639.

85 Michael Raoul-Duval, memo to Dick Cheney, August 5, 1976, Box 29, Folder "Republican Party Platform—Planning and Strategy (3)," Michael Raoul-Duval Files, GRFL.

86 Lou Cannon and Jules Witcover, "Reagan Forces Planning Early Test of Strength," *Washington Post*, August 10, 1976.

87 Shirley, *Reagan's Revolution*, 302, 306.

88 Christina Wolbrecht, *The Politics of Women's Rights: Parties, Positions, and Change* (Princeton, NJ: Princeton University Press, 2000), 41–42.

89 Jeremi Suri, "Détente and Its Discontents," in *Rightward Bound: Making America Conservative in the 1970s*, ed. Bruce J. Schulman and Julian E. Zelizer (Cambridge, MA: Harvard University Press, 2008), 227–45; Adam Clymer, *Drawing the Line at the Big Ditch: The Panama Canal Treaties and the Rise of the Right* (Lawrence: University Press of Kansas, 2008), 10–39.

90 The original language of "Morality in Foreign Policy" as well as proposed substitutions can be found in Box 76, Folder "Platforms 6/1/76–8/30/76," WHCF-PL 1–2, GRFL.

91 Spencer Rich, "Ford Team Defuses Policy Challenges," *Washington Post*, August 13, 1976.

92 Paul Huston, "Strongly Conservative Platform Criticizes Ford-Kissinger Policy," *Los Angeles Times*, August 19, 1976.

93 Tom Wicker, "The Paradox in Kansas City," *New York Times*, August 13, 1976.

94 Mark R. Arnold, "Republican Liberals Shun a Battle on Issues to Back Ford Candidacy," *National Observer*, August 28, 1976.

95 Gerald Ford's handwritten note, September 1, 1976, added to Ed Terrill, memo, August 30, 1976, and Jim Field, memo to Dick Cheney, September 9, 1976, both in Box 18, Folder "President—Telephone Calls, 9/76–11/76," Cheney Files, GRFL.

96 Text of speech, August 19, 1976, accessed at http://www.reagan.utexas.edu/archives/reference/8.19.76.html.

97 Witcover, *Marathon*, 539.

98 Philip Shabecoff, "Ford Sees Connally, Reagan, Rockefeller," *New York Times*, December 10, 1976.

99 Larry Winn Jr., letter to Ford, November 15, 1976, Box 4, Folder "Political Affairs," WHCF PL (Exec.), GRFL.

100 Kenneth Reich, "Ex-President: Avoid Contest Over Ideology," *Los Angeles Times*, April 17, 1977.

101 Phillip A. Klinkner, *The Losing Parties: Out-Party National Committees, 1956–1993* (New Haven, CT: Yale University Press, 1994), 134–36.

102 "Party Building Is What Bill Brock Does Best," *First Monday* (January–February 1977): 6.

103 Earl Black and Merle Black, *The Rise of Southern Republicans* (Cambridge, MA: Harvard University Press, 2002), 95.

104 Klinkner, *The Losing Parties*, 138. For an account of Brock's organizational efforts, see 139–46.

105 David Broder, "Brock Says Each State to Get a Full-Time Organizer," *Washington Post*, January 22, 1977.

106 M. Margaret Conway, "Republican Political Party Nationalization, Campaign Activities, and Their Implications for the Party System," *Publius* 13 (Winter 1983): 4.

107 Daniel K. Williams, *God's Own Party: The Making of the Christian Right* (New York: Oxford University Press, 2010), 105–86; Darren Dochuk, *From Bible Belt to Sunbelt: Plain-Folk Religion, Grassroots Politics, and the Rise of Evangelical Conservatism* (New York: W. W. Norton, 2011), 326–96.

108 This account draws from Daniel Schlozman's analysis of the Christian Right's emergence in the late 1970s as an "anchoring group" for the GOP in *When Movements Anchor Parties: Electoral Alignments in American History* (Princeton, NJ: Princeton University Press, 2015), 77–107.

109 Paul Boyer, "The Evangelical Resurgence in 1970s American Protestantism," in *Rightward Bound*, ed. Schulman and Zelizer, 29–51.

110 Klinkner, *The Losing Parties*, 147.

111 See Bill Brock, letter to invitees, November 19, 1979, Box 44, Folder 19, William E. Brock III Papers, Howard Baker Center for Public Policy, University of Tennessee, Knoxville (hereafter Brock Papers).

112 Klinkner, *The Losing Parties*, 139.

113 Brian Mathew Conley, "Party People: Bliss, Brock, and the Rise of the Modern Republican Party" (PhD diss., New School for Social Research, 2008), 187.

114 Niels Bjerre-Poulsen, "The Heritage Foundation: A Second-Generation Think Tank," *Journal of Policy History* 3 (October 1991): 158. On business mobilization, see Benjamin C. Waterhouse, *Lobbying America: The Politics of Business from Nixon to NAFTA* (Princeton, NJ: Princeton University Press, 2013); on PACs see Larry Sabato, *PAC Power: Inside the World of Political Action Committees* (New York: W. W. Norton, 1984).

115 Leo Berman, memo to Bill Brock, August 24, 1979, Box 44, Folder 9, Brock Papers; Bill Brock, "Learn to PAC—Effectively," *The Professional Agent* (February 1978).

116 Clarence Warner, letters to Brock, April 1 and April 12, 1977, Box 43, Folder 22, Brock Papers.

117 Minutes to RNC meeting, New Orleans, LA, September 30, 1977, Box 43, Folder 25, Brock Papers; Warren Weaver Jr., "Brock, Despite Unwritten Political Code, Cautiously Taking Sides in G.O.P. Primaries," *New York Times*, May 30, 1977.

118 William Lunch, *The Nationalization of American Politics* (Berkeley: University of California Press, 1987), 241–45.

119 "A 'Shadow Cabinet' Suggested by Ford," *New York Times*, January 16, 1977.

120 Bill Brock, letter to Gerald Ford, January 3, 1977, Box 4, Folder "Political Affairs 11/21/76–1/20/77," WHCF-PL (Exec.), GRFL. See also Brock, letter to David Leuthold, February 17, 1977, Box 43, Folder 6, Brock Papers.

121 Bill Brock, letter to John Connally, July 28, 1977, Box 43, Folder 19, Brock Papers.

122 David Broder, "Issues Session Heartens GOP," *Washington Post*, May 1, 1978.

123 Sidney Blumenthal, *The Rise of the Counter-Establishment: From Conservative Ideology to Political Power* (New York: Harper and Row, 1986), 166–209; Phillips-Fein, *Invisible Hands*, 166–84; Jonathan Chait, *The Big Con: Crackpot Economic and the Fleecing of America* (New York: Houghton Mifflin Harcourt, 2007).

124 Klinkner, *The Losing Parties*, 149.

125 Text of RNC Resolution Concerning Taxes, adopted September 30, 1977, Box 43, Folder 25, Brock Papers.

126 Roger Semerad, memo to Bill Brock, June 24, 1977, Box 43, Folder 8, Brock Papers.

127 Michael J. Malbin, "The Conventions, Platforms, and Issue Activists," in *The American Elections of 1980*, ed. Austin Ranney (Washington, DC: American Enterprise Institute, 1981), 101–2.

128 Bill Brock, letter to George Murphy, July 6, 1978, Box 65, Folder 6, Brock Papers.

129 Rowland Evans and Robert Novak, "A New Tax-Cut Theology for the GOP," *Washington Post*, June 8, 1978.

130 Bill Brock, letter to Howard Baker, July 24, 1978, Box 60, Folder 14, Brock Papers.

131 Bill Peterson, "GOP Plans 'Blitz' to Push Tax Cut Bill," *Washington Post*, July 7, 1978.

132 Itinerary for Republican Tax Cut Blitz in Box 60, Box 60, Folder 14, Brock Papers.

133 "Republican Party Platform of 1980," July 15, 1980, accessed online at John T. Woolley and Gerhard Peters, *The American Presidency Project* (Santa Barbara, CA), http://www.presidency.ucsb.edu/ws/?pid=25843.

134 Robert D. Novak, "Producers' Party," *National Review*, June 6, 1975.

135 Evans and Novak, "A New Tax-Cut Theology for the GOP."

136 Norman C. Miller, "Tax Cut Plan Gives GOP a New Issue," *Wall Street Journal*, September 19, 1978.

137 Quoted in Steven M. Gillon, *The Pact: Bill Clinton, Newt Gingrich, and the Rivalry that Defined a Generation* (New York: Oxford University Press, 2008), 38.

138 Kenneth Levin, letter to Bill Brock, April 22, 1977, and William Zimmerman, letter to Brock, April 24, 1977, Box 53, Folder 22, Brock Papers.

139 Examples include Bill Brock, letters to Roy Gibson Jr., April 12, 1978, and to O. J. Callahan, April 12, 1978, both in Box 65, Folder 5, Brock Papers; Brock to E. C. Hallstein, March 13, 1979, Box 65, Folder 6, Brock Papers.

140 Described in Bill Brock, letter to Wallace M. Davis Jr., July 13, 1979, Box 65, Folder 5, Brock Papers.

141 On conservative think tanks, see Blumenthal, *The Rise of the Counter-Establishment*; James Allen Smith, *The Idea Brokers: Think Tanks and the Rise of the New Policy Elite* (New York: Free Press, 1991); Michael Patrick Allen, "Elite Social Movement Organizations and the State: The Rise of the Conservative Policy-Planning Network," *Research in Politics and Society* 4 (1992): 87–109; and Andrew Rich, *Think Tanks, Public Policy, and the Politics of Expertise* (New York: Cambridge University Press, 2004). On conservative philanthropy's role, see Alice O'Connor, "Financing the Counterrevolution," in *Rightward Bound*, ed. Schulman and Zelizer, 148–68.

142 David M. Ricci, *The Transformation of American Politics: The New Washington and the Rise of Think Tanks* (New Haven, CT: Yale University Press, 1993), 160.

143 Blumenthal, *The Rise of the Counter-Establishment*, 37.

144 Les Francis, memo to Frank Moore, October 3, 1977, Box 37, Folder "Memoranda—Les Francis, 2/22/77–3/20/78," Office of Congressional Liaison, James Carter Library (JCL), Atlanta, GA.

145 Sasha Gregory-Lewis, "Right-Wing Finds New Organizing Tactic," *The Advocate*, June 29, 1977.

146 See, e.g., Paul Weyrich, letter to Orrin Hatch, September 18, 1978, Box 21, Folder 27, Weyrich Papers.

147 Rhodes Cook, "GOP Presidential Hopefuls Gave Plenty to Party Candidates in 1978," *Congressional Quarterly*, February 12, 1979.

148 Editorial, "Republican 'Cannibalism,'" *Washington Star*, November 16, 1977; Warren Weaver Jr., "G.O.P. Chairman Says Single Issue Groups Imperil Political System," *New York Times*, July 19, 1978.

149 Schlozman, *When Movements Anchor Parties*, 57, 75.

150 Bill Brock, letter to Andreas Moller, November 29, 1978, Box 53, Folder 1, Brock Papers.

151 Paul Weyrich to Richard Mellon Scaife, November 16, 1978, Box 3, Folder 10, Weyrich Papers.

152 Andrew E. Busch, *Reagan's Victory: The Presidential Election of 1980 and the Rise of the Right* (Lawrence: University Press of Kansas, 2005), 25.

153 Dennis Farney, "Republicans Have What Carter Wants: The Power of Votes," *Wall Street Journal*, April 20, 1979.

154 David Broder, "Brock Calls Independent Efforts for Reagan 'Divisive,'" *Washington Post*, July 1, 1980; Busch, *Reagan's Victory*, 203.

155 James L. Sundquist, "'Whither the American Party System?' Revisited," *Political Science Quarterly* 88 (Winter 1983–84): 580, 583, 596.

156 Myra MacPherson, "The GOP's Woman Without," *Washington Post Magazine*, July 1, 1980.

157 Richard E. Govignon, letter to Mary Crisp, Box 23, Folder 8, Mary Dent Crisp Papers, Schlesinger Library, Harvard University, Cambridge, MA (hereafter Crisp Papers).

158 Crisp lists her frustrations in an undated letter marked "Statement Never Made," Box 23, Folder 22, Crisp Papers.

159 Peter A. Brown, "GOP Faces the Music: No 'Bug' in Its Office," *Boston Globe*, June 23, 1980; Tom Sherwood, "The Bugging That Wasn't," *Washington Post*, February 11, 1981.

160 "RNC Co-Chairman Mary Crisp Comes from the Grass Roots," *First Monday* (March 1977), 8.

161 Thomas W. Ottenad, "Republican Battles Are Now Mostly Intramural," *St. Louis Post-Dispatch*, January 8, 1978.

162 James R. Dickinson, "Ford's Choice for GOP Post a Shrewd Move," *Washington Star-News*, September 5, 1974.

163 Donald T. Critchlow, *Phyllis Schlafly and Grassroots Conservatism: A Woman's Crusade* (Princeton, NJ: Princeton University Press, 2005), 244–48; Marjorie J. Spruill, "Gender and America's Right Turn," in *Rightward Bound*, ed. Schulman and Zelizer, 71–89.

164 Patricia Lahr Smith, letter to Mary Crisp, July 2, 1977, Box 27, Folder 5, Crisp Papers.

165 Mary Crisp to Tressa Crosner, November 18, 1977, Box 23, Folder 22, Crisp Papers.

166 United Press International, "Black Reagan Backer Seeks Key G.O.P. Post," *New York Times*, January 5, 1978.

167 George Murphy, letter to Bill Brock, June 28, 1978, Box 65, Folder 6, Brock Papers.

168 Wolbrecht, *The Politics of Women's Rights*, 88–89, 105–6.

169 Mary Crisp, letter to Horence Powell, May 23, 1979; Hilda Griffith, letter to Crisp, undated; Joan Williams, letter to Bill Brock, January 17, 1979; congressional letter to Brock, February 8, 1979—Box 28, Folder 1, Crisp Papers.

170 Mary Crisp, notes, "For Discussion with Chairman," June 1978, Box 23, Folder 16, Crisp Papers.

171 Quoted in MacPherson, "The GOP's Woman Without."

172 Brock, memo to Crisp, June 5, 1978; Crisp, memo to RNC Staff, June 9, 1978; Box 23, Folder 19, Crisp Papers.

173 MacPherson, "The GOP's Woman Without."

174 Compare the texts of "Republican Party Platform of 1976," and "Republican Party Platform of 1980," at http://www.presidency.ucsb.edu/ws/?pid=25843 and http://www.presidency.ucsb.edu/ws/index.php?pid=25844.

175 Arthur Siddon and Jon Margolis, "GOP Ignores Plea, Sticks to Its ERA Stand," *Chicago Tribune*, July 10, 1980.

176 Knight Ridder Service, "GOP's Cochairman Quits Over Platform," *Boston Globe*, July 10, 1980.

177 A convention-eve CBS poll of delegates found 62 percent reporting opposition to the ERA, versus 28 percent in favor. Adam Clymer, "Emotional Issue for GOP," *New York Times*, July 10, 1980.

178 Siddon and Margolis, "GOP Ignores Plea, Sticks to Its ERA Stand."

179 Mary Crisp, "Statement Never Made," undated, Box 23, Folder 22, Crisp Papers.

180 Wolbrecht, *The Politics of Women's Rights*, 45–47.

181 "Democratic Party Platform," August 11, 1980, at http://www.presidency.ucsb.edu/ws/index.php?pid=29607.

182 Referenced in Michael Harrington, letter to Gloria Steinem, July 25, 1980, Box 6A, Democratic Socialists of America Papers, Tamiment Library/ Robert Wagner Labor Archives, New York University, New York.

183 Pam Fridrich, letter to Mary Crisp, October 9, 1980, Box 25, Folder 13, Crisp Papers.

184 This is the process of "conflict extension" described by Layman et al. in "Activists and Conflict Extension in American Party Politics." On party divergence over environmental issues, for example, see Charles S. Shipan and William R. Lowry, "Environmental Policy and Party Divergence in Congress," *Political Research Quarterly* 54 (June 2001): 245–63.

CHAPTER 7

1 David Vogel, *Fluctuating Fortunes: The Political Power of Business in America* (New York: Basic Books, 1989); John B. Judis, *The Paradox of American Democracy: Elites, Special Interests, and the Betrayal of Public Trust* (New York: Pantheon, 2000), 109–55; Benjamin C. Waterhouse, *Lobbying America: The Politics of Business from Nixon to NAFTA* (Princeton, NJ: Princeton University Press, 2013).

2 Jeffrey M. Berry, *Lobbying for the People: The Political Behavior of Public Interest Groups* (Princeton, NJ: Princeton University Press, 1977), 18–109; Theda Skocpol, *Diminished Democracy: From Membership to Management in American Civic Life* (Norman: University of Oklahoma Press, 2003), 127–220.

3 Taylor Dark, *The Unions and the Democrats: An Enduring Alliance* (Ithaca, NY: Cornell University Press, 1999); Andrew Battista, *The Revival of Labor Liberalism* (Urbana: University of Illinois Press, 2008).

4 Michael Harrington, untitled roundtable contribution, *Dissent* (Fall 1968), reprinted as "Straight Lesser-Evilism" in Michael Harrington, *Taking Sides: The Education of a Militant Mind* (New York: Henry Holt, 1988), 149–50.

5 Maurice Isserman, *The Other American: The Life of Michael Harrington* (New York: PublicAffairs, 2000), 291–92. The quote is from Harrington's letter to the Socialist Party National Committee Members and Alternates of the Majority Tendency, May 18, 1971, Box 1, Folder 1, Democratic Socialists of America (DSA) Papers, Tamiment Library/Robert Wagner Labor Archives, New York University, New York (hereafter DSA Papers).

6 "For the Record: The Report of Social Democrats: U.S.A. on the Resignation of Michael Harrington and His Attempt to Split the Socialist Movement," Series RG0-003, Box 54, Folder "Michael Harrington, 1966–1974," George Meany Memorial Archive, Silver Spring, MD.

7   James Ring Adams, "Battle Royal among the Socialists," *Wall Street Journal*, December 8, 1972.

8   Quoted in Stephen C. Schlesinger, *The New Reformers: Forces for Change in American Politics* (Boston: Houghton Mifflin, 1975), 209–10.

9   Michael Harrington, "We are the socialist caucus of the democratic Left" draft statement, April 1973, Box 1, Folder 4, DSA Papers.

10   Michael Harrington, *The Long-Distance Runner: An Autobiography* (New York: Henry Holt, 1988), 21–23.

11   Peter Kihss, "Socialist Unit Is Founded Here," *New York Times*, October 13, 1973.

12   Bill Kovach, "A.F.L.-C.I.O. Unions Form McGovern Unit," *New York Times*, August 15, 1972.

13   Battista, *The Revival of Labor Liberalism*, 51; Harry Bernstein, "Unions Supporting McGovern Kick Off Blitz Voting Drive," *Los Angeles Times*, November 1, 1972.

14   Paul R. Wieck, "Labor's Al Barkan," *New Republic*, March 24, 1973.

15   Dorothy Sue Cobble, *The Other Women's Movement: Workplace Justice and Social Rights in Modern America* (Princeton, NJ: Princeton University Press, 2004), 201–5.

16   Doug Fraser, memo, September 27, 1977, Box 48, Folder 3, UAW President's Office, Douglas A. Fraser Collection, Walter P. Reuther Library, Wayne State University, Detroit, MI.

17   On the growing importance of public sector unions in the American labor movement from the 1960s onward, see Joseph A. McCartin, "Bringing the State's Workers In: Time to Rectify an Imbalanced U.S. Labor Historiography," *Labor History* 47 (February 2006): 73–94.

18   Battista, *The Revival of Labor Liberalism*, 146–62.

19   Harrington, *Long-Distance Runner*, 25–66; Isserman, *The Other American*, 320–22.

20   Harry Boyte, proposal, October 27, 1974, Box 5a, Folder "Harrington correspondence, 9-12/74," DSA Papers.

21   These activities are recounted in Booth's 1971 application for the Industrial Areas Foundation Training Institute, Box 251, Folder "Saul Alinsky—Industrial Areas Foundation Training Institute—July-August/1971,"

Midwest Academy Papers, Chicago History Museum, Chicago (hereafter Midwest Academy Papers).

22   Harry C. Boyte, Heather Booth, and Steve Max, *Citizen Action and the New American Populism* (Philadelphia: Temple University Press, 1986), 55.

23   For post-1968 discussions about a new party, see Eugene McCarthy, "A Third Party May Be a Real Force in '72," *New York Times Magazine*, June 7, 1970; and "A *New Democrat* Symposium: A Fourth Party in 1972?," *New Democrat* 1, no. 4 (1970).

24   Harrington, *Long-Distance Runner*, 114–15.

25   Harrington, "We are the socialist caucus of the democratic Left."

26   Robert Lenzer, "Socialist Role Eyed Among Democrats," *Boston Globe*, October 17, 1973.

27   Harrington, *Long-Distance Runner*, 14.

28   Quoted in Richard N. Goodwin, "A Divided Party," *New Yorker*, December 2, 1974.

29   Thomas E. Cronin, "On the American Presidency: A Conversation with James MacGregor Burns," *Presidential Studies Quarterly* 16 (Summer 1986): 536.

30   DSOC press release, January 14, 1975, Box 6A, DSA Papers.

31   On the origins of the full-employment idea and its development into Humphrey-Hawkins, see Jefferson Cowie, *Stayin' Alive: The 1970s and the Last Days of the Working Class* (New York: New Press, 2010), 266–71.

32   Isserman, *The Other American*, 328.

33   "Democracy '76: Program Proposals for the Democratic Party," undated, Box 2, Folder "DSOC—Organizational overview," DSA Papers.

34   Paul and Heather Booth, letter to Michael Harrington, October 18, 1975, Box 22, Folder "Democratic Socialist Organizing Committee—Michael Harrington—1973–79," Midwest Academy Papers.

35   Statement of purpose, undated, Box 22, Folder "Democracy '76 Conference—6/5/76," Midwest Academy Papers.

36   Dark, *The Unions and the Democrats*, 101–2.

37   The UAW's Leonard Woodcock was Carter's most important early labor supporter. Martin Halpern, "Jimmy Carter and the UAW: Failure of an Alliance," *Presidential Studies Quarterly* 26 (Summer 1996): 757.

38   Kathryn J. McGarr, *The Whole Damn Deal: Robert Strauss and the Art of*

Politics (New York: PublicAffairs, 2011), 187–89; Isserman, *The Other American*, 331.

39 Michael Harrington, testimony to the Resolutions Committee of the Democratic National Convention, May 18, 1976, Box 22, Folder "Democracy '76 Conference—6/5/76," Midwest Academy Papers.

40 "Democratic Party Platform of 1976," July 12, 1976, accessed online at John T. Woolley and Gerhard Peters, *The American Presidency Project* (Santa Barbara, CA), http://www.presidency.ucsb.edu/ws/index.php ?pid=29606#axzz1iweH8tcW.

41 McGarr, *The Whole Damn Deal*, 189.

42 David E. Rosenbaum, "Effort to Permit Speeches Foiled," *New York Times*, July 14, 1976.

43 Woodcock, "America's Unfinished Agenda" statement, May 18, 1978, Box 3, Folder 15, Douglas A. Fraser Papers, Walter P. Reuther Library, Wayne State University, Detroit, MI.

44 "Kennedy Criticizes Carter as Being 'Intentionally' Imprecise,'" *Boston Globe*, May 26, 1976.

45 Kandy Stroud, *How Jimmy Won: The Victory Campaign from Plains to the White House* (New York: Morrow, 1977), 277. On the election's substantive vacuity, see Laura Kalman, *Right Star Rising: A New Politics, 1974–1980* (New York: W. W. Norton, 2010), 172–73.

46 A. James Reichley, memo to Dick Cheney, June 25, 1976, Box 2, Folder "Constituency Analysis," A. James Reichley Files, GRFL.

47 Ford won 53 percent of the white southern vote, compared to Carter's 46 percent. Alexander P. Lamis, *The Two-Party South* (New York: Oxford University Press, 1984), 38.

48 James M. Perry, "Only Zealots Can Afford an Ideology," *National Observer*, March 1, 1975.

49 Daniel J. Galvin, *Presidential Party Building: Dwight D. Eisenhower to George W. Bush* (Princeton, NJ: Princeton University Press, 2010), 99–100.

50 Charles O. Jones, *The Trusteeship Presidency: Jimmy Carter and the United States Congress* (Baton Rouge: Louisiana State University Press, 1988).

51 Burton Kaufman, *The Presidency of James Earl Carter, Jr.* (Lawrence: University Press of Kansas, 1993), 28–49.

52 Agenda for Democratic Agenda conference, November 11–13, 1976, Box 4, Folder 71, Douglas Fraser Papers.

53   A. H. Raskin, "Nationwide Rallies for 'Decent' Jobs at 'Decent' Wages," *New York Times*, August 31, 1977; Cowie, *Stayin' Alive*, 273–74, 283.

54   Bob Pender, memo to Ralph Gerson, September 19, 1978, Box 16, Folder "COIN [O/A 6743]," Robert Strauss Files, Jimmy Carter Library (JCL), Atlanta, GA.

55   On labor-environmentalist alliances, see Harvey Wasserman, "Unionizing Ecotopia," *Mother Jones*, June 1978.

56   Galvin, *Presidential Party Building*, 220.

57   Elizabeth Drew, "Constituencies," *New Yorker*, January 15, 1979.

58   Donald Fraser, memo to Mid-Term Conference Delegates, October 11, 1978, Box 149.C.12.2(F), Folder "Democratic Conference," Donald M. Fraser Papers.

59   Isserman, *The Other American*, 334.

60   Harrington, *Long-Distance Runner*, 106.

61   Curtis Wilkie, "Democratic Parley to Get Compromise on Health Care," *Boston Globe*, December 7, 1978.

62   Harold Meyerson, "The D.S.O.C.—Radicals on a Tightrope," *The Nation*, April 7, 1979; Drew, "Constituencies."

63   Alan Ehrenhalt, "The Democratic Left Faces a Dilemma," *Congressional Quarterly*, December 16, 1978.

64   Michael Harrington, Margaret Phyfe, Jack Clark, and Libby Moroff, letter to "Key Contacts" of Democratic Agenda, December 27, 1978, Box 10A, Folder "Resolutions," DSA Papers.

65   See minutes to 1979 ADA board meeting, undated, Box 149.C.13.4(F). Folder "Misc.," Donald M. Fraser Papers.

66   Drew, "Constituencies."

67   Rhodes Cook, "New Party Rules: The Real Memphis Legacy," *Congressional Quarterly*, December 16, 1978.

68   Hendrick Smith, "The Message of Memphis," *New York Times*, December 11, 1978.

69   Ehrenhalt, "The Democratic Left Faces a Dilemma."

70   Editors, "The Tennessee Waltz," *The Nation*, December 23, 1978.

71   Timothy Stanley, *Kennedy vs. Carter: The 1980 Battle for the Democratic Party's Soul* (Lawrence: University Press of Kansas, 2010), 79.

72 David S. Broder and Bill Peterson, "Kennedy Warns of a Party Split by Arms Outlays," *Washington Post*, December 10, 1978.

73 Stanley, *Kennedy vs. Carter*, 86.

74 Jefferson Cowie, "'A One-Sided Class War': Rethinking Doug Fraser's Resignation from the Labor-Management Group," *Labor History* 44 (2003): 307–14.

75 Already in 1977, Fraser and his aides were discussing internally the "malaise in the labor movement," the resurgence of labor's enemies, and possible political strategies to address the problem. See Steve Schlossberg to Fraser, memo, October 20, 1977, Box 48, Folder 3, Douglas Fraser Papers.

76 Melvyn Dubofsky, "Jimmy Carter and the End of the Politics of Productivity," in *The Carter Presidency: Policy Choices in the Post-New Deal Era*, ed. Gary M. Fink and Hugh Davis Graham (Lawrence: University of Kansas Press, 1998), 106.

77 Douglas Fraser, letter, July 17, 1978, Box 1, Folder 27, Douglas Fraser Papers.

78 Doug Fraser, memo to Irving Bluestone, Steve Schlossberg, Howard Paster, Don Stillman, Howard Young, and Frank James, September 5, 1978, Box 68, Folder 21, Douglas Fraser Papers.

79 Douglas Fraser, letter to invitees, September 19, 1978, Box 3, Folder 13, Douglas Fraser Papers.

80 Battista, *The Revival of Labor Liberalism*, 86.

81 "Toward a Progressive Alliance," January 15, 1979, Box 10A, Folder 35, DSA Papers.

82 Ibid.

83 Interim Working Paper, September 21, 1978, Box 3, Folder 15, Douglas Fraser Papers.

84 Fred Barnes, "Q and A: UAW Chief Explains Goals of Liberals," *Washington Star*, October 27, 1978.

85 "A Bold and Balky Congress," *Time*, January 23, 1978.

86 See, e.g., Doug Fraser, letter to Thomas Murphy, July 17, 1978, Box 1, Folder 27, and Fraser's address to the National Conference on Social Welfare, Philadelphia, PA, May 13, 1979, Box 4, Folder 22, Douglas Fraser Papers.

87 Barnes, "Q and A."

88   Tom Matthews and Jon Lowell, "Liberals: Alive and Kicking," *Newsweek*, October 30, 1978.

89   A classic statement on the Watergate babies' neoliberal political legacy is William Schneider, "JFK's Children: The Class of '74," *Atlantic Monthly*, March 1989.

90   Barbara Sinclair, *Majority Leadership in the U.S. House* (Baltimore: Johns Hopkins University Press, 1983), 12.

91   Ibid., 12, 15.

92   Bruce J. Schulman, "Slouching Toward the Supply Side: Jimmy Carter and the New American Political Economy," in *The Carter Presidency*, ed. Fink and Graham, 54–57.

93   Dark, *The Unions and the Democrats*, 110–13.

94   Mark A. Peterson, *Legislating Together: The White House and Capitol Hill from Eisenhower to Reagan* (Cambridge, MA: Harvard University Press, 1990), 253–60.

95   "Summary Report—Democratic Agenda 1979 Project," February 1980, Box 2, DSA Papers; Leon Shull, Minutes to 1979 ADA board meeting, undated, Box 149.C.13.4(F), Folder "Misc.," Donald M. Fraser Papers.

96   Steve Schlossberg, memo to Doug Fraser, January 2, 1979, Box 68, Folder 22, Douglas Fraser Papers.

97   "Democrats Told 'New Right' Gains," *Albuquerque Journal*, July 23, 1978; Donald Fraser, speech at the NEA conference, August 7, 1979, Box 152.K.12.9, Folder "The New Right," Donald M. Fraser Papers.

98   Phillip Shabecoff, "Alliance Formed to Meet Challenge from Right Wing," *New York Times*, April 22, 1978.

99   "As Liberals Dig Out from Under," *U.S. News and World Report*, October 30, 1978.

100   Joy Horowitz, "NOW Flexes Muscle at Convention," *Los Angeles Times*, October 8, 1979; George McGovern, National Conference on Right-Wing Strategy speech, November 3, 1979, Box 187, Folder "Right Wing Issue File—1980 Campaign," George S. McGovern Papers, Seeley G. Mudd Library, Princeton University, Princeton, NJ.

101   See, e.g., Melvin Glasser, memo to Doug Fraser, December 9, 1980, Box 12, Folder 9, Douglas Fraser Papers.

102   Ed James, letter to Michael Harrington, May 30, 1980, Box 6A, DSA Papers.

103 Jake Rosenfeld, *What Unions No Longer Do* (Cambridge, MA: Harvard University Press, 2014), 10–30.

104 Battista, *The Revival of Labor Liberalism*, 96.

105 See Doug Fraser, memo to Progressive Alliance officers, May 3, 1979, Box 68, Folder 20, Douglas Fraser Papers.

106 Minutes to National Organizing Committee meeting, June 4, 1979, Box 10A, Folder 3, DSA Papers.

107 "Memo to Democratic Agenda," May 17, 1980, Box 2, Folder "DSOC—Organizational Overview," DSA Papers.

108 Skocpol, *Diminished Democracy*, 127–220; Gordon Silverstein, *Law's Allure: How Law Shapes, Constrains, Saves, and Kills Politics* (New York: Cambridge University Press, 2009).

109 Ehrenhalt, "The Democratic Left Faces a Dilemma."

110 Pennsylvania, Minnesota, and New Hampshire groups soon joined; Boyte, Booth, and Max, *Citizen Action and the New American Populism*, 48.

111 Tom Corrigan, undated report, Box 149, Folder "Citizen Action Organizing Conference—12/7–12/9/79," Midwest Academy Papers; see also Battista, *The Revival of Labor Liberalism*, 105.

112 Battista, *The Revival of Labor Liberalism*, 104.

113 David Moberg, "Activists Regroup for Reagan Years," *In These Times*, December 10–16, 1980; Florence Levinsohn, "On Bingo, Bankrolls, and Ballots: Public Action Goes Political," *Chicago Reader*, June 12, 1981; Renee Loth, "Fair Share Comes to the Electoral Crossroads," *Boston Phoenix*, June 15, 1982.

114 Heather Booth, notes, January 4, 1980, Box 150, Folder "CA Staff Meeting," Midwest Academy Papers.

115 Michael Harrington, speech, November 20, 1980, Box 150, Folder "CA Leadership Conference—11/20/80," Midwest Academy Papers.

116 Boyte, Booth, and Max, *Citizen Action and the New American Populism*, 153.

117 Dana Fisher, *Activism, Inc.: How the Outsourcing of Grassroots Campaigns Is Strangling Progressive Politics in America* (Stanford, CA: Stanford University Press, 2006), 11–15.

118 Michael Harrington, report to the DSOC National Office Committee, January 20, 1979, Box 10A Folder 36, DSA Papers; Steve Schlossberg, memo to Doug Fraser, January 2, 1979.

119 As Tim Stanley argues, the campaign capped "a renaissance of coalitional activity" on the left in the 1970s. Stanley, *Kennedy vs. Carter*, 7.

120 See, e.g., John Herbers, "The Party's Over for the Political Parties," *New York Times*, December 9, 1979.

121 David Broder, "Kennedy Exposed a 'Gaping' Carter Weakness," *Washington Post*, December 13, 1978.

122 Memo to Walter Mondale, Hamilton Jordan, Frank Moore, Jody Powell, Gerald Rafshoon, Phil Wise, Anne Wexler, and Jack Watson, May 22, 1979, Box PL 5-2, Folder "1/20/77–1/20/81," White House Central Files, JCL.

123 Kevin Mattson, *"What the Heck Are You Up To, Mr. President?" Jimmy Carter, America's "Malaise," and the Speech that Should Have Changed the Country* (New York: Bloomsbury, 2009), 125–66.

124 Adam Clymer, "Carter's Clash with Kennedy," *New York Times*, December 12, 1978; Max Fine, memo to Coalition for National Health Insurance members, September 27, 1979, Box 2, Folder 20, Douglas Fraser Papers.

125 Martin F. Nolan, "Mail Campaign Is Building Big War Chest for Kennedy," *Boston Globe*, September 6, 1979.

126 Mattson, *"What the Heck Are You Up To, Mr. President?"* 104–6; Susan M. Hartmann, "Feminism, Public Policy, and the Carter Administration," in *The Carter Presidency*, ed. Fink and Graham, 225.

127 David Broder, "Democrats," in David Broder, Lou Cannon, Haynes Johnson, Martin Schram, Richard Harwood, and the staff of the *Washington Post*, *The Pursuit of the Presidency 1980*, ed. Richard Harwood (New York: G. P. Putnam's Sons, 1980), 192–94. The CWA was another major progressive union to endorse Carter in 1980.

128 Harry Boyte, memo to DSOC National Office Committee, June 22, 1979, Box 10A, Folder 3, and Deborah Meier, "Draft on Election Policy," prepared for the National Executive Committee meeting, September 15–16, 1979, Box 10A, Folder "National Executive Committee Minutes," both in DSA Papers.

129 In addition to Stanley's account, see T. R. Reid, "Kennedy," in Broder et al., *Pursuit of the Presidency*, 65–82; and Adam Clymer, *Edward Kennedy: A Biography* (New York: William Morrow, 1999), 276–320.

130 Stanley, *Kennedy vs. Carter*, 116–17; and Reid, "Kennedy," 70.

131 Adam Clymer, "Kennedy Says that Leadership, Not Economic Policy, Is at Issue," *New York Times*, September 14, 1979.

132 "Transcript of Kennedy's Speech at Georgetown on Campaign Issues," *New York Times*, January 29, 1980.

133 Stanley, *Kennedy vs. Carter*, 99–111, 141–57.

134 This effort resulted in the odd spectacle of many leading lights of the McGovern-Fraser-era party reforms, now backing Kennedy, suddenly extolling the virtues of delegates retaining their autonomy from the wishes of primary voters. See, e.g., Joseph L. Rauh Jr., "A Lot Has Changed since the Primaries," *Washington Post*, July 6, 1980, and Barbara Mikulski's unpublished letter to the *Washington Post*'s editors, July 7, 1980, Box 1385, Folder "Kennedy '80 Rules Committee Material," DNC Records, National Archives, Washington, DC.

135 Bill Dodds, memo to Doug Fraser, July 9, 1980, Box 3, Folder 14, Douglas Fraser Papers.

136 Bill Dodds and Bob Corolla, memo to Doug Fraser, July 15, 1980, Box 3, Folder 14, Douglas Fraser Papers.

137 Robert G. Kaiser, "Carter Loyalists Reject Kennedy's Economic Plank, *New York Times*, June 23, 1980.

138 Brochure, "A Progressive Platform for the 1980s," Box 10A, Folder "Resolutions," DSA Papers.

139 Broder, "Democrats," 199–200.

140 Ruth Jordan, "Coalitions: Too Many or Not Enough?," *Newsletter of the Democratic Left*, November 1979.

141 George Meany's retirement as AFL-CIO president in 1979, followed soon after by Al Barkan's retirement from COPE, signified the departure of two of labor's most inveterate and determined opponents of "New Politics" liberalism. The departures helped to smooth the process by which the leading dissident union, the UAW, rejoined the AFL-CIO in 1982. The broader significance of these developments were discussed in a 1980 Citizen Action staff meeting; see Heather Booth's handwritten notes, January 4, 1980, Folder "CA Staff Meeting—1/4/80," Box 150, Midwest Academy Papers.

142 Matthews and Lowell, "Liberals"; Peter Kovler, "Democrats, Dismay, and Disarray," *Commonweal*, January 19, 1979.

143 "Toward a Progressive Alliance."

144 For an argument that the Democratic and Republican parties have embodied this core asymmetry for a long swathe of their twentieth- and twenty-first-century histories, see Matt Grossman and David Hopkins, *Asymmetric Politics: Ideological Republicans and Group Interest Democrats* (New York: Oxford University Press, 2016).

145 James Q. Wilson, "American Politics, Then and Now," *Commentary*, February 1979.

CHAPTER 8

1 James Reston, "Reagan's Startling Victory," *Washington Post*, November 5, 1980.

2 James L. Sundquist, *Dynamics of the Party System: Alignment and Realignment of Political Parties in the United States*, rev. ed. (Washington, DC: Brookings Institution, 1983), 445.

3 Sidney M. Milkis, *The President and the Parties: The Transformation of the American Party System since the New Deal* (New York: Oxford University Press, 1993), 262.

4 The term is Richard McCormick's. *The Party Period and Public Policy: American Politics from the Age of Jackson to the Progressive Era* (New York: Oxford University Press, 1988).

5 Sara Brandes Crook and John Hibbing, "Congressional Reform and Party Discipline: The Effects of Changes in the Seniority System on Party Loyalty in the U.S. House of Representatives," *British Journal of Political Science* 15 (1985): 207–26; David W. Rohde, *Parties and Leaders in the Postreform House* (Chicago: University of Chicago Press, 1991).

6 John M. Barry, *The Ambition and the Power: The Fall of Jim Wright—A True Story of Washington* (New York: Viking Press, 1989); John A. Farrell, *Tip O'Neill and the Democratic Century* (New York: Little, Brown, 2001); Barbara Sinclair, *Party Wars: Polarization and the Politics of National Policy Making* (Norman: University of Oklahoma Press, 2004), 67–109, 256–65.

7 Douglas L. Koopman, *Hostile Takeover: The House Republican Party, 1980–1995* (New York: Rowman and Littlefield, 1996); Sinclair, *Party Wars*, 110–42; Julian E. Zelizer, "Seizing Power: Conservatives and Congress since the 1970s," in *The Transformation of American Politics: Activist Government and the Rise of Conservatism*, ed. Paul Pierson and Theda Skocpol (Princeton, NJ: Princeton University Press, 2007), 105–34.

8 Editorial, "A Tip from Britain?," *Savannah Morning News*, July 7, 1979.

9 Paul Weyrich, letter to Pat Robertson, July 29, 1983, Box 16, Folder 20, Weyrich Papers.

10 See, e.g., Newt Gingrich's letter to Republican colleagues laying out a six-point plan for reforming conference procedures, June 8, 1983, in Box 4, Folder "W.H. Staff Memoranda—Legislative Affairs 1/83–6/83 [2 of 4]," James A. Baker III Files, Ronald Reagan Presidential Library, Simi Valley,

CA; and unsigned, undated memo to Robert Michel on Republican Task Force on Conference Rules, Box 11, Folder "Leadership, 100th. Task Force on Conference Rules: Procedures Committee Task Force (Lagamarsino)," Robert Michel Papers, Dirksen Congressional Center, Pekin, IL.

11   Lawrence J. Haas, "House GOP's Complicated Bottom Line," *National Journal*, February 13, 1988.

12   Sinclair, *Party Wars*, 120.

13   Joint letter of Robert Dole and Robert Michel, October 4, 1990, Box 13, Folder "Joint Letters: 10/4/90: Budget Resolution," Michel Papers.

14   Newt Gingrich, report, "Optimistic vs. Defeatist Republicans: The New Split in the GOP," circulated at August 3, 1983, meeting, Box 16, Folder 20, Weyrich Papers.

15   Koopman, *Hostile Takeover*, 144.

16   Ronald B. Rappaport and Walter J. Stone, *Three's a Crowd: The Dynamic of Third Parties, Ross Perot, and Republican Resurgence* (Ann Arbor: University of Michigan Press, 2005).

17   Dennis Hastert, address at the Library of Congress, November 12, 2003, accessed at http://www.congresslink.org/print_basics_histmats_hastert.htm.

18   Gary W. Cox and Matthew D. McCubbins, *Legislative Leviathan: Party Government in the House* (Berkeley: University of California Press, 1993).

19   Barbara Sinclair, *Unorthodox Lawmaking: New Legislative Processes in the U.S. Congress*, 3rd ed. (Washington, DC: CQ Press, 2007).

20   Sean M. Theriault, *The Gingrich Senators: The Roots of Partisan Warfare in Congress* (New York: Oxford University Press, 2013).

21   Sinclair, *Party Wars*, 191.

22   On contrasting consequences of polarization in the House and Senate, see Barbara Sinclair, *The Transformation of the U.S. Senate* (Baltimore: Johns Hopkins University Press, 1989), 71–140, and *Party Wars*, 185–233.

23   Quoted in David E. Rosenbaum, "Filibuster Foes Win the Key Test," *New York Times*, March 6, 1975.

24   Charles M. Cameron, "Studying the Polarized Presidency," *Presidential Studies Quarterly* 32 (2002): 647–63; Richard M. Skinner, "George W. Bush and the Partisan Presidency," *Political Science Quarterly* 123 (2009): 605–22; Daniel J. Galvin, "Presidential Partisanship Reconsidered: Eisenhower, Nixon, and Ford and the Rise of Polarized Politics," *Political Research Quarterly* 66 (2013): 46–60; Frances E. Lee, "Presidents and

Party Teams: The Politics of Debt Limits and Executive Oversight," *Presidential Studies Quarterly* 43 (2013): 775–91; Julia R. Azari, *Delivering the People's Message: The Changing Politics of the Presidential Mandate* (Ithaca, NY: Cornell University Press, 2014).

25   Frances E. Lee, "Dividers, Not Uniters: Presidential Leadership and Senate Partisanship, 1980–2004," *Journal of Politics* 70 (October 2008): 914–28.

26   Cornelius B. Cotter and John S. Bibby, "Institutional Development of Parties and the Thesis of Party Decline," *Political Science Quarterly* 95 (Spring 1980): 1–27; M. Margaret Conway, "Republican Political Party Nationalization, Campaign Activities, and Their Implications for the Party System," *Publius* 13 (Winter 1983): 1–17; A. James Reichley, "The Rise of National Parties," in *The New Direction in American Politics*, ed. John E. Chubb and Paul E. Peterson (Washington, DC: Brookings Institution, 1985), 175–200; Paul Herrnson, *Party Campaigning in the 1980s* (New York: Cambridge University Press, 1988); Phillip A. Klinkner, *The Losing Parties: Out-Party National Committees, 1956–1993* (New Haven, CT: Yale University Press, 1994), 71–196; Daniel J. Galvin, *Presidential Party Building: Dwight D. Eisenhower to George W. Bush* (Princeton, NJ: Princeton University Press, 2010), 120–59, 225–62.

27   Theda Skocpol, "Naming the Problem: What It Will Take to Counter Extremism and Engage Americans in the Fight Against Global Warming," prepared for the Symposium on the Politics of America's Fight against Global Warming, February 14, 2013, Harvard University; Steven Teles, Heather Hurlburt, and Mark Schmitt, "Philanthropy in a Time of Polarization," *Stanford Social Innovation Review* (Summer 2014).

28   Sinclair, *Party Wars*, 308–43; Katherine Krimmel, "Special Interest Partisanship: The Transformation of American Political Parties" (PhD diss., Columbia University, 2013), 22–72.

29   Krimmel, "Special Interest Partisanship," 62.

30   Nicholas Confessore, "Welcome to the Machine," *Washington Monthly* (July/August 2003).

31   Sidney Blumenthal, *The Rise of the Counter-Establishment: From Conservative Ideology to Political Power* (New York: Harper and Row, 1986); James Allen Smith, *The Idea Brokers: Think Tanks and the Rise of the New Policy Elite* (New York: Free Press, 1991); Michael Patrick Allen, "Elite Social Movement Organizations and the State: The Rise of the Conservative Policy-Planning Network," *Research in Politics and Society* 4 (1992): 87–109; David M. Ricci, *The Transformation of American Politics: The New Washington and the Rise of Think Tanks* (New Haven, CT: Yale University Press, 1993); Diane Stone, *Capturing the Political Imagination: Think Tanks*

and the Policy Process (New York: Routledge, 1996); Andrew Rich, *Think Tanks, Public Policy, and the Politics of Expertise* (New York: Cambridge University Press, 2004). O'Connor, "Financing the Counterrevolution," 148–68.

32 Jeffrey M. Berry and Sarah Sobieraj, *The Outrage Industry: Political Opinion Media and the New Incivility* (New York: Oxford University Press, 2014).

33 Paul S. Herrnson and Kelly D. Patterson, "Toward a More Programmatic Democratic Party? Agenda-Setting and Coalition-Building in the House of Representatives," *Polity* 27 (Summer 1995): 607–28; Kenneth S. Baer, *Reinventing Democrats: The Politics of Liberalism from Reagan to Clinton* (Lawrence: University Press of Kansas, 2000).

34 William Galston and Elaine Kamarck, *The Politics of Evasion: Democrats and the Presidency*, Progressive Policy Institute report, September 1989, http://www.progressivepolicy.org/wp-content/uploads/2013/03/Politics_of_Evasion.pdf.

35 Greg Easterbrook, "The Business of Politics," *Atlantic Monthly*, October 1986; Brooks Jackson, *Honest Graft: Big Money and the American Political Process* (New York: Knopf, 1988).

36 Geoffrey Kabaservice, *Rule and Ruin: The Downfall of Moderation and the Destruction of the Republican Party, From Eisenhower to the Tea Party* (New York: Oxford University Press, 2012).

37 James B. Booe, letter to Douglas Fraser, February 23, 1983, Box 70, Folder 16, UAW President's Office: Douglas A. Fraser Collection, Walter P. Reuther Library, Wayne State University, Detroit, MI; Rick Scott, memo to Gerald McEntee and William Lucy, October 29, 1991, Box 15, Folder 6, AFSCME President's Office: Gerald McEntee Collection, Walter P. Reuther Library, Wayne State University, Detroit, MI; Taylor Dark, *The Unions and the Democrats: An Enduring Alliance* (Ithaca, NY: Cornell University Press, 1999), 125–90.

38 Richard E. Cohen, "Citizen Action: Noah's Ark or a Sham?," *National Journal*, June 11, 1988.

39 Steven Greenhouse, "Link to Teamsters Forces a Liberal Group to Close Its National Office," *New York Times*, October 30, 1997.

40 Baer, *Reinventing Democrats*, 264.

41 Daniel DiSalvo, "The Death and Life of the New Democrats," *The Forum* 6, no. 2 (2008): art. 4.

42 In a 2002 book predicting the emergence of just such national majorities, John B. Judis and Ruy Tuxiera pointedly referred to this demographic

development as "McGovern's revenge." *The Emerging Democratic Majority* (New York: Scribner's, 2002), 37–68.

43 Focusing less on institutional crisis than the disaffection and drift induced by polarization, journalist E. J. Dionne Jr. offered an influential anatomy of the emerging era of ideological stalemate in *Why Americans Hate Politics* (New York: Simon and Schuster, 1991).

44 Joe Klein, "The Town That Ate Itself," *New Yorker*, November 23, 1998. The ironic invocation of the midcentury scholarly prescription of responsible parties soon enough became a staple of political science scholarship on polarization. As Nicol C. Rae put it, "Be Careful What You Wish For: The Rise of Responsible Parties in American National Politics," *Annual Review of Political Science* 10 (June 2007): 169–91.

CONCLUSION

1 Theda Skocpol and Vanessa Williamson, *The Tea Party and the Remaking of Republican Conservatism* (New York: Oxford University Press, 2012). In this sense the Tea Party typifies the "conflict extension" at work in modern party polarization. Geoffrey C. Layman et al., "Activists and Conflict Extension in American Party Politics," *American Political Science Review* 104 (May 2010): 324–46. See also Joseph Bafumi and Robert Y. Shapiro, "A New Partisan Voter," *Journal of Politics* 71 (January 2009): 1–24.

2 Marty Cohen et al., *The Party Decides: Presidential Nominations Before and After Reform* (Chicago: University of Chicago Press, 2008); Kathleen Bawn et al., "A Theory of Parties: Groups, Policy Demanders, and Nominations in American Politics," *Perspectives on Politics* 10 (September 2012): 571–97.

3 Juan Linz, "The Perils of Presidentialism," *Journal of Democracy* (Winter 1990): 51–69.

4 Dylan Matthews, interview with Juan Linz, "Monday we celebrated our presidential democracy. Juan Linz thinks that's mistaken," *Washington Post* online, January 22, 2013, accessed at: http://www.washingtonpost.com/blogs/wonkblog/wp/2013/01/22/monday-we-celebrated-our-presidential-democracy-juan-linz-thinks-thats-mistaken/. See also Harold Meyerson, "Did the Founding Fathers Screw Up?," *American Prospect*, September 26, 2011; Jeffrey Toobin, "Our Broken Constitution," *New Yorker*, December 9, 2013; and Matthew Yglesias, "American Democracy Is Doomed," *Vox*, October 8, 2015.

5 Jane Mansbridge and Catherine Jo Martin, eds., *Negotiating Agreement in Politics: Report of the Task Force on Negotiating Agreement in Politics* (Washington, DC: American Political Science Association, 2013).

6   Richard Pildes, "Romanticizing Democracy, Political Fragmentation, and the Decline of American Government," *Yale Law Journal* 124 (December 2014): 805-52; Raymond J. La Raja and Bryan F. Schaffner, *Campaign Finance and Political Polarization: When Purists Prevail* (Ann Arbor: University of Michigan Press, 2015); Jonathan Rauch, *Political Realism: How Hacks, Machines, Big Money, and Back-Room Deals Can Strengthen American Democracy* (Washington DC: Brookings Institution, 2015).

7   Richard Hofstadter, *The Idea of a Party System: The Rise of Legitimate Opposition in the United States, 1780-1840* (Berkeley: University of California Press, 1969).

8   Daniel Schlozman and Sam Rosenfeld, "The Hollow Parties," paper prepared for the SSRC Anxieties of Democracy Institutions Working Group conference, Princeton, NJ, October 2016.

9   Lee Drutman, "Donald Trump's Candidacy Is Going to Realign the Political Parties," *Vox*, March 1, 2016; Drutman, "American Politics Has Reached Peak Polarization," *Vox*, March 24, 2016.

BIBLIOGRAPHIC ESSAY

1   On the revival of political history, see Zelizer, Jacobs, and William Novak, eds., *The Democratic Experiment: New Directions in American Political History* (Princeton, NJ: Princeton University Press, 2003); and Zelizer, *Governing America: The Revival of Political History* (Princeton, NJ: Princeton University Press, 2012).

2   The most sustained recent argument against the traditional view that American parties have been historically less ideological than their European counterparts is John Gerring, *Party Ideologies in America, 1828-1996* (New York: Cambridge University Press, 1998). Using content analyses of national party platforms and campaign rhetoric, Gerring argues that both parties have demonstrated coherent and distinct ideological views since 1828. Gerring's methodology excludes from analysis the relative degree of internal party divisions over time, and thus has little to say about what might be significant about the parties' ideological sorting in the later twentieth century. Hans Noel, meanwhile, marshals quantitative evidence for a *longue duree* rise in ideological thinking over the course of the nineteenth and twentieth centuries, arguing that a "unidimensional" left-right ideological divide emerged in American society—gradually, but consistently in one direction. See Noel, *Political Ideologies and Political Parties in America* (New York: Cambridge University Press, 2013).

3   Joel H. Silbey, *The American Political Nation: 1838-1893* (Stanford, CA: Stanford University Press, 1991); Richard McCormick, *The Party Period* *and Public Policy: American Politics from the Age of Jackson to the Progressive Era* (New York: Oxford University Press, 1988); Frances Lee, "Patronage, Logrolls, and 'Polarization': Congressional Parties of the Gilded Age, 1876-1896," *Studies in American Political Development* 30, no. 2 (October 2016): 116-27. On partisan developments during the Gilded Age that presaged twentieth-century patterns, see Daniel Klinghard, *The Nationalization of American Political Parties, 1880-1896* (New York: Cambridge University Press, 2010).

4   On the decline of patronage politics in twentieth-century American parties, see Alan Ware, *The Breakdown of Democratic Party Organization, 1940-1980* (New York: Clarendon Press, 1985); A. James Reichley, *The Life of the Parties: A History of American Political Parties* (New York: Free Press, 1992), 304-15; and Katherine Krimmel, "Special Interest Partisanship: The Transformation of American Political Parties" (PhD diss., Columbia University, 2013). The distinct characteristics of issue-driven party activism— including the predominance of educated and middle-class participants—is emphasized in a line of empirical research starting with James Q. Wilson, *The Amateur Democrat: Club Politics in Three Cities* (Chicago: University of Chicago Press, 1962). The connection between education and ideological partisanship in the broader electorate was emphasized in 1964 by Herbert McClosky in "Consensus and Ideology in American Politics," *American Political Science Review* 58 (June 1964): 361-82; and is discussed more recently by Gerald Pomper and Marc D. Weiner, "Toward a More Responsible Two-Party Voter: The Evolving Bases of Partisanship," in *Responsible Partisanship? The Evolution of American Political Parties since 1950*, ed. John C. Green and Paul S. Herrnson (Lawrence: University Press of Kansas, 2000), 181-200; and Alan I. Abramowitz, *The Disappearing Center: Engaged Citizens, Polarization, and American Democracy* (New Haven, CT: Yale University Press, 2010).

5   Byron E. Shafer and Richard Johnston challenge the emphasis on race in *The End of Southern Exceptionalism: Class, Race, and Partisan Change in the Postwar South* (Cambridge, MA: Harvard University Press, 2006).

6   Brian D. Feinstein and Eric Schickler, "Platforms and Partners: The Civil Rights Realignment Reconsidered," *Studies in American Political Development* 22 (Spring 2008): 1-31; Anthony S. Chen, Robert W. Mickey, and Robert P. Van Houweling, "Explaining the Contemporary Alignment of Race and Party: Evidence from California's 1946 Ballot Initiative on Fair Employment," *Studies in American Political Development* 22 (Fall 2008): 204-28; Eric Schickler, Kathryn Pearson, and Brian D. Feinstein, "Congressional Parties and Civil Rights Politics from 1933 to 1972," *Journal of Politics* 72 (July 2010): 672-89; Hans Noel, "The Coalition Merchants: The Ideological Roots of the Civil Rights Realignment," *Journal of Politics* 74 (2012): 156-73; Christopher Baylor, "First to the Party: The Group Ori-

gins of the Partisan Transformation on Civil Rights, 1940–1960," *Studies in American Political Development* 27 (Fall 2013): 111–41; Eric Schickler, *Racial Realignment: The Transformation of American Liberalism, 1932–1965* (Princeton, NJ: Princeton University Press, 2016).

7   Jacquelyn Dowd Hall, "The Long Civil Rights Movement and the Political Uses of the Past," *Journal of American History* 91 (March 2005): 1233–63; Nelson Lichtenstein and Robert Korstad, "Opportunities Found and Lost: Labor, Radicals, and the Early Civil Rights Movement," *Journal of American History* 75 (December 1988): 786–811; Michael Honey, *Southern Labor and Black Civil Rights: Organizing Memphis Workers* (Urbana: University of Illinois Press, 1993); Patricia Sullivan, *Days of Hope: Race and Democracy in the New Deal Era* (Chapel Hill: University of North Carolina Press, 1996); Martha Biondi, *To Stand and Fight: The Struggle for Civil Rights in Postwar New York City* (Cambridge, MA: Harvard University Press, 2003).

8   This claim also complements arguments advanced recently by historians and APD scholars about the southern contribution to national conservative ideology in the postwar decades. See Matthew D. Lassiter, *The Silent Majority: Suburban Politics in the Sunbelt South* (Princeton, NJ: Princeton University Press, 2006); Kevin Kruse, *White Flight: Atlanta and the Making of Modern Conservatism* (Princeton, NJ: Princeton University Press, 2007); Joseph E. Lowndes, *From the New Deal to the New Right: Race and the Southern Origins of Modern Conservatism* (New Haven, CT: Yale University Press, 2008); Matthew D. Lassiter and Joseph Crespino, eds., *The Myth of Southern Exceptionalism* (New York: Oxford University Press, 2009); Crespino, *Strom Thurmond's America*; and Edward H. Miller, *Nut Country: Right-Wing Dallas and the Birth of the Southern Strategy* (Chicago: University of Chicago Press, 2015).

9   Howard L. Reiter and Jeffrey M. Stonecash, *Counter Realignment: Political Change in the Northeastern United States* (New York: Cambridge University Press, 2011); Matthew Levendusky, *The Partisan Sort: How Liberals Became Democrats and Conservatives Became Republicans* (Chicago: University of Chicago Press, 2009), 53–63.

10   E. E. Schattschneider articulated a theory of "conflict displacement" and its relationship to party realignment in *The Semi-Sovereign People: A Realist's View of Democracy in America* (New York: Holt, Rinehart, and Winston, 1960). The term "postmaterialist" is Ronald F. Inglehart's; see *The Silent Revolution: Changing Values and Political Styles among Western Publics* (Princeton, NJ: Princeton University Press, 1977). Later scholarly works emphasizing the reorientation of American politics around post-materialist issues include Jeffrey Berry, *The New Liberalism: The Rising Power of Citizen Groups* (Washington, DC: Brookings Institution, 1999); Gary Miller and Norman Schofield, "Activists and Partisan Realignment

in the United States," *American Political Science Review* 97 (2003): 245-60; and Jeffrey Smith, *Trading Places: The Two Parties in the Electorate from 1975-2004* (Saarbrucken, Germany: Lambert Academic Publishing, 2013). Thomas Frank popularized a conception of cultural politics as an electoral ruse deployed by economic elites in *What's the Matter with Kansas? How Conservatives Won the Heart of America* (New York: Metropolitan Books, 2004). Robert Self has reframed the story of a post-1960s conservative ascendancy by identifying the centrality of gender and family issues to even ostensibly "economic" controversies in *All in the Family: The Realignment of American Democracy since the 1960s* (New York: Hill and Wang, 2012).

11   Layman et al., "Activists and Conflict Extension in American Party Politics," 324-46. See also Larry Bartels, "What's the Matter with *What's the Matter with Kansas?*," *Quarterly Journal of Political Science* 1 (Summer 2006): 201-26; Jeffrey M. Stonecash and Mark D. Brewer, *Split: Class and Cultural Divides in American Politics* (Washington DC: CQ Press, 2007); Bafumi and Shapiro, "A New Partisan Voter," 1-24; and Noel, *Political Ideologies and Political Parties in America*, 144-64.

12   Lisa McGirr, *Suburban Warriors: The Origins of the New American Right* (Princeton, NJ: Princeton University Press, 2001); Lizabeth Cohen, *A Consumers' Republic: The Politics of Mass Consumption in Postwar America* (New York: Knopf, 2003); Donald T. Critchlow, *Phyllis Schlafly and Grassroots Conservatism: A Woman's Crusade* (Princeton, NJ: Princeton University Press, 2005); Kruse, *White Flight*; Lassiter, *The Silent Majority*; Darren Dochuk, *From Bible Belt to Sunbelt: Plain-Folk Religion, Grassroots Politics, and the Rise of Evangelical Conservatism* (New York: W. W. Norton, 2011); Michelle M. Nickerson, *Mothers of Conservatism: Women and the Postwar Right* (Princeton, NJ: Princeton University Press, 2012); Michael Stewart Foley, *Front Porch Politics: The Forgotten Heyday of American Activism in the 1970s and 1980s* (New York: Hill and Wang, 2013); Lily D. Geismer, *Don't Blame Us: Suburban Liberals and the Transformation of the Democratic Party* (Princeton, NJ: Princeton University Press, 2014).

13   Julian E. Zelizer, *On Capitol Hill: The Struggle to Reform Congress and its Consequences, 1945-2000* (New York: Cambridge University Press, 2004); Meg Jacobs, *Pocketbook Politics: Economic Citizenship in Twentieth-Century America* (Princeton, NJ: Princeton University Press, 2005); Eduardo Canedo, "The Rise of the Deregulation Movement in Modern America, 1957-1980" (PhD diss., Columbia University, 2008); Kimberly Phillips-Fein, *Invisible Hands: The Making of the Conservative Movement from the New Deal to Reagan* (New York: W. W. Norton, 2009); Benjamin C. Waterhouse, *Lobbying America: The Politics of Business from Nixon to NAFTA* (Princeton, NJ: Princeton University Press, 2013).

14   Catherine E. Rymph, *Republican Women: Feminism and Conservatism from Suffrage to the Rise of the New Right* (Chapel Hill: University of North Carolina Press, 2006); Timothy Stanley, *Kennedy vs. Carter: The 1980 Battle for the Democratic Party's Soul* (Lawrence: University Press of Kansas, 2010); Michael Bowen, *The Roots of Modern Conservatism: Taft, Dewey, and the Battle for the Soul of the Republican Party* (Chapel Hill: University of North Carolina Press, 2011); Jonathan Bell, *California Crucible: The Forging of Modern Liberalism* (Philadelphia: University of Pennsylvania Press, 2012); Geoffrey Kabaservice, *Rule and Ruin: The Downfall of Moderation and the Destruction of the Republican Party, From Eisenhower to the Tea Party* (New York: Oxford University Press, 2012); Leah Wright Rigueur, *The Loneliness of the Black Republican: Pragmatic Politics and the Pursuit of Power* (Princeton, NJ: Princeton University Press, 2015).

15   The term is from Abramowitz, *The Disappearing Center*.

16   The term is Feinstein and Schickler's—"Platforms and Partners," 6. Conceived broadly enough, this middle range also includes rank-and-file members of Congress and pressure groups who are able to hold party leaders accountable to sufficiently well-organized and articulated demands. See David W. Rohde, *Parties and Leaders in the Postreform House* (Chicago: University of Chicago Press, 1991); John H. Aldrich and Rohde, "The Logic of Conditional Party Government: Revisiting the Electoral Connection," in *Congress Reconsidered*, 7th ed., ed. Lawrence Dodd and Bruce Oppenheimer (Washington, DC: CQ Press, 2001), 26–92; and Barbara Sinclair, *Party Wars: Polarization and the Politics of National Policy Making* (Norman: University of Oklahoma Press, 2004), 67–184. In the world of interest groups and social movements, the key actors are those bridge-builders between activists in civil society and the parties who turn particular movements into long-term and transformational "anchoring groups" for one or the other party coalitions. See Daniel Schlozman, *When Movements Anchor Parties: Electoral Alignments in American History* (Princeton, NJ: Princeton University Press, 2015).

17   Noel, *Political Ideologies and Political Parties in America*.

18   Elizabeth Fones-Wolf, *Selling Free Enterprise: The Business Assault on Labor and Liberalism, 1945–1960* (Urbana: University of Illinois Press, 1994); Kevin Boyle, *The UAW and the Heyday of American Liberalism, 1945–1968* (Ithaca, NY: Cornell University Press, 1998); Thomas Sugrue, *The Origins of the Urban Crisis: Race and Inequality in Postwar Detroit* (Princeton, NJ: Princeton University Press, 1996); Jennifer Klein, *For All These Rights: Business, Labor, and the Shaping of America's Public-Private Welfare State* (Princeton, NJ: Princeton University Press, 2003); Kruse, *White Flight*; Phillips-Fein, *Invisible Hands*; Kathleen G. Donohue, ed., *Liberty and Justice for All? Rethinking Politics in Cold War America* (Amherst: University

of Massachusetts Press, 2012). Wendy L. Wall recounts the construction of the idea of a centrist American political consensus in *Inventing the "American Way": The Politics of Consensus from the New Deal to the Civil Rights Movement* (New York: Oxford University Press, 2008). Jennifer Delton reasserts the existence and efficacy of a postwar liberal consensus in *Rethinking the 1950s: How Anticommunism and the Cold War Made America Liberal* (New York: Oxford University Press, 2013).

19 Steve Fraser and Gary Gerstle, eds., *The Rise and Fall of the New Deal Order* (Princeton, NJ: Princeton University Press, 1990). For overviews of the vast literature on postwar conservatism, see Julian E. Zelizer, "Rethinking the History of American Conservatism," *Reviews in American History* 38 (June 2010): 367–92; and Kimberly Phillips-Fein, "Conservatism: A State of the Field," *Journal of American History* 98 (December 2011): 723–43. Historical accounts of liberalism during this period emphasizing fragmentation, decline, or convergence with conservative priorities include Allan Matusow, *The Unraveling of America: A History of Liberalism in the 1960s* (New York: Harper and Row, 1983); Dominic Sandbrook, *Eugene McCarthy: The Rise and Fall of Postwar American Liberalism* (New York: Anchor, 2005); Otis L. Graham Jr., "Liberalism after the Sixties: A Reconnaissance," in *The Achievement of American Liberalism: The New Deal and Its Legacies*, ed. William H. Chafe (New York: Columbia University Press, 2003), 293–325; Bruce Miroff, *The Liberals' Moment: The McGovern Insurgency and the Identity Crisis of the Democratic Party* (Lawrence: University Press of Kansas, 2007); Jefferson Cowie, *Stayin' Alive: The 1970s and the Last Days of the Working Class* (New York: New Press, 2010); Judith Stein, *Pivotal Decade: How the United States Traded Factories for Finance in the 1970s* (New Haven, CT: Yale University Press, 2010); and Geismer, *Don't Blame Us*.

20 Partial exceptions include Donald Critchlow, *The Conservative Ascendancy: How the GOP Right Made Political History* (Cambridge, MA: Harvard University Press, 2007); Sean Wilentz, *The Age of Reagan: A History, 1974–2008* (New York: HarperCollins, 2008); Laura Kalman, *Right Star Rising: A New Politics, 1974–1980* (New York: W. W. Norton, 2010); and Meg Jacobs and Julian Zelizer, *Conservatives in Power: The Reagan Years, 1981–1989—A Brief History with Documents* (New York: Bedford/St. Martin's, 2010).

21 The political science literature approaches empirical consensus on the asymmetric polarization of this period, a theme recently emphasized by Thomas Mann and Norman Ornstein in *It's Even Worse Than It Looks: How the American Constitutional System Collided with the New Politics of Extremism* (New York: Basic Books, 2012) and connected to the parties' differing coalitional structures and mass bases by Matt Grossman and David Hopkins in *Asymmetric Politics: Ideological Republicans and Group Interest Democrats* (New York: Oxford University Press, 2016).

22   On labor politics in the post-1960s period, see Taylor Dark, *The Unions and the Democrats: An Enduring Alliance* (Ithaca, NY: Cornell University Press, 1999); and Andrew Battista, *The Revival of Labor Liberalism* (Urbana: University of Illinois Press, 2008). A small but growing body of scholarship reassesses post-1960s developments in liberal and left politics and, to varying degrees, challenges the narrative of decline. See Sara Evans, "Beyond Declension: Feminist Radicalism in the 1970s and 1980s," in *The World the 60s Made: Politics and Culture in Recent America*, ed. Van Gosse and Richard Moser (Philadelphia: Temple University Press, 2003), 52–66; Stephen Tuck, "'We Are Taking Up Where the Movement of the 1960s Left Off': The Proliferation and Power of African American Protest in the 1970s," *Journal of Contemporary History* 43 (2008): 637–54; J. Zeitz, "Rejecting the Center: Radical Grassroots Politics in the 1970s— Second-Wave Feminism as a Case Study," *Journal of Contemporary History* 43 (2008): 673–88; Stanley, *Kennedy vs. Carter*; Bell, *California Crucible*; Jonathan Bell and Timothy Stanley, eds., *Making Sense of American Liberalism* (Urbana: University of Illinois Press, 2012); Foley, *Front Porch Politics*; and Geismer, *Don't Blame Us*.

23   Early statements on the reform of the parties' nominating procedures include Austin Ranney, *Curing the Mischiefs of Faction: Party Reform in America* (Berkeley: University of California Press, 1975); Jeane Kirkpatrick, *Dismantling the Parties: Reflections on Party Reform and Party Decomposition* (Washington, DC: American Enterprise Institute, 1978); Byron E. Shafer, *Quiet Revolution: The Struggle for the Democratic Party and the Shape of Post-Reform Politics* (New York: Russell Sage Foundation, 1983); and Nelson Polsby, *Consequences of Party Reform* (New York: Oxford University Press, 1983). Early assessments of congressional reform include Roger H. Davidson and Walter Oleszek, *Congress against Itself* (Bloomington: Indiana University Press, 1977), Thomas E. Mann and Norman J. Ornstein, eds., *The New Congress* (Washington, DC: American Enterprise Institute, 1981), and Burton D. Sheppard, *Rethinking Congressional Reform: The Reform Roots of the Special Interest Congress* (Cambridge, MA: Schenkman Books, 1985). The influence of that literature on subsequent historical scholarship can be seen, for example, in James T. Patterson, *Restless Giant: The United States from Watergate to Bush v. Gore* (New York: Oxford University Press, 2005), 76–85; and Kalman, *Right Star Rising*, 35, 39, 145. The major exception is Zelizer, *On Capitol Hill*.

24   Useful overviews of the political science literature on polarization include Geoffrey C. Layman, Thomas M. Carsey, and Juliana Menasce Horowitz, "Party Polarization in American Politics: Characteristics, Causes, and Consequences," *Annual Review of Political Science* 9 (2006): 83–110; Matthew Levendusky, "Partisan Polarization in the U.S. Electorate," in *Oxford Bibliographies Online: Political Science*, ed. Rick Valelly (New York:

Oxford University Press, 2013); and Michael Barber and Nolan McCarty, "Causes and Consequences of Polarization," in *Negotiating Agreement in Politics*, ed. Mansbridge and Martin.

25   Layman et al., "Activists and Conflict Extension in American Party Politics."

26   In this sense, Noel's account, in which ideological coalitions first rivaled the partisan coalitions and then won out and replaced them, is powerful but incomplete. Existing partisan arrangements influenced the work of ideological movement-building even in the process of those movements' altering the partisan arrangements. Noel, *Political Ideologies and Political Parties in America*. Similarly, Katherine Krimmel's argument that party nationalization rather than ideological activism drove the two parties' programmatic differentiation usefully revives E. E. Schattschneider's argument for the significance of scope in affecting political conflict. But, as this book documents, ideological activists were themselves the primary instigators of institutional reforms that would serve to nationalize the parties. In tracking the real-world work of partisan transformation, in other words, ideological and partisan influences cannot be so cleanly conceptually segregated. See Krimmel, "Special Interest Partisanship."

27   On national party organizations, see John Bibby, "Party Renewal in the National Republican Party," in *Party Renewal in America: Theory and Practice*, ed. Gerald M. Pomper (New York: Praeger, 1980), 102–14; A. James Reichley, "The Rise of National Parties," in *The New Direction in American Politics*, ed. John E. Chubb and Paul E. Peterson (Washington, DC: Brookings Institution, 1985), 175–200; Phillip A. Klinkner, *The Losing Parties: Out-Party National Committees, 1956–1993* (New Haven, CT: Yale University Press, 1994); John C. Green, ed., *Politics, Professionalism, and Power: Modern Party Organization and the Legacy of Ray C. Bliss* (Lanham, MD: University Press of America, 1994); Brian Mathew Conley, "Party People: Bliss, Brock, and the Rise of the Modern Republican Party" (PhD diss., New School for Social Research, 2008); Daniel J. Galvin, *Presidential Party Building: Dwight D. Eisenhower to George W. Bush* (Princeton, NJ: Princeton University Press, 2010); and Krimmel, "Special Interest Partisanship."

28   For two useful essays giving a historical overview of the debate over responsible parties, see John Kenneth White, "Intellectual Challenges to Party Government," in *Challenges to Party Government*, ed. John Kenneth White and Jerome M. Mileur (Carbondale: Southern Illinois University Press, 1992), 1–21; and John Kenneth White and Jerome M. Mileur, "In the Spirit of Their Times: 'Toward a More Responsible Two-Party System' and Party Politics," in *Responsible Partisanship? The Evolution of American Political Parties since 1950*, ed. John C. Green and Paul S. Herrnson (Lawrence: University Press of Kansas, 2000), 13–36. On party decline scholar-

ship, see Jeffrey E. Cohen, Richard Fleisher, and Paul Kantor, eds., *American Political Parties: Decline or Resurgence?* (Washington, DC: CQ Press, 2001).

29 John H. Aldrich, *Why Parties? A Second Look* (Chicago: University of Chicago Press, 2005), 5.

INDEX

Page numbers in italics refer to figures.

Nelson, Robert, 135, 151
New American Movement, 229
New Deal: and conservative coalition, 11,
67–69; and nationalization of politics, 10–11; and party machines, 9, 26;
policy agenda of, 32, 57, 64, 85–86, 126,
187, 257, 289; political coalition for, 11,
61, 119–20, 135, 141, 221, 223, 260, 275,
291, 380n19, 381n22; and Republican
Party, 59–60, 62, 76, 85–86; and responsible party advocates, 10–12, 16,
64
New Democratic Coalition, 135, 137, 145–
46
New Democrats, 275–78
New Left: and Michael Harrington, 224–
26, 229; and New Politics, 126; and
organized labor, 114–15, 251; on political system, 79, 95–97, 112–13
New Politics: coalitional vision of, 127, 135,
137, 141, 226, 278, 337n16, 373n42; and
New Left, 126; organized labor and,
136–37, 148, 225–26, 228; and party reform, 135, 141, 147, 152, 155; on political
system, 135, 162, 362n23; and the Social
Issue, 126–27
New Right, 5; as coalitional brokers, 202–3,
214, 252, 274, 352n66; and economics,
193–94, 352n68; liberals' analysis of,
241, 247–48; on party system, 188, 191,
210–11. See also "Social Issue"
New York Committee for Democratic
Voters, 52
Nixon, Richard, 84, 88, 134, 148; and conservative movement, 87, 89, 103, 126,
179, 186; and Modern Republicanism,
52, 76–77, 86; and Operation Switch
Over, 173–75; on party system, 2–3; and
the Social Issue, 126–27, 175–76, 201,
348nn5–6; and Watergate, 165, 180
Noel, Hans, 375n2, 382n26
Nofziger, Lyn, 196
North American Free Trade Agreement,
278
Novak, Robert, 105, 107, 206–8
NOW (National Organization for
Women), 219–20, 248, 254
NWPC (National Women's Political Cau-
cus), 140, 145, 152, 216, 239

O'Donnell, Peter, 91
O'Hara, James, 150–54, 169
O'Neill, Tip, 171, 247, 259, 268

Operation Dixie (Republican Party), 87,
90–91
Operation Switch Over, 173–77, 348nn3–4
Ornstein, Norman, 380n21
Oswald, Lee Harvey, 103
Overacker, Louise, 15

Packwood, Bob, 205
PACs (political action committees): driven
by ideology, 182, 191, 210–11, 212, 248;
proliferation of, 204, 274
Panama Canal, 196–98, 211, 237
party decline: and ideology, 177, 194–95,
211; and party reform, 132–33, 168–70,
337n15, 381n23; in popular discourse,
128–30, 244–45, 265; scholarship on,
129, 244–45, 282, 292, 347n141
Paster, Howard, 239
Patman, Wright, 166
Percy, Charles, 57–58, 83–84
Percy Committee. See Republican Com-
mittee on Program and Progress
Perlman, Philip, 37–38
Pew, J. Howard, 82
Phillips, Channing Emery, 137
Phillips, Howard, 188, 191
Phillips, Kevin, 127, 188
Phillips-Fein, Kimberly, 352n68
Phyfe, Marjorie, 231–32, 237
Pipes, Richard, 341n64
pluralism, 17–18, 43–44, 273
Poage, W. R., 162, 164–66
Podhoretz, Norman, 341n64
polarization: and 2016 election, 284–85;
civic maladies of, 3–4, 6, 374n43; in
civil society, 273–75; in Congress, 267,
270–72, 281–82, 371n22; definitions of,
305n9; and governmental dysfunction,
5–6, 278–79, 282; across issue dimensions, 177, 207–8, 219–20, 223–24, 262,
281, 289, 360n184, 374n1; measurement of, 130–31, 336n9; in political
science, 262–63, 282, 292–93, 374n44;
predictions of, 2, 19–20, 43, 44, 73, 93,
262–63
political action committees: driven by
ideology, 182, 191, 210–11, 212, 248;
proliferation of, 204, 274
Polsby, Nelson, 120, 169, 279
Pomper, Gerald M., 187, 350n33
Porter, Jack, 75
Port Huron Statement, 95–98, 108
Potter, I. Lee, 91–92